Anna S. Berger
Spectres of Masculinity

AF285518

GenderScripts: Literary and Gender Studies | 5

Editorial

There are few literary texts that do not deal with issues of gender and sexual identity, the gendered constitution of literary protagonists, or with sexual orientation.
Long before gender studies became institutionalised as an academic discipline, authors reflected on gender relations and explored role assignments, performativity,
power dynamics, and norms in their writing. In doing so, they have not only formed
cultural archives of historically diverse conceptions of gender, but also contributed
– sometimes consciously, sometimes unconsciously – to the social construction of
gender. The "GenderScripts" series aims to do justice to the highly productive interplay between literary studies and gender studies in the most inclusive way possible
by including all 'subcategories', such as women's and masculinity studies, queer,
trans* and intersex studies as well as sexuality and intersectional gender studies.
The series is anchored in the disciplines of English, American, German, and Romance studies but is open to proposals from all literary studies with text-analytical,
cultural and media studies approaches.
The series is edited by Gregor Schuhen, Maren Lickhardt and Stefan Horlacher.

Anna S. Berger is a literary scholar and journalist. She works as a postdoctoral
researcher in English didactics at Universität Augsburg and as a journalist for
the *Schwäbische Zeitung*. Previously, she was involved in journalism education at
Hochschule Magdeburg-Stendal. Her research focuses on Victorian literature –
particularly Gothic literature –, comics and graphic novels, as well as critical media
education.

Anna S. Berger

Spectres of Masculinity

Manhood in Victorian and Edwardian Ghost Stories, 1860-1914

[transcript]

This work was supported by a scholarship from the Studienstiftung des Deutschen Volkes.

Bibliographic information published by the Deutsche Nationalbibliothek
The Deutsche Nationalbibliothek lists this publication in the Deutsche Nationalbibliografie; detailed bibliographic data are available in the Internet at https://dnb.dnb.de

2025 © transcript Verlag, Bielefeld
Hermannstraße 26 | D-33602 Bielefeld | live@transcript-verlag.de

Cover design: Maria Arndt
Cover illustration: @theo.berger
Printing: Elanders Waiblingen GmbH, Waiblingen
https://doi.org/10.14361/9783839440568
Print-ISBN: 978-3-8376-7956-4 | PDF-ISBN: 978-3-8394-4056-8
ISSN of series: 2751-2029 | eISSN of series: 2751-2037

Printed on permanent acid-free text paper.

Ghosts, we hope, may be always with us
– that is to say, never too far out of the reach of fancy.
Elizabeth Bowen

Contents

Acknowledgements

This book is the revised version of my doctoral dissertation. I would like to express my deep appreciation and gratitude to all those who have supported and guided me throughout my research and writing of this dissertation.

First and foremost, I am indebted to my supervisor, Professor Ingrid Hotz-Davies, for her constant support, intellectual curiosity, and constructive feedback, which has haunted me in the best possible way, inspiring me to push my research further.

I would like to extend my appreciation to Professor Russell West-Pavlov and Professor Christoph Reinfandt for their invaluable input and thought-provoking feedback that has helped me to approach my research from new perspectives.

I further wish to express my gratitude to the Studienstiftung des Deutschen Volkes for the scholarship and the workshops I had the opportunity to attend.

Anya Heise-von der Lippe also deserves a special mention for the inspiring talks we had in-between the oral exams we conducted together. Our discussions about ghosts, vampires, and other monsters have been a constant source of inspiration and have always motivated me to continue my project. I would also like to express my gratitude to Gero Bauer for his help and encouragement, especially in the early stages of my project.

Many thanks also go to the participants of our PhD colloquium for their constructive feedback, which has helped me to sharpen my ideas and to refine my arguments. In particular, I am grateful to Amina ElHalawani, Rebecca Hahn, David Lo, Katharina Luther, Sara Vakili, Nathalie Walker, and Mascha Wieland. I could not have wished for better "comrades in arms" during those sometimes difficult times. Thank you for your support, friendship, and the "Tuesday-Lunches" in Tübingen which have always provided me with fresh energy, happiness, and a sense of belonging.

I am incredibly grateful to my parents, Dorothee and Theo Berger, for a childhood full of books and stories. Thank you for always believing in me and encouraging me to pursue my dreams. Your moral support and unwavering love have been a constant source of strength and motivation for me.

Warmest thanks go to my siblings Jonas Berger, Rosa Berger-Keller, and Jennie Eggstein, for being my constant companions through the journey that life is. I am also grateful to my friend Nicole Lang and my office mate in Magdeburg, Carolin Alexander, for their friendship and constant support throughout the last stages of my dissertation.

A spectral thank you also to my Godmother, Ann Reynolds, who is not here anymore to witness this moment, but who has been so instrumental in sparking my love and interest for English literature. I will always miss you and feel your ghostly presence in my life!

Most of all, I wish to express my heartfelt gratitude to my husband Claudius Richter and my daughter Pippa. Claudius, thank you for your love, understanding, and support during the ups and downs of my PhD journey. Pippa, you have been the best baby a PhD student can wish for. You have grown into a wonderful, life-hugging little person whose joy and happiness are infectious. I love you more than I can say.

Introduction

In H. G. Wells's ghost story "The Red Room", which was first published in the monthly magazine *The Idler* in 1896, the young male protagonist spends a night in a haunted room in Lorraine castle, determined to prove that the stories surrounding the room are nothing but superstitious belief. "I can assure you … that it will take a very tangible ghost to frighten me" (Wells 172), the narrator declares at the onset of the story. However, he soon loses control over his impulses and cannot keep a cool head, "in spite of my efforts to keep myself to a matter of fact phase" (ibid. 174), as he stresses. When the candles are snuffed out in the draughty room, the protagonist suffers a hysterical fit. In a panic-stricken attempt to find the door in the pitch-black room, he eventually hits his head against a piece of furniture and loses consciousness. Humbled by the experience, he admits to the housekeepers the next day that he was not defeated by "a very tangible ghost" (ibid. 179), but by spectres produced by his own mind: "there is no ghost there at all; but worse, far worse … The worst of all the things that haunt poor mortal man, … and that is, in all its nakedness – *Fear!*" (ibid., emphasis in original).

H. G. Wells's "The Red Room" is characteristic for a number of ghost stories written in the latter decades of the nineteenth century and the onset of the twentieth century, not only because it makes use of the haunted house trope, which is one of the most frequent literary devices employed in ghost stories, but also because it undercuts male superiority and the belief in the steadfastness of male rationality in an age of scientific advancement. Many Victorian ghost stories utilize the tension between science and the supernatural "in presenting a sceptical observer whose rationalist worldview is profoundly shaken by the narrative's close" (Bissel, "Science" 40). In doing so, these stories are not only critical of the contemporary belief in scientific advancement and progress, but also undermine dominant scripts of maleness and masculinity.[1]

In "The Red Room", the narrator's rationalist worldview is repeatedly shaken by his belief in spirits and the supernatural, which he is unable to suppress. In spite of his willingness to keep himself to "a matter of fact phase" (Wells 174), he is susceptible to "fanciful suggestions" (ibid. 175), "in a state of considerable nervous tension" (ibid. 176), and "frantic with the horror of the coming darkness" (ibid. 177) – reactions commonly associated with women, especially in the nineteenth century which witnessed a considerable output of pseudoscientific texts testifying to women's nervous excitability.[2] The personification of darkness in the following passage is indicative of the narrator's own excitability: "darkness closed upon me like the shutting of an eye, wrapped about me in a stifling embrace, sealed my vision, and crushed the last vestiges of reason from my brain" (ibid. 178). The passage also reveals that the narrator loses something which was considered an essentially masculine trait at the time the story was written: reason.[3] By portraying a male narrator who is controlled by fear and superstition rather than rationality, "The Red Room" blurs the seeming binary between male rationality and female irrationality. Wells's

---

1   Following numerous gender and queer studies theorists, I understand sex and gender as categories that are ascribed to people at birth, and which may stand at odds with a person's identity. Accordingly, when I talk about men or women in the course of this study, I refer to groups of people who are read as female/male and/or feminine/masculine. Although the term masculinity did not come into use until the 1970s, I will employ it alongside the words manliness and manhood. Whereas manliness has often been used to describe attributes men were happy to possess, masculinity is a more neutral term (Tosh, *Manliness* 2–3).

2   For instance, the American neurologist George Beard maintains in *American Nervousness* (1881) that "women are more nervous, immeasurably, than men, and suffer more from general and special nervous diseases" (207). In the same vein, Havelock Ellis writes in *Man and Woman* (1894) that "[t]here is general agreement that ... [nervous disorders] are much more common in women" (279). According to Sarah Bissell, "[f]or some nineteenth-century commentators, this designation justified women's subjugation" (*Haunted Matters* 8) and exclusion from the public sphere.

3   Moira Gatens has remarked that, in Western philosophical texts about corporeality, women are often seen as more affected by their bodies than men and are therefore more often associated with irrational behaviour. As a consequence, "the ideal conception of the rational is ... articulated in direct opposition to qualities typical of the feminine" (Gatens 50).

story thus complicates the idea that women are prone to nervous diseases while men can keep a cool head.

By calling fear "[t]he worst of all the things that haunt poor mortal *man*" (Wells 177, my emphasis), the narrator explicitly frames his reaction in terms of the sex and gender identity assigned to him. The nineteenth century was a period of "exploration and Imperial expansion" (Beynon 30) and an age "of unprecedented male achievement in engineering, the sciences ... and medicine" (ibid.). In order to serve the demands of the time, men were expected to be "strong, authoritative [and] decisive", on the one hand, and rational, "disciplined and resourceful" (ibid.), on the other hand. By losing his conviction in "the impossibility of ghosts and haunting" (Wells 176) and by showing fear, the unnamed male narrator in Wells's story is shown as unable to adhere to these parameters of masculinity. It is noteworthy though that he describes his panic as something that actively dispels reason from his brain, thus presenting himself as a victim of some foreign force rather than owning up to his susceptibility to superstitious belief. In this way, the story illustrates the narrator's need to justify his seemingly emasculating behaviour.

The present study shows that the prevalent concept of masculinity is challenged in various ways in Victorian and Edwardian ghost stories. As in "The Red Room", men are repeatedly punished for their unquestioned belief in science and materialism. Yet, for most of them, their ignorance has more fatal consequences than for the unnamed protagonist of Wells's story. In Bram Stoker's "The Judge's House" (1891), for instance, the protagonist is killed by the ghost of a cruel judge whose house he dared to inhabit. And in Lettice Galbraith's "In the Séance Room" (1893), the protagonist ends up committing suicide after having attended a séance during which he was exposed as a murderer.[4] Other stories concerned with masculinity focus less on ghostly punishments but are more concerned with the abysses of the human psyche. Some of these stories express anxieties about Britain's imperial project by hinting at the cultural and racial decay of the supposedly superior Englishman, whereas others blur gender boundaries and contest the heteronormative concept of marriage by suggesting that gender and sexuality are not fixed categories that fit into a binary system but, rather, are fluid entities that allow for a multiplicity of gender and sexual identities. In many of these tales, the figure of the ghost functions as a metaphor for feelings, desires, and anxieties that are not compatible with the ideal of masculinity prevalent in Great Britain in the latter decades of the

---

4   Both stories will be discussed in more detail in chapter 4.

nineteenth century and the beginning of the twentieth century. In this way, these stories suggest the damaging impact of a heteronormative concept of masculinity. They further expose the female/male binary as unstable and undermine assumptions that sex, gender, and sexuality can be classified as either normal or abnormal. Ultimately, the ghost stories discussed in the following chapters present the patriarchal system as problematic for both men and women.

Until now, studies on the ghost story have largely ignored the preoccupation of the genre with men and masculinity. That is not to say that there has been no research on ghost stories written by men. Until recently, male writers of supernatural fiction "have received the lion's share of critical attention" (Dickerson 7). Ghost stories by women writers, in contrast, have been subject to neglect for a long time – a neglect that mirrors women's marginalisation within the patriarchal structures of Victorian society. Julia Briggs, for example, almost exclusively interrogates ghost stories written by male writers in her early study on the genre *Night Visitors: The Rise and Fall of the English Ghost Story* (1977). Glen Cavaliero even goes so far as to bluntly dismiss supernatural tales by Charlotte Riddell, Amelia B. Edwards, and Mary Elizabeth Braddon in *The Supernatural and English Fiction* (1995), arguing that "the strange events they describe are merely intrusions on ordinary life, and, as such, good for no more than an agreeable shudder" (36). Instead, Cavaliero focuses on ghost stories by authors like Charles Dickens, Bram Stoker, and M. R. James.[5] However, only rarely do these critics pay attention to the ways in which the genre was used in order to blur, question, and undercut the superiority of the white middle-class male, despite their preference of male authors – or maybe precisely because of that. Anthony Easthope has argued in his introduction to *What a Man's Gotta Do: The Masculine Myth in Popular Culture* (1986) that the disregard for issues concerning white, middle-class masculinity has perpetuated the myth of a hegemonic masculine identity: "masculinity has stayed pretty well concealed. This has been its ruse in order to hold on to its power. Masculinity tries to stay invisible by passing itself off as normal and universal" (1). As an example, Easthope

---

5   In addition to the scholarly focus on ghost stories written by men, critics of women's writing have tended to see ghost stories "as less important than other facets of a writer's work" (Stewart, "Weird" 114–5). As we shall see in chapter 2, this is particularly the case with Edith Nesbit, whose biographers have repeatedly ignored or dismissed her Gothic contributions, and with Elizabeth Gaskell, whose social image as good and homely is at odds with her wild and transgressive short supernatural fiction.

uses the words "man" and "mankind" which "treat masculinity as if it covered everyone" (1) and present it as normative. This study shows that ghost stories written in the latter half of the nineteenth century and the onset of the twentieth century contest the idea of a universal masculinity. It is noteworthy that many of these stories were written by women. Michael Cox and R. A. Gilbert have maintained that women, being themselves on the margins of society, might have been impelled "to write about the margins of the visible, for the ghost story (as Dorothy Sayers observed) deals with power and thus might be expected to appeal to those who felt the absence of self-determination in their own lives" (*English* xiii). As much as I agree with the first part of their argument, which suggests that women might have been more aware of the margins of society because of their marginalised position, I think that the second part does not do them justice. They did not only write ghost stories in order to put themselves in a position of power. The ghost stories by women discussed in this work show a deep understanding for the gender role expectations confronting men and the problems these expectations caused. In much the same way as male authors like Wilkie Collins interrogated the difficulties women had to face in the nineteenth century, female authors explored gender role restrictions imposed on men in this time period, as we shall see.

In the last two decades, research on women's ghost stories has shown that women did not only write spine-chilling and entertaining ghost stories, but also made "use of the ghost as a figure of social critique" (Makala 18).[6] Several critics have noted that there is a striking parallel between the figure of the ghost and the liminal position women were assigned in Victorian society, for Victorian domestic ideology rendered women both visible and invisible, "removed from the power-wielding occupations of the world ... [,] yet relegated to the higher realm of moral influence" (Dickerson 5), especially if they belonged

---

6   Some of the most notable monographs on the topic include, but are not limited to, Diana Basham's *The Trial of Woman: Feminism and the Occult Sciences in Victorian Literature and Society* (1992), esp. chapter 5, Vanessa D. Dickerson's *Victorian Ghosts in the Noontide: Women Writers and the Supernatural* (1996), Clare Stewart's *Fighting Spirit: Victorian Women's Ghost Stories* (2000), Melissa Edmundson Makala's *Women's Ghost Literature in Nineteenth-Century Britain* (2013) and her more recent study *Women's Colonial Gothic Writing, 1850–1930* (2018), Sarah Bissell's *Haunted Matters: Objects, Bodies, and Epistemology in Victorian Women's Ghost Stories* (2014), and Victoria Margree's *British Women's Short Supernatural Fiction, 1860–1930* (2019).

to the middle class.[7] This in-betweenness, Vanessa D. Dickerson contends in *Victorian Ghosts in the Noontide: Women Writers and the Supernatural* (1996), finds a parallel in the ghost, "a figure of indeterminacy, of imperilled identity, of substance and insubstantiality" (ibid). It adds to Dickerson's interpretation to point out that the idealised image of the "Angel in the House"[8] also places women in a position of indeterminacy between heaven and earth. In *The Trial of Women: Feminism and the Occult Sciences in Victorian Literature and Society* (1992), Diana Basham further maintains that "Victorian ghosts and Victorian women had much in common, ... for both ghosts and women were subject to the same kind of criticism and liable to be met with the same dismissive hostility in their attempts to gain recognition" (152). It is hardly surprising, therefore, that many ghost stories written by women "share a concern about cultural visibility which is key to understanding their configurations of the spectral" (Smith, *Ghost Story* 93).

However, in most stories, the ghost is more than just a metaphor for women's liminal position in Victorian society. Women writers repeatedly used the figure in order to draw attention to "the ways in which their limited

---

7   It is worth noting that studies about women's supernatural writing generally focus on the experience of white middle-class women and thus have a "limited range, insofar as a heterosexual, middle-class, white woman's experience cannot adequately represent *all* female experience" (Bissell, *Haunted Matters* 25). As Sarah Bissell has pointed out, some of these studies fail to acknowledge this bias (ibid.). A notable exception is Melissa Edmundson's work on women's colonial Gothic literature. Even though she focuses on Gothic stories by white middle-class women who lived in the far-flung corners of the British Empire, Edmundson is very conscious of their status and illustrates how their stories might have worked as "a critique of the empire from within" (Procter and Smith 97). Referring to Kimberlé Crenshaw's concept of intersectionality, Victoria Margree also points out that "Victorian and early twentieth-century women writers may have been marginal to dominant culture in respect of being women, but in relation to other axes of social power many of them possessed relative privilege" (*British* 16). On the term "intersectionality" see especially Crenshaw's 1989 paper "Demarginalizing the Intersection of Race and Sex: A Black Feminist Critique of Antidiscrimination Doctrine, Feminist Theory and Antiracist Politics".

8   The term stems from Coventry Patmore's poem "The Angel in the House" (1854). In the poem, the speaker describes his pure and submissive wife, who is devoted to her children and controlled in her behaviour. This depiction of womanhood is indicative of the hegemonic ideal of femininity in the Victorian period. It is not my intention to overestimate the influence Patmore's poem and the ideas proposed in it exerted over Victorian women. Not all women were willing to accept the ideal. Nevertheless, the representation of one form of femininity as normative had (and has) a disciplinary effect.

property and legal rights were routinely justified on a range of contradictory assumptions about womanhood" (Bissel, *Haunted Matters* 11). Just like the ghosts in their stories, women writers refused to be silenced and rebelled against their marginalisation: "women writers of ghost stories 'troubled' the present by raising awareness of unsafe domestic spaces, gender relations, economic conditions and the consequences of imperialism" (Makala 5).

Considering this focus on power structures and the marginalisation of women within the patriarchal system, it is perhaps not surprising that some of the first investigations of men and masculinity in Victorian and Edwardian ghost stories emerged in studies on women's ghost stories. As Richard Nemesvari has remarked, "novelistic depictions of proper/improper femininity can only take place in the context of carefully delineated proper/improper masculinity" (88). In her 1992 study on women and the occult, Basham has noted that "[o]ne feature which is strikingly common in women's ghost stories is the use, either of a masculine narrator, or of a masculine narrative focus" (Basham 158). One reason for this might have been that, just like male pseudonyms or the anonymous publication of women's writing, male narrators offered a way for women to disguise their female identity and gain greater acceptance in the literary marketplace. However, to reduce women's use of the male narrative voice to this point, does not do their ghost stories justice. As Basham maintains, "[i]t is the male consciousness which is made to encounter, puzzle over, interpret or be haunted by the mysterious 'otherness' of the supernatural agent" (ibid.). Accordingly, "the challenge of the supernatural" is not only made to men but "directly to notions of masculinity itself" (ibid.). Unfortunately, Basham does not pursue these observations further in her chapter on women's ghost stories. Instead, she focuses on the ways in which the absence of women echoes "the exclusion of women and their inadequate representation" (ibid. 171) in ghost stories by Amelia B. Edwards, Margaret Oliphant, and Vernon Lee. Another insightful description of how ghost stories by Victorian women challenge men and masculinity is given by Jennifer Uglow. In her introduction to *The Virago Book of Victorian Ghost Stories* (1988), Uglow observes that, in many ghost stories written by women, men "are made to feel (as the women of their day so often did) that their destiny is out of their hands and their world is governed by uncontrollable, relentless, probably hostile powers" (xvii). This observation is not exclusive to women's ghost stories but applies to the genre in general, as will be shown in this study. Numerous Victorian and Edwardian ghost stories by both male and female authors show how "men of authority and science – doctors, priests, fathers – lose their confidence, become oppressed, doubtful, unsure of their status, vulnerable to swings of emotion" (Uglow xvi).

More recently, Ruth Heholt has taken Uglow's and Basham's observations one step further. In "Science, Ghosts, and Vision: Catherine Crowe's Bodies of Evidence and the Critique of Masculinity" (2014), Heholt convincingly illustrates how Crowe uses the supernatural in order to destabilise contemporary ideas about masculinity. Additionally, in "Visible Yet Immaterial: The Phantom and the Male Body in Ghost Stories by Three Victorian Women Writers" (2018), Heholt investigates the deconstruction of Victorian masculine identity in ghost stories by three women writers: Catherine Crowe, Rhoda Broughton, and Edith Nesbit. In her insightful study *Women's Ghost Literature in Nineteenth-Century Britain*, Melissa Edmundson Makala also takes a big step away from discussions that focus solely on female concerns by including issues such as imperialism, race, and numerous other political and economic concerns. She further explores "the troubled place of marginalized men" (Makala 18). However, in contrast to Heholt, she does not specifically turn to hegemonic concepts of masculinity. To my knowledge, this work constitutes the first full-length study on representations of men and masculinity in Victorian and Edwardian ghost stories.

It is by no means my intention to imply that recent scholarship on the Victorian ghost story was wrong in focusing on female-authored tales and women's ghostly position within patriarchy. With their work, scholars like Vanessa D. Dickerson, Melissa Edmundson, and Victoria Margree successfully worked against the long neglect of women's supernatural writing in academia. I would like to expand on their research by illustrating how the genre was also used to counter gender expectations confronting men. The only thing that I take issue with is the claim that women's supernatural writing is inherently different from men's in its tendency to reject materialism and science in favour of spiritualism and the occult and that women are generally more sensitive to social and cultural issues.[9] Even though I agree that in a

---

9   For instance, in her acclaimed *Victorian Ghosts in the Noontide*, Vanessa D. Dickerson maintains that "men and women write ghost stories … in different voices" (6–7). She further points out that men "tend to be more diagnostic, clinical, journalistic, vested in mensuration" (Dickerson 7) than their female counterparts. Similarly, Rosemary Jackson claims that male authors "investigate 'horror' for its own sake", while women "extended our sense of the human, the real, beyond the blinkered limits of male science, language, and rationalism" (xviii). And Mike Ashley writes in his introduction to the 2008 ghost story collection *Unforgettable Ghost Stories by Women Writers* that "men liked

society that privileges men and masculinity, the experiences of people who are read as female invariably differ from those who are read as male, I find such generalisations problematic. For one, they further reinforce the gender binary and "risk reinscribing the gendered nature/culture dualism historically used to exclude women from the traditions and practices of rationalism" (Ferguson 433). Sarah Bissell has rightly remarked that by overstating "women's designation as invisible, powerless, and supernaturally-receptive" critics of women's ghost writing risk "presenting these features as integral female traits rather than culturally-ascribed positions" (Bissel, *Haunted Matters* 25). Accordingly, they reinforce the socially constructed "myths they purport to explode" (ibid. 26). Furthermore, the claim that female-authored ghost stories are more concerned with social issues is built on the underlying assumption that men, being themselves in a privileged position, are not interested in or oblivious to marginalised people and the injustice they experience – an assumption which "ignores the complexities and variations" (ibid.) of male-authored ghost stories. In this study, I hope to break up the binary enforced by earlier research regarding the author's sex and gender. While I agree that it is significant to counter the neglect women's writing has suffered, I believe that it is equally important not to reinforce the gender binary any further at this point. For this purpose, I will look at ghost stories by both female and male authors in this study.

The overall aim of *Spectres of Masculinity: Manhood in Victorian and Edwardian Ghost Stories, 1860–1914* is to shed light on the ways in which the ghost story was used in order to engage with prevalent concepts of masculinity between 1860 and 1914. I chose this period of study because it encompasses a relatively consistent concept of masculinity which was very much influenced by the needs of the British Empire and marked by a rigorous rejection of various Others[10] – most notably women, colonised people, and homosexual men. The ghost stories discussed in the following chapters show a deep understanding for the conflict many men found themselves in during the latter decades of

---

to create stories of vengeful ghosts and sinister hauntings, [whereas] women tended to go for something more subtle" (qdt. in Bissell, *Haunted Matters* 6). Melissa Edmundson Makala is more careful in acknowledging that "[c]lassifying Gothic by gender has its limits". Nevertheless, she states that "women, in their ghost literature, concentrated on the limits of this world and were generally more interested than their male counterparts in changing the public's mindset" (*Women's Ghost* 16).

10   For emphasis, the words "Other" and "Otherness" are generally written with a capital letter throughout this work.

the nineteenth century and the years preceding the Great War. By exploring men's struggle to live up to prevalent ideas about masculinity, these stories suggest that what was seen as manly is not a natural condition, but a socially constructed role designed to discipline men. Before going into detail regarding the dominant ideal of manliness, I would like to spend some time on the ghost story as a distinct literary genre and showcase why the form lends itself particularly well to the interrogation of social, political, and cultural issues.

The Ghost Story as a Genre: Entertainment, Uncanny Minds, and the Political Dimension of Haunting

Stories of ghosts and spirits are an integral part of British culture. There is almost no ancient town, no old manor house, no abandoned ruin, no lonely moor in the United Kingdom that is not haunted by a ghost – or rather said to be so. Many of those tales are hundreds of years old and continue to haunt British public consciousness to this day.[11] Ghosts also feature prominently in Shakespeare's plays[12] – from *Richard III* (1592–1593) to *Julius Caesar* (1599–1600), *Hamlet* (1600–1601) and *Macbeth* (1605–1606) – and they recur in the early Gothic novels of Anne Radcliffe.[13] However, it was not until the 1820s that the ghost story as a distinct literary genre came into being. The first contribution to the genre is commonly considered to be Walter Scott's "Wandering Willie's Tale", inset into his novel *Redgauntlet*, published in 1824 (Cox and Gilbert, *English* xii).

---

11   Peter Ackroyd has compiled a selection of "true" ghost stories from various centuries in *The English Ghost: Spectres Through Time*. In the introduction to his anthology, Ackroyd traces the history of the English ghost from the Middle Ages to the present day. He maintains that the "English ghost tradition … is deeply rooted in its peculiar mingling of Germanic, Nordic and British superstitions" (1).

12   Shakespeare was not the only playwright of his day who made use of ghosts, of course. Mike Ashley has observed that ghosts were often utilized as a "stage device" and signified "a melodramatic warning, a harbinger of doom, or an outward manifestation of individual guilt" (403) in the Elizabethan and Jacobean periods.

13   It is worth pointing out that most of Radcliffe's novels offer a rational explanation for the seemingly supernatural events at some point and therefore belong to the explained supernatural. A notable exception is the real ghost in *Gaston de Blondeville*, published posthumously in 1826. Radcliffe's contemporaries also made use of ghosts in their writing. In Matthew Lewis's *The Monk* (1796), for instance, the real ghost of the "Bleeding Nun" haunts the castle – and elopes with the protagonist, who mistakes her for his beloved.

A few years later, Scott created one of the first self-contained ghost stories, "The Tapestried Chamber", which appeared in *The Keepsake* in 1829. Scott seems to have met the *zeitgeist*, for, from its inception onwards, the ghost story quickly developed into one of the most popular genres of the time. Some of the most well-known authors of the nineteenth century excelled in the form – among them authors who are today mainly remembered for their social realism like Charles Dickens, Elizabeth Gaskell, and Margaret Oliphant, but also more notorious writers of Gothic and sensation fiction such as Robert Louis Stevenson, Bram Stoker, and Mary Elizabeth Braddon. If one has a look into the various ghost story anthologies that have been put together in the past thirty or so years, it almost seems as if no literary reputation could have been complete in the Victorian era without the publication of at least one ghost story.

The ghost story's success can partly be attributed to changes in the literary marketplace in the nineteenth century. While the novel and its little sister, the short story, were regarded "as a morally suspect form of amusement rather than a serious literary form" at the beginning of the century, they "had become the dominant form of literature" (Pykett, *Wilkie Collins* 71) as the century drew to its close. "Population growth and rising literacy rates also fuelled [the] demand" (Seville 215) for fiction. While the population of the UK doubled from just over ten million in 1801 to more than 20 million in 1851, "and almost doubled again (to 37 million) by the end of the century" (Seville 215), "literacy rates continued to rise, reaching around 98 per cent by the end of the century" (Mandal 29).[14] The demands of this new "monster audience" (Wilkie Collins's term, "The Unknown Public" 187) were satisfied by the circulating libraries and the emergence of numerous literary magazines in the 1840s.[15] Ghost stories featured regularly in these magazines (Pykett, "Sensation" 198). Many of them were published at Christmas and/or have their setting at Christmas like Henry James's *The Turn of*

---

14 For information on the population growth in the UK between 1801 and 1981, see also B. R. Mitchell, *British Historical Statistics*.

15 As Deborah Wynne has pointed out, there was a "marked divide" (15) between the cheap penny dreadfuls, which aimed at a working-class readership, and the more respectable monthlies such as *Fraser's* and *Blackwood's*, bought mainly by middle- and upper-class readers. Charles Dickens's two-penny weekly *Household Words*, first published in 1850, was one of the first periodicals affordable and acceptable to both working- and middle-class readers. Dickens thus created a "new market for serialized magazine fiction" (Pykett, *Wilkie Collins* 76).

the Screw (1898) and Charles Dicken's *A Christmas Carol* (1843).[16] The spine-chilling plot of the ghost story stands in strong contrast to the cosy and familiar atmosphere at Christmas. This tension arguably made the supernatural happenings appear more shocking to the Victorian audience.[17] By the middle of the century, no extra Christmas number of the popular family magazines was "complete without something about ghosts" (Martin 28). However, the growing readership and the increased availability (and respectability) of fiction does not fully account for the particular popularity of ghost stories.

Critics have repeatedly tried to get to the bottom of the genre's attraction – to authors and readers alike. The answers they propose are as multifaceted as the ghost stories themselves. While some suggest that authors, women in particular, have been partly motivated to produce ghost stories out of financial necessity,[18] others stress the craving for the supernatural in an increasingly secular age that was shaped by fundamental transitions in everyday life following the invention of the steam locomotive at the beginning of the nineteenth century. Ghost story writer Vernon Lee, for instance, emphasises the function of the supernatural as a way to escape the reality of the modern world in her

---

16   More than any other author, Charles Dickens tightened the link between Christmas and ghosts, not only with his own ghost stories, but also by publishing ghost stories in the extra Christmas issues of his periodicals *Household Words* and *All the Year Round*: "His own stories 'The Trial for Murder' and 'The Signalman' both appeared in the latter; Mrs. Gaskell's 'The Old Nurse's Tale' [sic.] and Wilkie Collins's 'The Dream Woman' were commissioned by Dickens for Christmas issues of the former" (Briggs, "Ghost" 180). Louise Henson also stresses Dickens's role in this context: "Dickens had a central role in the development of the Victorian ghost story. His hugely successful Christmas Books of the 1840s forged the cultural association of ghosts and Christmas. These popular seasonal hauntings continued throughout the 1850s and 1860s in many of the collaborative Christmas stories carried by his weekly miscellanies" (44).

17   As Julia Briggs has pointed out, "Victorian ghost stories, in particular, often employed this contrast as their central effect, either by using a setting such as Christmas at Dingley Dell or alternatively through their publishing context: ghost stories typically appeared in periodicals intended for family consumption, like those Dickens edited, or later magazines such as the *Strand*" (Briggs, "Ghost" 181). A related framing device is the telling of the ghost story by the fireside. As ghost story writer Sheridan Le Fanu has remarked, ghost stories "may be read with very good effect by a blazing fire on a shrewd winter's night" ("Chapelizod" 117). Sarah Bissell has suggested to "connect this convention to the genre's oral roots" (*Haunted Matters* 5).

18   See, for instance, Julia Briggs in "The Ghost Story" (2012), Michael Cox and R. A. Gilbert in their introduction to *The Oxford Book to English Ghost Stories* (1986), and Lyn Pykett in "Sensation and the Fantastic in the Victorian Novel" (2005).

essay "Faustus and Helena: Notes on the Supernatural in Art", published in the *Cornhill Magazine* in 1880: "We moderns seek in the world of the supernatural a renewal of the delightful semi-obscurity of vision and keenness of fancy of our childhood; when a glimpse into fairyland was still possible, when things appeared in false lights, brighter, more important, more magnificent than now" (Lee, *Hauntings* 312). What Lee stresses here is "a nostalgia for an older, more supernatural system of beliefs" (*Night Visitors* 19) which, according to Julia Briggs, "provides the foundation of the ghost story" (ibid.) as a literary form. In an age governed by scientific advancement, "[g]hosts challenge or at least question the authority of science and reason" (Byron and Punter 27), Glennis Byron and David Punter argue. Likewise, Briggs maintains that "the symbolic meaning of the ghost story most consistently exploited was the most obvious one – its rejection of materialism" (*Night Visitors* 24). Srdjan Smajic makes a similar point: "ghosts in the Victorian era ... channel the dissatisfaction with mechanistic models of the universe and the displacement of intuition- and faith-based forms of knowledge by materialism and scientific naturalism" (55). In a similar vein, Cox and Gilbert note that "the ghost story seemed to thrive precisely because it dealt in possibilities that were in fundamental opposition to the explicatory march of science" (*Victorian* xv).

While these arguments are valid and can partly account for the genre's popularity, I believe that they are also too short-sighted. To begin with, to reduce women's interest in the genre to financial reasons ignores the sociocultural critique inherent in many of their ghost stories. As Sarah Bissell has rightly pointed out, it makes more sense to look at it the other way around: "The ghost story ... supplied a platform through which women writers could negotiate the troubled dynamics between 'masculine' materialism and 'feminine' ethereality .... Encouragingly, to engage these ideas through popular fiction simultaneously allowed women to alter their material circumstances by earning money" (Bissell, *Haunted Matters* 9). The production of ghost stories thus furthered women's independence on more than one level. Bissell has also warned that "the form's relationship with materialism is far more complex" (*Haunted Matters* 18) than many scholars suggest. I concur with Bissell on that point. After all, the problem with ghosts is that they *do* materialise and often draw attention to very real political and social issues. Some psychic investigators of the time even believed that ghosts might constitute some kind of unknown matter (Owen xvii). It is therefore problematic to view the ghost story primarily as a means of escaping the material world. Simon Hay in *A History of the Modern British Ghost Story* (2011) even goes so far as to argue that the supernatural genre of the ghost story is representative of British natural-ism. Rather than being a genre that is marked by a rejection of materialism, the ghost story "is in fact an extremely useful genre for representing 'reality'" (Hay 92), he argues. For naturalist writers, Hay contends, "'reality' and 'life' are increasingly understood as psychological rather than social categories" (ibid.) and the ghost is particularly suitable for the expression of this aspect of human existence.

Regarding the ghost story primarily as an expression of nostalgia is also problematic, for the past (and ghosts as representations of the past) can be unsettling and bring back unwanted memories. As Nickianne Moody has remarked in her 1996 essay "Visible Margins: Women Writers and the English Ghost Story", the genre's "preoccupation with the past ... is not necessarily nostalgic. ... As with horror writing, nostalgia is often inverted and childhood, previously thought of as a safe haven, is the source of fear and terror" (78). In *Specters of Marx* (1994), Jacques Derrida likewise stresses the darker aspects of ghosts and haunting by pointing out that ghosts represent "a threat that some would like to believe is past" (39). In his work, Derrida notes the ghostly persistence of political and social ideas, particularly those of Karl Marx, "de-spite the triumphant celebration of the supposed 'end of Marxism' since the 1990s, with the collapse of Eastern European Communism and the seemingly irresistible ideological dominance of neoliberalism and global capitalism" (Sy-rotinski 48–9). He argues that Marx's theories still have relevance after the fall of the Berlin Wall and warns us not to embrace "the ideal of liberal democracy and of the capitalist market" (Derrida, *Specters* 106) uncritically: "no degree of progress allows one to ignore that never before, in absolute figures, have so many men, women, and children been subjugated, starved, or exterminated on the earth" (ibid.).

Derrida employs the figure of the ghost in order to disrupt the idea of his-tory as a linear development that can overcome the past. Instead, he proposes a "looping circularity of history, ... whereby the past refuses to be entirely oc-cluded but remains to haunt the apparent site of enlightened new beginnings" (Punter, "Spectral Criticism" 262). According to Derrida, "a spectre is always a *revenant*" (*Specters* 11) and as such it naturally disrupts the idea of a linear tem-porality:

> What is the time and what is the history of a specter? Is there a present of the specter? Are its comings and goings ordered according to the linear suc-cession of a before and an after, between a present-past, a present-present,

and a present-future, between a "real time" and a deferred time? ... If there is something like spectrality, there are reasons to doubt this reassuring order of presents. (Derrida, *Specters* 39)

As a revenant, a being "whose very nature is to violate chronological time" (Margree, *British* 2), the figure of the ghost calls our attention to the fact that the present is inevitably haunted by the past. Ideas from the past or deeds committed in the past have an impact on the present. Just like a spectre, they may come back and "re-incarnate" (Derrida, *Specters* 48) themselves in the present or the future.

Derrida's insistence on the ghost's status as a revenant provides a helpful framework for the discussion of literary ghosts. As Melissa Edmundson Makala has noted, the "idea of repetition is key to understanding the force of meaning inherent in a ghost" (6). She argues that the "unsettling nature of the ghost ... exists beyond a specific moment, representing the past and influencing the future" (Makala 6). The ghost is thus a constant reminder of the past. According to Derrida, "this being with specters would also be, not only but also, a *politics* of memory, of inheritance, and of generations" (*Specters* xviii, emphasis in original). It comes as no surprise, then, that ghost stories are particularly concerned with questions of inheritance, trauma, and transgenerational haunting[19]. Hence, ghosts often carry a cultural and "political consciousness that must be recognized and dealt with" (Makala 7). I suspect that it is this socio-political dimension of ghosts and haunting that attracted many authors of the nineteenth and early twentieth centuries to the genre.

In order to refer to the atemporal nature of the ghost, Derrida employs the term "hauntology" (*Specters* 10, 202) – a pun on the words "haunting" and "ontology", which is even more striking in Derrida's original French, in which the words "ontologie" and "hauntologie" are homophone as the "h" is silent in the language. The term not only stresses the nature of the ghost as a haunting, but calls attention to the liminality of the spectre, its in-betweenness. A ghost is neither dead nor alive, neither material nor immaterial, neither past

---

19   The term "transgenerational haunting" has strongly been influenced by Nicolas Abraham and Maria Torok. Building on Sigmund Freud's concept of repression, Abraham and Torok have established the idea that trauma, when unresolved, can be passed on to the next generation: "what haunts are not the dead, but the gaps left within us by the secrets of others" (Abraham 287). In many Victorian and Edwardian ghost stories, it is both the dead and their unresolved traumas that haunt the living.

nor present. "Phantom bodies take up no space, they have no corporeality ... and yet are present and visible" (Heholt, "Visible" 149), as Ruth Heholt has put it. Ghosts invade and inherit "different bodies, [are] able to break the boundaries of time and space, or to transcend the ordinary limits of matter" (R. Jackson xvi). The figure of the ghost is thus inherently paradoxical, "both fundamental to the human, fundamentally human, and a denial or disturbance of the human, the very being of the inhuman" (Bennett and Royle 160). This liminal existence of ghosts carries a potential for social and political criticism. Just like the ghosts themselves, stories about ghosts and haunting transgress the boundaries of probability and blur binary thinking. As Rosemary Jackson has observed, supernatural literature "explores and thereby threatens to dissolve many of the structures upon which social definitions of reality depend, those rigid boundaries between life and death, ... past and future, reason and madness" (xviii). Similarly, Lowell T. Frye points out that "[b]y calling into question these binary oppositions, the ghost story undermines the authority of such dualisms as well as the socially constructed hierarchies they mask" (Frye 169).

In *The Fantastic* (1973), Tzvetan Todorov offers another useful explanation of why fantastic literature lends itself particularly well to social critique. Todorov notes that "the social and the literary functions coincide" (166) in supernatural writing: "in both cases, we are concerned with a transgression of the law" (ibid.). He argues that, with regard to content, supernatural writing has the tendency to transgress the boundaries of what is considered acceptable by society: "incest, homosexuality, love for several persons at once, necrophilia, excessive sensuality... It is as if we were reading a list of forbidden themes, established by some censor" (ibid. 158). By addressing these themes, "the fantastic is a means of combat against ... censorship" (ibid. 159). On the narrative level, Todorov maintains, the supernatural likewise has the function to break with established rules. The fantastic element "disturb[s] the stable situation of the beginning ... [w]hereby the plot is amazingly advanced" (ibid. 165). Todorov concludes that "[w]hether it is in social life or in narrative, the intervention of the supernatural element always constitutes a break in the system of pre-established rules, and in doing so finds its justification" (166).

Clare Stewart has made a similar point. With regards to women's ghost stories, she notes that "the supernatural element and the social comment, were, cleverly, so indistinguishable as to make vague misgivings difficult to identify and vocalize" ("'Weird'" 111). In other words: the message is "hidden" in the supernatural realm of the story. The "fun of the shudder" (Wharton 63) thus functions to distract readers from the subversive content of these stories. An important point that Stewart makes in this context is that the ghost story's status as a form of entertainment rather than a respectable literary genre worked to establish it as a privileged space for the critique of societal issues. "Under the guise of a 'harmless' ghost story" (Stewart, "Weird" 111), Stewart contends, social criticism could be expressed more directly than in more highly regarded genres. Lowell T. Frye has also argued this position. He maintains that the ghost story "constituted something of a secret or submerged corner of the Victorian literary universe – because it was and is lacking the respectability of the realistic novel" (Frye 168). In the same vein, Diana Wallace argues that women used the supernatural guise of the ghost story in order "to offer critiques of male power and sexuality which are often more radical than those in more realist genres" ("Uncanny" 57). Kate Kruger further notes that while sensation fiction was often criticised "for the physical and moral damage it could do to impressionable readers" (66), the ghost story somehow could get away with the same transgressions of societal taboos. Victoria Margree suspects that this has also to do with the ghost story's identification as short fiction which "has, of course, long been considered an inferior form of the novel … . But as we know from other marginalised kinds of fiction such as children's literature, 'inferior' status has often afforded writers particular kinds of freedom" (*British* 9). According to Margree, the short story provides the perfect foundation for ghost narratives:

> the very brevity of short fiction frees it from certain requirements placed upon novels …, such as to explain events by establishing cause and effect, or to end with narrative closure. … It is also these qualities that have arguably made short fiction particularly hospitable to ghosts. Ghosts are not always so well accommodated in narratives that require suspension of readerly disbelief over a sustained duration, but they flourish in the intensely charged, unfamiliar and uncertain moments in which the short story specialises. (Margree, *British* 10)

In line with these observations, we will see time and again in the course of this work, how the ghost story subverts the literary conventions of the realist novel, thereby expressing dissatisfaction with the status quo. It is worth adding that the ghost story as a popular form that was mainly published in the successful family magazines also offered writers an opportunity to engage with cultural, social, and political debates in front of a vast audience. As Laurel Brake and Julie F. Codell have pointed out, the flourishing periodical press provided "a major public space for discourses about society, politics, culture, public order, and larger worlds of foreign and imperial affairs" (2).

In many Victorian ghost stories, especially those written in the early and mid-Victorian periods, it is literally the dead who refuse to be silenced and come back to haunt the living: "the seduced, betrayed, persecuted, wronged, or dispossessed return to right or avenge their wrongs or repossess what has been taken away" (Pykett, "Sensation" 198). In other ghost stories just as numerous, it is not the dead who return but the repressed feelings, desires, and memories of the ghost seer. These tales, Virginia Woolf remarks in her essay "The Supernatural in Fiction", published in the *Times Literary Supplement* on 31 January 1918, are characteristic for the latter decades of the nineteenth century and the onset of the twentieth century and "seek to terrify us not by the ghosts of the dead, but by those ghosts that are living within ourselves" (Woolf, "Supernatural" 294). For Woolf, it is nothing alien that is frightening but "the power that our minds possess for such excursions into the darkness" ("Supernatural" 295). In her essay, Woolf cleverly shifts the focus from the ghost story genre to the writers and readers of the form. Instead of wondering why the British are so intrigued by ghost stories, she asks what this attraction tells us about the writers and readers: "So much evidence of the delight which human nature takes in stories of the supernatural will inevitably lead one to ask what this interest implies both in the writer and in the reader" (Woolf, "Supernatural" 293). Woolf then attributes "our love for ghost stories" to a "strange human craving for the pleasure of feeling afraid" (ibid.). She notes that "[i]t is pleasant to be afraid when we are conscious that we are in no kind of danger" (ibid.). For Woolf, this does not mean that ghost stories constitute a rather superficial kind of entertainment. On the contrary, she argues that "the fear which we get from reading ghost stories of the supernatural is a refined and spiritualized essence of fear" (ibid.).[20] Woolf thus counters assumptions that the ghost story's "purpose to

---

20   Virginia Woolf's observations can be traced back to Edmund Burke's concept of the sublime and Anne Radcliffe's distinction between horror and terror. In his influential *A Philosophical Enquiry into the Origin of Our Ideas of the Sublime and Beautiful* (1757), Burke discusses the affects produced by the sublime and the beautiful. Whereas the beautiful describes everything that is little and contained and results in love (affect that is experienced), the sublime originates in a fear of death or pain and "is triggered by extremes – vastness, extreme height, difficulty, darkness, excessive light" ("Burke's") etc. – and excites awe. When we experience danger and pain from a distance, Burke argues, we experience what he calls "delightful horror" (Burke 14, 32), a mixture between fear and admiration. Anne Radcliffe has taken Burke's ideas one step further in her essay

entertain and frighten limit[s] its cultural value" (Bissell, *Haunted Matters* 18).[21] Similarly to Vernon Lee, Woolf remarks that "the craving for the supernatural in literature coincided in the eighteenth century with a period of rationalism in thought, as if the effect of damming the human instincts at one point causes them to overflow at another" ("Supernatural" 293–94). Woolf then links the "delight which human nature takes" (ibid. 293) in writing and reading ghost stories to the subconscious: "perhaps [we] unconsciously welcome the chance for the licit gratification of certain instincts which we are wont to treat as outlaws" (ibid.), she writes in her essay and surmises whether "some psychological law lies hidden beneath the hundreds of stories about ghosts and abnormal states of mind" (ibid.).

The idea that ghosts are mental constructs and can be ascribed to an overstimulated imagination was not a new thought in the Victorian period. "The recognition that certain subjective experience might be the result of mental disturbance had begun as early as the sixteenth century" (Briggs, *Night Visitors* 142).[22] However, it was during the nineteenth century that apparitions became increasingly linked to psychological illnesses (ibid. 143). This process goes

---

"On the Supernatural in Poetry" (1826), arguing that the sublime is produced by a feeling of terror rather than horror. Terror, Radcliffe argues, depends on "obscurity" ("Supernatural" 149). That which is perceived as threatening is indicated but not explicitly shown. In fiction evoking horror, by contrast, the threat is shown explicitly. According to Radcliffe, this open display of threat leads to a feeling of disgust which freezes the mind: "Terror and horror are so far opposite, that the first expands the soul, and awakens the faculties to a high degree of life; the other contracts, freezes, and nearly annihilates them" (ibid.). Woolf at least implicitly builds on Radcliffe's definition of terror when she describes "the fear which we get from reading ghost stories ... [as] a refined and spiritualized essence of fear" (Woolf, "Supernatural" 293).

21   Julia Briggs, for instance, asserts that "[m]any of the most effective ghost stories are quite reasonably concerned with entertaining rather than making a serious contribution to literature" (*Night Visitors* 8).

22   In her study on the ghost story genre, Briggs refers to the Swiss theologian and clergyman Ludwig Lavater who declares in his work on ghosts *De spectris* (which was published in England in 1572 under the title *Of ghostes and spirites walking by nyght*) that ghosts do not have a supernatural origin: "True it is, that many men doo falsly persuade themselves that they see or heare ghostes: for that which they imagin they see or heare, proceedeth eyther of melancholic, madnesse, weaknesse of the senses, fear or of some other perturbation" (Lavater 9). The assumption that ghosts might not be something supernatural is also expressed in William Shakespeare's play Hamlet, in which Queen Gertrude suggests to Hamlet that his father's ghost is nothing but "the very coinage of your brain" (*Hamlet* 97).

hand in hand with developments in mental science and psychology, which repeatedly linked hallucinations to the troubled psyche (McCorristine 4–5).[23] It
is hardly surprising, therefore, that the mind repeatedly becomes "a kind of
space, filled with intrusive spectral presences" (Castle, *Female Thermometer* 164)
in nineteenth-century Gothic. By hinting at the possibility that ghosts are
nothing but a hallucination and are therefore not located in external forces
but within the mind of the ghost-seer, the ghost story contributed to the
psychologization of Gothic themes.

The interest of ghost story writers in the genre's potential to suggest mental
phenomena is well documented. Vernon Lee, for instance, clearly seems to have
been interested in imagined ghosts. In the preface to her short story collection
Hauntings (1890), Lee comments on the nature of the supernatural narratives
collected in her book:

> [M]y four little tales are of no genuine ghosts in the scientific sense; they
> tell of no hauntings such as could be contributed by the Society for Psychi-
> cal Research, of no spectres that can be caught in definite places and made
> to dictate judicial evidence. My ghosts are what you call spurious ghosts (ac-
> cording to me the only genuine ones), of whom I can affirm only one thing,
> that they haunted certain brains, and have haunted, among others, my own
> and my friends'. (Lee, *Hauntings* 39–40)

Vernon Lee clearly distances herself and her writing from the illustrious Society for Psychical Research (SPR). Founded in London in 1882, the SPR sought
to place supernatural encounters on a scientific footing. What is remarkable
about the SPR is the intellectual quality of its members, among them fellows
of the universities of Cambridge and Oxford, influential psychologists such as
Sigmund Freud and Gustav Jung, and well-known authors such as Robert Louis
Stevenson and Arthur Conan Doyle. As Shane McCorristine notes, "the SPR re-
sembled a *Who's Who* of the *fin-de-siècle* world" (104). Considering that Vernon
Lee saw ghost stories as a means to escape scientific modes of thinking, it is
not surprising that she rejected the activities of the SPR. The above quote also
reveals that Lee did not see her ghosts as external, supernatural forces but as
mental constructs that have their origin in "the haunted recesses of the subject's own mind" (Botting and Townshend 2). In line with Virginia Woolf, Lee

---

23   Sigmund Freud and Joseph Breuer, for instance, describe multiple symptoms for hysteria, among them "visual hallucinations" (8) in *Studies on Hysteria* (1895).

was fascinated by the psychological meaning of imagined ghosts, spectres that haunt "certain brains", as she puts it.

Likewise, Charles Dickens valued the psychological dimension of ghosts and haunting. In a letter to Elizabeth Gaskell, dated 25 November 1851, he praises the ghost story's potential to illustrate mental phenomena:

> My dear Scheherazade – for I am sure your powers of narrative can never be exhausted in a single night, but must be good for at least a thousand nights and one. ... I hope I have not damaged the incident of the Face? It came into my mind (you remember that it struck me when you told it) as a very remarkable instance of a class of mental phenomena ... Ghost stories, illustrating particular states of mind and processes of the imagination, are common property, I always think – except in the manner of relating them, and O who can rob some people of *that* (Dickens, Letter to Mrs Gaskell 545, emphasis in original).

The above letter reveals that Dickens was particularly interested in the ways in which the ghost story could be used in order to interrogate the complexities of the human psyche and showcase "particular states of mind and processes of the imagination". [24]

Dickens wrote numerous ghost stories and published even more in his popular family magazines *Household Words* (1850–1859) and *All the Year Round* (1859–1895). Most of his own contributions to the genre preserve an ambiguity that makes it impossible to tell whether the ghosts really exist or whether they are the projection of an overwrought imagination. In one of Dickens's most gruesome ghost stories, "The Trial for Murder", which was first published in 1865 in the extra Christmas number of *All the Year Round* and later republished

---

24   The letter is not only interesting because it testifies to Dickens's interest in mental phenomena and their relation to the ghost story genre. It also constitutes Dickens's response to Elizabeth Gaskell's accusation that he stole one of the ghost stories she used to relate at parties. In his letter, Dickens's justifies his decision to write down and publish Gaskell's story by presenting it as "common property" (Dickens, Letter to Mrs Gaskell 545) – an idea which stresses the genre's origin in oral tradition and folklore. Gaskell seems to have disagreed with Dickens on that point, however. A letter Gaskell sent to her friend Eliza Fox reveals that she was furious about Dickens's behaviour: "How are the Dickens wretch that he is to go and write MY story of the lady haunted by the face; I shall have nothing to talk about now at dull parties" (Gaskell, Letter to Eliza 172), she complains. Nevertheless, Gaskell continued to contribute stories to Dickens's magazines.

under the title "To Be Taken With a Grain of Salt", the protagonist, who is summoned to serve at a jury in a murder trial, is not sure whether the ghostly figure, the spectre of the murdered person, is real or whether he is suffering from an illusion. The latter interpretation is supported by the later title of the story, "To Be Taken With a Grain of Salt", for it warns the reader not to take everything for granted. On one level, the tale can be read as a critique of Britain's judicial system, which seems to need supernatural invention to function properly. Yet, on another level, it is also possible to read it as a story about the narrator's repressed homosexuality and the subsequent homophobia, which drove him to kill the object of his illicit desire. The ghost would then serve as an embodiment of the narrator's guilty conscience. According to this reading, the narrator not only participates in one murder, but two, as he ensures that the man falsely accused of the deed is sentenced to death at the end of the story. Although not all of Dickens's stories can be read as profound interrogations of the human psyche, most of them leave a "loophole for a natural explanation" (M. R. James's term, qdt. in Briggs, *Night Visitors* 143) of the seemingly supernatural events.[25]

---

25   In *A Christmas Carol* (1843), for instance, the ghosts are only seen by Ebenezer Scrooge. Likewise, the goblins only appear to Gabriel Grub in "The Story of the Goblins Who Stole a Sexton" (1836), and in "The Signal-Man" (1866) only the signalman is able to see the supernatural appearances. For this reason, the reader should be warned not to accept the ghosts as real. This ambiguity seems to have been something Dickens was also looking for in the stories he published. In another letter exchange with Elizabeth Gaskell, Dickens disputed with her over the ending of her ghost story, "The Old Nurse's Story", which was published in the extra Christmas number of Dickens's *Household Words* in 1852. In a letter dated 6 November 1852, he writes that "the turn is greatly weakened by their all seeing the ghosts" and suggests that "it would be very new and very awful" (Letter to Mrs Gaskell 800) if the ghosts were only seen by the child who then cries out what it sees. Dickens's ending would have made the story ambiguous. It would have been impossible to tell whether we are dealing with actual ghosts or an illusion. Unfortunately, Gaskell's reply to Dickens's proposal is not available to us. Hopkins suggests that her letter disappeared when Dickens destroyed a huge part of his correspondence shortly before his death (Hopkins 357). However, Gaskell must have rejected Dickens's idea. In a letter dated 4 December, Dickens grudgingly accepts Gakell's version of the denouement: "I have no doubt, according to every principle of art that is known to me from Shakespeare downwards, that you weaken the terror of the story by making them all see the phantoms at the end. And I feel a perfect conviction that the best readers will be the most certain to make this discovery. Nous verrons." (Letter to Mrs Gaskell 815)

For Walter Scott, the understanding of ghosts as figments of the imagination and expressions of disordered mental states is inevitable in an age ruled by rational materialism: "the belief in prodigies and supernatural events has gradually declined in proportion to the advancement of human knowledge" (341), he states in an 1827 essay on the German writer E. T. A. Hoffmann and concludes that "the occurrence of tolerably attested anecdotes of the supernatural characters are so few, as to render it more probable that the witnesses have laboured under some strange and temporary delusion, rather than that the laws of nature have been altered or suspended" (ibid.).

Freud's discussion of the uncanny in his essay by the same name, published in 1919, has frequently been used by critics as an interpretative framework for the analysis of ghosts and spectrality in literature.[26] Freud describes *das Unheimliche* (translated as "the uncanny") as "that class of the frightening which leads back to what is known of old and long familiar" ("The Uncanny" 220). Like Virginia Woolf and Vernon Lee, Freud does not see external terrors and supernatural beings as the origin of that which is frightening but regards the human psyche as the source of the uncanny. To argue his position, Freud compares the German word "unheimlich" (uncanny) with its etymological root word "heimlich" (homely/secret). He observes that the word "heimlich" is ambiguous: "On the one hand it means what is familiar and agreeable, and on the other, what is concealed and kept out of sight" ("The Uncanny" 225). Freud points out that "unheimlich" is usually used as the contrary only of the first meaning of the word "heimlich" (homely). He then contends that there is also a connection to the second meaning of the word (secret). He concludes that "this uncanny is in reality nothing new or alien, but something which is familiar and old-established in the mind and which has become alienated from it only through the process of repression" (ibid. 241). What is really frightening is the return of that which has been repressed: just like a ghost that is defined by its coming back and the consequential refusal to be forgotten, repressed feelings, desires,

---

26   These scholars include but are by no means limited to Terry Castle in *The Female Thermometer: Eighteenth-Century Culture and the Invention of the Uncanny* (1995), David Punter in "Spectral Criticism" (2002) and "The English Ghost Story" (2018), Andrew Smith in "Hauntings" (2007) and *The Ghost Story 1840–1920: A Cultural History* (2010), esp. pp. 22, 120, Srdjan Smajic in *Ghost-Seers, Detectives, and Spiritualists: Theories of Vision in Victorian Literature and Science* (2010) and Julian Wolfreys in *Victorian Hauntings: Spectrality, Gothic, the Uncanny and Literature* (2002).

and memories ultimately refuse to be banished from consciousness and come back to haunt the individual. In Freud's words:

> if psycho-analytic theory is correct in maintaining that every affect belonging to an emotional impulse, whatever its kind, is transformed, if it is repressed, into anxiety, then among instances of frightening things there must be one class in which the frightening element can be shown to be something repressed which *recurs*. This class of frightening things would then constitute the uncanny. (Freud, "The Uncanny" 241, emphasis in original)

Freud then explicitly links the uncanny to secrecy, or rather the loss of it: "This reference to the factor of repression enables us ... to understand ... the uncanny as something which ought to have remained hidden but has come to light" (ibid.). The feeling of the uncanny thus erupts in a moment when something cannot be hidden and kept secret anymore.

Not all scholars have been eager to apply Freudian theory to their analysis of Victorian and Edwardian ghost fiction. Julia Briggs, for instance, has pointed out that numerous "psychological ghost stories were written before Freud's work was known to more than a handful of specialists" (*Night Visitors* 159). She further contends that "[i]t is difficult to assess at what point Freud's theories began to make an impact in England, but it seems probable that they were known mainly to specialists before the outbreak of the war in 1914" (Briggs, *Night Visitors* 159–60). Hence, it is unlikely that Freudian psychoanalysis has influenced the writing of ghost stories in the Victorian and Edwardian periods. Simon Hay has further argued that to "explain the ghost story in terms of psychoanalysis ... will get us nowhere. Yes, we will be able to say: this ghost story looks like it references the psyche; but only because Freud's conception of the psyche was always built out of references to ghost stories anyway" (Hay 5). I disagree with Briggs and Hay on that point. I do not see why it should be problematic to read ghost stories retrospectively through the lens of Freudian theory. It is also not particularly helpful to maintain that psychoanalysis should be abandoned as a means of understanding literary ghosts because "Freud's version of the psyche and of the psychoanalytic process are ... modelled on the ghost story" (Hay 5). I believe that it works both ways: ghost stories can help us to understand the human psyche, and psychoanalysis can help us to understand ghost stories. In fact, there is a striking parallel between psychoanalysis and Gothic fiction which "lies in the manner in which both disclose what ought to have remained concealed" (Botting and Townshend 2). By bringing to light that which has been repressed, Freudian theory and Gothic fiction reveal society's abandoned Others. As Fred Botting and Dale Townshend stress, "emotions, wishes, fears and desires, everything pertaining to sexuality in the broadest sense of the term, underlie a culture whose values ostensibly rely on their exclusion. The uncanny, then, serves as a strange reminder of all those elements from which culture emerges, and rigorously distances itself" (ibid.). Gothic fiction thus serves as a mirror that shows society its disavowed aspects. This is especially true for ghost stories, for the figure of the ghost is arguably the most suitable metaphor for the return of the repressed.

Raewyn Connell has also drawn attention to the importance of Freud for discussions about masculinity. As she has pointed out in her acclaimed study *Masculinities* (1995), Sigmund Freud contested the idea of maleness as normative with his research: "It was Freud, more than anyone else, who let the cat out of the bag. He disrupted the apparently natural object 'masculinity', and made an enquiry into its composition both possible and, in a sense, necessary" (Connell 8). Accordingly, any study concerned with masculinity rightly considers Freudian theory as a way of understanding male gender performance and identity.[27]

If ghosts are expressions of mental phenomena, and if stories about them are indicative of "our sense of our own ghostliness" (Woolf, "Supernatural" 294), to employ Virginia Woolf's words again, what does it mean, then, to see ghosts and to write and read about them? Which brains do they haunt and why? Andrew Smith has suggested that ghosts are "ciphers for models of subjectivity which refer to culturally specific notions of psychological trauma" ("Hauntings"

---

27   Antony Easthope has rightly remarked that "psychoanalysis is still in part contaminated by the patriarchal assumptions it sets out to analyse" (3) and that "it regards as general something that is only or mainly masculine" (ibid.), thus further reinforcing the idea of maleness as the norm as opposed to a deviant femininity. This is undoubtedly a valid criticism and a point which is also inherent in Freud's "The Uncanny", in which he argues that "the anxiety about one's eyes, the fear of going blind, is often enough a substitute for the dread of being castrated" (231). Freud also only uses examples of men in order to underpin his thoughts, thus excluding women from his theory. However, scholars like Juliet Mitchell have shown that psychoanalysis might also be used for feminist purposes. In her acclaimed *Psychoanalysis and Feminism* (1974), which is informed by Lacanian thinking, Mitchell argues that "a rejection of psychoanalysis and of Freud's work is fatal for feminism … . Psychoanalysis is not a recommendation *for* a patriarchal society but an analysis *of* one" (xv, emphasis in original). In line with this argument, this work seeks to make apparent the uncertainties and anxieties that underlie normative concepts of masculinity.

148). Simon Hay makes a similar point: "the ghost is something that comes back, the residue of some traumatic event that has not been dealt with and that therefore returns, the way trauma always does" (Hay 4). What Hay and Smith stress here is the historical dimension of ghosts and haunting and the trauma that is bound up with it. For Smith, a spectre is "a strangely historical entity that is haunted by the culture which produced it" ("Hauntings" 147). Melissa Edmundson Makala similarly remarks that "literary ghosts are … direct products of their time, and as such, have a vast amount to tell us about the many significant cultural shifts that occurred in the nineteenth century" (8). In order to fully understand a ghost story, it is therefore imperative to take the context in which it was produced into account. For this reason, this study takes a literary historicist approach. To fully understand male gender performance in the ghost story genre, I place literary texts within the social and cultural context in which they were created. At the same time, I treat the ghost stories discussed in this work as historical texts which do not only reflect the discourse on manliness in the nineteenth century but contribute to it. In short, this is an attempt to understand literature through its historical context and to comprehend history through literary texts.

John Kucich has rightly remarked that we must be careful not to exaggerate the extent of repression experienced by Victorian society:

> twentieth-century culture – both popular and intellectual – has been eager to view the Victorians as fearful, dishonest, silly, or coercive because of their refusal of emotional expression. Sometimes, the motive for the attack is only to see ourselves, by comparison, as part of a teleological movement toward freedom and authenticity. Often, too, we are able to distance our own ambivalence about desire … by attacking the Victorians for being overtly more inhibited and covertly more perverse. (Kucich 4–5)

While I concur with Kucich that it is problematic to dismiss the Victorians as a society of sexually repressed hypocrites, I think that it is also important to acknowledge that any form of hegemony has an impact on the individual – in both the Victorian period as well as in our world today. As Elaine Showalter has pointed out with regards to masculinity in Britain at the fin de siècle,

> many men found their part of the equation as difficult to sustain as women did theirs, and the source of as much anxiety. Opportunities to succeed at home and in the Empire were not always abundant; the stresses of maintain-

ing an external mask of confidence and strength led to nervous disorders, such as neurasthenia; suppressing "feminine" feelings of nurturance and affection created problems for many men as well. (Showalter, *Anarchy* 9)

In many of the ghost stories which we will encounter, the ghostly visitations make apparent these anxieties and point to the nervous disorders developed by men as a consequence of a too rigidly defined concept of manliness that they were not able to conform to. Time and again, these stories suggest that the protagonists are not troubled by supernatural forces but by the ghosts produced by their own minds.

The "golden age" of the ghost story roughly coincides with the heyday of the British Empire. Both stories of haunting and the belief in Britain's imperial mission never occupied a more prominent place in British public consciousness than in the latter half of the nineteenth century and the advent of the twentieth century. It is perhaps no coincidence, therefore, that ghost stories "are, in complicated ways, insistently about Empire" (Hay 10), as Simon Hay has declared. Hay links his observation to Edward Said's claim in *Culture and Imperialism* that "nineteenth-century British novels can make the British Empire, on which the way of life depicted in such novels absolutely depends, visible only as a kind of structuring absence" (ibid.). For Hay, this invisible presence of the British Empire becomes the focal point in many Victorian ghost stories: "because ghost stories systematically focus on invisible presences, on liminality generally, such invisibility is actually central, while seeming marginal" (ibid.). The same can be said about the ideal of imperial masculinity, which was prevalent in the years between 1860 and 1914. Although only a minority of men could draw on first-hand experience regarding Britain's colonial project, imperialism came to haunt white middle-class men and their perception of masculinity in one way or another, as we shall see in the next section of this introduction.

What needs to be addressed before I move on to the predominant ideal of masculinity in the years between 1860 and 1914, however, is the question of what counts as a ghost story. The ghost story is not a clearly defined genre. While most critics regard it as "a special category of the Gothic" (Briggs, "Ghost" 177) or "a major extension of Gothic writing" (Blair xvii), there has been a debate over the exact definition of the ghost story. As Julia Briggs has pointed out, the term "ghost story" has been employed with a certain latitude: "it can denote not only stories about ghosts, but about possession and demonic bargains, spirits other than those of the dead, including ghouls, vampires, werewolves, the 'swarths' of living men and the 'ghost-soul' or *Doppelgänger*" (*Night Visitors* 12).

In their introduction to *The Oxford Book of English Ghost Stories*, Michael Cox and R. A. Gilbert suggest a more rigid definition of the genre:

> The ghostly protagonists must act with deliberate intent; *their* actions – or the consequences of their actions – rather than those of the living must be the central theme; and, most important of all, each ghost, whether human or animal phantom or reanimated corpse, must unquestionably be dead. From this it follows that there can be no rationalization of the ghost, no explanation of events by natural causes. (Cox and Gilbert, *English* ix, emphasis in original)

While I find a definition of the genre which includes ghouls, vampires, and werewolves not specific enough, Cox's and Gilbert's definition is too narrow, especially because it does not encompass the kind of ghost story notable contributors of the genre like Vernon Lee and Charles Dickens found so compelling: tales illustrating internal states and processes of the imagination rather than external terrors. Nickianne Moody has provided a very useful definition of the genre which acknowledges psychological ghost stories: "all narratives labelled as ghost stories will at some point address a haunting – a return of the dead or the past in some manner" (Moody 77). Very much in agreement with this definition of the genre, my own work considers texts of the explained and unexplained supernatural as well as ambiguous tales which have a moment of haunting at the core of the narrative – be that in the form of actual ghosts, imagined ones, *Doppelgängers*, or possessions.

Political Bodies: Empire, Englishness, and the Ideal of Imperial Masculinity

To understand the social and cultural expectations placed on men in a particular society, it is important to spend some time on the term "masculinity" itself and its implications. Compared to the focus on women and femininity in academia, masculinity studies is a relatively young field of research. It began to form in the early 1980s and, in its beginnings, "can be characterized as largely non-literary in nature, with the social sciences taking the most visible lead in what was then a new and sometimes controversial approach to gender" (Reeser, "Concepts" 12).[28]

To illustrate the extent to which questions of masculinity and male identity have been neglected in both academic and cultural discourse, the sociologist Michael S. Kimmel felt compelled to make the seemingly bold claim in 1993 that "men have no history" (28). What he means by that is not that men have been ignored or subjected to discrimination. On the contrary, "virtually every history book is a history of men. If a book does not have the word 'women' in its title, it is a good bet that the book is about men" (ibid.). However, in line with what I have pointed out earlier regarding research on the ghost story genre that has thus far largely ignored the implications of male ghost seeing, these "[b]ooks feel strangely empty at their centres, where the discussion of men should be. Books about men are not about men as men" (ibid.). More than 30 years have passed since Kimmel's claim that "men have no history as gendered selves" (ibid.). While arguably still "a minority interest in the field of gender research worldwide" (Horlacher 53), masculinity studies has evolved into a fully-fledged and fertile field of research.

Masculinity, scholars agree, is made up of multiple masculinities.[29] It is expressed in numerous ways by different people – or even by the same person at different times and/or in different contexts. However, despite this consensus, "masculinity is still a highly problematic and controversial field of study that is located at the intersection of the humanities and the arts, the social sciences and natural sciences" (Horlacher 53), as Stefan Horlacher points out. He maintains that, in this field of study, "most pressing questions can only be answered through approaches that are historical, comparative, intersectional, trans- and

---

28   There are some notable exceptions, of course, such as Coppélia Kahn's *Men's Estate: Masculine Identity in Shakespeare* (1981), Alfred Habegger's *Gender, Fantasy, and Realism in American Literature* (1982), and Eve Sedgwick's *Between Men* (1985) – a work that also informs the current study. Today, research navigating the interception between literary and masculinity studies is no longer the exception. As Todd W. Reeser stresses, "literary analysis in the twenty-first century constitutes a crucial and vibrant wing of masculinity studies" ("Concepts" 12).

29   See, for instance, David Buchbinder's *Masculinities and Identities* (1990), Raewyn Connell's *Masculinities* (1995), John Beynon's *Masculinities and Culture* (2002), John Tosh's *Manliness and Masculinities in Nineteenth-Century Britain* (2005), Todd W. Reeser's "Concepts of Masculinity and Masculinity Studies" (2015), and Stefan Horlacher's "Masculinity Studies: Contemporary Approaches and Alternative Perspectives" (2018).

interdisciplinary, and which incorporate findings from LGBTI studies and reject reductive and limiting definitions of masculinity" (ibid. 55).

A crucial point to be made is that we cannot talk about different expressions of masculinity without considering other identity categories such as race, class, sexual orientation and identification, religion, ethnicity, age, and physical ability. As a social code of behaviour, masculinity is "unavoidably involved with other social structures" (Connell 75). However, at the same time, it would be misleading to assume that there is such a thing as "gay masculinity" or "black masculinity". As Raewyn Connell has noted in her influential study *Masculinities* (1995), such labels risk "oversimplification" (76). Likewise, John Beynon has pointed out in *Masculinities and Culture* (2002) that "any easy generalizations like 'working class', 'middle class', 'gay' or 'black' masculinities are greatly misleading because within each of these broad categories there is considerable variation in both experience and presentation" (2). Therefore, I concur with Connell that "[t]o recognize more than one kind of masculinity is only the first step" (76).

Notions about masculinities are also products of time and geographical location, "shaped and expressed differently at different times in different circumstances in different places by individuals and groups" (Beynon 2). It is therefore important not to impose Western ideas about masculinity onto other cultures. Likewise, one must bear in mind the historical context when discussing gender performance in a past decade or century. As Connell emphasises, "we are 'doing gender' in a culturally specific way" (68). As our culture changes, ideas about masculinity shift and reshape themselves.

One of the most contested topics in the field of masculinity studies is the notion of the male body and the role biological determinism plays in this context. In their ground-breaking study *Gender Trouble* (1990) Judith Butler not only famously announces that gender is a social construct, a behaviour that is learned and performed within a particular culture, but questions the sex/gender binary altogether: "perhaps this construct called 'sex' is as culturally constructed as gender; indeed, perhaps it was always already gender, with the consequence that the distinction between sex and gender turns out to be no distinction at all" (Butler 7). Butler supports their thesis by arguing that the idea of sex is inseparable from and only accessible through notions of gender. As Kevin Floyd has so eloquently rephrased it, the distinction between sex and gender "quickly devolves into the nonsensical because the only way we can ever access the supposed hard truth of the material body is through the same 'constructed' categories from which we also seem, persistently, to want to distinguish that body" (33–4). While about gender in general and not about masculinity in particular, Butler's "theoretical concepts can be brought to bear on masculinity in productive ways" (Reeser, "Concepts" 30). When applying Butler's framework to masculinity, "'maleness' or 'manhood' in its biological configuration (as influenced by testosterone, the male sex drive, or the penis, for instance) can be understood as elements of gender as constructed through the medium of language" (ibid. 30–1). From this point of view, maleness and masculinity are seen as inherently instable and fluid constructs, always liable to change and possibly even interchangeable.

Jack Halberstam also blurs the seemingly natural link between masculinity and the male body. In *Female Masculinity* (1998), he raises questions about the definition of masculinity as "the social and cultural and indeed political expression of maleness" (1), arguing that female masculinity is not simply an imitation of maleness but rather a particular expression of masculinity. For Halberstam, "female masculinities are framed as rejected scraps of dominant masculinity in order that male masculinity may appear to be the real thing" (1).[30]

Eve Kosofsky Sedgwick also maintains that masculinity is not necessarily about men. In her essay "'Gosh Boy George, you must be awfully secure in your masculinity'" (1995), Sedgwick states that, just like men, she as a woman is a consumer, producer, and performer of masculinities (13). What Sedgwick means by that is that her own behaviour and attitudes as a woman are simultaneously shaped by and reinforce ideas about gender. In this way, women can reaffirm the idea that "everything that can be said about masculinity pertains in the first place to men" (Sedgwick, "Gosh" 12). But they can also actively participate in the dissolution of the gender binary and the creation of new gender categories by displaying what is perceived by others as masculinity. Sedgwick particularly focuses on the gender performance of femme and butch women in this context and the negotiation of her own gender identity.

---

30   The concept of female masculinity has also attracted criticism. According to Lynne Segal, attributes that are usually assigned to men should also be acknowledged as aspects of femininity, not just as markers of masculinity: "When women display power, assertiveness, physical prowess, intellectual rigour, aggression or simply black leather boots, how useful is it, I wonder, to view this as 'performing masculinity' rather than aspects of 'femininity' ...?" ("Back" 235, emphasis in original). I agree with Segal on that point.

In a related but slightly different vein, Connell and Messerschmidt point out that "focusing only on the activities of men occludes the practices of women in the construction of gender among men. As is well shown by life-history research, women are central in many of the processes constructing masculinities" (Connell and Messerschmidt 848). They therefore suggest to "give much closer attention to practices of women and to the historical interplay of femininities and masculinities" (ibid.) in research on hegemonic masculinity.

Disassociating men and masculinity is particularly difficult, however. As Halberstam states in an interview with Annamarie Jagose for the online journal *Genders*, "we have an easier time understanding [femininity] as transferable, mobile, fluid. But masculinity has an altogether different relation to performance, the real and the natural and it appears to be far more difficult to pry masculinity and maleness apart than femininity and femaleness" (Jagose). Stefan Horlacher suspects that this may stem "from the fact that while the relationship between femininity and performativity is accepted or even taken for granted, masculinity often tends to deny its performative quality, presenting itself as non- or anti-performative, or masquerading as nature" (61).

Recent work in the field of transgender studies further erodes the correlation between masculinity and maleness: "if both masculinity and a male body can be acquired by a body born or sexed female, then it is extremely difficult to argue or to assume that masculinity ever belongs to men" (Reeser, *Masculinities* 139). At the same time, transgender and transsexual subjects may even "envision sex in a non-Butlerian way as biological" (Reeser, "Concepts" 33):

> When a transsssexual [sic] wants to become a man, and not a woman, to pass as a man, to live life as a man, to create a coherent gender identity where sex and gender correspond in a stable way, to acquire gender advantages traditionally accorded to the male body, then masculinity may appear desirable over femininity, perhaps even hegemonic, and may not be destabilized but in fact (re)affirmed. (Reeser, *Masculinities* 141)

In *Second Skins: The Body Narratives of Transsexuality* (1998), Jay Prosser argues this position. In his book, Prosser highlights the materiality of the body as central to trans experience, arguing that "transition does not shift the subject away from the embodiment of sexual difference but more fully into it" (6). For Prosser, who shares his own experiences with female-to-male transition in his book, the "figure of being trapped in a wrong body" has become a "transsexual leitmotif" (69) for a reason: "because being trapped in the wrong body is simply what transsexuality feels like" (ibid.). Body image therefore "has a material force for transsexuals" (ibid.). This focus on bodily materiality, Prosser argues, "reveals queer theory's own limits: what lies beyond or beneath it's favoured terrain of gender performativity" (6).

Prosser's view is far from being universally accepted. Sandy Stone, for instance, maintains in her landmark essay "The Empire Strikes Back: A Post-transsexual Manifesto" (1987) that "[f]or a transsexual, as a transsexual, to generate a true, effective and representational counterdiscourse is to speak from outside the boundaries of gender, beyond the constructed oppositional nodes which have been predefined as the only positions from which discourse is possible" (230). Building on Stone's argument, Kevin Floyd highlights the importance to think outside the binary structure of gender for many transsexual subjects, "[b]ecause the transition is so frequently *not* into the comfortably knowable space of maleness or femaleness, but into a gendered space that remains inconceivable" (46, emphasis in original). A discourse that embraces trans as an identity is therefore, according to Floyd, a "necessary response to the persistent technological *inability* to effect a full or complete or successful 'transition.'" (ibid., emphasis in original).

It is not possible within the scope of this study to get into more detail regarding this discussion. What it clearly shows, however, is that "[m]asculinity is neither innate nor necessarily liked to a male body" (Horlacher 67). There is no "fixed masculine essence" (Beynon 2).

Nevertheless, it is often assumed that there is such a thing as a unified masculinity, "a standardized container, fixed by biology, into which all 'normal' men are placed, something 'natural' that can even be measured in terms of psychological traits and physical attributes" (Beynon 2). As Horlacher states, "although a large number of human beings do not fit into the culturally produced, traditional heteronormative system of being either male or female, Western culture, even in the twenty-first century, still vigorously defends this system of enforced binaries" (69). This monolithic idea of masculinity is mostly reduced to five features: "[m]ale, white, middle class, heterosexual, and able-bodied" (Schmidt 52).

The myth of a normative masculinity was firmly established in Victorian culture, as we will see in the following. In their introduction to *The Victorian Male Body* (2018), Ruth Heholt and Joanne Ella Parsons point out that while there never is "one, unified, complete, (perfect?) construction of ... [the] male body" (15), there certainly "existed a discourse around this ideal" (ibid.) in the Victorian period. This claim can be expanded beyond Victorian Britain. Building on

Antonio Gramsci's concept of "cultural hegemony", according to which the ruling class secures its supremacy by presenting itself as the societal norm,[31] Connell has shown that the discourse about ideal masculinity fosters the notion of a normative masculine identity that "occupies the hegemonic position in a given pattern of gender relations" (76). According to Connell, hegemonic masculinity "embodies the currently accepted answer to the problem of the legitimacy of patriarchy, which guarantees (or is taken to guarantee) the dominant position of men and the subordination of women" (77). In addition, it legitimises the subjugation of men who do not represent the hegemonic ideal. An important aspect of hegemonic masculinites is that they do not necessarily "correspond closely to the lives of any actual men. Yet these models do, in various ways, express widespread ideals, fantasies, and desires" (Connell and Messerschmidt 838). As Connell and Messerschmidt point out, "there is a circulation of models of admired masculine conduct, which may be exalted by churches, narrated by mass media, or celebrated by the state" (ibid.).[32]

---

31   See Antonio Gramsci's *Selections from the Prison Notebooks*, esp. pp. 257–63.

32   While widely acknowledged as an important critical framework that "challenges us to understand how some masculine models enjoy a privileged relationship to institutional power" (Deane 7), Connell's definition of hegemonic masculinity has also been subject to criticism. For instance, in "Hegemonic Masculinity and Gender History", John Tosh criticises "that the priority which Connell gives to patriarchy is overstated" (53–4). Tosh argues that this emphasis "drastically simplifies the homosocial dynamic ... . Strength, self-reliance, bread-winning capacity, and sexual performance are all in their different ways patriarchal attributes, but they are also celebrated among men in ways which have as much to do with peer-group standing as with sexual dominance" ("Hegemonic" 54). Bradley Deane has defended Connell's approach, stating that her "framework is flexible enough to accommodate this additional dimension" (233n20). I concur with Deane and would like to add that peer-group standing and sexual dominance over women are but two sides of the same patriarchal coin. After all, homosociality has always been one of the pillars of patriarchy. Also, as Connell has pointed out, even if most men do not adhere to the hegemonic standards of masculinity, they still benefit from the presentation of masculinity as normative: "The number of men rigorously practising the hegemonic pattern in its entirety may be quite small. Yet the majority of men gain from its hegemony, since they benefit from the patriarchal dividend, the advantage men in general gain from the overall subordination of women" (Connell 79). Connell is therefore right in emphasising the relationship between hegemonic masculinity and patriarchal structures. Together with James W. Messerschmidt, Connell also responds to critiques and misconception of her concept of hegemonic masculinity in "Hegemonic masculinity: Rethinking the Concept", emphasising that hegemonic masculinity is not "a fixed character type" (Connell and Messerschmidt 854) but a dy-

Antony Easthope has argued that the presentation of the white, male body as normative provides people belonging to this group with a cloak of invisibility (1). The spotlight is on everyone who differs from the norm. Jonathan Rutherford also argues this position in his introduction to *Male Order: Unwrapping Masculinity* (1988): "masculinity remains the great unsaid. The contestation is over the bodies of black and gay people and women" (11). Heholt and Parsons similarly emphasise that "everyone else has formed the spectacle and white men have been invisible, or at least less visible, powerful surveyors" (2). This invisibility, critics agree, ensures the supremacist position of white, heterosexual, middle-class men in Western societies. This argument can be traced back to Foucault's concept of disciplinary power. According to Foucault, power was traditionally linked to "what was seen, what was shown. ... Disciplinary power, on the other hand, is exercised through its invisibility; at the same time, it imposes on those whom it subjects a principle of compulsory visibility" (*Discipline* 187). Building on Foucault's concept, Heholt and Parsons have remarked that "[i]f power cannot be seen, it cannot be resisted; if it is obscured it is less likely to be questioned, more likely to be taken-for-granted and left in place. ... [The] powerful gaze is turned outward, illuminating the marginalised, whilst itself remaining in the shadows" (2–3). Drawing upon research about women and the ghost story, I have pointed out earlier that women were rendered invisible and ghostlike in the Victorian and Edwardian periods. This seems to stand in opposition to women's forced visibility as the Other. This apparent contradiction, Heholt and Parsons point out, "is resolved quite easily. ... [The] compulsory visibility for othered people slips quite easily into compelled invisibility. What is not seen is the humanity and agency of the other, partly through the very visibility and objectification of their bodies. ... [I]t is the bodies of the oppressed that are seen, whilst their individuality and agency are not" (4).

With hegemonic masculinity it is the other way around: while white, heterosexual, middle-class masculinity might be invisible, the individual is not. As Stephanie M. Wildman and Adrienne D. Davis have maintained, the

namic and intersectional system of power that varies by context. It can be described as the way "men position themselves through discursive practices" (ibid. 841). Connell and Messerschmidt further emphasise that "it is a mistake to deduce relations among masculinities from the direct exercise of personal power by men over women. At the least, we also must factor in the institutionalization of gender inequalities, the role of cultural constructions, and the interplay of gender dynamics with race, class, and region" (ibid. 839).

trademarks of the privileged group do not only define the societal norm, but the "normalization of privilege means that members of society are judged, and succeed or fail, measured against the characteristics that are held by those privileged" (890). With regards to hegemonic concepts of masculinity, this means that men are constantly judged on whether they conform to the normative standards of manliness "as tough, heterosexual, authoritative, successful" (Segal, "Back" 239). Those who do not live up to the socially accepted norm risk being seen as inferior.[33] Accordingly, men are subjected to an omnipresent gaze and are thus in constant danger that their behaviour might be recognised as unmanly by their environment. As with normative categories in general, hegemonic masculinity therefore "face[s] the problem that not many men actually meet the normative standards" (Connell 79).

Hegemonic masculinity is therefore not only an attempt to ensure patriarchal structures, but also functions as a system of oppression for men. As Donald E. Hall has noted, "[w]hile the male body has often served as a paradigm and metaphor for male-dominated culture and society, it has also served as a site for struggle" (6). In a similar vein, Lynne Segal stresses that hegemonic masculinity is tightly linked to "images of power and control over anything indicative of weakness – whether in women, other men or, importantly[,] in repudiated aspects of oneself" ("Back" 239). That is not to say that the privileged class of men face the same kind of oppression that women, men of colour, homosexual men, transgender men etc. often endure. Nevertheless, the representation of one form of masculinity as hegemonic functions as a mechanism of control that seeks to constrain male gender performance. This is a particularly important point which lies at the heart of most ghost stories discussed in the following chapters. By portraying men who fail to display the prevalent hallmarks of masculinity, these stories suggest that hegemonic masculinity might not be that predominant after all and that the majority of men occupy a margin

---

33   Connell notes that this does not necessarily mean "that the most visible bearers of hegemonic masculinity are always the most powerful people. ... Individual holders of institutional power or great wealth may be far from the hegemonic pattern in their personal lives" (77). However, "hegemony is likely to be established only if there is some correspondence between cultural ideal and institutional power" (ibid.).

of abject masculinities.[34] In doing so, they expose "the fractures, imperfections and failures" (Heholt and Parsons 14) of the prevalent concept of masculinity. The ideal of masculinity under scrutiny in this study is the concept of imperial masculinity, as it has been termed by several critics.[35] It refers to the dominant expression of masculinity in the second half of the nineteenth century and at the onset of the twentieth century in the British Empire. At its heart is the image of the courageous, resolute, and self-disciplined man who would sacrifice himself for the greater good. As with hegemonic masculinity in general, the ideal of imperial masculinity seemed to describe the societal norm. In reality, however, it was very class-specific and pertained to a privileged group of white, middle-class men. The scope of this study is therefore limited to the situation of this group and does not pertain to all men.

David Newsome has identified the middle of the nineteenth century as a turning point in the perception of manliness in Victorian Britain. In his often-cited *Godliness and Good Learning: Four Studies on a Victorian Ideal* (1961), Newsome notes that while "the tendency to emotionalism and to passionate friendship" (83) was seen as an integral part of male gender identity in the early Victorian period, "displays of emotion came in time to be regarded as bad form" (26). Emotions like affection and sensitivity were rejected as markedly feminine qualities which were incompatible with true manliness. Vulnerability had to be concealed beneath a masquerade of confidence. As John Tosh has put it: "the door was shut on emotional disclosure for men by the new cult of the 'stiff upper lip'" (*Manliness* 22). David Newsome causally links this "change of spirit" (26) to the demands of the growing Empire, arguing that "it would never

---

34   The "abject" as a concept in Gothic fiction was introduced by Julia Kristeva in her influential *Powers of Horror* (1982). According to Kristeva, the abject transgresses the boundaries between the self and the Other and reminds the self of its rejected aspects. As Kristeva notes, the abject "takes the ego back to its source on the abominable limits from which, in order to be, the ego has broken away" (15). Building on Kristeva's ideas, Elisabeth Bronfen has identified the monster as an exemplary embodiment of the abject: "Monstrous bodies can fruitfully be seen as symptoms of anxiety regarding the fragility of identity because they embody a blurring between human and inhuman" (3). A similar point can be made about ghosts: the liminality of the spectre, its status as a being that is neither dead nor alive, neither past, present nor future, undermines the boundaries between being and non-being, subject and object, and thus evokes abjection.

35   See, for instance, Beynon, *Masculinities and Culture*, p. 26, and Deane, *Masculinity and the New Imperialism*, p. 7.

have done for Empire builders ... to exhibit their emotions" (83). The hegemonic concept of masculinity was influenced by the expansion of the British Empire in so far as character traits needed for combat and service in the Empire became fundamental to male gender performance. As Tosh has pointed out, the Empire's "acquisition and control depended disproportionally on the energy and ruthlessness of men" (*Manliness* 193). Men had to be both physically and mentally strong in order to ensure British supremacy (Beynon 32). To this end, "[p]hysical strength and valour" as well as "psychological toughness and self-discipline" (ibid.) became exemplary virtues that every man should possess, or at least aspire to.

The British Empire had grown throughout the eighteenth and nineteenth centuries and was at its height at the *fin de siècle* with the occupation of parts of Africa. Especially in the time period investigated in this work (1860–1914), the British Empire expanded significantly. As Robert Young has observed, "between 1860 and 1900 the geographical area of the British Empire more than quadrupled" (*Postcolonialism* 34).[36] This emphasis on the expansion of British borders can partly be attributed to the rise of other political and economic powers such as Germany and the United States, which "forced the British to seek new protected markets and raw material" (Ledger and Luckhurst 133). In addition, the "empire became a new locus for making the nation cohere" (ibid. 134). Even though imperial expansionism was attacked by socialists for whom the Empire meant "wars, bloodshed, exploitation and a sordid search for profits" (Eldridge 2), imperialism as an ideology rose to the centre of the national psyche and forged notions of racial and national superiority – concepts which came to replace religion as a form of identification at a time when Charles Darwin's *On the Origin of the Species* (1859) had "encouraged wide scale religious doubt" (Jamieson 72).[37] This was the time of what is now referred to as "New

---

36   According to Sally Ledger and Roger Luckhurst, "[b]etween 1870 and 1900, the British empire was extended by 4.75 million square miles, annexing thirty-nine separate areas and adding 88 million new 'subjects' for Queen and Empress Victoria, taking her tally to 420 million people" (133).

37   For an excellent selection of imperialist and anti-imperialist primary texts, see Sally Ledger's and Roger Luckhurst's *The Fin de Siècle: A Reader in Cultural History c. 1880–1900* (2000), which contains, for instance, a socialist reading of imperialism by J. A. Hobson. In his text, Hobson argues that imperialism is less "the product of blind passions" (162), but "primarily a struggle for profitable markets of investment" (164). Written in 1902, Hobson's text anticipates many of the issues we have today regarding globalisation, consumerism, and capitalism.

Imperialism", when the Empire was seen as "the source and proof of Britain's Glory" (Deane 9).

The conviction in the racial and cultural superiority of white people, in general, and the English, in particular, was also reflected in the ideal of masculinity. As Newsome has pointed out, "patriotism and doing one's duty for country and Empire became the main sentiments" (26) for men. This development was accompanied by a "marked appetite of the British public for conquest, combat and heroism" (Tosh, *Manliness* 192). Accordingly, there was a close link between the prevalent concept of masculinity and the imperialist ideologies which fuelled British expansionism.

In *Masculinity and the New Imperialism* (2014), Bradley Deane notes a particularly revealing feature of imperial masculinity: "just as the New Imperialism was not merely an escalation of earlier political commitments but a seismic revision of the Empire's purpose, so too was imperial masculinity marked by its readiness to reject earlier masculine values" (Deane 7). Where earlier notions of masculinity "stress personal development and moral maturation as exemplary virtues" (Berger 3), the concept of imperial masculinity is characterised by an emphasis on physical strength and mental resilience (Tosh, *Manliness* 22). Role models like "the entrepreneur, the missionary, and the affectionate family man [...] [were] elbowed aside by the untamed frontiersman, the impetuous boy, and the unapologetically violent soldier" (Deane 1).

The most striking difference between earlier models of masculinity and the new hypermasculine ideal arguably lies in the relationship with domesticity and femininity. While a respectable household "signified not only a man's success as a breadwinner, but also a haven in which his manly character could be bolstered by the moral influence of his wife" (Deane 5) in the first half of the nineteenth century, femininity and domestic life gradually came to be regarded as damaging influences in the second half. The mother was increasingly perceived as a hindrance in the acquisition of true manliness. It was believed that only a tough environment could forge boys into "real" men. To this end, upper- and middle-class fathers sent their sons to public schools, which they regarded as a "crash course in manliness" (Tosh, *Masculinity* 2). They hoped that far away from the softening influence of the feminine, boys could grow into manly men (ibid.).

The Victorian public schools, in turn, saw it as their duty to maintain British supremacy through their members (Mangan, *Games Ethic* 21). As J. A. Mangan has pointed out, most headmasters "had a view of education that was not only national but also imperial" (ibid. 43). Interestingly, they "did not base their claim to service the empire on academic grounds. What they specialized in was manliness" (Tosh, *Manliness* 197). This is evidenced, for instance, in an article which H. H. Almond, headmaster of Scotland's oldest boarding school Loretto from 1862 until 1903, wrote for *The New Review* in 1897. Referring to the so-called Indian Rebellion of 1857, he maintains that "[i]t should be remembered that it is not the scholar or mathematician, but the man of nerve, endurance, high courage, and animal spirits who may avert disaster in any future mutiny" ("Public School" 96). In another article for *Macmillan's Magazine*, published in 1881, Almond further maintains that physical robustness should be central to the school curriculum. On that, he asserts, "depended the future maintenance of the physical vigour of our imperial race" ("Athletics and Education" 293). "Team sports, which formed an integral part of the school curriculum at that time, played a significant role in this context" (Berger 3). It was assumed that they would instill in boys a sense of subordination to the team and the ability to obey or issue commands (Mangan, *"Manufactured"* 60). Military heroes like General Robert Baden-Powell, who founded the "Boy Scout Movement" in 1907, reinforced this link by claiming that the playing field served as preparation for the battlefield (Mangan, *Games Ethic* 47–48).[38]

---

38   In a letter dated 22 July 1900, which was addressed to the pupils of his former preparatory school in Brighton, Baden-Powell directly links skills acquired on the playing-field to the success of the imperial project: "while you are yet boys is the time to learn to do your duty. ... At football you do your duty not by playing to show yourself off to the onlookers but to obey the orders of the Captain of the team and to back up so that your side win the game. And you do your duty in carrying out the orders of your masters ... If you can get into the way of thinking only of doing your duty while you are still boys at school it will come quite naturally to you when you grow up, to continue to do it for your Sovereign and your country, and you will never dream of trying to save your own life if your duty requires you to risk it" (qtd. in Mangan, *Games Ethic* 47–8). Reverent J. E. C. Welldon, headmaster of Harrow School from 1881 to 1895, likewise asserts in a speech at the Royal Colonial Institute's Seventh Ordinary General Meeting of 1895 that team sports not only contribute to mental and physical toughness, but nurture skills that ensure Britain's supremacy: "Englishmen are not superior to Frenchmen or Germans in brains or industry or the science and apparatus of war; but they are superior in the health and temper which games impart. ... For it is not the physical value of athletic games that is the highest. The pluck, the energy, the perseverance, the good temper, the self-control, the discipline, the co-operation, the esprit de corps, which merit success in cricket or football, are the very qualities which win the day in peace or war" (qdt. in Mangan, *Games Ethic* 34).

An equally important nurturing ground for the development of imperial masculinity were the popular adventure tales. Published mainly in magazines for juvenile male readers, they constituted "one of the most widely consumed forms of entertainment" (Boyd 34) in the second half of the nineteenth century. As Kelly Boyd has pointed out, "adventure tales offered a canvas on which dramas of character could be played out. ... Character in this instance was a code word for manliness and masculinity" (49). By featuring resourceful young men who prove their manly vigour in a series of trials somewhere in the far reaches of the British Empire, they promoted "to a wide and enthusiastic audience new fantasies of an imperialist masculinity" (Deane 1–2). It is noteworthy that adventure tales did not only provide boys and juvenile men with plucky role models but reinforced imperial ideologies by using foreign countries and native people as a counterpart against which the white, male heroes could define themselves as rightful leaders of the world. In this way, adventure tales reinforced the link between Britain's imperial mission and the definition of masculinity.

John Tosh has pointed out that ideas about hegemonic masculinity are not only maintained by institutional power but reaffirmed "by cultural means such as education and the popular media, which establish many of the assumptions of hegemonic masculinity in the realm of 'common sense', where they are particularly difficult to dislodge" (Tosh, "Hegemonic" 43). As we have seen, both of these cultural means were particularly relevant in the shaping and dissemination of imperial masculinity.

Another factor that marked the concept of imperial masculinity was its emphasis on a healthy mind and body – a thought which ties the ideal to the muscular Christianity movement of the mid-Victorian period. Popularised through the novels of Charles Kingsley and Thomas Hughes, the movement promoted the idea that bodily activities enhance the workings of the mind and make a man a better Christian. With their emphasis on physical and mental strength, the advocates of muscular Christianity certainly influenced the hegemonic concept of masculinity in the second half of the nineteenth century. However, as the century progressed, the stress of the muscular Christians on a "healthy body as the temple for the moral person" (Boyd 40) was replaced by a more reckless attitude which was less concerned with morality. "Christianity drops out of the picture" (Vance 191), as Norman Vance has adequately put it in *The Sinews of the Spirit* (1985).[39]

The preoccupation with health was also not particular to the muscular Christianity movement but is part of a larger discourse about health in the second half of the nineteenth century. As Bruce Haley has noted in *The Healthy Body and Victorian Culture* (1978), "no topic more occupied the Victorian mind than Health" (3). Michel Foucault has argued in his landmark work *The History of Sexuality* (1976) that what is often seen as the repression of sexuality in the Victorian period can partly be attributed to a concern for the healthy body, "a body to be cared for, protected, cultivated, and preserved from the many dangers and contacts" (122) it is exposed to. What blood is to the aristocracy, Foucault maintains, is the cultivation of a healthy body to the newly rich and influential middle class. "Its dominance was in part dependent on that cultivation" (Foucault, *Sexuality* 125).

In addition to Foucault's argument, I believe that the Victorian preoccupation with health is also indicative of anxieties about the decay of Great Britain as a nation – anxieties that were fuelled by a discourse about degeneration in the latter decades of the nineteenth century. Even though the British Empire was still growing, there was a feeling of crisis. As John Beynon has put it: "The major concern was that ... [the British Empire], like the Roman Empire, would rot from within" (38). Especially the fear "that the national 'stock' of men was degenerating" (ibid. 27) became an issue in the last quarter of the nineteenth century. In 1882, an inquiry into the constitutional robustness of British civil servants in India revealed that "of a total of thirty-seven civilians, five had gone insane, seven had retired, and thirteen were in poor health" (Sinha 107). In an attempt to explain these alarming figures, a commentator with *The Times* in London detected unmanliness as one of the reasons for the poor health of the civil servants (ibid.), thus establishing a direct link between healthiness and manliness. Concerns about the mental health of men were further reinforced by accounts of male hysteria. While long recognized as a disease in women, physicians and psychologists started to diagnose men with hysteria in the 1880s (Showalter, *Hystories* 66). The fitness of British men also rose to the centre of attention during the Second Boer War in South Africa between 1899 and 1902, first due to the loss of important battles of the British army against

---

39   For more information on the muscular Christianity movement, see Vance's *The Sinews of the Spirit* and J. A. Mangan's and James Walvin's *Manliness and Morality* (1987) respectively.

"a handful of Dutch farmers, and second through the recruiting campaign that discovered the physical inadequacies of the men from London's East-End slums, who were alarmingly undersized, frail, and sickly" (Spencer 311). Both events hint at the inability of Englishmen to defend the Empire. Fears about national and individual decline became inextricably linked and unsettled the confidence in the future of both the British Empire and the English race. The ideal of imperial masculinity with its marked emphasis on a robust mind and body was motored by these fears. It was an attempt to revitalise the nation through the display of "true" manliness.

However, it would be short-sighted to see the prevalent concept of manliness only as a product of Britain's imperial needs and concerns about the Empire's decline. John Tosh has suggested that the harsh definition of masculinity at the end of the century was also caused by the "fear of women in the social arena" (Tosh, *Manliness* 22). He proposes to reverse "the relationship between imperialism and masculinity by locating the primary sense of crisis, not in the empire, but in the pattern of gender relations. According to this perspective, enthusiasm for the empire at the end of the century was a symptom of masculine insecurity within Britain" (*Manliness* 194). In fact, the Empire confirmed male gender identity at a time which saw growing enthusiasm for the feminist cause which culminated in the New Woman movement in the 1890s and the suffrage movement at the beginning of the twentieth century. It served as a "site of 'masculinist imaginings' in which men could enjoy homosocial comradeship in physically challenging, arduous circumstances far from what they perceived to be the damaging influences of 'the feminine'" (Beynon 31). Joanna de Groot is therefore correct in suggesting that the relationship between imperialism and hegemonic masculinity was reciprocal: "manliness and empire confirmed one another, guaranteed one another, enhanced one another" (Groot 122).

This brings us back to the beginning of our discussion of masculinity and Connell's assertion that hegemonic masculinity serves as the foundation of patriarchal structures. Connell has argued that masculinity is "inherently relational" (68) and "does not exist except in contrast with 'femininity'" (ibid.). It is hardly surprising, therefore, that a perception of masculinity which is defined by the rigorous rejection of feminine virtues established itself as a powerful social imperative exactly at a time when women increasingly questioned the binary division of gender which had ensured male supremacy up to that point.

The ghost stories discussed in this work show that the concept of imperial masculinity was influenced by a multitude of factors – among them concerns about the crumbling Empire, the agitation for women's rights, and new findings in psychology which suggested the deep and potentially terrifying abysses of the human mind. By revealing the pitfalls of the prevalent concept of manliness, they question hegemonic gender categories and invite readers to rethink their own ideas about sex and gender.

The Structure of this Book

In *Spectres of Masculinity: Manhood in Victorian and Edwardian Ghost Stories, 1860–1914*, I examine a wide range of ghost stories from the mid-Victorian period to the Great War. While most of these stories were penned by well-known authors such as Arthur Conan Doyle, Rudyard Kipling, and Elizabeth Gaskell, I also look at tales written by less prominent writers such as Lettice Galbraith, whose dark supernatural tales are threatened to fall into oblivion. The stories are divided into four chapters.

My first chapter focuses on what is arguably the most common trope found in ghost literature: the haunted house. My central argument is that the gendered space of the domestic family home represents a site where patriarchal assumptions of male dominance can be questioned and undermined. In order to illustrate this, I look at ghost stories by Charlotte Riddell, Lettice Galbraith, and Algernon Blackwood. Contrary to "the emphatic Victorian development of the idea of home as a place of peace, safety, and protection" (Warwick 30), these stories disturb the idea of the domestic space as a site where men bolster their masculinity. On the contrary, they become fearful and helpless, unable to face the supernatural with manly vigour and determination. Women, by contrast, display power in these narratives, thereby usurping the territory of the domestic space as female dominion.

My second chapter looks at the ways in which male sexual desire was "spectralised" in the latter decades of the nineteenth century. Based on Michel Foucault's *The History of Sexuality* and more recent research on the closet, I argue that the ambiguous readability of the ghost story provided a means for authors to express sexual and gender identities that were deemed unacceptable or even unlawful by society. The chapter is divided into two sections. In the first section, I look at how homosexual love and desire are articulated in coded ways in ghost stories written by Vernon Lee and Henry James. The second section focuses on a question which has received little scholarly attention so far: how did the idea of the sexually pure and submissive "Angel in the House" affect men and their perception of their own sexual identity? In an attempt to answer this question, I examine supernatural tales by Elizabeth Gaskell and Edith Nesbit which feature male narrators who struggle against their supposedly unruly desire for sexually expressive and active women.

Building on Patrick Brantlinger's description of imperial Gothic fiction as "that blend of adventure story with Gothic elements" (227), my third chapter[40] argues that imperial ghost stories form a sort of antithesis to the popular adventure fiction of the period: while adventure fiction reaffirms the belief in the imperial mission and the racial superiority of the white Englishman through the display of hypermasculine heroes, imperial ghost stories establish connections between imperial decline and masculine failure. In order to illustrate the ways in which imperial ghost fiction functions to destabilise the binary construction between civilised Western Self and savage Eastern Other, I will first pinpoint the narrative formula of imperial adventure fiction and then compare it to ghost stories by Amelia B. Edwards, Rudyard Kipling, and Arthur Conan Doyle. One of my central arguments is that both adventure fiction and imperial ghost stories ultimately reflect anxieties about the decay of the British Empire.

My final chapter engages with the relationship between science and spiritualism. While the former was tightly associated with educated, middle-class men and their supposedly masculine rationality, spiritualism was linked to women and their "feminine" emotionalism. The stories analysed in this chapter subvert the hierarchical dualism between manly rationality and womanly emotionalism by privileging allegedly female forms of knowledge such as intuition and the belief in the supernatural over scientific epistemology. The chapter is split up into two sections. In the first section, I look at ghost stories by Bram Stoker and Lettice Galbraith which feature sceptical male materialists whose rationalist worldview prevents them from considering the possibility of ghosts and haunting – with fatal consequences. By proving these men wrong, the stories problematise the elevation of rational materialism as

---

40   Parts of my third chapter were previously published as a research article in *Humanities*, vol. 9, no. 4, Oct. 2020, titled "Haunted Oppressors: The Deconstruction of Manliness in the Imperial Gothic Stories of Rudyard Kipling and Arthur Conan Doyle". They appear here with permission and are supplemented by new, previously unpublished insights and interpretations. The present paragraph also draws on material from the earlier publication. The original open-access article can be accessed at https://www.mdpi.co m/2076-0787/9/4/122.

a basis for male gender performance. In the second section, my analysis focuses on supernatural tales by Margaret Oliphant and Rudyard Kipling which propose a transformed concept of masculinity that accommodates emotions like affection, sensitivity, and tenderness as important facets of male gender identity, thereby countering the prevalent ideal of imperial masculinity with its stern rejection of supposedly female character traits. The encounter with ghost children plays an important role in both stories. For one, it is through their interaction with the ghost children that the protagonists develop a spiritual awareness which enables them to assume a modified form of masculinity. Furthermore, the children's emotional dependence on the male ghost-seers opposes ideas of fatherhood as unemotional and reserved. In this way, these stories stress the importance of paternal involvement.

Overall, the stories discussed in this work expose the myth of the hyper-masculine soldier hero as a socio-cultural and political tool that was used to ensure the supremacist position of white, middle-class men, on the one hand, and to control, confine, and discipline them, on the other hand. By questioning normative ideas about masculinity, they ultimately promote healthier and more diverse ways of being a man.

Chapter 1
Uncanny Places: Haunted Houses and Male Discomfort

The house is arguably the most common location for ghosts and haunting to occur. "Everybody has heard of haunted houses; and there is no country, and scarcely any place, in which something of the sort is not known or talked of" (Crowe 273), Catherine Crowe remarks in her popular collection of paranormal phenomena *The Night Side of Nature, or Ghosts and Ghost-Seers*, which was first published in 1849. Weary of the figure of the haunted house, Charles Dickens complains about the stereotypical repetition of the trope in his 1850 essay "A Christmas Tree": "There is no end to the old houses, with resounding galleries, and dismal state-bedchambers, and haunted wings shut up for many years, through which we may ramble, with an agreeable creeping up our back, and encounter any number of ghosts, but (it is worthy to remark perhaps) reducible to a very few general types and classes; for, ghosts have little originality, and 'walk' in beaten track" (Dickens, "Christmas" 242–3). Despite his apparent boredom with clichés surrounding the haunted house, Dickens still seems to have remained fascinated by the feature and even dedicated the 1859 extra Christmas number of his popular family magazine *All the Year Round* to "The Haunted House".[1]

We will encounter at least one haunted house tale in each chapter of this book. While in some stories we are made to encounter malicious spectres whose motive for disturbing a house is not revealed to us, others feature ghosts that are animated by a trauma or an injustice they wish to overcome and share with the present inhabitants or visitors of the houses they haunt:

---

1   For the issue, he asked writers, including Elizabeth Gaskell and Wilkie Collins, to invent a story for each room in a supposedly haunted country house. Dickens also contributed three stories – among them the opening and the closing tales. See Dickens, Charles. *The Haunted House*. Mineola, Dover Publications, 2008.

they seek to undo past wrongdoings, be reunited with loved ones, deliver some kind of message, or take revenge, often on their murderer.

The present chapter focuses exclusively on houses and haunting. It uses ghost stories by Charlotte Riddell, Lettice Galbraith, and Algernon Blackwood as an example of the ways in which Victorian writers engage with male discomfort and gendered domestic spaces in their haunted house narratives. While Riddell's "Nut Bush Farm" (1882) and Blackwood's "The Empty House" (1906) feature male protagonists whose reaction to ghosts and haunting stands in contrast to dominant scripts of masculinity and forces them to re-evaluate their perception of their own masculine identity, Galbraith's "A Ghost's Revenge" (1893) undermines patriarchal power structures by demonstrating female superiority within the haunted domestic space. Before delving into a discussion of these three stories, I believe it is necessary to spend some time on the haunted house trope itself and the gendered aspects of what Anthony Vidler has termed "the architectural uncanny" (ix) in his influential work on the subject.

Remnants of the Past: History, Architecture, and Gendered Domestic Spaces

To this day, the figure of the haunted house has remained a key element in supernatural fiction. "The haunted house is a stock structural and narrative figure, whether one thinks of Henry James' *The Turn of the Screw*, Charles Dickens' *A Christmas Carol*, or Stephen King's (and Stanley Kubrick's) *The Shining*, to take some obvious examples" (5), Julian Wolfreys writes in *Victorian Hauntings: Spectrality, Gothic, the Uncanny and Literature* (2002), thus referring to popular works from the mid-Victorian period to the late twentieth century.[2] By including Kubrick's film adaptation of King's *The Shining*, Wolfreys draws attention to the fact that the trope of the haunted house is not restricted to writing, but has entered other forms of entertainment in the course of the twentieth and twenty-first centuries. In addition to films, it recurs in graphic novels, features in video games, and is a stock element at almost every funfair.

---

2   Charles Dickens' *A Christmas Carol* was published in 1843, Henry James' *The Turn of the Screw* appeared in 1898, and Stephen King's *The Shining* was printed in 1977 and followed by the film release three years later.

What, however, is it that turned the haunted house into such an enduringly popular narrative feature? In "Archive Fever: A Freudian Impression" (1995), Derrida states that "haunting implies places, a habitation, and always a haunted house" (55). My analysis complicates this observation insofar as haunting is also shown as a state of mind in many of the tales discussed in this and the following chapters. It also stands in opposition to Derrida's own concept of hauntology and his insistence on the spectral persistence of political thoughts. His comment is nevertheless helpful for a discussion of ghost stories, for it makes clear that ghosts do not exist except in relation to particular locations – be that a lonely moor, a haunted house, or the human mind. Also, as Wolfrey's choice of works in the above quote illustrates, haunted minds and haunted houses do not necessarily stand in opposition to one another. Quite the contrary: while *The Turn of the Screw* and *A Christmas Carrol* are constructed in a way that makes it impossible to tell whether the protagonists are confronted with real ghosts or whether they are a figment of their imagination, the house and the mind of the story's protagonist are likewise haunted in *The Shining* – in both King's novel and Kubrick's film adaptation. The same can be said about many of the ghost stories discussed in this work, as we shall see.

However, the close relationship between ghosts and houses cannot be explained merely by the fact that ghosts need places in order to exist. Reminiscent of Dickens's comment on haunted houses, Stephen King writes in his nonfiction book about horror fiction, *Danse Macabre* (1981), that a good haunted house narrative needs more than simply "a repertory company of ghosts, complete with clanking chains, doors that bang open or shut in the middle of the night, and strange noises in the attic or cellar" (King, *Danse* 281). For King, "the haunted-house tale demands a historical context" (ibid. 282). I agree with King on that point and would suggest that it is the interplay between past and present that makes the house particularly suitable as a haunted location. As Nick Freeman has pointed out, the house is a place which "exists in the present as both a historical artefact and a contemporary residence" ("Haunted" 328). A house, if it is not newly built, wears the marks of its former inhabitants, thus reminding the present owners of its history and the people who used to live in it. Even haunted house narratives that "spectralise newness" (Liggins, *Haunted House* 28), as Emma Liggins has put it, are often in some way connected to the past and stir up buried memories: "compact modern households, more sparkly than sullen, did still include 'family vaults' in the form of undisclosed secrets and haunting memories. ... The new is rapidly invaded by memories and unseen presences" (ibid. 243). This invasion of the present/future by the past evokes Derrida's concept of hauntology, according to which the ghost as a revenant naturally disrupts the idea of a linear temporality (*Specters* 48). As Derrida points out, the "being-with specters" is always also "a *politics* of memory, of inheritance, of generations" (ibid. xviii, emphasis in original). Houses and ghosts, therefore, have much in common: both are inevitably bound up with the past, thereby undermining the assumption that the present can overcome the past. This striking parallel between ghosts and houses is foregrounded in the haunted house narrative, where the history of a house and its past inhabitants is brought to the attention of the present occupant or visitor through the manifestation of a ghost/ghosts.

The three haunted house narratives discussed in this chapter highlight what Glennis Byron and David Punter have described as "the domestication of Gothic figures, spaces and themes" (26). While the haunting was distanced from the everyday life of the British audience in early Gothic fiction through the setting of the story in a remote castle or monastery somewhere in a catholic country on the continent, horrors became located within the world of the reader in Victorian Gothic fiction. As Fred Botting has noted, "the castle gradually gave way to the old house; as both building and family line, it became the site where fears and anxieties returned in the present" (Botting, *Gothic* 3). In a similar vein, Alexandra Warwick has argued that the transition from early Gothic to Victorian Gothic fiction is primarily marked by a shift of location: "first to a bourgeois domestic setting, and second to the urban environment" (Warwick 30). The three ghost stories investigated below showcase the whole range of Victorian Gothic settings – from prosperous country estate in Galbraith's "A Ghost's Revenge" to rural farmhouse in Riddell's "Nut Bush Farm", to urban townhouse in Blackwood's "The Empty House".

But how did these new settings affect the reading experience of the Victorian audience? In an essay on the thrills and horrors of the short-lived but nonetheless popular sensation novels of the 1850s and 1860s,[3] Henry James remarks that the genre confronts the reader with

> those most mysterious of all mysteries, the mysteries which are at our own doors. This innovation gave a new impetus to the literature of horrors. It was fatal to the authority of Mrs. Radcliffe and her everlasting castle in the Alpennines. What are the Alpennines to us, or we to the Alpennines? Instead of the

---

3   On the popularity of the genre, see, for instance, Lyn Pykett's "Collins and the Sensation Novel", esp. 50–55.

horrors of "Udolpho", we are treated to the horrors of the cheerful country house and the busy London lodgings. And there is no doubt that these are the more horrible. (James, "Miss Braddon" 110)

According to James, the "literature of horrors" (James, "Miss Braddon" 110) is more shocking when the story is located within the world of the contemporary reader and not far away in some "castle in the Alpennines" (ibid.). The middle-class home, which is often depicted as a "haven of tranquillity" (Pykett, *Wilkie Collins* 88–89) in the domestic novel, becomes "the source and scene of violence" (ibid. 89) in the Victorian Gothic.[4] In line with James's observations, several scholars have argued that the shift of the setting to the house as the locus of the family home makes the haunting appear more shocking. As Wolfreys has remarked, "[t]he act of haunting is effective because it displaces us in those places where we feel most secure, most notably in our homes, in the domestic scene. Indeed, haunting is nothing other than the destabilization of the domestic scene, as that place where we apparently confirm our identity, our sense of being, where we feel most at home with ourselves" (Wolfreys 5). Anthony Vidler similarly emphasises that the familiar atmosphere of the domestic space and "its role as the last and most intimate shelter of private comfort sharpened by contrast the terror of invasion by alien spirits" (17). While I largely agree with these critics, I nonetheless would like to contest the view that the disturbance of the homely domestic space by "alien spirits" (ibid.) is the *primary* source of

---

4   It is perhaps worth noting that the Brontë sisters were among the first British authors who transported Gothic elements into a modern setting. By turning the family home into a prison, Emily Brontë's *Wuthering Heights* (1847) and Anne Brontë's *The Tenant of Wildfell Hall* (1848) both echo the incarceration and persecution of Walepole's and Radcliffe's heroines. Similarly, the fate of Bertha Mason, the madwomen in the attic in Charlotte Brontë's *Jane Eyre* (1847), draws on these tales of female imprisonment. The wrongful incarceration of Laura Fairlie in a lunatic asylum in Wilkie Collins's *The Woman in White* (1860) – one of the novels Henry James is referring to in his essay – is another modernized version of the Gothic element. As Warwick has pointed out, "[i]n contrast with the emphatic Victorian development of the idea of the home as a place of peace, safety and protection, the Brontë's domestic spaces, and the state of marriage or family life that the spaces embody, are terrifyingly ambiguous" (30). However, there is a crucial difference between the incarceration of the vulnerable female characters of Walepole's and Radcliffe's fiction and the incarceration of Bertha in *Jane Eyre*, for Mr Rochester's first wife does not represent a sexually submissive and pure domestic angel, but a woman whose uncontrollable passion was often associated with madness in Victorian society.

terror in Victorian Gothic fiction. Instead, I would like to propose that what is really frightening in these narratives is the fact that the domestic household itself becomes the source of terror, thereby revealing the abysses of the bourgeois family home.

An important point to be made about spectre-smitten houses in this context is that haunting often represents a violation of domestic privacy. Ilse Bussing has identified the Victorian period as a time marked by "an excessive concern for privacy and concealment" (100). This concern, Bussing maintains, is evident in Gothic texts which "are haunted by issues of privacy, concealment and secrecy" (107). As Anne Williams has pointed out, "[a] house makes secrets in merely being itself, for its function is to enclose spaces. … The walls of the house both defend it from the outside world ('A man's home is his castle') and hide the secrets it thereby creates" (44). Ghosts threaten to disclose those secrets. As Emma Liggins has remarked, "[t]he return of the dead may destroy the intimacy of the home by revealing its secrets" (*Haunted House* 3).

Sigmund Freud's investigation of the etymological entanglements of the German words *heimlich* (secret/homely), *unheimlich* (uncanny), and *Heim* (home) in his 1919 essay "The Uncanny" also points to the home as the locus of the uncanny. The home is a secretive and therefore potentially uncanny place; a space that can turn from homely and private to unhomely and secretive. This "disquieting slippage between what seems homely and what is definitely unhomely" (Vidler ix-x) is at the core of what Anthony Vidler has described as the architectural or "spatial" (ibid. x) uncanny.

Several scholars have also emphasised the importance of gender to discussions of Gothic spatiality. Kate Kruger defines gendered spaces as "locations wherein social interactions are governed by expectations surrounding masculine and feminine behaviors" (1). In her insightful *British Women Writers and the Short Story, 1850–1930: Reclaiming Social Space* (2014), Kruger argues that ghost stories by M. E. Braddon and Rhoda Broughton "disturb a particular social definition of home that hinges upon conventional Victorian gender relations" (98), thus exposing "the undeniable instability of the Victorian home as an ideological space" (100). According to Kruger, this is achieved by the spectral transgression of spatial boundaries and the subsequent disclosure of marital secrets: "Spaces purportedly designed for a heightened sense of privacy and segregation of the household – the garden, the bedroom, the dressing room, and the stairwell – expose the untenable behaviors of spouse and parent" (K. Kruger 98). Liggins also draws attention to "the gendered implications of haunted space" (*Haunted House* 12) in her recent study *The Haunted House in Women's Ghost Stories: Gender, Space and Modernity, 1850–1945* (2020): "As most of the haunted houses that appeared in women's ghost stories were domestic spaces, concepts of home and domestic organisation are crucial to understanding the haunted house narrative, as if in this period what is most haunting is domesticity itself" (Liggins, *Haunted House* 6).

The constructions of home and domesticity to which Kruger and Liggins are referring are closely linked to the Victorian separate spheres ideology, whose long shadow arguably still influences ideas about ideal gender performance to this day. According to this ideology, men and women are inherently dissimilar. While men are best suited for the active role of the breadwinner, women are designed to occupy the private sphere of the Victorian middle-class home. These binary ideas about gender reflect the assumption that human beings are determined by their biological sex. It is a notion that equates gender with the chromosomal sex of a person. Scientific research, such as Darwin's ground-breaking study *The Descent of Man, and Selection in Relation to Sex* (1871), reaffirmed and fuelled such ideas, arguing that "women had evolved differently from men, that their nurturant domestic capabilities fitted them for home and hearth, while men had evolved aggressive, competitive abilities that were meant to be exercised in the public arena" (Kahane 287). This female/male dichotomy has, of course, always been a myth. For one, it did not apply to working class women who, out of necessity, had to enter into the world of business and trade in order to support their families. Furthermore, the conduct books for adolescent men and women, which proliferated in the nineteenth century, indicate the concern that the attributes pointed out above are not innate qualities but have to be cultivated.[5] Nevertheless, the representation of one form of femininity/masculinity as normative has a disciplinary effect and marks those who deviate from the norm as "the Other". As Christine Junker has pointed out, "the influence of the separate spheres worked concurrently with the cult of domesticity to spatialize identity" (3).

Despite women's association with domesticity, the Victorian family home was "heavily patriarchal in terms of territory, control, and meaning" (L. Walker 826). While gender functioned as "an organizing principle in architecture ... since antiquity" (ibid.), the gendering of houses and the rooms they contain was particularly prevalent in the construction of houses during the Victorian

---

5   In an article for *The British Library*, Holly Furneaux also argues this position. See Furneaux, Holly. "Victorian Sexualities." *The British Library*. 15 May 2014. https://www. bl.uk/romantics-and-victorians/articles/victorian-sexualities.

period. This is evident in the work of the well-known British architect Robert Kerr, who advises architects on the spatial organisation of houses in his *The Gentleman's House; or, How to Plan English Residences* (1864). The title of Kerr's book already suggests the power of the male head of the household. In his book, Kerr then also allocates the majority of rooms to the male members of the household. He also situates them near the front of the house, whereas the women's rooms are placed at the back, thereby reinforcing the association of women with the private sphere and men with the public sphere. Normative ideas about gender thus "get translated into domestic space" (L. Walker 823). Furthermore, women's spaces, such as the drawing room, though furnished and decorated "entirely ladylike" (Kerr 119), can be used by both sexes according to Kerr. By contrast, the men's rooms form "an exclusively male territory within the house" (Chase 114), thus creating "spatial boundaries that produced and upheld dominant gender definitions and relations" (L. Walker 826). Kerr's architectural ideas clearly privilege men and masculinity over women and femininity: "it is the men of the house who hold the real power; it is they who have access to all architectural space and knowledge" (Chase 145).

This comparative powerlessness of women within the domestic space and the male privilege of architectural knowledge is reflected in many nineteenth-century haunted house narratives that stage the family home as the site of female incarceration and abuse, on the one hand, and of male secrecy, on the other hand.[6] Scholarly explorations of haunted house stories have often focused on the exploration of such stories and established them as examples of the female Gothic, "finding in the haunted house an expression of women's discomfort in the social and economic space assigned to them by a patriarchal culture" (Schaper 6).[7]

However, as Susan E. Schaper has noted, the house does not only function as a place of female disempowerment in Victorian ghost fiction; in her insightful exploration of Victorian haunted house narratives, Schaper illustrates that many ghost stories "portray the house as a palimplest inscribed by both domestic and patriarchal values, admitting competing definitions of home and expressing anxiety that occurs when either sex finds itself disempowered in

---

6   A prime example for this is Elizabeth Gaskell's "The Grey Woman" (1961) in which the intimidated heroine, Anna, is likewise imprisoned in the house and excluded from the male quarters.

7   On this issue, see also Diana Wallace's influential article "Uncanny Stories: The Ghost Story as Female Gothic" (2004).

an *unheimlich* perception of home" (6, emphasis in original). For Alexandra Warwick, the home constitutes a place that can potentially disturb traditional ideas
about gender. It is a place "where women are active and often dangerous" (Warwick 31). Emma Liggins similarly remarks that "[w]omen's spatialities can be
paradoxical, ostensibly constrained by patriarchal rules yet also challenging hierarchies within the domestic economy, a realm where female power becomes
a possibility" (Liggins, *Haunted House* 19). The same can be said of men's spa-
tialites. While the architecture of the home reflects male superiority, as we have
seen, Victorian domestic ideology undermines the idea of the home as a masculine sphere, pushing men into "an exile from the refuge of home, now the
special province of women" (K. Ellis xiii). In the ghost stories discussed in the
following, the house more often than not becomes a place of unease for the
male guests, inhabitants, or intruders.

Female Spaces, Monstrous Women, and the Effeminising Effect of Ghost-Seeing in Charlotte Riddell's "Nut Bush Farm", Lettice Galbraith's "A Ghost's Revenge", and Algernon Blackwood's "The Empty House"

In the three ghost stories discussed in the following, patriarchal anxieties
about female power and superiority within the domestic space resurface.
While at first seemingly confident in their representation of normative masculinity, the protagonists of Riddell's "Nut Bush Farm" and Blackwood's "The
Empty House" are shown as insecure and vulnerable to swings of emotion in
the course of the haunted house narratives, while the female characters display
characteristics traditionally associated with men like courage, self-reliance,
and self-control. In Galbraith's "A Ghost's Revenge", the case is somewhat different. While the encounter with the ghostly bolsters the masculine identity
of the story's male protagonist, other male characters are portrayed as feeling
surrendered to an unyielding female power within the domestic sphere which
not only pushes them into a feminised position but threatens their lives. The
house is depicted as an equivocal space in the story. While first established as
a patriarchal territory, the supernatural eventually enables female domination
over the domestic space.

Charlotte Riddell "Nut Bush Farm" (1882)

The figure of the haunted house is particularly prevalent in the supernatural writing of Charlotte Riddell (1832–1906). Five of the six narratives compiled in her well-known short story collection *Weird Stories* (1882) involve haunted properties. In these stories, Riddell generally follows a particular narrative formula, as Victoria Margree has observed:

> a house, rumoured to be haunted, has been deemed uninhabitable by its owners or tenants; a young man, dismissive of the rumours of haunting, takes up occupation of the house (as owner, tenant, or temporarily as investigator) determined to uncover the mystery; greatly to his surprise, his investigations confirm the reality of supernatural possession; the ghost is found to be seeking exposure of a crime, and once this is achieved, the house becomes habitable again. (Margree, "(Other)Wordly" 71)

Part of this narrative formula is the use of a male protagonist who either functions as the narrator or narrative focus of the tale. Margree surmises that Riddell's use of the male narrative voice "might be partly conditioned by the central place within her supernatural fiction of the haunted-house narrative, it being, of course, men much more than women who, in this period, acted as house purchasers, lease-holders and accountant clerks" ("(Other)Wordly" 70). I concur with Margree but would like to add that the use of the male narrative voice also ensures that readers are afforded an insight into the minds of the male protagonists of these stories. In this way, their experience of masculinity is put on display.

In addition, the spectral invasion in Riddell's *Weird Stories* is usually related to money and the deeds people commit for that money: "Misdirected inheritances, missing wills, lack of money, stolen money, squandered money and miserliness all summon restless spirits" (Makala 97). For instance, in "The Open Door", the ghost of a murdered man materialises in order to ensure that property ownership is not passed on to his wife. The story is told by a young clerk who is trying to resolve the mystery surrounding the haunted Ladlow Hall and is almost killed by the young widow who is seeking to get hold of her late husband's will which would disown her. In "The Old House in Vauxhall Walk", a young man encounters the ghost of the former inhabitant, a miserly old woman who was killed by two burglars in search of her money. Murder for money is also the source of haunting in the story that I am shortly going to discuss in more detail: "Nut Bush Farm", which was also published in *Weird Stories*. In this sensational ghost story/detective story hybrid, the new tenant of Nut Bush Farm tries to solve the murder of his predecessor who has returned to the place as a ghost. In all three stories, "spectral trouble is the direct result of monetary trouble" (Makala 97). Riddell's stories thus clearly foreground "the Gothic potential of money to dehumanise" (Margree, "(Other)Worldly" 66).

Given their entanglement with questions of money, property, and inheritance, it is perhaps not surprising that Riddell's haunted house narratives have often been read in light of her own financial situation, which was greatly influenced by the financial mismanagement of the men in her life: while born into a wealthy family as the daughter of a High Sheriff in Cerrickfergus, Ireland, in 1832, she was forced to migrate to London to make her living when her father left her and her mother with a pile of debt after his death in the early 1850s; and then, later in Riddell's life, her husband's failed business ventures repeatedly threatened her with ruin (Bleiler v, Killeen 93–94). Like other female writers of the period, such as Edith Nesbit and Margaret Oliphant, whose ghost stories will also be discussed in this study, Riddell "experienced particularly acutely a conflict between literary aspiration and the responsibilities of financially supporting a family" (Margree, "(Other)Worldly" 67). While I agree with existing research that Riddell's knowledge about the world of business and her own experiences with both "prosperity and pennilessness" (ibid.) greatly influenced her ghost stories as well as her non-supernatural writing, I do not intend to reproduce former discussions on her writing which foreground the economic theme.[8] Instead, my analysis of "Nut Bush Farm" will focus on how the protagonist and his perception of his masculine identity are impacted by the haunting of Nut Bush Farm and explore the ways in which ideas about gender are brought to the forefront of the story. That is not to say that I am going to ignore Riddell's preoccupation with questions of money, wealth, and property altogether, for monetary issues are closely tied to gender issues in "Nut Bush Farm", as we shall see.

---

8   For detailed analyses on how Charlotte Riddell "blended economic concerns with the haunted house motif" (Makala 100–1) see Melissa Edmundson Makala's chapter "'Uncomfortable Houses' and the Spectres of Capital" in *Women's Ghost Literature in Nineteenth-Century Britain*, Victoria Margree's "(Other)Worldly Goods: Gender, Money and Property in the Ghost Stories of Charlotte Riddell", and Andrew Smith's chapter "Love, Money, and History: the Female Ghost Story" in *The Ghost Story, 1840–1920*.

The narrative is told by Jack, a young husband and father, who leaves his office job in London following an accident for which his employers "recompensed [him] with a liberty [he] never can feel sufficiently grateful for" (Riddell, "Nut Bush" 1). In an attempt to change his life, he travels to Kent and starts looking for a farm, while his wife and son stay in London with Jack's father-in-law. No property suits him until he comes across the eponymous Nut Bush Farm, which is owned by the self-made businesswoman Miss Gostock. Smitten by the farm, which he describes as "the prettiest place I had ever seen or ever desire to see" (Riddell, "Nut Bush" 4), Jack immediately decides to rent it, convinced that his health will improve in such a place. When he is just about to get the farm up and running, he hears rumours about the property being haunted by the ghost of its former tenant Mr. Hescot – to his great annoyance:

> I do not know when I was more put out than by this intelligence. It is unnecessary to say I did not believe in ghosts or anything of that kind, but my wife being a very nervous, impressionable woman, and our only child a delicate weakling, in the habit of crying himself into fits if left alone at night without a candle, I really felt at my wits' end to imagine what I should do if a story of this sort reached their ears. (Riddell, "Nut Bush" 1)

This is an interesting passage not only because it introduces us to the haunting of Nut Bush Farm, but also because it gives us an insight into the protagonist's world view. By stressing that he does not believe in ghosts while his wife and "delicate weakling" (Riddell, "Nut Bush" 1) of a son might be affected by the rumours, Jack echoes Victorian binary constructions of gender which present men as rational and controlled and women as irrational and excitable. By emphasising that Jack's wife and child might be terrified by the rumours in the same way, the story highlights children's supposed "alliance with the feminine" (Schaper 9). Susan E. Schaper has pointed out that a number of ghost stories focus on patriarchal anxieties over "the figure of the ghost-seeing son" (ibid.).[9] Generally, the juvenile ghost-seer is "'cured' from his infantile affliction simply through naturally maturing into adult masculinity, with a little help from male institutions and rituals" (ibid.). In "Nut Bush Farm", the reader is left to

---

9   As examples Schaper cites R. H. Benson's "Father Brent's Tale" (1907), E. F. Benson's "The Psychical Mallards" (1911) and Louisa Baldwin's "The Uncanny Bairn: A Story of Second Sight" (1892). Margaret Oliphant's "The Open Door", which will be discussed in the final chapter of this book, also dwells on boyish ghost-seeing.

imagine the boy's susceptibility to ghost-seeing, for he and his mother remain absent from the tale.

Jarlath Killeen has illustrated that ghost stories have been regarded as the product of "the weak-minded, the fanciful or the plain old deluded" and were "dismissed as old wives' tales'" (81) at least since the sixteenth century.[10] The association of women with ghost-seeing was particularly prevalent in the Victorian and Edwardian periods. This was often attributed to women's supposedly innate qualities such as "intuition, compassion, spirituality" (Schaper 7). For this reason, women played an important role during the growing spiritualist movement which originated in Hydesville, New York, in 1848, arrived in the United Kingdom in late 1852 and turned into "something of a national obsession" (Cox, *English* xiii) in the second half of the nineteenth century. "By the 1870s, years during which the most successful metropolitan séances obtained a certain glamour and cachet, women constituted some of the most popular mediums of the day", Alex Owen points out in her influential *The Darkened Room* (1989). However, a woman's strength was also seen as her weakness, as Schaper has observed: "If women were more sensitive to the supernatural, it was due to their affective natures, and as creatures of emotion rather than reason, they were subject to poor self-discipline" (Schaper 7). Hence, women's association with spiritualism and ghost-seeing was "double-edged" (Killeen 83): "women could be blessed with particular gifts which enabled them to contact the dead or to channel spirits, but these very gifts could also be a reason for continuing to deny women the right to educational and political power" (ibid.). The association of women with the paranormal became particularly problematic when practitioners of "the emerging discipline of psychology suggested a link between apparent occult powers and hysteria" (ibid.) in the latter decades of the nineteenth century: "Eminent doctors diagnosed spiritualism as a pathology linked to transgressions of the home, including child-abandonment, intense erotic desire, a tendency to refuse to obey orders issued by husbands and extreme religious piety" (ibid.). Ghost-seeing was, therefore, a risky business, not

---

10   This is testified by what Killeen calls a "classic manifesto of the sceptic" (ibid): *De spectris* (which was published in England in 1572 under the title *Of ghostes and spirites walking by nyght*), a text on ghost-seeing by the Swiss theologian and clergyman Ludwig Lavater. In his work, Lavater declares that ghosts are nothing but a figment of the imagination and that "wemen, which for the most parte are naturally geven to feare more than men ... do more often suppose they see or heare this or that thing, than men do" (14).

only for women, but also for men whose rational minds were supposed to prevent them from ghost-seeing. This is particularly relevant with regards to the then prevalent ideal of imperial masculinity which emphasised "the interaction of a healthy mind and a healthy body" (Allen 116).

In this context, it is worth noting that Jack might himself not be as psychologically stable as he pretends to be in the above passage. While Jack never provides any specific information about the accident which preceded his decision to become a farmer, there are hints that his suffering might have mental rather physical causes. Early in the narrative, Jack reveals that his doctors specifically told him to "give up office work and leave London", otherwise they "would not give a year's purchase for [his] life" (Riddell, "Nut Bush 1), which implies that life in the big city and deskwork rather than a physical injury affect his well-being. This impression is strengthened when the narrator states that "the sweet, pure air" at the farm has "braced up my nerves and given me fresh energy" (Riddell, "Nut Bush" 3), thus further suggesting that his mental health was impacted by the accident. The most obvious hint at the protagonist's mental instability, however, is provided towards the end of the narrative when Jack witnesses the mental breakdown of his neighbour Mrs. Waite. Jack describes her condition as "an attack of violent hysterics – a malady with the signs and tokens of which I was not altogether unacquainted" (Riddell, "Nut Bush" 32), thus hinting at his own medical history.

Elaine Showalter has pointed out that while "men were far more likely to be confined as insane" ("Insanity" 315) than women in the first half of the nineteenth century, the case was reversed in the second half of the nineteenth century. The increase of women admitted to lunatic asylums was accompanied by a considerable output of pseudoscientific texts which stated that women are more affected than men by their bodies, especially by their reproductive organs, and consequently more prone to mental illnesses. By the 1880s, the time when Riddell published her *Weird Stories*, "gynaecologists and psychologists ascribed nearly all female diseases to uterine malfunction" (Showalter, "Insanity" 327). The notion that women are more susceptible to nervous diseases soon established itself as a cultural narrative. As early as 1851, Charles Dickens remarks in an article he published following a visit to St. Luke's Hospital for the Insane that "[t]he experience of this asylum did not differ, I found, from that of similar establishments in proving that insanity is more prevalent among women than men" (Dickens, "Curious Dance" 387). Dickens also singles out a group that he considers particularly vulnerable: "Female servants are, as is well known, more frequently afflicted with lunacy than any other class of person" (ibid.). As we shall see, Jack has internalised contemporary ideas about the susceptibility of women to nervous excitement and believes in their biological disposition. It is therefore possible to read the fact that Jack does not give any details about his accident (and the long illness that followed) as an attempt to disclose what he perceives as a humiliatingly feminising illness.

In the course of the story, Jack is further established as a person who firmly believes in the Victorian separate spheres ideology. When he describes his sister Lolly, who has come to the farm to "help get the furniture a little to rights" (Riddell, "Nut Bush" 12) and to keep him company, his ideas about proper female appearance and behaviour are brought to the forefront:

> She was as pleasant and fresh to look upon as a spring morning, with her pretty brown hair smoothly braided, her cotton or muslin dresses never soiled or crumpled, but as nice as though the laundress had that moment sent them home – a rose in her belt and her hand never idle – for ever busy with curtain or blind, or something her housewifely eyes thought had need of making or mending. (Riddell, "Nut Bush" 13)

The passage reads like a dream vision of the perfect housewife whose hair is always neat and tidy and whose clothes magically stay clean while she is doing whatever "her housewifely eyes thought had need of making" (Riddell, "Nut Bush" 13). It is evident that Jack views Lolly as the perfect "Angel in the House". She also ensures that Jack is provided with a cooked meal every day and serves as his partner while his wife and son are still in London. Sarah Bissell has argued that Lolly represents "a healthy and productive femininity" (*Haunted Matters* 62) which the protagonist values more than the sickly femininity of his wife.[11] It is crucial to note, however, that he still considers Lolly as mentally instable simply because she is a woman. When he finds her lost in thought,

---

11   It is tempting for twenty-first-century readers to read more than brotherly affection into Jack's interaction with his sister. Besides his depiction of Lolly as "pleasant and fresh to look upon" (Riddell, "Nut Bush" 13), the siblings also seem to be very intimate. For instance, Lolly takes Jack "by the button-hole" (ibid. 14) when she wants his attention and "put[s] up her lips for [him] to kiss her" (ibid. 17) when he leaves the house. However, as Valerie Sanders has maintained, "[f]or many Victorians, the brother-sister relationship was the very cornerstone of middle-class family life" (11) and "there was emotional intensity of a kind that now seems alien" (12). For the Victorians, a kiss between brother and sister did not imply sexual desire (ibid. 15–6). It would therefore be misleading to read any kind of unnatural intimacy into their behavior.

he decides not to press her for details: "I was so accustomed to women, even the best and gayest of them, having occasional fits of temper or depression – times when silence on my part seemed the truest wisdom – that, taking no notice of my sister's manner, I occupied myself with the newspaper till dinner was announced" (Riddell, "Nut Bush" 14). When Lolly confides in him shortly afterwards that she has seen the ghost of a man on the property, he does not take her seriously and calls her a "silly little woman" (ibid. 17), thus suggesting the infantility of her behaviour.

From the farm's servants Jack then learns that they too believe that Nut Bush Farm is haunted. According to them, the ghost is that of the former tenant, Mr. Hascot, who has been murdered for his money. It is a generic convention of Victorian and Edwardian ghost fiction that the uneducated local population often knows more about the ghosts than the middle-class men who are affected by the haunting. In the course of this work, we will repeatedly encounter middle-class men who initially reject information about ghosts and haunting as the local superstition of an ill-educated working-class population, but who are forced to question their beliefs as the story progresses. This is also the case in "Nut Bush Farm".

In an attempt to dispel the rumours of the farm being haunted, Jack takes on the role of a detective and tries to get to the bottom of the mystery. He discovers that other locals suspect Hascot has run away with a pretty local girl, Sally Powner, "leaving his wife and children on the parish" (Riddell, "Nut Bush" 11). An inquiry at the local bank reveals that the late tenant of Nut Bush Farm had withdrawn "a cruel lot of money" (ibid. 18) from his account on the day he disappeared, which might account for both theories, that he was murdered for the money or that he eloped with a young girl. Jack's suspicion soon falls on his landlady, Miss Gostock: "It was an ugly idea, and yet it haunted me" (ibid. 30), he remarks. It is significant that Jack uses the term "haunted" with regards to the idea that Miss Gostock might have murdered Mr Hascot and not in reference to the ghost that supposedly haunts his property. In fact, the story strongly implies that Jack perceives Miss Gostock as more spectral than the actual ghost of the story, as I will illustrate in the following.

Uncertain about her biological sex when he first encounters her, the narrator describes Miss Gostock as "a figure wearing a man's broad-brimmed hat, a man's coat, and a woman's skirt. I raised my hat in deference to the supposed sex of this stranger" (Riddell, "Nut Bush" 5–6). By showing that Miss Gostock's unconventional mix of clothes makes it impossible for the narrator to clearly identify her as female, the story draws attention to the fact that clothing plays

a crucial role in the gendering of people (Crane 16). As Diana Crane has established in *Fashion and Its Social Agendas: Class, Gender, and Identity in Clothing*
(2000), "[f]ashionable clothes are used to make statements about social class
and social identity, but their principal messages are about the ways in which
women and men perceive their gender roles or are expected to perceive them"
(16). At the time "Nut Bush Farm" was published, women's clothing involved
long skirts and, for middle-class and upper-class women, usually also a corset
– items which restrict women's bodies and prevent them from pursuing certain activities. As we shall see, Miss Gostock engages in hard physical work, an
activity that requires practical clothing. Her refusal to wear gender-appropri-
ate clothes is therefore part of a more general rejection to assume the passive
feminine role required of women in the 1880s. Miss Gostock also wears "her
hair short like a man" , her "old-fashioned parlour ... [does] not contain a single feminine belonging" (Riddell, "Nut Bush" 8), and her laugh is "not musical"
(ibid. 9), as the male narrator is careful to point out.

But even more than by her gender deviant appearance, the narrator is taken
aback by Miss Gostock's unconventional behaviour:

> she went to a corner cupboard, and producing a square decanter half full of
> spirits, set that and two tumblers on the table.
> "You don't like much water, I suppose," she said, pouring out a measure
> which frightened me.
> "I could not touch it, thank you, Miss Gostock," I exclaimed; "I dare not do so;
> I should never get back to Whittleby."
> For answer she only looked at me contemptuously and said, "D—d non-
> sense."
> "No nonsense, indeed," I persisted; "I am not accustomed to anything of that
> sort."
> Miss Gostock laughed again ... and raised the glass to her lips.
> "To your good health and prosperity," she said, and in one instant the fiery
> potion was swallowed.
> "You'll mend of all that," she remarked, as she laid down her glass, and
> wiped her lips in the simplest manner by passing the back of her hand over
> them.
> "I hope not, Miss Gostock," I ventured to observe.
> "Why, you look quite shocked," she said; "did you never see a lady take a
> mouthful of brandy before?"
> I ventured to hint that I had not, more particularly so early in the morning.
> "Pooh!" she said. "Early in the morning or late at night, where's the differ-

ence? ... Good-bye for the present, and I hope we shall get on well together."
I answered I trusted we should, and was half-way to the hall-door, when she
called me back.

"I forgot to ask you if you were married," she said.

"Yes, I have been married some years," I answered.

"That's a pity," she remarked, and dismissed me with a wave of her hand.

"What on earth would have happened had I not been married?" I considered
as I hurried down the drive. "Surely she never contemplated proposing to
me herself? But nothing she could do would surprise me." (Riddell, "Nut
Bush" 10–11)

Miss Gostock refuses to play the gendered role demanded of her. She drinks,
wipes her lips unceremoniously with her hand, and mocks her male tenant
who appears to be shocked by her unwomanly behaviour, as she observes with
feigned astonishment. She actively breaks with societal expectations which she
has no desire to fulfil and even dares to imply her interest in Jack. What Jack
does not seem to understand is that it is, at the very least, questionable that a
woman like Miss Gostock might actually be interested in marriage. It is more
likely that she deliberately transgresses societal rules. By reversing the traditional script of the marriage proposal which – to this day – expects women to
passively wait until the man is willing to propose, Miss Gostock undercuts patriarchal superiority.

An unbiased presentation of Miss Gostock is denied to us because everything we get to know about her is filtered through Jack's consciousness. However, Jack's depiction of Miss Gostock both provides us with information about
his landlady and reflects on the narrator himself (Margree, "(Other)Worldly"
75). As Sarah Bissell has pointed out, Miss Gostock's resistance to gender
stereotypes "throws Jack's own sense of masculinity into question" (*Haunted
Matters* 60). In his conversations with Miss Gostock, Jack is repeatedly pushed
into the supposedly female role of the silent and submissive listener – a
role which stands in opposition to his understanding of his masculinity as
superior. In this way, the story undercuts traditional power structures. Jack
attempts to undermine Miss Gostock's superiority by calling her "ludicrous"
(Riddell, "Nut Bush" 6), thereby hinting at the contemporary association of
women with insanity.[12] When Jack finally signs his lease contract with Miss

---

12   In this context it is worth noting that women who rebelled against patriarchal struc-
      tures were sometimes sent to lunatic asylums. As Elaine Showalter points out: "It was
      easy for fathers, brothers, and husbands to find doctors willing to certify that sexually

Gostock, he further "tries to contain the economic power of the propertied female by insisting on the spectralness of the business deal" (Dickerson 140):

> Like one in a dream, I sat and watched Miss Gostock while she wrote. Nothing about the transaction seemed to me real. ... Miss Gostock appeared to me but as some monstrous figure in a story of giants and hobgoblins. The man's coat, the woman's skirt, the hobnailed shoes, the grisly hair, the old straw hat, the bare, unfurnished room, the bright sunshine outside, all struck me as mere accessories in a play – as nothing which had any hold on the outside, everyday world. (Riddell, "Nut Bush" 9)

Miss Gostock's transgression of normative feminine behaviour makes her appear as "some monstrous figure" (Riddell, "Nut Bush" 9) to Jack who feels he has entered "a story of giants and hobgoblins" (ibid.). The narrator uses words related to dreams and fairy tales to "cast an air of ghostly twilight over the harsh material reality created by the writing" (Dickerson 140). By insinuating that a woman like Miss Gostock has no "hold on the outside, everyday world" (Riddell, "Nut Bush" 9) but only exists in a kind of parallel universe, Jack attempts to disempower his landlady.

When Jack meets Miss Gostock at his farm later in the story, he is also shocked to see that she is doing the repairs he requested as part of their business deal herself, working "under a sun which would have killed anybody but a negro or my landlady" (Riddell, "Nut Bush" 11). By comparing his landlady to the colonial Other, Miss Gostock's Otherness is stressed. To make matters worse for the male narrator, she even offers to teach him how to mow a lawn. By pushing Jack into the role of the ignorant pupil, Miss Gostock again redefines the hierarchical relation of male and female to a degree that "significantly troubles his masculine identity" (Bissell, *Haunted Matters* 61).[13]

---

rebellious women were lunatics" ("Insanity" 325). The wrongful incarceration of women in asylums "fed a good deal of the Sensation fiction genre of the 1860s" (Ledger and Luckhurst 243). It is likely that contemporary readers were familiar with both fictional and real-life cases of wrongful incarceration and would have picked up on Jack's remarks about Miss Gostock's supposed lunacy.

13   The figure of the unruly woman who transgresses gender boundaries in one way or another (she might be a criminal, sexually active, or a genderqueer woman) often appears in Victorian literature. It is one of the literary conventions of the time to either reintegrate these female characters into patriarchal structures (through marriage, for instance) or to punish them for their transgressive behaviour and thus remove them from society. As Kate Kruger remarks with regards to the short-lived genre of sensa-

The story strongly implies that Jack's suspicion that Miss Gostock has murdered the late tenant of Nut Bush Farm is caused by her refusal to comply with
Victorian ideas about femininity:

> When I remembered the woman's masculine strength, when I recalled her
> furious impetuosity when I asked her a not very exasperating question, as
> I recalled the way she tossed off that brandy, when I consider her love of
> money, her eagerness to speak ill of her late tenant … . I hated myself for the
> suspicion; and yet, do what I would, I could not shake it off. (Riddell, "Nut
> Bush" 30–31)

Besides the fact that Mr Hascot and Miss Gostock apparently did not get along
well, all reasons Jack lists for his accusation refer to his landlady's transgression of societal rules and her markedly masculine gender performance: her
"masculine strength", her habit of drinking brandy, and what Jack calls "furious
impetuosity" (ibid.). Money also plays a role in Jack's considerations. Victoria
Margree describes Miss Gostock as "a prime example of women in Riddell's
ghost fiction who are depicted in terms of monstrosity for their possession of,
or desire for, money. Other examples include the witch-like figure of the female miser in 'The Old House in Vauxhall Walk', and the murderous dowager
of 'The Open Door'" ("(Other)Worldly" 74). Considering that all three stories are
related by male narrators or through a male narrative focus, it is possible to link
the demonisation of the propertied and/or money-seeking female to male anxieties about female economic independence, especially given their publication
in 1882, the year of the extension of the Married Women's Property Act, which
"allow[ed] married women to have complete personal control over all of their

tion fiction, which dominated the literary market in the 1860s and incorporates many
of the topics of Gothic fiction like transgressive sexuality, madness, and murder, "de-
viance is at first recognized but is ultimately eliminated; the end of sensation is a return
to normalcy" (K. Kruger 68). For instance, in Elizabeth Gaskell's ghostly tale "The Grey
Woman" (1861), the mannish Amante is killed in the end, leaving the female protagonist, Anna, dependent on the help of a man. Similarly, Lucy ends up dead in a mental institution in Belgium at the end of Mary Elizabeth Braddon's *Lady Audley's Secret*
(1862). "The transgressor is punished and the protagonist, Robert Audley, rewarded
with a marriage and the preservation of his family's wealth" (K. Kruger 68). By contrast, Miss Gostock remains untouched, as we shall see. This is a departure from the
expectations of the Victorian audience.

property" ("Marriage").[14] With her habit of drinking brandy, her candour, and her taste for men's clothes, the economically independent character of Miss Gostock anticipates "the press caricatures of the late Victorian 'New Woman'" (Bissell, *Haunted Matters* 61), a figure who would become the icon of the feminist movement ten years after the publication of Riddell's story.

Several critics have argued that the development of a hypermasculine ideal in the second half of the nineteenth century was partly induced by the feminist movement and the figure of the New Woman, who presents an outright antithesis to the idealised notion of women as angelic housewives. The term "New Woman" was coined in the mid-1890s by the feminist writer Sarah Grand (pseudonym of Frances Elizabeth Clarke) and the novelist Ouida (pseudonym of Maria Louise Ramé) in a pair of articles (Ledger 9). The figure itself, however, had been around some time by then, as the character of Miss Gostock illustrates. It was the result of forty years of feminist activism (Heilmann 16). Among her contemporaries, the New Woman was both celebrated and reviled. Those in favour of the movement saw in her a figure of social change, "the advanced woman of to-day", "the woman of the period", the "Novissima" – terms which stress the "avant-gardist and trend-setting effect" (ibid.) she had in the 1880s and 1890s, especially on educated, middle-class women, who felt that the patriarchal society, which saw marriage and motherhood as the only proper occupations for women, bereaved them of their personal fulfilment. Her many opponents, however, condemned the New Woman as "chain-smoking spinster", "wild woman" and "modern man-hater" (ibid.). By pursuing professional aspirations, the supporters of the feminist movement did not only question the traditional Victorian perception of women, but the binary division of gender in general, which had ensured male supremacy up to this point. Even though women were still far from being an economic threat to men,[15] women's call

---

14   Before 1870, a woman's legal identity was subsumed under her husband's upon marriage, which meant that married women could neither own money nor property. The Married Woman's Property Act of 1870 enabled married women to take possession of the money and property they earned or inherited during their marriage. The extension of the act in 1882 allowed women to also keep money and property they had acquired before their marriage. For more information see the section on "Marriage: Property and Children" on the official website of the UK Parliament.

15   In *Sexual Anarchy* Elaine Showalter presents some figures which bear witness that women were still extremely underrepresented and discriminated against in the world of employment by the end of the nineteenth century: "Overall, women in the workforce earned only 50 percent of what men earned, and only 8 percent of trade union mem-

for a self-sufficient, independent life gave cause to gender insecurity.[16] Elaine Showalter has maintained that this redefinition of womanhood also led to "an awakening consciousness of what it meant to be a man" (*Anarchy* 9). John Tosh further argues that the "[f]ear of women in the social arena was closely associated with fear of the feminine within" (*Manliness* 22). This development is tangible in most of the stories discussed here who generally portray men who struggle to live up to the masculine ideal and who are deeply troubled if the hierarchical relation of man and woman gets reversed. Jack in "Nut Bush Farm" is one such example.

Jack's refusal to believe that Mr Hascot has returned to the farm as a ghost is conditioned by his perception of his (masculine) identity as rational: "I did not believe it – I could not, and I added, 'if I saw it with my own eyes, I would not.' Having arrived at which decided and sensible conclusion, I went in to supper" (Riddell, "Nut Bush" 19). Jack's internal monologue highlights that rationality and scepticism are part of his perception of himself as a "decided" and "sensible" man whose convictions do not allow a belief in ghosts – even if he saw them with his own eyes.

However, in stark contrast to his initial remarks about ghost-seeing, Jack immediately starts to believe in the supernatural return of Mr Hascot when he sees the ghost with his own eyes: "If I had been incredulous before, I was not so now – I could not distrust the evidence of my own eyes" (Riddell, "Nut Bush" 24). The ghost story's preoccupation with visual epistemology is part of a larger discourse on the reliability of vision in the Victorian period. As Sarah Bissell has pointed out, "[t]he nineteenth century saw a significant reconfiguration of vision in science and culture, one which radically altered the ways in which Victorians thought about visual experience. Although sight had formerly been perceived as a dependable and relatively straightforward means through which one could interpret the world, nineteenth-century scientific theories increasingly presented vision as variable, disjointed and subjective, complicated further by new hypotheses regarding hallucination and the mind" (Bissell, *Haunted*

---

bership was female. Furthermore, universities were far from feminized. By 1897, there were only 844 women in all the English universities put together" (Showalter, *Anarchy* 7).

16   Lynne Segal has identified this feeling of crisis as symptomatic for hegemonic masculinity: "while men everywhere express their anxieties and loss of former privileges, overall they are conceived of and remain the dominant sex" ("Back" 239).

Matters 68).[17] While Jack initially believes vision to be unreliable, he quickly changes his mind when he encounters the ghost himself.

The ghost appears to Jack half-way through the narrative when he, unable to find rest, goes for a night-time walk "in the clear light of a most lovely moon" (Riddell, "Nut Bush" 20). In sharp contrast to Miss Gostock, who seems unreal like a ghost to Jack, the phantasmal Mr Hascot's looks so real to him that he mistakes the spectre for a living man: "A middle-aged man, so far as I could judge, with a set, determined expression of countenance, dark hair, no beard or whiskers, only a small moustache. A total stranger to me" (ibid. 25). It is only when the stranger passes through him that Jack realises that he has encountered a ghost. Seeking to expose the remnants of his body and thus solve the secret of his disappearance, the ghost beckons Jack to follow him. Jack, however, is lacking the resolution and courage to follow the ghost's request:

> I could not follow. My limbs refused their office. He turned his head, and lifting his hand on which the ring glittered, beckoned me to come. He might as well have asked one seized with paralysis. On the confines of the wood he stood motionless as if awaiting my approach; then, when I made no sign of movement, he wrung his hands with a despairing gesture, and disappeared. ... – and I fainted." (Riddell, "Nut Bush" 26)[18]

At the end of the narrative, Jack succeeds in solving the mystery of Nut Bush Farm and can put Mr Hascot's spirit to rest. However, the direct encounter with the ghost is marked by failure. Instead of helping the spectre who is wringing his hands in despair, Jack is paralysed by fear and falls into "a womanly faint" (Margree, "(Other)Worldly" 76) – reactions which stand in opposition to dominant scrips of masculinity that foreground resolution and courage as essentially male attributes. Jack lacks both. His display of what was seen as a rather

---

17   On this topic see also Sarah Bissell's "The Ghost Story and Science" (2017), Shane McCorristine's *Spectres of the Self: Thinking About Ghosts and Ghost-Seeing in England, 1750–1920* (2010), and Srdjan Smajic's *Ghost-Seers, Detectives, and Spiritualists: Theories of Vision in Victorian Literature and Science* (2010).

18   The ring Hascot's ghost is wearing is one of the items that are used to identify the victim when his body is eventually found at the end of the story: "I had the wood thoroughly examined, and there in a gully, covered with a mass of leaves and twigs and dead branches, we found Mr. Hascot's body. His watch was in his waistcoat pocket – his ring on his finger; save for these possessions no one could have identified him" (Riddell, "Nut Bush" 37).

feminising behaviour is framed by the setting of the scene in the light of the moon, which Jack repeatedly genders female during his encounter with the ghost (for instance, he calls the moon "the queen of night" (Riddell, "Nut Bush" 23)).[19]

In addition to Jack's affective reaction to the apparitional Mr Hascot, the male ghost body also undermines the contemporary image of masculinity as active and self-reliant. Unable to act for himself and take revenge on his murderer, the revenant needs help to ensure justice. Ruth Heholt contends that the "question of 'need' arises many times in relation to ghosts" ("Visible" 160) and that it places the male phantom "in a feminised position of powerlessness" (ibid.). Heholt explains: "In Victorian times it was far more usual for a woman to need a man to act for her outside of the domestic space and the Victorian ideal for men is one of self-reliance and an ability to take responsibility for oneself" (ibid.). Dependent on Jack's help, Hascot is pushed into a traditionally female role.

Jack's detective work finally reveals that not his unconventional landlady but his neighbour, Mr Waite, killed Mr Hascot. As usual in Riddell's haunted house narratives, the murder was motivated by money: Mr Waite, who had repeatedly borrowed money from Mr Hascot, killed the late tenant of Nut Bush Farm in order to get his hands on the sum he had withdrawn from the bank the day he went missing. Jack further finds out that Mr Hascot did not have an affair with Sally Powner but helped the girl to get away from her abusive grandparents. Jack's detective work thus reveals "the hidden realities of familial abuse, and the morally corrupting effects of avarice" (Margree, "(Other)Worldly" 76). By disclosing not only the murder of Mr Hascot but also the brutal realities of the domestic household, Riddell's story suggests that "there is no real closure, protection, or final burial of secrets" (K. Kruger 72), even within the enclosed space of the family home.

It is possible to argue that Jack re-establishes his masculine identity by solving the mystery and releasing Hascot's ghost, who disappears after his murder has been revealed. However, the story's ending makes clear that Jack's masculine gender identity has suffered irreversibly. In order to solve Mr Hascot's murder, he had to reposition himself and assume a gender identity that brings him "closer to the perspectives of women and the lower classes" (Margree, "(Other)Worldly" 77). Just as he looked down upon Lolly at the onset of

---

19   On this point see also Margree's "(Other)Worldly Goods: Gender, Money and Property in the Ghost Stories of Charlotte Riddell", pp. 75–76.

the story when she confesses to have seen Hascot's ghost, Jack is now ridiculed by his brother: "He says the place never was haunted – that I never saw Mr Hascot except in my own imagination – that the whole thing originated in a poor state of health and a too credulous disposition!" (Riddell, "Nut Bush" 37). It does not matter that Jack has solved the mystery of Nut Bush Farm and has brought peace to the place. The only thing that matters in his brother's evaluation of Jack's male behaviour is that he shows qualities that were coded feminine at the time. By presenting Jack's experiences within the haunted space as a narrative of masculine failure, Riddell's story implies that gender identity must be acted out according to societal rules and that everyone who breaks with predefined gender roles is frowned upon.

Lettice Galbraith: "A Ghost's Revenge" (1893)

In Lettice Galbraith's "A Ghost's Revenge", the ghost of Katharine Deverel haunts Ravenshill Hall and no man can survive New Year's Eve within the house but is forced to die the way she and her infant son did: by drowning in the garden pond. The ghost is animated by a past wrong done to her and her son, who, following the death of Katharine Deverel's husband, were driven out of Ravenshill Hall by a man who took her "choild's birthright" and slurred her "fair naame" (Galbraith, "Revenge" 225).[20] Disowned and homeless, Katharine Deverel committed suicide the same night, taking her baby son with her. As a ghost, she is determined to avenge herself on every man who dares to take possession of Ravenshill Hall.

Until recently, almost nothing was known about the story's author, Lettice Galbraith. Literary critics and anthologists regarded her as "no less mysterious than the stories she wrote", as is stated in the blurb of *The Shadow on the Blind and Other Stories*, a 2007 collection of supernatural tales by Louisa Baldwin (Rudyard Kipling's aunt and mother of Prime Minister Stanley Baldwin) and Lettice Galbraith. As we further learn there, "[s]he appeared on the literary scene in 1893, published a novel and two collections of stories in that year, a further story ('The Blue Room') in 1897, and then nothing more." Her story "A Ghost's Revenge" was originally published in one of the 1893 collections: *New Ghost Stories*. The book "was probably one of the most popular and widely-read

---

20   The unhappy fate of Katharine Deverel is embedded in the narrative and retold by a farmer who is speaking in a Northern English dialect. Quotes from the story may therefore contain words written in dialect.

ghost story collections of that decade as it ran through three best-selling editions in a five year period", the publisher states on the jacket of *The Blue Room
and Other Stories*, a compilation of ghost fiction by Galbraith, which was issued
as part of Richard Dalby's *Mistresses of the Macabre* series in 1999.[21]

Considering Galbraith's success, it comes as a surprise that the author disappeared from the literary scene after the 1890s, almost as if she was but "a
'ghost' herself" (qtd. in Gunn 175).

In his recent, ground-breaking new edition of Galbraith's ghost stories, Al-
istair Gunn reveals that this is actually not true but that "'Lettice Galbraith' was
in fact a pseudonym of Lizzie Susan Gibson (1859–1932), a native of Kingston
upon Hull (usually abbreviated to 'Hull'), in the East Riding of Yorkshire" (Gunn
176) and that, from 1905 onwards, she wrote novels, which were published under her real name L. S. Gibson (ibid. 185). "Thanks to this new edition of Lettice Galbraith's supernatural stories and the extensive biographical research
undertaken by Alastair Gunn, we can finally put a name – and indeed a life –
to this most mysterious of Victorian-era writers" (Edmundson, Foreword 2),
Melissa Edmundson points out in her foreword to the book.

Galbraith was born into a wealthy family and grew up living "a comfortable
life supported by a cook and a housemaid" (Gunn 177). She lost her father in 1874
and then relocated with her mother to the south of England sometime during
1886 and 1888, presumably to be closer to some of her family members. After
her mother's death in 1901, Galbraith moved in with her brother Alfred, a vicar.
The author published her last novel in 1912, 20 years prior to her death in 1932
(ibid. 177–89).

Gunn's research, which he describes as "a labour-of-love … [which] involved
a great deal of detective work, trawling of archives (both digital and physical),
genealogical research, and the occasional stroke of good luck" (Gunn 176), is
likely to spark new literary attention – and rightly so.

The story discussed in the following, "A Ghost's Revenge", demonstrates not
only her talent as a writer of spooky tales; it also reveals social concerns about
the vulnerability of women within the patriarchal system – a topic that repeatedly resurfaces in Galbraith's ghost fiction. Her brilliant tale "In the Séance
Room", for instance, features the ghost of a woman who returns to expose her

---

21   Richard Dalby's collection of Galbraith's ghost fiction is out of print and very rare. The
       jacket text of the book is available on Dalby's official website https://richarddalbyslib
       rary.com.

murderer, a distinguished gynaecologist and magnetiser, who killed her to secure his marriage with a wealthy woman.[22] Another example is "The Missing
Model", which offers a subtle commentary on the objectification of women in
the art scene. Both stories, which were originally published in Galbraith's *New
Ghost Stories*, use male focalizers for their critiques of male dominance, thereby
exposing the frame of mind that leads to the subjugation of women. I believe
that the following discussion of "A Ghost's Revenge" illustrates that the author's
work is deserving of further critical attention.

The domestic family home as a "refuge from evil" (K. Ellis xiii) is decon-
structed in multiple ways in the story: on the one hand, the house is presented
as a patriarchal space that leaves women (and their children) vulnerable and
helpless. Although the reader is not provided with any details about the man
who disowned Katharine Deverel and her son (we do not even learn his name),
the story implies that he committed fraud and that the legal system could not
protect the family from losing their home (Galbraith, "Revenge" 225). The story
thus points to the inequalities of the legal system that privileges men, who
made and executed British laws at the time the story was written, while women
were excluded from the process of law-making. On the other hand, the supernatural allows Katharine Deverel to reclaim power and to take possession of
her home, again, turning it into a place of nightmares for any man who dares
to inhabit it. Hence, the family home is presented as an equivocal space that is
fundamentally defined by patriarchal rules and yet also constitutes a territory
where women can be powerful and potentially dangerous.

The theme of female financial insecurity and dependence is also articulated
in "Nut Bush Farm" through the wife and children of the murdered Hascot,
who are left homeless and penniless after the farmer's death. Both stories thus
express anxieties about the economic dependence of women within a society that restricts women's opportunities to earn their livelihood and privileges
men when it comes to matters of inheritance, education, and career opportunities. However, while Jack in "Nut Bush Farm" shows concern for Hascot's family
and even helps them to retrieve the money that was stolen from the murdered
man, the men that appear in "A Ghost's Revenge" do not express sympathy for
the wronged female, even though she is clearly a victim of a society that failed
to protect her from homelessness. Instead, her ghostly repossession of Ravenshill Hall and her supernatural power is coded as monstrous throughout the

---

22   "In the Séance Room" will be discussed in detail in the last chapter of this work.

story. The publication of the story in 1893 is relevant in this context, for the final decade of the nineteenth century was marked by growing enthusiasm for women's rights and female independence, as has been pointed out above. It is possible, therefore, to read Katharine Deverel's demonization as an articulation of cultural anxieties over female empowerment.

The story is focalised through a London businessman, Gerald Harrison. He first hears about the haunting at Ravenshill Hall when he visits an old college chum, Reverend Richard Forster, who lives near the mansion in Mallowby and has invited its present inhabitant, Philip Granville, for dinner the same evening that Harrison arrives at his place. Granville instantly strikes Harrison as a "man who has received some severe mental shock" (Galbraith, "Revenge" 220). It bothers Harrison that, though intelligent, he never "wholly give[s] his attention to the subject in hand", but "seem[s] to be constantly listening for some unexpectant sound" (ibid.). Not unlike Jack at the beginning of "Nut Bush Farm", Harrison is presented as a man who believes in the socially constructed picture of masculinity with its stress on determination and fearlessness as essentially male attributes. When it is nearing midnight, Granville urges Reverend Forster to bring his cart around and declines his host's offer to spend the night at his house – much to Harrison's relief:

> "No, thanks; no," [he said] with the nervous haste of one who fears that his resolution may fail him, "I cannot do that. ... I dare not show the white feather to the servants. They would think me a fool; but, my God! They don't hear it as I do. Tell them to bring the cart round, Forster. ..."
>
> The order was given. As the minutes wore on, Granville became increasingly uneasy. He could not restrain his restless anxiety to be off, and it was a relief to everyone when the grating of wheels outside announced that the trap was in readiness. (Galbraith, "Revenge" 221)

This is an interesting passage because it suggests that both social and gender roles are performative and subject to the scrutiny of others. While Granville is concerned that his authority as the master of Ravenshill Hall might suffer when he admits fear and spends the night at another man's place, his nervous behaviour is judged upon by Harrison as the focaliser of the tale who sees in Granville's demeanour a sign that his manly resolution might fail him. By pointing out Granville's inability to "restrain" (Galbraith, "Revenge" 221) his nervous behaviour, the passage further suggests that it is not his anxiety that poses the problem, but his lack of self-control. Self-discipline was one of the key qualities of hegemonic masculinity in the second half of the nineteenth century and the onset of the twentieth century. In his best-selling advise book *Self-Help* (1859), the government reformer Samuel Smiles even describes "the victory over ourselves" as "the highest virtue" (291). Self-discipline was regarded as a virtue that distinguished civilised men from the supposedly savage people the British fought and suppressed in their colonies (Deane 5). While not depicted as savage, Granville's lack of self-discipline reflects badly on his gender performance. The fact that it is a relief for the whole group to get rid of Granville further implies that there is little tolerance for men who fail to embody normative masculinity.

Granville is aware that his behaviour reflects badly on his masculine gender performance, as the following comment suggests: "I am like Cinderella. I must be indoors before midnight" (Galbraith, "Revenge" 220), he explains before his departure. By comparing himself with the heroine of a well-known fairy tale, Granville deconstructs gender boundaries and suggests his identification with qualities that were generally coded feminine. When he has left, Harrison asks his host if there is something wrong with the man: "does he drink, or is he off his head?" (ibid.). For him, Granville represents an unhealthy masculinity which he associates with alcoholism and mental illness.

When Harrison learns from Reverend Forster that Granville is convinced that Ravenshill Hall is haunted, he dismisses the belief in ghosts as superstitious folly and makes fun of Granville:

> "No-one but a lunatic believes in ghosts these days. …"
> "There is something queer about the old Hall, though", persisted Forster. "I do not believe that any consideration you could offer would induce a Mallowby man to sleep there alone. The place has a bad name. It stood empty for years before Granville bought it. He spent no end of money in repairs and furniture, too, which makes it additionally hard on him to be driven out by –"
> "A ghost," concluded Harrison, with a shout of laughter. "My dear Dick, it is too absurd. Let us exorcise the place. I will back my six-shooter at thirty feet against any combination of goblins and blue fire. We will arrange a match tomorrow. Fifty pounds a side, to be paid in material currency only. Come admit now that the thing is a huge joke." (Galbraith, "Revenge" 221–2)

According to Harrison, only "a lunatic" (Galbraith, "Revenge" 221) believes in ghosts and other supernatural beings like goblins. Given the problematic contemporary association of ghost-seeing not only with women but also with madness, it is hardly surprising that he perceives Granville as both effeminate and mentally instable. By contrast, Harrison presents himself as a man who is not afraid of anything and for whom a tale about ghosts and haunting is nothing but "a huge joke" (Galbraith, "Revenge" 222). His offer to exorcise the place is more than just mockery, though, for it enables Harrison to assume the position of the resolute man of action who is capable of helping the effeminate Granville. Furthermore, it foreshadows the protagonist's confrontation with Katharine Deverel's ghost later in the story.

Harrison's judgmental attitude towards Granville turns into dismay when he and Reverend Forster learn that the master of Ravenshill Hall was found dead on the edge of the garden pond on the morning of New Year's Eve. The two men hurry to the scene, hoping to be able to revive the body:

> It was a relief to be able to do something, but long before the surgeon arrived they knew that his services would be useless. Death had sealed the master of Ravenshill for his own. The cold and rigid limbs refused to respond to the revivifying influences of hot blankets and artificial respiration.
> Harrison was of the opinion, as he assisted in his friend's frantic endeavours to restore some semblance of life, that poor Granville had been dead for several hours.
> It was a painful task. In vain Forster tried to close the dull, lack-lustre eyes, fixed in a wide stare of indescribable horror. The tense features would not relax. Never had a human being passed away from life leaving behind him so terrible an impression of fear. (Galbraith, "Revenge" 223)

The men's relief at being able to do something at the beginning of the passage is instructive because it reflects ideas about gender that see men as active rescuers – as opposed to the presumed passiveness of women. The main focus of the passage, however, is on Granville and the horror that apparently preceded his death and still seems to seize the dead body. The expression of fear that is visible on Granville's face evidently has an impact on Harrison, for he objects to Reverend Forster's idea to stay the night with the dead body:

> To Forster th[e] desertion of the helpless corpse seemed terrible. He would have spent the night in watching beside the poor fellow who had so lately been his guest, and was only dissuaded from his purpose by the earnest solicitations of his churchwarden, a stalwart farmer, on whose grey head seventy odd years sat lighter than most men's fifty. ...

"Mr Dawson is right, Dick," urged Harrison; "you can't do the poor fellow any good. Your nerves are shaken, and I am free to confess, ghost or no ghost, to spend the night in that dismal house with a dead man is more than I should care about." (Galbraith, "Revenge" 224–5)

While willing to exorcise the house less than 24 hours earlier, Harrison now perceives Ravenshill Hall as an uncanny place where he would not spend the night. Harrison's remark "ghost or no ghost" (Galbraith, "Revenge" 225) even implies that he is now willing to consider the possibility of haunting.

From Forster's churchwarden, the two men also learn that Katharine Deverel's ghost has supposedly claimed other victims in the past: "Mony an' mony a good mon has met that death, sin' the noight that Katharine Deverel stood in yon winter and cursed the mon who had robbed her of her husband's name, an' theer lad of his lawful inheritance" (Galbraith, "Revenge" 225). As so often in ghost stories, the middle-class men have to rely on "the working-class locals for detailed information on the story behind the haunting" (Makala 108). The churchwarden also tells the two friends that Katharine Deverel's curse befalls every man who dares to take possession of the place, "be he young or auld, good or evil" (Galbraith, "Revenge" 225).

Katharine Deverel is a tragic figure. Although the reader does not learn anything about her life before the fatal night in which she lost her life, it is clear that she turned from the nurturing mother of a little baby boy into a vengeful revenant, determined to terrorise and murder every male owner of Ravenshill Hall. Jarlath Killeen has suggested that the ghost story as a genre has served as a means for women writers to subvert the hierarchical order of Victorian society and to push men into the role of the vulnerable victims of relentless female oppressors: "The ghost-in-the-house terrorizing the male owner may be a means by which the 'angel-in-the-house' might sublimate her desire to subject her husband to oppression and terror" (Killeen 84). Katharine Deverel's ghostly attack on male superiority is twofold: in a first step, she terrorises the male owners of Ravenshill Hall until they turn into nervous wrecks whose gender performance stands in opposition to dominant scrips of masculinity. In a second step, she kills those men.

In contrast to the emasculated ghost in Riddell's story, who is dependent on a living person who can act for him, the female ghost in "A Ghost's Revenge" is an empowered version of the living woman, who was powerless against the man who drove her and her son out of their home. According to Vanessa Dickerson, female spectres in late-Victorian ghost fiction by women tend to be "less

humble and more aggressive than their predecessors" (144). Ruth Heholt adds
that in these tales "the female ghost body can be seen as liberated, radical and
transformative" ("Visible" 164). It would be a mistake to assume, however, that
it is possible to generalise about female and male phantom bodies and that female ghosts generally represent an empowered version of femininity, while
male ghosts undermine notions of active masculinity. Heholt contends that
male spectres can also execute a "manly version of active determined masculinity" which is indicative of "the survival of the masculine will from beyond the
grave" ("Visible" 150). As an example, Heholt refers to Edith Nesbit's "John Char-
rington's Wedding", a tale in which the main figure returns from the dead in order to execute his wedding to a young woman he is determined to possess. In "A
Ghost's Revenge" we are certainly dealing with a very powerful female spectre.
It is unclear, however, if the ghost can actively harm its victims or if Katharine
Deverel drives them into suicide by terrorising them night after night.

What is noteworthy about the way Granville has died is that he stayed in the
library before his death – a room conventionally coded as masculine. The servants, who found their master later beneath the willows by the garden pond,
also report that the "odour of tobacco" (Galbraith, "Revenge" 223) still hung in
the air when they entered the library. Since smoking was an exclusively male
pastime in the nineteenth century (smoking women were looked down upon
and condemned as half-men), the smell of tobacco stresses the library's identification as a room for the male owner of the house. It is telling that Granville,
who has the impression that his home is haunted by a female ghost, refrains
from staying in the bedroom – a room used by men and women alike – and
withdraws to the library, evidently hoping that the male space would protect
him from the female intruder. However, in a reversal of the Victorian architectural hierarchy that excluded women from certain parts of the house, the ghost
can penetrate the masculine space and even make the male occupant leave the
room through the window and walk into the often-feminised space of the garden where he finds his death.[23]

The purpose of the ghost is to exact revenge. Just as in Riddell's "Nut Bush
Farm" and numerous other haunted house narratives, the haunting of Raven-

---

23   In a striking parallel, women and gardens were supposed to be cultivated, fertile and
      beautiful. Furthermore, the garden belonged to the private sphere of the house. As
      Lynne Walker has pointed out: "In keeping with 'proper' social relations …, women's
      rooms [were] placed at the back or … on the garden side of the house, protected from
      the street and the gaze of strangers" (L. Walker 826).

shill Hall exists only because of the crime that occurred within its walls. The house is haunted by its own history that refuses to be forgotten and comes to the fore whenever Katharine Deverel claims another victim. However, unlike many other Victorian and Edwardian ghosts, who are released from their liminal existence when the crime that led to their ghostly afterlives is revealed (in "Nut Bush Farm" the phantasmal Mr Hascot disappears, for instance), Deverel's ghost cannot be consoled but is caught in an endless cycle of revenge as long as the hall exists. The revenant does not only seek justice by avenging herself on the man who committed the crime against her and her son but on every male inhabitant of Ravenshill Hall, regardless of his age and character. Katharine Deverel's revenge is directed against men in general and thus forms a rebellion against the patriarchal system that enables the subjugation of women who, without male protection, are vulnerable to fraud and disinheritance. It is only when the building burns down at the end of the story that Katharine Deverel's ghost disappears, vanishing with the structure to which it is attached. Before it comes to this, however, the ghost of Katharine Deverel threatens another man's life.

Five years after Granville's death, Harrison has almost forgotten about the incident and his friend Richard Forster has left England for Honduras, where he, as Bishop of the country, "was doing good work for God and man in his far-off colonial diocese" (Galbraith, "Revenge" 225).[24] However, the gruesome events are brought back to his mind when Harrison, who had been staying in Italy for a couple of months on business and has just put his feet on British soil again, receives a letter from a friend of his schoolboy days, Jack Chamberlayne, stating that he is considering buying a country mansion and would like his advice. From the description of the location, Harrison intuitively knows that his friend is talking about Ravenshill Hall. Unaware of the danger in which

---

24   As has been argued in the introduction, the hegemonic concept of masculinity was largely influenced by the needs of the British Empire in the second half of the nineteenth century and the onset of the twentieth century. While chapter 3 of this work specifically focuses on imperial ghost stories, the Empire is also present as an underlying structure on which the hegemonic concept of masculinity is based in the other ghost stories discussed in this work. In this context, it is worth noting that Forster is described as somebody who is doing good work for "God and *man*" (Galbraith, "Revenge" 225, my emphasis) instead of "God and country" or "God and Queen", which were common pairings in New Imperialist propaganda texts and speeches. By substituting the second element with "man", the story stresses the importance of the imperial project for constructions of masculinity at the time the story was published.

he finds himself, Chamberlayne merrily reports that the house is "going for a mere song" and that "even a family ghost is thrown in" (Galbraith, "Revenge" 226). Through an unfortunate succession of events, Harrison receives the letter with delay "at noon on the last day of the year" (ibid.).[25] Shocked that his friend is to celebrate the New Year in Ravenshill Hall, Harrison jumps on the next train to Mallowby. From this point onwards, it is clear that he has shed his incredulity and now believes in the supernatural power of Katharine Deverel's ghost. During the train ride, he even calls up imaginary ghosts:

> then the heavy velvet curtains trembled, parted, and a woman's figure stood framed in the long window – a woman with dripping garments and a white set face, lighted by strange, lurid eyes – eyes which were dead, and yet alive in their fierce hatred and unquenchable thirst for revenge. How they glittered! They were close to him now, looking in through the carriage window, and Harrison, who had once laughed contemptuously at the mere notion of supernatural manifestations, was perilously near raising a ghost for himself from the intensity of his nervous excitement. ... With a half-laugh at his own weakness, he drew the curtains across the windows. (Galbraith, "Revenge" 229)

The ghost that Harrison imagines is inspired by the story he heard five years earlier. While the "dripping garments" (Galbraith, "Revenge" 229) function as reminders of Katharine Deverel's unhappy fate, her depiction as a creature with glittering eyes who is consumed by a "fierce hatred and unquenchable thirst for revenge" (ibid.) is the result of her perceived monstrosity. Considering the rise of the feminist movement at the time the story was written, it is even possible to see Harrison's imaginary ghost as an embodiment of male anxieties over female empowerment. Subconsciously, he seems to believe that women have cause for revenge. Harrison is aware that the ghost is not real but a figment of his imagination and that the spectre testifies to his frenzied state of mind – a condition which he perceives as weakness and thus tries to shake off. However, while he was able to dismiss the possibility of ghosts with "a shout of laughter" (Galbraith, "Revenge" 221) at the beginning of the story, he can only utter a "half-laugh" (ibid. 229) now.

The climax of the story occurs when Harrison arrives at the train station in Mallowby and, together with the stationmaster, hurries to the haunted man-

---

25   The letter had been sent to Italy, where it arrived after Harrison had left, and was then forwarded to England.

sion. When they arrive at Ravenshill Hall, the church bells strike midnight. While the stationmaster is too scared to enter the gates, Harrison swallows some spirit he brough along in a flask and approaches "the haunted house" (Galbraith, "Revenge" 231). He arrives just in time to witness how his friend, in a re-enactment of Granville's fate, climbs out of the library window and walks towards the garden pond. Just as Granville before him, Chamberlayne is consumed by horror and pain:

> Suddenly from within the closed windows of the library issued a wild cry. The shutters were flung back, as if by magic the casement was thrown open, and the dark shadow of a man crossed the sill.
> The moon emerging suddenly from behind a bank of clouds poured down a flood of silvery light on the stone wall, the snow-covered path, and on the figure of Jack Chamberlayne, who, with hands clenched as if in mortal pain, his eyes fixed with an expression of nameless horror on some object, invisible to all but him, was slowly following the ghostly vision along the drive ... With supreme effort Harrison threw off the paralysing numbness which was creeping over him. Instinctively he dashed across the grass and stood between Chamberlayne and the fatal pond. (Galbraith, "Revenge" 233)

What is interesting here is that Chamberlayne's pain is characterised as "mortal pain" (Galbraith, "Revenge" 233), which contrasts with the ghost's immortal thirst for revenge and draws attention to the fact that the man is not yet dead. The passage further suggests that the female ghost has taken control over Chamberlayne's mind and body and that he is compelled to follow her to the garden pond. Harrison is not able to see the ghost, however, which might be conditioned by the fact that the ghost only preys on the male owners of Ravenshill Hall and not on men in general (the male servants of the hall are also immune to Katharine Deverel's curse). Harrison can only hear voices singing, "with ghastly reiteration[,] 'We shall have him tonight'" (ibid.). In contrast to Jack in "Nut Bush Farm", who is paralysed by fear and whose ghost-seeing experience ends in a feminising faint, Harrison is able to shake off the "paralysing numbness" (Galbraith, "Revenge" 233) that threatens to overcome him. Thanks to his knowledge in wrestling, he is able to tackle the significantly taller Chamberlayne and save him from certain death, thereby breaking Katharine Deverel's curse. Only moments after Harrison's interference, flames are licking out of the library window and soon expand to cover the whole house. The story suggests that it was Katharine Deverel's ghost who has set the house on fire, for Harrison hears a "hideous peal of shrill triumphant laughter" amidst "the continuous roar of the flames" (Galbraith, "Revenge" 235). Ravenshill Hall burns down to the ground. As has been pointed out above, haunting is inevitably tied to certain places. It comes as no surprise, then, that Katharine Deverel's ghost disappears with the house.

Harrison is established as the hero of the story: the "man who, single-handed, had braved the Deverel ghosts and baulked them of their prey ranked, by the Mallowby standard, above Gordon, and only a little lower than Nelson" (Galbraith, "Revenge" 236), the reader learns. By referring to the heroes of the British Empire, General Charles George Gordon and Admiral Horatio Lord Nelson, the story draws attention again to the entanglement of British imperial thinking with questions of ideal masculinity. Harrison is presented as the epitome of imperial masculinity, a man willing to give his own life in his attempt to destroy the murderous plans of the monstrous female Other. He fails, however, to undo the crime committed by the man who wronged Katharine Deverel and her infant child. Instead, Harrison treats the ghost with the same hostility that led to the haunting of Ravenshill Hall in the first place. In this context, it is important to note that there are no female characters in the story except for Katharine Deverel's ghost, who largely remains silent and is eventually exorcised. Even the servants in the story are exclusively male. This absence of women from the narrative echoes the hierarchy of Victorian society, where women were pushed into the role of the silent object. The narrative strategy is thus part of a larger preoccupation of the story with questions of gender and power.

Algernon Blackwood: "The Empty House" (1906)

The last story discussed in this chapter was written by Algernon Blackwood (1869–1951), who was arguably one of the most prolific ghost story writers of the early twentieth century. He wrote twelve ghost story collections and "several forgotten fantasy novels" (Sullivan 115). "The Empty House" is one of Blackwood's earliest ghost stories. It served as the eponymous tale for his first ghost story collection *The Empty House and Other Ghost Stories*, which was published in 1906. In the collection, Blackwood utilizes the "'man-in-the street' figure, Jim Shorthouse, as a link between several of the tales" (Briggs, *Night Visitors* 61). This "very ordinary young man" (Blackwood 224) also functions as the focalizer in "The Empty House". Though often anthologised in ghost story collections, the tale has received almost no critical attention so far. The narrative constitutes a classic example of what Nick Freeman calls "the 'knowing encounter'" ("Haunted Houses" 331) with the supernatural, meaning that the protagonists enter the haunted space willingly. In the story, Jim Shorthouse spends the weekend with his "elderly spinster aunt" (Blackwood 223) Julia, who nurtures "a mania for psychical research" (ibid.) and asks him to accompany her to an allegedly haunted house – a request that he willingly fulfils when his aunt reassures him that, with him on her side, she "should be afraid of nothing in the world" (ibid. 224), thus "appeal[ing] to his vanity" (ibid.), as the heterodiegetic narrator of the story observes.

The subsequent analysis of "The Empty House" demonstrates that the story erodes the seeming binary between manly courage and female sensitivity – a dualism that was not only reinforced at the time the story was written but continues to influence ideas about gender to this day. The tale also displays Blackwood's belief in the ability to expand human faculties beyond the ordinary under particular circumstances. Born into an evangelical family, Blackwood broke free from the strict doctrine of his parents and, after only one term at Edinburgh University, spent a decade in the US and Canada, where he performed various jobs before returning to England in 1899 (Willard 7). Several of the ghost stories that he would later produce are inspired by his time abroad. After his return to England, Blackwood turned to psychic phenomena and was briefly a member of the Order of the Golden Dawn, a secret hermetic society for the study and practice of occultism (Joshi 116). Blackwood was particularly interested in what he called "the Extension of Human Faculty" (qtd. in Sullivan 117). In his autobiography *Episodes before Thirty* (1923), Blackwood points out that "[t]o be known as the 'ghost man' is almost a derogatory classification ... . My interest in psychic matters has always been the interest in extended or expanded consciousness" (qtd. in Sullivan 117). The question of whether or not ghosts exist was of secondary interest to Blackwood. He believed that, "under exceptional stimulus" (ibid.), human faculties are capable of extending "beyond the normal gamut of seeing, hearing, feeling" (ibid.). According to Blackwood, this is evident in his ghost narratives: "in most of these stories there is usually an average man who, either through a flash of terror or beauty, becomes stimulated into extra-sensory experience" (ibid.).

In "The Empty House", the extra-sensory experience of the male protagonist is triggered by flashes of terror. Even before Shorthouse and his aunt enter the haunted house, his senses seem to be amplified by the adventure. This is evidenced by the fact that Shorthouse ascribes animate properties to inanimate objects as they walk to the haunted house: "Slowly they walked among the empty streets of the town; a bright autumn moon silvered the roofs, casting deep shadows; there was no breath of wind; and the trees in the formal gardens by the sea front watched them silently as they passed along" (Blackwood 225). The wind has a "breath", the trees "watch[...] them silently", and the moon "silver[s] the roofs". These anthropomorphisms of the objects surrounding Shorthouse can be interpreted as an example of what Blackwood has termed "the Extension of Human Faculty" (qdt. in Sullivan 117). However, the broadening of the senses is not experienced as mind-expanding by Shorthouse, but results in a feeling of shame that is rooted in his inability to adhere to the contemporary parameters of masculinity, as we shall see. Shorthouse's struggle to keep up an appearance of manly self-control and the feeling of failure he experiences within the haunted space will be the focus of my reading of "The Empty House".

Like the protagonist in H. G. Well's "The Red Room" (1896), which I have briefly discussed in the introduction of this work, Shorthouse sets out on the adventure with the conviction that he can preserve his manly self-control:

> He agreed to go.
> Instinctively, by a sort of sub-conscious preparation, he kept himself and his forces well in hand the whole evening, compelling an accumulative reserve of control by that nameless inward process of gradually putting all the emotions away and turning the key upon them – a process difficult to describe, but wonderfully effective, as all man who have lived through severe trials of the inner man well understand. (Blackwood 224)

The passage illustrates Shorthouse's notions about manly willpower and fearlessness. Like a soldier preparing himself for war, Shorthouse supposedly locks away his emotions and compels "an accumulative reserve of control" (Blackwood 224). By referring to this inner process as an act that "all men who have lived through severe trials of the inner man well understand" (ibid.), the narrator explicitly frames Shorthouse's preparation for the adventure in terms of the masculine gender identity assigned to him. It is also important to note that Shorthouse's accumulation of self-control is described as something he does instinctively. This way, self-control is presented as an innate quality which men like Shorthouse naturally seem to possess. The remainder of the story complicates this idea, however.

Throughout the story, the heterodiegetic narrator generally adopts Jim Shorthouse's point of view. The internal focalization on Shorthouse is crucial in order to understand the text's critique of contemporary gender expectations, for it ensures that we get an insight into his thoughts. It is important to note, however, that we are dealing with a very complex narrative voice here. As the narrative unfolds, the narrator also uses their narrative voice in order to comment on the events. Irony is used as a narrative device time and again in order to show that there is a tension between what the male protagonist is doing and what he is actually feeling. The reader thus learns that, rather than mastering his feelings, Shorthouse cannot keep a stiff upper lip and is susceptible to swings of emotion. In this way, the story draws attention to the fact that the idea of compartmentalization (arguably *the* male achievement, even today) is a social construct that is rooted in an understanding of manliness as unemotional and rational.

From the onset of the story, there are numerous hints at Shorthouse's nervous excitability and his lack of self-control: suffering from a "wave of nervousness" (Blackwood 225), Shorthouse has to "fumble[…] a long time with the key" (ibid.) before he is able to fit it into the lock and open the door to the haunted house, for instance. Additionally, when he opens a box of matches in order to light a candle shortly afterwards, he opens it upside down and spills the matches all over the floor (ibid. 226). Both instances suggest the protagonist's inability to keep calm. In addition, Shorthouse is unable to control his voice, which "sounded like someone else's and was only half under control" (ibid. 228). It is telling that Shorthouse's voice does not sound like his own when he has lost control over it. The story thus emphasises that such a bodily reaction does not comply with his perception of himself as a man who is capable of holding his emotions in check.

However, instead of admitting his fear and emotional distress, Shorthouse acts as if his aunt is the vulnerable party in need of his protection. When he takes her arm, it is because "[s]he needed support" (Blackwood 225), and when he hesitates, it is "on his aunt's account" (ibid. 224). He even believes that his task during the adventure is "to carry his aunt's fear as well as his own" (ibid. 224) and we learn that he has "confidence in his own power to stand against any shock that might come" (ibid. 225). Given the numerous narratological hints at Shorthouse's excitability and nervousness, these assertions have a comic quality. The irony of the situation arises from the fact that, while the reader is acutely aware of the obvious gap between what the protagonist wants to feel and what he actually experiences, Shorthouse himself seems oblivious of this tension.

When Shorthouse finally manages to fit the key into the lock at the beginning of their adventure, we also learn that, "[f]or a moment, if truth were told,

they both hoped that ... [the door] would not open" (Blackwood 225). This remark not only points to Shorthouse's unwillingness to enter the haunted space,
but also indicates that he feels that he has to hide his true feelings. Later in the
story, the heterodiegetic narrator also tells us that Shorthouse and his aunt investigate the haunted house with "a great appearance of boldness" (ibid. 229)
while "over his body the skin moved as if crawling ants covered it" (ibid.). Shorthouse's bodily reaction is again indicative of the terror he experiences within
the haunted space. At the same time, the story exposes his manly vigour as
nothing but "a great appearance" (ibid). By emphasising Shorthouse's struggle to keep up appearances, the story not only draws attention to Shorthouse's
failure to compartmentalize his feelings but also counters the idea that determination and self-control are innate qualities that men naturally possess.

The narrative further suggests that Aunt Julia is actually more vigorous
than her nephew. When the candle, which he and his aunt use to illuminate
the rooms inside the house, is extinguished, Shorthouse utters a cry, "[i]n
spite of himself" (Blackwood 230). In contrast to her nephew, Aunt Julia seems
to remain calm: "She made no sound ... [and] her control returned almost at
once" (ibid.), the narrator points out, thereby suggesting that Aunt Julia is less
affected by the adventure than her nephew.

More than just "a setting for supernatural activity", the house is also "the
protagonist" (Bussing 99) in Blackwood's tale: "Certain houses, like certain persons, manage somehow to proclaim at once their character for evil ... . [P]er-
haps ... it is the aroma of evil deeds committed under a particular roof, long
after the actual doers have passed away, that makes the gooseflesh come and
the hair rise" (Blackwood 222), the narrator describes the house. The comparison of the house with "certain persons" stresses its status as a quasi-human
subject rather than an inanimate object. It is something evil that can do harm
to the people who dare to invade its spaces. However, apart from the "aroma of
evil deeds" (ibid.), the house shows no outward sign of being haunted. Quite
the contrary:

> There was manifestly nothing in the external appearance of this particular
> house to bear out the tales of the horror that was said to reign within. It was
> neither lonely nor unkempt. It stood, crowded into a corner of the square,
> and looked exactly like the houses on either side of it. It had the same num-
> ber of windows as its neighbours; the same balcony overlooking the gardens;
> the same white steps leading up to the heavy black front door; and, in the
> rear, there was the same narrow strip of green, with neat box borders, run-

ning up to the wall that divided it, from the backs of the adjoining houses. Apparently, too, the number of chimney pots on the roof was the same; the breadth and angle of the eaves; and even the height of the dirty area railings.

And yet this house in the square, that seemed precisely similar to its fifty ugly neighbours, was as a matter of fact entirely different – horribly different. (Blackwood 222)

The townhouse in Blackwood's story is apparently one of "those most mysterious of all mysteries" (James, "Miss Braddon" 10), as Henry James has put it. It looks just like any other townhouse in the street, which implies that any urban family home can become the locus of horror and haunting.

It is noteworthy, however, that, just like the house itself, the evil that resides in it is manmade. As Aunt Julia tells Shorthouse before they start their nightly adventure,

"[i]t has to do with a murder committed by a jealous stableman who had some affair with a servant in the house. One night he managed to secrete himself in the cellar, and when everyone was asleep, he crept upstairs to the servants' quarters. Chased the girl down to the next landing, and, before anyone could come to rescue threw her bodily over the banisters into the hall below." (Blackwood 224)

Shorthouse's knowledge of the brutal deed that happened within the house is crucial for the understanding of the story, for he is the only ghost-seer in the narrative. When he and his aunt enter the "large double drawing-rooms" (Blackwood 229) of the house,

a face thrust itself forward so close to his own that he could almost have touched it with his lips. It was a face working with passion; a man's face, dark, with thick features, and angry, savage eyes. It belonged to a common man, and it was evil in its ordinary normal expression, no doubt, but as he saw it, alive with intense, aggressive emotion, it was a malignant and terrible human countenance. (Blackwood 230)

Shorthouse evidently sees the ghost of the stableman who murdered the young woman. It is important to be aware, however, that everything we come to know about the spectral figure is filtered through Shorthouse's consciousness. It is possible, therefore, that the story about the murderous stableman has set

Shorthouse's imagination in motion and that he imagines the ghostly appearance. The heterodiegetic narrator does not validate Shorthouse's perception of the event. Likewise, Aunt Julia does not witness the emergence of the spectre: "Aunt Julia always declared that at this moment she was not actually watching him but had turned her head towards the inner room" (Blackwood 230). One cannot but wonder if Shorthouse would have seen the ghost if Aunt Julia had not told him about the murder that happened within the walls of the haunted house. The story's title also suggests that there are no real ghosts in the house, but that it is essentially "empty".

In any case, the act of ghost-seeing and its contemporary association with femininity and mental instability mark Shorthouse as effeminate. If the ghost is real, Shorthouse's ability to see the spectre aligns him with the numerous female mediums of the time and thus further highlights his embodiment of supposedly feminine qualities like sensitivity. If the ghost is just a figment of his imagination, it might be regarded as a sign of a weak mind or even mental illness.

As a figment of his imagination, the phantom stands in allegorically for Shorthouse's desires and anxieties. In this context, it is important to note that Shorthouse perceives the stableman as racially Other with a "dark" complexion, "thick features", and "savage eyes" (Blackwood 230). In Aunt Julia's narration of the murder, there is nothing which hints at the Stableman's foreign appearance. It rather seems that, for Shorthouse, an evil deed is more likely to be committed by a "dark" person. In this way, the story indicates the protagonist's racialised anxieties, which are rooted in the imperialist thinking of the time which denotes the Orient as dangerous and savage. What is also striking is that Shorthouse becomes the object of the stableman's angry passion in the passage. It is he at whom the ghost gazes "with intense, aggressive emotion" (Blackwood 230). Shorthouse apparently stands in for the servant girl who has been murdered by the stableman. By taking the girl's position, Shorthouse is pushed into the role of the vulnerable female and presented as a victim of sexualized violence. The homoerotic tension Shorthouse experiences at this moment is signalled by the terms that are used to describe the spectral stableman like "passion" (ibid.) and "intense ... emotion" (ibid.), on the one hand, and by the way he experiences the distance between himself and the ghost, on the other hand. The spectre is so close that "he could almost have touched it with his lips" – a remark which can be read as a hidden desire to kiss the stableman. It is even possible to argue that what is experienced as frightening by Shorthouse is his homoerotic desire for the dark, working-class man – a figure that represents

racial, social, and sexual Otherness. Shorthouse simultaneously rejects and desires this embodiment of Otherness, a feeling that may best be described with
Allon White's and Peter Stallybrass's concept of "phobic enchantment" (124). According to White and Stallybrass, "phobic enchantment occurs when the dominant culture uses its political power to abject and reject what it defines as a
debased other" (Hoeveler 114). This process, they argue, "conflicts powerfully
and predictably with a desire for this Other" (Stallybrass and White 5).

It is further noteworthy that Shorthouse encounters the ghost in the drawing room, a space conventionally coded as feminine. This is relevant for several reasons: by letting the ghost appear in a female space, the story highlights
Shorthouse's embodiment of supposedly feminine qualities. Furthermore, the
narrative presents the female domestic space as uncanny and the locus of male
discomfort – a place where men are vulnerable and powerless. What is also
noteworthy about the location of haunting is the association of the drawing
room with middle-class family life. It is a space from which the stableman was
excluded in life, but which he now usurps, thus transgressing class boundaries.

After the ghostly visitation of the murderous stableman, Shorthouse and
Aunt Julia further invade the haunted space and come across the room into
which the murderer allegedly chased his victim and finally caught her:

> he felt less master of himself here than in any other part of the house. There
> was something that acted directly on the nerves, tiring the resolution, enfee-
> bling the will. He was conscious of the result before he had been in the room
> five minutes, and it was in the short time they stayed there that he suffered
> the wholesale depletion of his vital forces, which was, for himself, the chief
> horror of the whole experience. (Blackwood 231)

In this passage, the inability to embody the prevalent hallmarks of masculinity
and to remain "master of himself" (Blackwood 231) is identified as the real horror of the nightly adventure. Here the story is again reminiscent of H. G. Well's
"The Red Room", in which the protagonist similarly states that the most terrifying occupant of the supposedly haunted room is fear itself. By showcasing that
the loss of qualities like resolution and a strong will is experienced as outright
terrifying, "The Empty House" points to the pressure that a heteronormative
construction of masculinity exerts on men.

At the end of the story, Shorthouse finally gives up his struggle to keep up
appearances:

The woman's courage amazed him; it was so much greater than his own; and, as they advanced, holding aloft the dripping candle, some subtle force exhaled from this trembling, white-faced old woman at his side that was the true force of his inspiration. It held something really great that shamed him and gave him the support without which he would have proved far less equal to the occasion. (Blackwood 234)

Shorthouse finally admits to himself that his elderly aunt is, in fact, more courageous than he and that she helps him to get through the adventure – rather than the other way round. By referring to Aunt Julia as "the woman", the narrative draws attention to the gender assigned to Shorthouse's aunt, thereby undermining contemporary assumptions about women's sensitivity and excitability. It is important to note, however, that the gender role reversal is something that Shorthouse experiences as shameful. Bradley Deane has detected "a growing emphasis on shame in late Victorian constructions of male behavior" (103), a feeling which came to replace "the discourses of guilt, self-criticism, and sin that had been more characteristic of mid-century fiction" (ibid.). As Deane points out, guilt and shame differ significantly from one another: "the former represents the sanction of conscience according to internalized laws of right and wrong and the latter the external sanction of a group concerned primarily with behavior rather than motive" (ibid.). Accordingly, the emphasis on shame draws attention to the pressure men like Shorthouse experience regarding their "flawed" gender performance.

The story's deconstruction of the stereotypical depiction of men as active and fearless rescuers and of women as passive and frightened victims is also relevant when seen in the context of the Gothic tradition which often reinforces the female/male binary by depicting dominant male oppressors and female victims, so-called damsels in distress, especially in its early texts. Blackwood's ghost story diverges from this tradition by featuring a mentally strong elderly woman, on the one hand, and an excitable young man, on the other hand. By undermining the contemporary association of men with rationality and self-discipline and women with irrationality and emotionality, the narrative suggests that what was seen as manly and womanly is not a natural condition, but a socially constructed role.

The feeling of fear experienced by Shorthouse in the haunted house can also be interpreted as an allegory for the growing discomfort upper- and middle-class men seemed to feel towards the end of the century regarding domesticity. For instance, Robert Louis Stevenson complains in an 1881 essay that "marriage, if comfortable, is not at all heroic. It certainly narrows and damps the spirits of generous men. ... The air of the fireside withers out all the fine wildings of the husband's heart" (*Virginibus* 5–6). In a similar vein, W. R. Greg lists the disadvantages of marriage in an 1869 essay: "the fetters of a wife, the burden and responsibility of children, and the decent monotony of the domestic hearth" (21). In his 1885 advice book on matrimony with the telling title *How to Be Happy Though Married*, E. J. Hardy even detects a general reluctance among young men to get married: "it is often said that they are giving up matrimony as if it were some silly old habit suited to their grandfathers and grandmothers" (12). We do not get to know much about Shorthouse's family background; but since a wife or a family is never mentioned, it is likely that he is, in fact, a bachelor. What we do know for certain is that Aunt Julia is a "spinster" (Blackwood 223), a figure often portrayed in a bad light and looked down upon – very much in contrast to her male equivalent. By portraying Aunt Julia as fearless, sympathetic and mentally stronger than her nephew, the story reverses this dynamic.

* * *

Despite their apparent otherworldliness, ghosts that haunt properties often have a clear connection with worldly matters (Margree, *British* 30). They return to the living in order to expose or re-enact crimes, take revenge, reveal hidden wills, and influence the passing on of properties. In the ghost stories by Riddell, Galbraith, and Blackwood discussed above, the ghosts that appear exist because of a crime that has been committed in the past. Their existence brings these crimes to the awareness of the present owners or visitors of the houses they haunt. They are, as Ruth Heholt has so accurately put it, "material evidence" ("Raising") of the crime. In this chapter, I have focused on the ways in which their presence affects the male ghost-seers and their ideas of masculinity. What all three stories share is that the manifestation of the ghost has a shattering effect on the ghost-seers. While the protagonists of Riddell's "Nut Bush Farm" and Blackwood's "The Empty House" lose their confidence in their gender performance as exemplary for the ideal of imperial masculinity, the male owners of Ravenshill Hall in Galbraith's "A Ghost's Revenge" are not only forced to re-evaluate their representation of normative masculinity but are in danger of losing their lives. In all three stories, the gendered territory of the domestic family home serves as a site where traditional ideas about femininity and masculinity are being subverted, thereby undermining patriarchal assumptions of male dominance. In Riddell's text, Miss Gostock's refusal to comply with dominant scripts of femininity and to decorate her house according to the expectations of Victorian society make her appear as less real and more spectral than the actual ghost that haunts the eponymous Nut Bush Farm. The narrator finds himself in an inferior position that is further reinforced when he starts seeing the spectre of the farm's late tenant. In Galbraith's story, the revenant of a disowned woman returns to reclaim the patriarchal space of Ravenshill Hall. The protagonist, at first disbelieving of the existence of ghosts, is forced to acknowledge the superior power of the spectral woman, whose attack on the male owners of her former home represents a rebellion against the patriarchal system in general. And in Blackwood's "The Empty House", the protagonist's nervous excitement is juxtaposed to his aunt's courage, thereby exposing dominant conceptions of gender as social constructs.

The motif of the haunted house will recur in various forms throughout this work. In the chapter that is to follow, two of the authors, Henry James and Edith Nesbit, appropriate the haunted house narrative and its entanglement with questions of secrecy and disclosure in order to articulate what has arguably been *the* secret in Victorian and Edwardian society: illicit sexual desire.

Chapter 2
Spectral Sexualities: Guilty Desire and the Male Sexual Body

In the ghost stories discussed in this chapter, it is male sexual desire that is experienced as frightening because it is not acceptable within the moral code of Victorian society. In a way that Freud would term "the uncanny" in 1919, these stories suggest that it is not something alien that haunts the mind of the ghost-seers but, rather, the Other within the self. The protagonists are troubled by a dawning consciousness of their supposedly "unruly" sexuality. The ghosts we will encounter in this chapter can therefore be regarded as metaphors for the ghost-seer's sexual anxieties.

The chapter is structured as follows: Section One draws attention to the subject of male sexuality in the Victorian and Edwardian eras. Even though male sexual desire was acknowledged, and it was common for men to visit prostitutes (and pass on sexual diseases like syphilis to their wives),[1] the public elevation of "the virginial ideal of the 'Angel in the House'" (Furneaux) suggested to bourgeois men that there is only one type of woman worthy of their attention. Hence, bourgeois codes of conduct restricted heterosexual men in the open expression of sexual desire. At the same time, the prosecution of homosexual men criminalised gay men and same-sex desire. This is not to say there was no gay subculture and men shrunk from desiring sexually affirmative women. On the contrary, one of my central arguments in this chapter is that, despite the attempts to regulate sexual desire, there existed a discourse about the normality and naturality of erotic desire in the Victorian and Edwardian eras and that the ghost as a literary figure was used by writers to partake in

---

1   On syphilis and the cultural fears associated with the infection, see Andrew Smith, *Victorian Demons* (2008), chap. 4 in particular.

this discourse. However, as my subsequent discussion will demonstrate, het-eronormative assumptions about gender and sexuality caused problems for many men who felt that they would harbour "forbidden" desires.[2] The figure of the ghost functioned as both a means to make visible taboo sexual desires and to illustrate the "spectralization" of non-normative sexual behaviour, thereby exposing the repressive nature of Victorian moral doctrine.[3] Section Two and Three then illustrate the particular ways in which the supernatural realm of the ghost story enabled writers to think and speak about desire, eroticism, and sexual anxieties. Section Two considers Vernon Lee's "A Culture Ghost: or, Winthrop's Adventure" (1881)[4] and Henry James's "The Real Right Thing" (1899). In both stories, homoerotic desire surfaces. Section Three looks at Elizabeth Gaskell's "The Poor Clare" (1856) and Edith Nesbit's "The Ebony Frame" (1891). In this section, I analyse how ghost story writers commented on the "Angel in the House"/"Fallen Woman" dichotomy, ultimately suggesting that the latter is much more desirable.

Closeted Desire: Secrecy, Disclosure, and the Ghost Story

Michel Foucault's *The History of Sexuality* (1976) serves as a good starting point for an investigation of male sexuality in the Victorian and Edwardian periods. In the first volume of his work, Foucault illustrates how eighteenth- and nine-teenth-century medical and sexological discourse contributed to the repres-sion of sexuality. He contends that while society had "almost certainly con-stituted a whole restrictive economy" (Foucault, *Sexuality* 18) which "deprived [people] of a certain way of speaking about sex" (ibid. 30), "[a]t the level of dis-courses and their domains, however, practically the opposite phenomenon oc-

---

2   It is certainly not my intention to suggest that men faced greater oppression than women regarding sexuality in Victorian Britain. Female sexuality was repeatedly sup-pressed, pathologized, or even denied its existence, especially in the latter decades of the nineteenth century. In the following, I will illustrate how the mechanisms that were used to control female sexuality also influenced men in their perception of their own sexual identity.

3   I would like to stress that I only look at texts that deal with sexual desire between con-senting adults in this chapter. I strongly reject every form of sexual expression that involves children or non-consenting adults.

4   Subsequently referred to as "Winthrop's Adventure". Lee republished the story in 1927 under this shortened title.

curred" (ibid. 18). At first glance, these developments might appear contradictory. However, as Sally Ledger has pointed out, "[s]cientifically to classify and
medically to analyse sexuality was institutionally to control it, and in this way it
is possible to see how Victorian sexual repression and prohibition actually went
hand in hand with the discursive explosion around the subject of sex" (95).

One of the major strands in nineteenth-century sexological theory was
"the study of the sexually 'sick', as the title of the most famous bible of sexology,
Richard von Krafft-Ebing's *Psychopathia Sexualis* (1886), suggests" (Downing
88). The classification of sexuality as part of an individual's identity led to
the identification of what was perceived as perverse sexualities and, more
importantly, to the labelling of deviant subjectivities. Foucault contends that
while in the pre-Victorian period the performance of a disallowed sexual act
did not reflect on the person's personality but marked the act itself as a sin,
an individual could be labelled as sexually abnormal even "in the absence of
any genital activity" (Sedgwick, *Epistemology* 83) in the latter decades of the
nineteenth century. "Sin, in this view, was no longer something you did, but
something you 'were', as part of a whole range of scientifically 'explained'
pervations, malfunctions or aberrations" (Skovmand 53).

Along with other forms of sexuality, Foucault argues, the homosexual was
invented as an identity category: while sodomy "[a]s defined by the ancient civil
or canonical codes ... [as] a category of forbidden acts" (Foucault, *Sexuality* 43)
had been seen as "a temporary aberration; the homosexual was now a species"
(ibid.). As Lisa Downing has remarked, "Foucault's ... claim here is that the 'sexual scientists' of the nineteenth century did not invent techniques and methods for *uncovering* the hidden truths about sex; rather they *produced* sexuality
as a new category of knowledge, a historically specific field" (89, emphasis in
original).

Several critics have identified cracks in Foucault's theories. Especially the
assumption that (homo-)sexuality as an identity category has not existed before the end of the nineteenth century has been criticised repeatedly – and
rightly so. Eve Kosofsky Sedgwick, for instance, takes issue with Foucault's idea
that a modern concept of sexual identities has superseded an earlier notion
that focused on acts. She argues that "issues of modern homo/heterosexual
definition are structured, not by the super-session of one model and the con-
sequent withering away of another, but instead by the relations enabled by the
unrationalized coexistence of different models during the times they do coexist" (*Epistemology* 47). In *Homosexuality in Renaissance England* (1982), Alan Bray
further illustrates that a gay male subculture already existed in the seventeenth

century. Similarly, Terry Castle posits in her acclaimed *The Apparitional Lesbian* (1993) that women have identified as women-loving women long before the emergence of the term lesbian around 1900 (9–10). In *Houses, Secrets, and the Closet* (2016), Gero Bauer concludes that the concept of sexual identity "has to be dated back at least to the two centuries between 1600 and 1800" (14).

John Fletcher has pinpointed another inconsistency in Foucault's theory. In his work, Foucault stresses "the social construction of homosexuality by the dominant discourses of law, medicine and sexology" (Fletcher 53–54). Fletcher points out, however, that the term "homosexuality"[5] was first used by gay activists and concludes that it was therefore an act of *"self*-naming and *self*-definition within what was a discourse of civil rights and not a medical or sexological discourse" (54–55, emphasis in original).

While I concur with these critics, I think it is nevertheless important to maintain that Foucault is right in pointing out that the labelling of sexual types and supposed abnormalities in Victorian medical and sexological discourse had serious consequences. The identification of the deviant relies heavily on a definition of the normal. That is, to look at it the other way around, the very idea of the normal cannot exist without that which has been labelled abnormal (S. Kruger 337). By pathologizing everything that does not serve a reproductive purpose (masturbation and homosexuality, for instance), a normative heterosexuality was reinforced. The heightened focus on sexuality in the social sciences thus furthered a system of surveillance that monitored and restricted sexual behaviour.

While the categorisation of supposedly deviant sexualities contributes to a system of power that regulates the sexual expression of the individual, it also invites what Foucault has called a "'reverse' discourse" (Foucault, *Sexuality* 101):

---

5   The term "homosexuality" was coined in 1868 by the German-Hungarian writer and human rights activist Károly Márià Kertbeny (born Karl Maria Benkert, 1824–1882) who used the word in a letter to Karl Heinrich Ulrichs in order to describe same-sex attraction. Both men campaigned against the Prussian law statute that criminalised sex between men. Kertbeny argued that homosexuality was natural and should therefore not be treated as a crime (Norton, "Homosexual"). Since sexual intercourse between women was to a great extent overlooked in Europe and often not prohibited by law, it is noteworthy that Kertbeny used the term "Homosexualisten" for male homosexuals and "Homosexualistinnen" for female homosexuals. However, these terms were not used by anyone else until 1880, when a text by Kertbeny was published in the popular science book *Entdeckung der Seele*. Kertbeny used the pseudonym "Dr M" which led to the "mistaken belief that Kertbeny was a doctor or scientist" (ibid.).

"We must make allowance for the complex and unstable process whereby discourse can be both an instrument and an effect of power, but also a hindrance, a stumbling-block, a point of resistance and a starting point for an opposing strategy" (ibid.). By naming certain types of deviant sexuality, Foucault argues, sexologists provide groups of people with the necessary vocabulary and information they need for their resistance to social control: "homosexuality began to speak in its own behalf, to demand that its legitimacy or 'naturality' be acknowledged, often in the same vocabulary, using the same categories by which it was medically disqualified" (ibid.).[6] We have seen above that regarding homosexuality "sexologists took their terms and categories from the emergent and polemical self-consciousness of apologists for same-sex love" (Fletcher 55) and not the other way around. To speak of a "reverse" discourse is therefore misleading. For this reason, I propose to use the term counter discourse. This term is often used to describe a discourse that "challenge[s] dominant narratives around socio-political issues" (Feltwell et al. 345). This is also how the term will be used here. In the following, I argue that the ghost stories discussed in this chapter can be regarded as a contribution to this counter discourse.

The ambiguous readability of ghost stories gave authors an opportunity to navigate their way through the restrictions of the Victorian society, as we have seen before. On one level, ghost stories can be read as thrilling pieces of literature and the ghosts that appear in them can be regarded as mere spectres. Yet, on another level, ghosts can often be interpreted as hallucinations and thus function as metaphors for the ghost-seer's feelings and desires. This ambiguity made it possible for writers to hide their criticism in the supernatural framework of the story.[7] In the ghost stories discussed in this chapter, it is the ghost-

---

6   It is crucial to note that not all sexologists treated homosexuality as an abnormality or sickness. Havelock Ellis, for instance, hoped that the scientific discourse about homosexuality might actually lead to the social acceptance of same-sex desire. In his *Sexual Inversion* (1897), Ellis presents a series of case studies which "indicate that the link between masculinity and heterosexuality was not a necessary or inevitable one" (Smith, *Demons* 29). Homosexuality is shown as a normal and natural expression of sexual desire. As Chiara Beccalossi has argued, "*Sexual Inversion*'s radical proposition rested on the broader implications of the book: if sexual inversion was neither a sin nor a sickness, it followed that the difference between heterosexuality and homosexuality was simply in the choice of object of desire" (172).

7   I am not claiming that every Victorian and Edwardian ghost story is ambiguous. There are, of course, ghost stories which belong to the category of the explained supernatural, on the one hand, and tales which are clearly supernatural, on the other hand. An example of the latter is "The Poor Clare", which is discussed in this chapter. Even though

seers' "unruly" sexuality that needs concealment. This camouflage is twofold: the information about the protagonists' sexuality is not only buried in the supernatural realm of the story but also linguistically encoded.

In a society in which non-normative love and desire were regarded as dangerous, degenerate, and, in the case of gay love, even punishable by law, writers had to "find discreet ways and discrete discourses of speaking to each other and the world, and also to invent a literature of their own" (White 116). By using "unclear references, … gaps and silences that can but need not be filled by the reader" (N. Walker 13), this way of "writing relies on an encoded framework there to be read by those in the know" (White 116). Another strategy to "evoke recognizant knowledge in those who already possess it without igniting it in those who may not" (Sedgwick, *Epistomology* 101) is to make use of the "'slipperiness' of language" (Hotz-Davies 277), its ability to suggest a meaning besides the obvious one. As Ardel Haefele-Thomas has pointed out, in the nineteenth century "'[s]trange' and 'peculiar' were often coded words between queer people and 'unaccountable' is yet another word signalling something not yet named" (Haefele-Thomas 127). By relying on the ambiguity of language, a text can suggest same-sex desire, "even in the absence of explicit homosexual terminology and activity" (E. Cohen 803).

A text which conveys homoeroticism in a hidden way is generally referred to as closeted. This term was first used in relation to homosexuality in the 1950s (Janes 13). However, authors employed the concept of the closet long before that to express same-sex desire and eroticism.[8] Henry Urbach describes the closet as "a social and literary convention that narrate[s] homosexuality as a spectacle of veiled disclosure" (67).[9] In *Configurations of the Female Closet: 1800–1930* (2019), Nathalie Walker criticises that "closet research has basically created the

---

the spectral figure is clearly supernatural, the text deals with unruly sexualities in a veiled way and the ghost can be seen as an embodiment of suppressed sexual desires, as we shall see.

8   This has been persuasively illustrated by Eve Kosofsky Sedgwick in her ground-breaking study *Epistemology of the Closet* (1990).

9   Urbach also comments on the connection between the spatial and the metaphorical closet: "These two closets are not as different as they might appear. Taken together, they present a related way of defining and ascribing meaning to space. They both describe sites of storage that are separated from, and connected to, spaces of display. Each space excludes but also needs the other. The non-room, the closet, houses things that threaten to soil the room. Likewise, in a social order that ascribes normalcy to heterosexuality, the closet helps heterosexuality to present itself with authority" (Urbach 63).

closet as a *per se* male concept" (13, emphasis in original). She argues that the relative neglect of the female closet is symptomatic of a society which "lend[s] the concealment and disclosure of male secrets an aura of greater importance, in that women's secrets can seemingly only pertain to private, personal content, while a man's greater participation in public discourses gives any kind of knowledge he possesses political relevance" (N. Walker 13–14). My aim is not to further reinforce the connection between the closet and masculinity but to show that any sexual identity that is deemed unacceptable by society might be pushed into the closet and is thus vulnerable to what Terry Castle describes as the "ghost effect" (Castle, *Apparitional* 2). In her ground-breaking study *The Apparitional Lesbian*, Castle demonstrates the denial of lesbian relationships in Western culture: "Lesbian contributions to culture have been routinely suppressed or ignored, lesbian-themed works of art censored and destroyed" (Castle, *Apparitional* 5).[10] This cultural erasure of female homosexuality has forced the lesbian into an apparitional existence.[11] In a similar way, male sexual desire was often "spectralized" in the Victorian and Edwardian eras. The reason for this might have been that the contemporary ideal of imperial masculinity was based on the idea of the "male body as heroic rather than erotic, ... the body's depiction as 'under control' rather than 'out of control'" (Budd 77). But it was also the result of contemporary sexological discourse which privileged and elevated the reproductive function of sexual intercourse. It is not my intention to suggest that the extent of repression felt by men who harbour "forbidden" desires is comparable to the denial of female homosexuality. My aim is to show

---

10   In line with Castle, Paulina Palmer has remarked in *The Queer Uncanny* (2012) that "whereas male gay sexuality has been suppressed by society instituting laws and devising brutal or humiliating penalties for their infringement, lesbianism in many periods and cultures has been rendered well-nigh invisible" (Palmer 17). Similarly, Earl Jackson maintains that "[a]lthough marginalized, male gay sex is still recognisable under patriarchy. Lesbianism is inconceivable" (147). Lilian Faderman, in *Surpassing the Love of Men* (1981), points out that this disregard of female homosexuality is closely linked to the view that women are sexually dormant: "a sexual act without a male initiator, one which required autonomous drive, would be unthinkable" (Faderman 154). According to Sally Ledger, same-sex love between women started to be seen as a threat when the New Woman emerged in the 1890s; until then, she maintains, "same-sex love between women had been regarded as 'harmless'" (Ledger 124).

11   As Castle has maintained, the ignorance of female homosexuality nonetheless has not deprived the lesbian of her power. On the contrary: "the very frequency with which the lesbian has been 'apparitionalized' in the Western imagination also testifies to her peculiar cultural power" (Castle, *Apparitional* 7).

that "[t]here ... [are], potentially, as many forms of sexual secret and closeted life as there ... [are] varieties of personal identity and desire" (Janes 12).

Initially, it appears contradictory that of all things the figure of the ghost seems to have served as a useful metaphor for the articulation of "spectralized" sexualities. However, the ghost's very nature as a revenant arguably turns it into the most suitable metaphor for the articulation of repressed feelings, desires, and thoughts. The ghost is also a very potent figure. Despite its immateriality, its power and presence nevertheless are felt. The same is true for sexual desire. In Castle's words: "Only something very palpable – at a deeper level – has the capacity to 'haunt' us so thoroughly" (Castle, *Apparitional* 7).

Homospectrality and Queer Men in Vernon Lee's "Winthrop's Adventure" and Henry James's "The Real Right Thing"

The end of the nineteenth century witnessed a marked homosexual panic that peaked during the trials of Oscar Wilde in 1895. This "panic of same-sex desire" (Liggins, "Gendering" 41) was partly induced by a change in the law. In 1885, Section 11 of the Criminal Law Amendment Act (commonly known as Labouchère Amendment after the Radical MP Henry Labouchère who initiated the act) was passed. The clause states that

> [a]ny male person who, in public or private, commits, or is a party to the commission of, or procures, or attempts to procure the commission by any male person of, any act of gross indecency with another male person, shall be guilty of a misdemeanour, and being convicted thereof, shall be liable at the discretion of the Court to be imprisoned for any term not exceeding two years, with or without hard labour. (Bodkin and Mead 68)

Sodomy had been a crime in the UK since 1533 when the Buggery Act was initiated by Henry VIII. Under the statute, homosexual intercourse was punishable by death (C. Arnold 255). However, "the law was hardly enforced at all before the 1720s" (Cocks, "Secrets" 110) and it was only in the late eighteenth century that "the numbers of men arrested for homosexual offences began to rocket" (ibid.). In 1861, the maximum penalty was lowered to life imprisonment (ibid. 111). Considering that sodomy had been a capital offence, the Labouchère Amendment with its maximum penalty of two years with hard labour appears almost moderate. However, while homosexual acts were grouped together with other crimes under the umbrella term "unnatural offences" before 1885, the Labouchère Amendment "made it clear that sodomy was finally equated with male homosexual sex acts, more or less ignoring heterosexual sodomy" (Haefele-Thomas, *Queer* 173). This led to a heightened focus on same-sex relations between men, "the hitherto uninterrogated bachelor [became] a candidate for the suspicion of secrets" (Fletcher 63).

However, even more than this change in the law, a series of events which took place in Britain between 1870 and 1895 marked "the male homosexual as a criminal in the British public imagination" (Haefele-Thomas, *Queer* 121). In 1870, the transvestites Ernest Boulton and Frederick William Park, who had paraded about London's West End in women's clothes as "Lady Stella Clinton" and "Fanny Winifred", were arrested. The public imagination became obsessed with their case: "it was sensational and enormously popular, widely reported in all the major papers of the day" (W. Cohen 75). What made their case so compelling was not only the act of cross-dressing and the gender transgression associated with it, but also the fact that "Stella" and "Fanny" managed to attract a considerable number of admirers. Some of them stated in court that they had mistaken Boulton and Park for women – arguably to protect themselves from prosecution (Kaplan 22). Places where homosexual men could go in order to have sex with other men were not new in the late nineteenth century. Brothels for homosexual men, so-called Molly Houses, date back to around 1700. In these clubs, men could find other men dressed as women. However, homosexual desire and intercourse was largely confined to an underworld that remained unseen by those who did not set out in search of it (Kaplan 19).[12] With Boulton and Park, the homosexual subculture became visible. "This 'coming out'" (Kaplan 21), as Morris Kaplan has appropriately called it, "challenged conventional assumptions about gender and sexuality, domesticity and publicity, commerce and pleasure" (ibid.). Notwithstanding the scandal the case caused, Ernest Boulton and Frederick William Park, who both belonged to highly respected middle-class families, were eventually found not guilty by the jury (C. Arnold 263).

The first scandal which seized the public imagination after the initiation of the Labouchère Amendment in 1885 was the Cleveland Street affair (Kaplan 167). The scandal was prompted in 1889 by a police raid on a male homosexual brothel in which telegraph messenger boys earned extra money by selling

---

12   On this topic, see also Rictor Norton's *Mother Clap's Molly House: The Gay Subculture in England 1700–1830*.

themselves off to gentlemen, among them, it was rumoured, Prince Albert Victor who was then second-in-line to the British throne (Haefele-Thomas, *Queer* 120, 173). To the sexual transgression, the Cleveland Street scandal added a class transgression (ibid. 129). Furthermore, the lead investigating officer linked the scandal "with monstrosity and criminality" (ibid. 131): Chief Inspector Frederick G. Abberline, who had unsuccessfully hunted for Jack the Ripper the previous year, was assigned to the case (Hyde 24), thus linking "the male prostitutes and their costumers ... [to] the single most monstrous entity that London of the late nineteenth century had known" (Haefele-Thomas, *Queer* 131). The socio-cultural connection of homosexual men with monstrosity is attested by *More Sprees in London – A Guide for Every Green-Horn*, a guidebook which recommends various brothels to male visitors of London – but also warns them of "the increase of these monsters in the shapes of men" (qdt. in Haefele-Thomas, *Queer* 129). The most prominent public persona who was convicted under the Labouchère Amendment was, of course, Oscar Wilde, who was sentenced to two years of hard labour at Reading Goal in 1895. Wilde, who was a celebrated writer in both the United Kingdom and the United States, received the maximum penalty a person could get for the offence under the Labouchère Amendment.

Just as the Cleveland Street scandal and the "Men in Petticoats" (Kaplan 24), as Boulton and Park were often referred to, the conviction of Oscar Wilde was extensively reported on in the media. What is interesting about these reports is the tendency to avoid direct references to the crime of gross-indecency, as the following review on Oscar Wilde's *The Picture of Dorian Gray*, published anonymously on 4 July 1890 in the *Scots Observer*, illustrates: "Mr Wilde has brains, and art, and style; but if he can write for none but outlawed noblemen and perverted telegraph-boys, the sooner he takes to tailoring (or some other decadent trade) the better for his own reputation and the public morals" (qtd. in Wilde 372). The author refers to the Cleveland Street affair rather than addressing the novel's "homosexual undercurrent" (Cocks, *Nameless* 2) directly. In much the same way, journalists have relied on coded language in order to report on the Cleveland Street affair, as the following excerpt from *The Pall Mall Gazette*, published on 20 November 1889, demonstrates:

> The foul scandal which has filled London with purulent gossip since the end of September seems likely now to come into open court. The facts of the case are simple. In a house of evil fame in Cleveland Street, off Tottenham Court road, last September, the police seized two persons ... who were accused of

offences similar to those which led to the Cornwall-French trials in Dublin. ("The Scandal of Cleveland Street" 6)

Instead of addressing same-sex love between men, the article alludes to the scandal as "foul" and uses a reference to another homosexual affair, the Cornwall-French trials, in order to talk about the crime. This reluctance to speak directly about homosexual intercourse can also be observed in other newspaper articles of the time: "From newspapers in Ireland to Australia and throughout Britain, the news about the Cleveland Street scandal was full of coded language, innuendo and the unnameable nature of the crime" (Haefele-Thomas, *Queer* 129). The Cornwall-French trials were used particularly often as a substitute for the actual events that had happened in Cleveland Street (ibid.).

This unwillingness to call homosexuality by its name is part of a larger process of silencing around the subject of homosexuality: "Christian Europe, from the fourth century onward, regarded same-sex relations as anathema, and its nations competed in devising punishments for 'unnatural' crimes. Homosexuality became the *precatum non nominandum inter Christianos*, 'the sin not even to be mentioned among Christians'" (Crompton 1). The words "unspeakable" and "unmentionable" were often used as coded words in this context (Sedgwick, *Between* 94).

The necessity to talk about same-sex desire in a veiled way is indicative of the restrictions imposed on the subject of homosexuality, especially after the conviction of so prominent a figure as Oscar Wilde. Homosexuality's "very namelessness, its secrecy, was a form of social control" (Sedgwick, *Between* 94) which contributed to the "ghosting" of homosexuals in society. However, in a way that actually corresponds with Foucault's idea of a "reverse discourse", writers also employed the very closeting strategies used by the popular press and in legal treatises in order to find a way to describe "publicly that which was assumed to be indescribable" (Cocks, *Nameless* 1). By using the "unspeakability" of homosexuality as a trope for same-sex desire, homosexuality is not silenced anymore but can be referred to in a language that makes heavy use of allusions, metaphors, and ambiguity. The subsequent ghost stories both use this "closet-speak" (N. Walker 308, 345) in order to voice homosexual desire.

Vernon Lee: "Winthrop's Adventure" (1881)

The heightened focus on same-sex love in the media and scientific discourse posed a threat to many men and evoked a feeling of paranoia. They felt that they were surrendered to a seemingly omnipresent gaze which constantly judges their gender performance. In her influential *Between Men* (1985), Eve Kosofsky Sedgwick therefore describes homophobia as "a mechanism for regulating the behaviour of the many by the specific oppression of a few" (Sedgwick, *Between* 88). Even though felt by all men, this mechanism of control weighed particularly heavy on the shoulders of homosexual or bisexual men, of course. It is in "this atmosphere of heightened fear and paranoia" (N. Walker 305) that Vernon Lee wrote her ghost story "Winthrop's Adventure", which was published in January 1881 in *Frazer's Magazine*.

Vernon Lee (1856–1935) was born Violet Paget near Boulogne, France, to a Welsh mother and a father descended from French gentry. She spent much of her youth travelling around Europe until the family finally settled in Florence, Italy. Even though she had British citizenship, Vernon Lee spent most of her life on the continent. She did not even visit England until 1881 (N. Wilson 325). Nevertheless, she kept herself informed about current events in the British Empire (Kane 7). She assumed the male pseudonym "Vernon Lee" when she started publishing for *Fraser's Magazine* in 1878, allegedly because she wanted to avoid that her sex would influence the perception of her writing (Denisoff 249). However, even though her real identity was soon discovered, she decided to keep the pen name. As Ardel Haefele-Thomas points out, the masculine Vernon Lee developed into something more than a mere pen name: "over the course of her life, she became less and less known as 'Violet' and preferred 'Vernon'" (Haefele-Thomas, *Queer* 173), which is indicative of her own genderqueer identity.[13]

Ruth Robbins has maintained that Lee's fiction is "haunted" by Walter Pater's "psychological aesthetics" and his "fascination with sexual indeterminacy" (188). Lee knew Pater and the focus on haunting portraiture in many of her Gothic texts indicates her involvement with Aestheticism. Furthermore, nonnormative gender and sexual identities feature prominently in Lee's writing,

---

13   Lee's sexual orientation was presumably also not or not solely heteronormative. At least, she lived in close relationships with other women for most of her life, "the first being her friendship with Annie Meyers in the 1870s. From 1881 to 1887, her main companion was A. Mary F Robinson …, followed by what Lee called her 'new love and new life' with Clementina (Kit) Anstruther-Thomson" (Denisoff 249). However, scholars have never been able to prove that Lee actually entertained sexual relationships with these women (Haefele-Thomas, *Queer* 173). Several critics of Lee's work, however, have illustrated that she belonged to a markedly queer community. On this topic see, for instance, Vineta Colby's *Vernon Lee: A Literary Biography* (2003) and Martha Vicinus's *Intimate Friends: Women Who Loved Women* (2006).

most strikingly so perhaps in her queer fairy tale "Prince Alberic and the Snake Lady" (1896). However, as Angelia Leighton has remarked, Lee's "understanding of the aesthetic is in some ways more ambiguous and morally inflected than [Pater's]. She rejected 'art for art's sake', [...] and advocated in its place 'art for the sake of life'" (Leighton 101). I concur with Leighton and suggest that it is possible to read Lee's Gothic writing as a form of resistance against the homophobic panic of the time.[14]

"Winthrop's Adventure" is one of Lee's earliest ghost stories. First published in 1881, Lee rewrote the story a couple of years later and republished it 1890 under the title "A Wicked Voice". "A Wicked Voice" is often regarded as the more sinister version of the tale – probably because the spectral encounter deprives the story's protagonist, a Scandinavian composer named Magnus, of his own creative power. What both stories share is that the protagonist is seduced by the ghost of a dead singer. I chose to focus on "Winthrop's Adventure" primarily because of the story's frame narrative, which provides us with an additional narrative voice – something which is missing in the later version of the tale. In my reading of Lee's "Winthrop's Adventure" the focus will be on the protagonist's difficulty to conform to Victorian assumptions about gender and sexuality.

What Lee's ghost story demonstrates particularly well is that there is a close connection between Sigmund Freud's idea of the uncanny and the concept of the closet. Both concepts focus on "the moment of the shift or the reversal of the *heimlich* into ... its opposite the *unheimlich*" (Fletcher 60). In *Epistemology of the Closet*, Eve Kosofsky Sedgwick illustrates the connection of "secrecy and disclosure" (71) to the concept of the closet. Building on John L. Austin's speech act theory, she remarks that "'[c]losetedness' itself is a performance initiated as such by the speech act of a silence" (Sedgwick, *Epistemology* 3). This silence is double-edged: on the one hand, people can be pushed into the closet because their sexual identity is deemed unacceptable or even unlawful. In this instance, the closet works as "the defining structure for gay oppression" (ibid. 71). On the other hand, the closet can function as "a device that enable[s] ... people to develop their sexual lives in private" (Janes 18). Accordingly, the closet can be both a speech act of forced and of chosen silence. But even in the case of chosen silence, the closet is never a safe space, for a person's sexuality can also be "outed"

---

14   Ardel Haefele-Thomas has made a similar argument. According to them, Lee's decadent Gothic "makes a political statement and defends a victimized queer community – if the reader is able to follow the coded language" (*Queer* 121).

by others. As is generally the case with knowledge, especially when it is supposed to remain secret, sexual knowledge gives rise to blackmail and equips those in the know with power. The closet is therefore necessarily concerned with the concealment and disclosure of information. However, knowledge is a dangerous commodity in more than one way in this context, for knowing of the sexual desires of the other implies that one knows what to look for, meaning that one knows the code. As Sedgwick has pointed out, "'knowledge' and 'sex' [became] conceptually inseparable from one another ... so that knowledge means in the first place sexual knowledge; ignorance, sexual ignorance" (*Epistemology* 73).

The disclosure of (sexual) knowledge is also at the core of Freud's theory. John Fletcher, therefore, has aptly referred to the uncanny as "a closet effect" (58). For Freud, what is uncanny is not something alien or unknown but "something which ought to have remained hidden but has come to light" (Freud 241). This is implied by the German word *unheimlich* which "includes the element of exposure, the moment of coming to light or coming out" (Fletcher 59). Something is not *heimlich*, not secret, anymore and that is what is experienced as frightening. Freud links his observations to the human subconscious and the return of repressed feelings and desires. This return is at the core of Lee's "Winthrop's Adventure". What the protagonist struggles with in this story is his homoerotic desire which he can no longer repress. Winthrop's closet, as we shall see, is a "space of *Heimlichkeiten* which is undecidedly both *heimlich* and *unheimlich*" (Fletcher 60). By addressing Winthrop's homosexual panic, Lee's text makes apparent the "dialectic between homosexuality and homophobia" (Sedgwick, *Between Men* 92).

In Lee's narrative, a young painter, Julian Winthrop, is invited to a party at a villa in Florence. When the hostess, Countess S---, performs a song for her guests, Winthrop starts breathing "spasmodically" (Lee, "Winthrop's" 105) and appears to be "quivering" (ibid.) all over. He then admits that he recognises the song and tells the group how he has come across the piece.

In the embedded narrative, which takes place a year and a half previous to Winthrop's breakdown at the villa, Winthrop is "rambling about Lombardy" (Lee, "Winthrop's" 110), Northern Italy, with some of his cousins, "poking into all sorts of odd nooks and corners" (ibid.) There they make the acquaintance of "a highly learned and highly snuffy" (ibid.) old nobleman who gave away all he owned for "a collection of things musical, a perfect museum" (ibid.). Among his possessions is the portrait of the singer Ferdinando Rinaldi dating back to 1782. From the old man, who goes by the nickname Maestro Fa Diesis, Winthrop learns that the singer attracted too much attention from a lady in high favour at Court in his lifetime and was subsequently stabbed to death:

> Who had done it, no one ever knew or cared to know. A packet of letters, which his valet said he always carried on his person, was all that was found missing. The lady left Parma and entered the Convent of the Clarisse here; she was my father's aunt, and this portrait belonged to her. A common story, a common story those days. (Lee, "Winthrop's" 115)

The text's engagement with sexual desire is established early in the narrative. First, the singer's own sexual transgressiveness is attested by Fa Diesis's story. The homoerotic content of the story is also already hinted at by the setting, for the story takes place in Italy, "a 'queer' coded location" (Haefele-Thomas, *Queer* 121) due to the fact that, in Italian Renaissance, homoerotic relationships between men were tolerated. As Ardel Haefele-Thomas has remarked, "Italy keeps appearing alongside queer desire" (ibid. 123), for instance in the writing of the known homosexual John Addington Symonds and in Anne Lister's diaries, where lesbian sex is referred to as "going to Italy" (ibid.).

We soon also learn about Winthrop's (homo-)sexual secret. To Fa Diesis, the portrait of Rinaldi is a common one. Winthrop, however, becomes obsessed by it. Even though his eye as a painter sees "faults of drawing here and there" (Lee, "Winthrop's" 112), he feels an irresistible attraction to the portrait:

> It returned to my mind as something strange and striking. … There was something peculiar and unaccountable in the look of that face, a yearning, half-pained look, which I could not well define to myself. I became gradually aware that the portrait was, so to speak, haunting me. Those strange red lips and wistful eyes rose up in my mind. (Lee, "Winthrop's" 113)

In this passage, Lee makes heavy use of the "'slipperiness' of language" (Hotz-Davies 277) in order to suggest same-sex desire. The description of singer's "strange red lips and wistful eyes" as something that rises up in his mind is indicative of Winthrop's sexual arousal, suggesting the rising up of the male sexual organ. In addition, Lee employs a number of homoerotically charged code words: "For her specific audience, … the terms 'peculiar', 'unaccountable' and even 'strange' … would have signalled the homoeroticism of his first encounter with the portrait" (Haefele-Thomas, *Queer* 127). Winthrop's description of the portrait as something that haunts him further indicates his obsession with the singer eternalised in it. This obsession is also attested by the fact that Winthrop keeps referring to the portrait in his conversations with his cousins: "I instinctively and without knowing why reverted to it in our conversation. ... My cousins paid no attention to my speech, for they did not share that vague, *unaccountable* feeling with which the picture had inspired me" (Lee, "Winthrop's" 113, my emphasis). It is apparent that Winthrop cannot resist his desire for the man in the portrait. But it is also important to note that Winthrop experiences this attraction as "unaccountable" and something he "[can]not well define to [himself]" (ibid.). In this way, the story suggests that Winthrop feels confused about his sexual identity. The fact that he feels haunted by the portrait is further indicative of Winthrop's homoerotic panic. It is one of the implications of haunting that one does not choose to be haunted. By presenting the portrait as something that forces its way into Winthrop's mind and takes possession of it, the story highlights the young man's "panic of same-sex desire" (Liggins, "Gendering" 41). Like in *The Picture of Dorian Gray* the portrait functions as a mirror: it reveals more about the narrator himself than about the object of his gaze (Kane 30).

Winthrop's confusion about his attraction to the singer in the portrait turns into a severe inner conflict when he revisits the painting one year later. During this second encounter, his homoerotic desire evokes a feeling of shame: "The sun streamed brightly on the brown face and light powdered locks. I know not how, I felt a momentary giddiness and sickness, as if of long desired, unexpected pleasure; it lasted but an instant, and I was ashamed of myself" (Lee, "Winthrop" 117). Winthrop is simultaneously fascinated by the portrait and disgusted by his desire for the dead singer. It is a highly ambivalent feeling which ties in with Allon White's and Peter Stallybrass's term "phobic enchantment" (124) according to which the dominant culture is irrevocably attracted to what it has come to view as abject and Other. The Other here is a man who is both feminised and exoticized with his "brown face" (Lee, "Winthrop's" 117) and "light powdered locks" (ibid.), the antithesis to the late-Victorian ideal of masculinity, and Winthrop's repulsion is both homophobic and xenophobic. But it is also Winthrop who is Othered here because of his gay desire for the man. By describing the feeling as a momentary sickness, the story further highlights that same-sex desire was considered unnatural and even monstrous in the Victorian period, an illness which befalls certain men. It is not surprising, therefore, that Winthrop immediately experiences a feeling of shame. Furthermore, the passage shows that the young man tries to repress his homoerotic feelings. He only lets his feelings get the better of him for "an instant" (ibid.).

Towards the end of the narrative, the story displays Winthrop's same-sex desire – and panic – most explicitly. When Winthrop visits Rinaldi's former mansion, he encounters the singer's ghost, who is delivering an air.

> The wonderful sweet, downy voice glided lightly and dexterously through the complicated mazes of the song; it rounded off ornament after ornament, it swelled imperceptibly into glorious, hazy magnitude, and diminished, dying gently away from a high note to a lower one, like a weird, mysterious sigh; then it leaped into a high, clear, triumphant note, and burst out into a rapid, luminous shake. (Lee, "Winthrop's" 130–31)

Winthrop describes the encounter in terms of a sexual experience which culminates in an orgasm. The song "swells" like the male sexual organ and climaxes in one "triumphant" moment in a "rapid luminous shake". The moment of haunting provides a space for expressing (and experiencing) a more ambiguous sexuality and satisfies Winthrop's longing for the fulfilment of his homoerotic desires. At the same time, he experiences homosexual panic, for shortly after the sexualized encounter with the spectre reaches its climax, Winthrop flees the scene. The ghostly is thus experienced as erotic and liberating as well as frightening (Liggins, "Gendering" 41). By presenting same-sex desire as both fulfilling and something to fear, the story "illuminates the violence of a homophobic ... fin-de-siècle culture of panic" (Haefele-Thomas 121). Lee thus utilises the spectral in order to advocate for homosexual eroticism and desire.

The ghostly figure of Rinaldi remains ambiguous throughout Winthrop's stay at the mansion. Even Winthrop himself is not sure whether he saw a spectre or whether the figure was the product of his imagination. "Tell me, is it reality or fiction" (Lee, "Winthrop's" 134), he asks the people who have listened to his adventure when the story returns to the frame narrative. There are several hints at Winthrop's impressionable nature throughout the narrative. Even before he encounters the portrait of Rinaldi, he imagines the artefacts in Fa Diesis's villa to come to life. This suggests that the figure of Rinaldi belongs to the kind of spectres which Vernon Lee describes as ghosts which haunt brains in the preface to her well-known short story collection *Hauntings* (1890): "things of the imagination, born there, bred there" (Lee, *Hauntings* 39). In line with Freud's idea of the uncanny, it is not something strange and unfamiliar that haunts Winthrop, but his suppressed same-sex desire. As Melissa Edmundson Makala notes, Lee's spectres find "their dramatic force not in 'real' ghosts and the trauma that first caused their haunting, but in the terror and anxiety that exists within the ghost-seer" (75).

It is not only Winthrop's homoerotic desire which blurs prevalent ideas about gender and sexuality in the story. As has been pointed out above, the portrait itself also counteracts hegemonic ideas regarding gender, sexuality, and race:[15]

> The features were irregular and small, with intensely red lips and a crimson flush beneath the transparent bronzed skin; the eyes were slightly upturned and looking sidewards, in harmony with the turn of the head and the parted lips, and they were beautiful, brown, soft like those of some animals, with a vague, wistful depth of look. (Lee, "Winthrop's" 112)

With its intensely "red lips", "crimson flush", soft eyes, and small features the figure in the portrait displays attributes generally associated with femininity. These feminine facial features strike Winthrop as "irregular" which suggests that the portrait undermines the binary division of gender. By confronting the reader with the strikingly feminine portrait of Rinaldi, the story blurs the idea of a hegemonic masculine appearance. Rinaldi's dark skin tone and eyes are also stressed in this passage, thereby signalling the singer's racial Otherness, an Otherness that reminds Winthrop of "some animals". The portrait further functions as a mirror which reflects Winthrop's wishes and desires. As Melissa Edmundson Makala has observed, "[i]n Rinaldi's sexual 'betweenness' Winthrop sees a freedom that he himself wishes to possess" (80). Winthrop continues to project his feelings onto the portrait when he further describes the look on Rinaldi's face: "it seemed as if there were life in those soft, velvety eyes, and as if those red lips were parting in a sigh – a long, weary sigh" (Lee, "Winthrop's" 115). Having suppressed his homoerotic desire for so long, Winthrop, just as the man in the portrait, is weary and in need of a sigh.

An interesting but often overlooked aspect of the story is the frame narrative. While the embedded narrative focuses on the protagonist as someone who is "in the closet", the frame hints at the danger of public disclosure, thereby

---

15   Ardel Haefele-Thomas has argued that, in contrast to "A Wicket Voice", "gender is very clearly marked as male on both sides: the man gazing at the portrait and the man in the portrait" (*Queer* 128) in "Winthrop's Adventure". While I generally find their interpretation of both stories very insightful and share most of their views, I decidedly disagree with Haefele-Thomas on this point, as my interpretation of the subsequent passage illustrates.

stressing the difficulty of keeping secrets. We have already seen that Winthrop is presented as the narrator of the embedded narrative. The frame narrative, by contrast, is told by an unnamed narrator, who is not involved in the supernatural events. This homodiegetic narrator describes Winthrop as an "odd sort of creature" (Lee, "Winthrop's" 104) with a "too impressionable" (ibid.) nature and "feelings and moods gliding strangely into each other" (ibid.). These remarks can be read as commentaries on Winthrop's queer gender performance. For one, the word "too" transports a judgement. It implies that Winthrop is not as rational as men were supposed to be in this time of scientific advancement. By contrast, he is impressionable and thus displays a characteristic usually assigned to women, who were generally seen as irrational, controlled by their bodies rather than their minds (Gatens 50). Furthermore, Winthrop's mood swings stand in opposition to the ideal of the cool-headed, confident, and controlled soldier and hint at the contemporary perception of homosexual men as effeminate. Homosexual men posed a threat to the idea of normative, heterosexual masculinity and the gender binary in general. According to Alan Sinfield, Victorian society was able to secure "the demarcation masculine/female" (73) by viewing homosexual men not as real men but as "displaced versions of the 'feminine'" (72). By presenting Winthrop as someone who is not in control of his feelings, the narrator highlights his "improper" gender performance. In addition, Winthrop is dehumanised by the narrator, who does not describe him as a man but a "creature", thus suggesting his status as an invert with a supposedly unnatural craving. The narrator's remarks make apparent an important aspect of the Victorian idea of manliness: it does not matter what kind of man you are, but how others judge your gender performance.

The story's engagement with the prevalent ideal of masculinity is also hinted at by the title "Winthrop's Adventure", which evokes associations with the adventure literature of the time. However, in contrast to the manly heroes portrayed in adventure stories, Winthrop cannot live up to heteronormative ideas about masculinity in his adventure. By portraying a man whose repressed sexual identity comes back to haunt him, the story further implies that while gender may be performative, human nature is not.

Henry James: "The Real Right Thing" (1899)

The 1890s were the time in which Henry James (1843–1916) produced most of his ghost fiction, his famous novella *The Turn of the Screw* (1898) included. T. J. Lustig has suggested that James's preoccupation with ghosts was influenced by the death of several of his close friends and family members: "mortality had been much on James's mind for some years: his sister Alice had died in 1892 and his friend Robert Louis Stevenson in 1894. In the same year, James's close friend Constance Fenimore Woolson died in Venice, possibly by her own hand" (Lustig 142). That the loss of his family and friends haunted James is also suggested by a letter he wrote in 1895 to the American composer Francis Boott in response to the death of yet another artist: the American sculptor William Wetmore Story:[16] "I see ghosts everywhere" ("Francis" 293), he states there.

And yet, despite his own experiences with death and mourning, James's ghost stories are not conventional Gothic tales that focus on the return of loved ones. More often than not, James's spectral tales sustain their ambiguity until the very end and thus belong to what Tzvetan Todorov has termed "the fantastic". "[R]eality or dream? truth or illusion?" (Todorov 25), according to Todorov, it is for the reader to decide (ibid. 41). With the exception of James's first ghost narrative "The Romance of Certain Old Clothes" (1868), there is always a possibility that, in reality, the haunting is "the product of the subliminal consciousness" (Sausman 368) of the ghost-seer. As Justin Sausman has accurately observed, "James' ghosts are ... both literal and metaphorical, not only the spirits of the dead, but spectres of the self, ghostly doubles that represent a divided psychology of characters who are haunted by their own pasts or alternate lives" (ibid.).

James's ambiguous ghost fiction mirrors the writer's general in-betweenness. Born in America, James spent a great deal of time on the continent before eventually settling in London. More than anything, he was a man of the world (or rather a man between worlds) and this is reflected in "the 'international theme' in novels such as *The Portrait of a Lady* (1881)" (Sausman 366). Also, his writing vacillates between Victorian realism and literary modernism – much like that of Vernon Lee.

James and Lee were well acquainted. The already renowned James helped Lee to find her way in the literary scene of London in the 1880s (Gettmann 47). Lee even dedicated her first novel, *Miss Brown* (1884), to Henry James. However, their friendship cooled when Lee based one of her characters on James in "Lady Tal" (1892), a satire which shows James as self-centred and "implicates him in the literary establishment's hostility toward women writers" (Murphy 281). In a letter to his brother William James, who was spending the winter of 1893 in

---

16   James would later write a biography about Story: *William Wetmore Story and his Friends* (1903).

Italy, Henry James praises Lee as someone whose "vigor and sweep of intellect are most rare" but also warns him not to "caress her, ... she is as dangerous and uncanny as she is intelligent" and advises him to "draw it mild with her on the question of friendship. She's a tiger-cat" (qdt. in Weber 683).

Notwithstanding their personal rift, Vernon Lee and Henry James seem to have been preoccupied with similar topics and their writing has often been compared (Zorn xvi). There is also a marked similarity between the two stories discussed in this chapter. In both stories, the spectral functions as a site where homoeroticism and same-sex desire can be played out. In an attempt to break the unspeakability of gay love and desire, these stories use "the spectral encounter at the centre of the story to address what remained 'unseen'" (Liggins, "Gendering" 38).

Henry James's ghost story "The Real Right Thing" was published a year after his masterpiece *The Turn of the Screw* in December 1899 in *Collier's Weekly*. In the story, a young journalist and critic, George Withermore, is commissioned by the wife of the recently deceased author Ashton Doyne to write a biography about her late husband.

Withermore's gay identity is hinted at from early on in the narrative when he proclaims that "he wasn't a person ... [Mrs Doyne] could have an interest in flattering" (James, "Real" 268). It is also evident from the onset that Doyne's wife is in the know. At the beginning of the story, she justifies her decision for Withermore as Doyne's biographer in this way: "'My thought went straight to *you*, as his own would have done'" (ibid. 268, emphasis in original), she explains. "'You're the one he liked most, oh, *much!*'" (ibid., emphasis in original). The emphasis which Doyne's wife puts on "*you*" and her assertion that her husband liked Withermore "*much*" suggest that she is aware that George Withermore and Ashton Doyne were more than friends. What is striking is that she first proclaims that Withermore is the person her husband liked "most" but then corrects herself. This signals that Mrs Doyne knows that, as his wife, she should have been the person he liked most.

Since his occupation as a journalist keeps him busy during the day, Withermore works on the biography in the evenings. He is permitted by Doyne's wife to conduct his work in the late author's study. When Withermore first steps into the room, he is overwhelmed by the memories the place brings back to him:

The place was full of their lost friend, everything in it had belonged to him, everything they touched had been part of his life. It was for the moment too

> much for Withermore – ... memories still recent came back to him, ... his heart beat faster and his eyes filled with tears. (James, "Real" 269)

It is apparent that Withermore is still suffering from the recent death of his friend, yet he is also intrigued by the intimacy the study promises. Withermore fetishizes the room and the things it contains and his excitement to be able to touch the deceased writer through his belongings is palpable. Yet there is also a "suggestion of intrusion" (Fletcher 67) and appropriation. Withermore is able to touch everything without Doyne's permission and this puts him into a position of power.

Withermore's feeling of loss is then also soon replaced by the impression that Doyne's spirit is with him in the study, that he is, in fact, acting as "his mystic assistant" (James, "Real" 273). It is a feeling which does not frighten Withermore. Rather, he "quite cherishe[s] it" and is "looking forward all day to feeling ... [Doyne's presence] renew itself in the evening, and waiting for the growth of dusk very much as one of a pair of lovers might wait for the hour of their appointment" (ibid. 271–72). By comparing Withermore's feelings to that of lovers who longingly await their reunification, the story rather overtly hints at the journalist's gay love for the dead author.

It is during these "homospectral" (Fletcher 62) meetings with Doyne's spirit that Withermore feels "an intimacy so rich" (James, "Real" 270) and "the possibility of an intercourse closer than that of life" (ibid.). While it is possible to interpret Withermore's feelings as "sentimental and platonic" (Hoeveler 116), James clearly offers "a knowing wink to [his] intended readership" (ibid.) here. By using words like "intercourse" and "intimacy", which are loaded with sexual innuendo, the text expresses homosexual eroticism and carries the suggestion of sexual encounters with a spectral Doyne. The narrative also implies that the deceased and his biographer entertained a sexual relationship before Doyne's sudden death, as Withermore reminisces about their past meeting "in the narrow passage" (James, "Real" 272) where he felt Doyne's "tight squeeze" (ibid.).

Withermore's homospectral relationship with Doyne's ghost is again hinted at later on in the narrative: "the special state of his own consciousness ... wasn't a thing to talk about – it was only a thing to feel. There were moments for instance when, while he bent over his papers, the light breath of his dead host was as distinctly in his hair as his own elbows were on the table before him" (James, "Real" 272). While hinting at the unspeakability of homosexual love and desire, something to feel but not to talk about, the passage also alludes to a closeness beyond friendship, a closeness that is clearly sexual. With

Withermore leaning forward on his elbows and the spectral Doyne behind him breathing into his hair, there is even "the latent metaphor of anal penetration" (Fletcher 68), a metaphor which, according to John Fletcher, keeps recurring when the narration turns to Withermore's research: "there were times of dipping deep into some of Doyne's secrets when it was particularly pleasant to be able to hold that Doyne desired him, as it were, to know them. He was learning many things he hadn't suspected – drawing many curtains, forcing many doors, reading many riddles, going, in general, as they said, behind almost everything" (James, "Real" 272). Withermore imagines that he is the person Doyne would have wanted to share his secrets with, that, even in death, he desires to invite Withermore into his homospectral closet. The metaphor of "going behind", in this context, may well be linked to anal penetration. However, Withermore's "fantasy of an intimate encounter with the dead man" (Fletcher 68) is mixed with a feeling of intrusion and violation of privacy. While Withermore might imagine that "Doyne desired him" (James, "Real" 272) to unlock his secrets, the metaphor of "forcing ... doors" (ibid.) suggests otherwise. It is a metaphor that implies violence on Withermore's part – and resistance on the part of Doyne.

The suggestion of intrusion intensifies as the story progresses. Like the spirit that he is, Doyne begins to "hover[...] and linger[...]" (James, "Real" 272) about the room, fixing Withermore with a look that is "the least bit harder than in life" (ibid. 273). Eventually, the spectre appears on the threshold to his study before the biographer can enter the room, "guarding it" (ibid. 277). Withermore starts to doubt that writing a biography about Doyne is "the real right thing" to do and turns to the dead man's wife for advice:

"I'm afraid."
"Of *him*?" asked Mrs Doyne.
He thought. "Well – of what I'm doing."
"Then what, that's so awful, *are* you doing?"
"What you proposed to me. Going into his life."
She showed, in her present gravity, a new alarm. "And don't you *like* that?"
"Doesn't *he*? That's the question. We lay him bare. We serve him up. What is it called? We give him to the world."
Poor Mrs Doyne, as if on a menace to her hard atonement, glared at this for an instant in deeper gloom. "And why shouldn't we?"
"Because we don't know. There are natures, there are lives, that shrink. He mayn't wish it," said Withermore. "We never asked him."
"How *could* we?"

He was silent a little. "Well, we ask him now. ..."
"Then – if he has been with us – we've had his answer."
Withermore spoke now as if he knew what to believe. "He hasn't been 'with'
us – he has been against us."
"Then why did you think –"
"What I *did* think at first – that he wishes to make us feel is his sympathy?
Because I was in my original simplicity mistaken. I was – I don't know what to
call it – so excited and charmed that I didn't understand. But I understand at
last. He only wanted to communicate. He strains forward out of his darkness,
he reaches toward us out of his mystery, he makes us dim signs out of his
horror."
"'Horror'?" Mrs Doyne gasped with her fan up to her mouth.
"At what we are doing." He could by this time piece it all together. "I see now
that at first –"
"Well, what?"
"One had simply to feel he was there and therefore not indifferent. And the
beauty of that misled me. But he's there as a protest."
"Against *my* Life?" Mrs Doyne wailed.
"Against *any* Life. He's there to *save* his Life. He's there to be let alone."
"So you give up?" she almost shrieked.
He could only meet her. "He's there as a warning."
For a moment, on this, they looked at each other deep. "You *are* afraid!" she
at last brought out. (James, "Real" 275–76, emphasis in original)

This is an immensely dense dialogue full of allusions to the unnameable crime
and the danger of being outed as a homosexual within the "repressive sexual
climate" (Sedgwick, *Epistemology* 197) of late-Victorian Britain. It is, in fact, a
prime example for the ways in which language can convey "hidden meanings
and evasions" (Cocks, *Nameless* 2). While Withermore implies his own homoerotic longing for the dead Doyne by pointing out that he does not "know how
to call it" (James, "Real" 276), thereby evoking the unspeakability of same-sex
desire, there are also several hints at Doyne's gay identity. Disclosing Doyne's
sexual secret, to "lay him bare" (ibid. 276), is to expose him and his work "to the
world" (ibid.). Withermore's concerns suggest that even in death writers have
to fear that they might share the fate of Oscar Wilde, who had to endure "legal,
journalistic and public onslaught" (Haefele-Thomas, *Queer* 123) only four years
prior to the publication of James's story. Also evident here is a more general
anxiety that writing about the life of an author might affect the impact of their
writing, that Doyne and his work might "shrink" (James, "Real" 276) when "the

secret of the writer's creativity" (Fletcher 69) is revealed. The story thus draws attention to the theme of "the dead author who no longer has the power to author or to authorize a text" (Matterson 210).[17]

What is also interesting about this passage is Mrs Doyne's reaction to Withermore's doubts. On one level, she seems to be entirely dependent on Withermore's judgement in order to figure out what it is that her husband would have wanted and to decipher the ghost's messages to them. Yet, on another level, it is also possible to interpret her questions as a form of resistance, an unwillingness to accept Withermore's point of view. When Withermore states that he is afraid of "[g]oing into … [Doyne's] life", she replies with a question that sounds more like a statement: "'And don't you *like* that?'" (James, "Real" 276). The stress on *"like"* implies that Mrs Doyne is conscious of how much Withermore enjoys penetrating the secret corners of the dead writer's life and that she knows about her husband's homoerotic relationships.[18] There are also hints in the above passage that suggest that Doyne's wife wants to expose her late husband's sexual secret. She certainly does not seem to share Withermore's fear that the biography might harm his legacy. "'And why shouldn't we?'" (ibid. 276), she gloomily asks when Withermore explains to her that his work jeopardises Doyne's privacy, almost as if this is what she wanted all along. The seemingly misplaced assumption that her life might be the target of Doyne's protest can also be interpreted as an admission of guilt. She has the authority to decide whether or not there will be a biography on her late husband and this puts her in a position of power she is not willing to give up. What first appears to be a male invasion of male privacy (Withermore "going … behind almost everything" (James, "Real" 272)), turns out to be a female desire to intrude male secrets. This

---

17   Stephen Matterson has read James's story as a meditation on his own legacy: "'The real right thing' is fictively prophetic of James' actions in blocking or complicating posthumous biographical and critical access through actions such as the burning of his papers, the preparing of his own editions of his work and the directive autobiographies" (Matterson 214).

18   We can only suspect that Withermore is not the only man with whom Doyne entertained a homoerotic relationship. The only thing we learn from the narrative regarding Doyne's social life is that Doyne had "many friends gilded with greatness" (James, "Real" 268). That Doyne might have been intimate with some of them is suggested when Mrs Doyne appoints Withermore as Doyne's biographer. While Mrs Doyne asserts that he is the person Doyne liked "most"/"*much*" (ibid. 268), Withermore wonders "if she had known Doyne enough, when it came to that" (ibid.). The "that" here is highly ambiguous and suggests that there are more people whom Doyne liked "*much*".

is an interesting twist considering that women were generally more vulnerable to male intrusion in the Victorian period.

From the onset of the narrative, Mrs Doyne's control over her husband's legacy is stressed: "These materials – diaries, letters, memoranda, notes, documents of many sorts – were her property and wholly in her control, no conditions at all attaching to any portion of her heritage; so that she was free at present to do as she liked" (James, "Real" 267). What we see here is an anxiety about female control, particularly that of widows who come to own what once belonged to their husbands – personal items included. Mrs Doyne is not only able to unlock her husband's secrets, but is "free at present to do as she liked" and Doyne, having died "too soon and too suddenly" (ibid.) to leave a will, now, in death, is vulnerable to exposure. That this might be dangerous is also implied early in the narrative. In the first three paragraphs we learn that "Doyne's relations with his wife had been to Withermore's knowledge a special chapter" (ibid.) and that "[s]he hadn't taken Doyne seriously enough in life" (ibid. 268). Both comments suggest that Mrs Doyne's relationship with her husband was a difficult one and that they were estranged. This impression is reinforced by the fact that Doyne and his wife inhabited different parts of their home before the author's death. While he spent his time upstairs in his study, Mrs Doyne inhabited a room downstairs, a "small bright room in which, night after night, she had been living her life as he had been living his own upstairs" (ibid. 274). While it was not uncommon for domestic spaces to be assigned to one sex or the other, as we have seen in the previous chapter, the strict spatial seclusion between Doyne and his wife in its intensity mirrors their emotional seclusion. Since the story is focalized through Withermore's consciousness, it is possible to read many of the comments on Mrs Doyne and her relationship to the deceased as jealousy on the young man's part. The heterodiegetic narrator does not offer us an insight into Mrs Doyne's thoughts. However, there are also no narrative hints that contradict Withermore's point of view.

Withermore's intimacy with the deceased and his spirit is then also repeatedly juxtaposed to the relationship Doyne entertained with his wife: while the married life of Doyne and is wife is primarily marked by seclusion, Withermore is "conscious, abundantly, of how close he had stood to him" and even though Mrs Doyne presents herself with a "large array of mourning – with her big black eyes, her big black wig, her big fan and gloves" (James, "Real" 268), it is Withermore who bursts out into tears when "memories still recent come back to him" (ibid. 269): "while his heart beat faster and his eyes filled with tears, the pressure of his loyalty seemed almost more than he could carry. At the sight of his tears Mrs Doyne's own rose to her lids, and the two for a minute only looked at each other. He half-expected her to break out 'Oh help me to feel as I know you know I want to feel!'" (ibid.). What is interesting about this passage is not only that Withermore views Mrs Doyne's mourning dress as a sort of masquerade that the widow uses to simulate grief, but that he, above all, is overwhelmed by a feeling of loyalty. This loyalty stands in stark contrast to Mrs Doyne's apparent intension to publish a biography against her dead husband's will.

More than Vernon Lee's "Winthrop's Adventure" Henry James's "The Real Right Thing" is thus concerned with the dangers of coming out. While the frame narrative of Lee's story offers us an outside view on Winthrop and his seemingly inappropriate mood swings, there is no real threat of public exposure. In James's narrative, by contrast, the threat of exposure is at the core of the narrative and leads to Doyne's ghostly afterlife. The ghost, we come to realise, has not returned to his study to be reunited with Withermore, but to guard his study which is quintessentially the locus of his sexual secret.

Longing for the Female Sexual Body: Elizabeth Gaskell's "The Poor Clare" and Edith Nesbit's "The Ebony Frame"

A part of the myth which was built around the ideal of womanhood in the Victorian period was that "women (happily for society) are not very much troubled with sexual feeling of any kind" (Acton 212), as the British medical doctor William Acton put it in 1875. He claimed that "[t]he best mothers, wives and managers of households, know little of or are careless about sexual indulgences. Love of home, of children, and of domestic duties are the only passions they feel" (Acton 213). Only in rare occasions do women experience sexual pleasure, he further points out. But "[a]s a general rule, a modest woman ... *submits to her husband's embraces* ... principally to gratify him; and, were it not for the desire of maternity, would far rather be relieved from his attentions" (ibid.). Acton's theory is clearly built on the assumption that women only have sex for procreative purposes. This erasure of female sexual desire was systematic in Victorian society. It is noteworthy that the Labouchère Amendment only made gross-indecency between men a crime. It explicitly labels all male homosexual acts as illegal, but does not refer to women getting involved in same-sex relationships. When it was brought to Queen Victoria's attention that women are not mentioned in the statute, she allegedly said that "no woman would do that"

(Ellmann 409). If the good and proper housewife was presumed sexually dormant, sexual relationships between women were unthinkable (Ledger 125–26).

The reality was, of course, more complicated than this. As Terry Castle has pointed out, there has been "a whole slangy mob of [words] ... for pointing to (or taking aim at)" (*Apparitional* 9) women loving women: *"tribade, fricatrice, sapphist, roaring girl, amazon, freak, romp, dyke, bull dagger, tommy.* Even the seemingly innocent *odd woman* or *odd girl* occur with such enticing regularity in early lesbian-themed writing as to suggest the possibility of a host of lost or suppressed code terms" (ibid., emphasis in original).

Also, the medical discourse on female sexuality was manifold. While some physicians and psychologists shared William Acton's view that women could not enjoy sexual pleasures (L'Esperance 114), others insisted that sexual desire was natural to women.[19] The American gynaecologist Robert T. Morris even feared that academic pursuits might diminish the clitoris, "leading to lessened sexual desire and therefore more female independence of men" (Showalter, *Anarchy* 130). Many doctors also viewed the clitoris as the pivotal organ in the treatment of hysteria and used the professional stimulation of the clitoris to "hysterical paroxysm" – a euphemism for orgasm – as a therapy for nervous illnesses.[20] Still others regarded the female sexual organ as an expendable, if not threatening organ. In the 1860s Western gynaecologists pioneered in the operation of clitoridectomy, the surgical excision of the clitoris, as a cure to female nervous diseases and disorders of the reproductive system. They maintained that these illnesses were caused by sexual arousal and that the excision

---

19   The physician George Drysdale believed, for instance, that sexual desire is natural and beneficial to both men and women. He unmasked the gendered stereotype of the chaste and pure wife and mother as an unrealistic image imposed on women by the patriarchal system: "If we examine the origins and meaning of these singular ideas with regards to women, we shall find that they are based upon no natural distinction between sexes, but upon the erroneous views of man, and especially upon the mistaken ideas as to the virtue of female *chastity*" (qdt. in L'Esperance 111–12, emphasis in original).

20   As Rachel P. Maines points out in *Technology of Orgasm: Hysteria, the Vibrator, and Women's Sexual Satisfaction*, "[t]here is no evidence that male physicians enjoyed providing pelvic massage treatments. On the contrary, this male elite sought every opportunity to substitute other devices for their fingers, such as the attentions of husbands, the hands of a midwife, or the business end of some tireless and impersonal mechanism" (4).

of the clitoris would cure women (Kent 47). One of the most prominent practitioners of clitoridectomies was Isaac Baker Brown. In 1866 he published a
study in which he claims to have cured numerous women from maladies like
epilepsy, catalepsy and hysteria – illnesses which were supposedly caused by
"peripheral excitement", a term Baker Brown used as euphemism for masturbation.[21] Baker Brown and his colleagues performed about "600 [clitoridec-
tomies] … between 1860 and 1866, at which time they were discontinued in
England" (Kent 48). Baker Brown's career ended in 1867 when he was accused
of having performed clitoridectomies on women without their knowledge and
consent (Fennell 68). The medical debate about the clitoris was also used to
stigmatize queer and homosexual women: "Lesbians were rumoured to have
grossly enlarged clitorises, and in addition to homosexuality, other 'diseases'
of the New Woman, such as masturbation, depression, martial dissatisfaction,
and nymphomania, were attributed to clitoral over-development" (Showalter,
Anarchy 130). Female sexuality was thus repeatedly pathologized and perceived
as something monstrous that had to be controlled by (male) physicians.

It has been subject to much scholarly debate how women writers questioned heteronormative ideas regarding female sexuality and gender in their
writing. However, only little attention has been paid to how the Victorian ideal
of femininity affected men's perception of their sexual identity. Acton makes it

---

21   One of the cases he describes in his book is that of a young woman of twenty who suffered from "spinal irritation" (Baker Brown 34). Baker Brown diagnosed her with "peripheral irritation of the pudic nerve" (ibid.) – a euphemism for sexual arousal. This diagnosis was at first strongly rejected by the strictly religious young woman. But Baker
Brown assured her that "the illness was to be attributed solely to a physical condition,
and was not at all necessarily immoral" (ibid.). He was then met with the objection that
the "operation might interfere with marital happiness and prevent procreation" (ibid.).
These concerns, however, were also brushed aside by the gynaecologist: "I explained
how, physiologically, these objections were untenable" (ibid.). This advice seems rather
contradictory considering that he used the treatment to rid women of sexual arousal.
The excision might not lead to infertility, but it largely interferes with marital happiness. Nevertheless, the young woman eventually gave her consent to the operation.
Another woman was "cured" from her "great distaste for her husband" (Baker Brown
84) by Baker Brown. The physician diagnosed her with an "irritable clitoris and labia"
and "pursued the usual surgical treatment" (ibid.) which resulted in the desired outcome: [A]fter two months' treatment, she returned to her husband, resumed cohabita-
tion, and stated that all her distaste had disappeared; soon became pregnant, resumed
her place at the head of her table, and became a happy and healthy wife and mother"
(ibid.).

sound like a good thing that women are supposedly not "troubled with sexual feeling of any kind" (212). However, the idea of the pure "Angel in the House" was also highly problematic for men. How can they desire something that is considered asexual? This question is at the core of Elizabeth Gaskell's "The Poor Clare" and Edith Nesbit's "The Ebony Frame". In both stories, the male narrators appear conflicted about their sexual identity because they desire what they should not: the sexually transgressive, "forbidden" fallen woman. While the narrator of E. Nesbit's story eventually embraces his sexual desire, the protagonist of Gaskell's tale succeeds in suppressing not only his fiancée's supposedly improper sexuality but also his own.

Elizabeth Gaskell: "The Poor Clare" (1856)

> In my recollections of her there is no "brilliance" of any kind, but a large, firm, homely figure, furnished far beyond the common with a kindly wisdom. (qdt. in Allott 3)

This is how Elizabeth Gaskell (1810–1865) was described by Frederick Greenwood, editor of *The Cornhill Magazine*, in which Gaskell's unfinished last novel *Wives and Daughters* (1866) was serialized. Her oeuvre comprises six novels, about thirty short stories, a number of novellas and articles, a few poems, and a biography about her close friend Charlotte Brontë – all of which Gaskell, wife of a Unitarian minister in Manchester and mother of four daughters, managed to write "[i]n the intervals of her busy housekeeping" (Allott 3). Greenwood met Gaskell shortly before her death in 1865 and his description of her as kind and homely rather than brilliant reflects a more general denigration of women writers in the Victorian period. Interestingly though, it is also echoed in an essay by the feminist writer Edna Lyall, which was published three decades after Gaskell's death:

> Few writers, we think, have exercised a more thoroughly wholesome influence over their readers than Mrs Gaskell. Her books, with their wide human sympathies, their tender comprehension of human frailty, their bright flashes of humour and their infinite pathos, seem to plead with us to love one another. Through them all we seem to hear the author's voice imploring us to "seize the day" and to "make friends". (Lyall 145)

While acknowledging Gaskell's influence over her reading public, Lyall attributes the success of Gaskell's work to the writer's tenderness and compassion, thus reinforcing the picture Greenwood has painted of her. It is an image that is at odds with Gaskell's shorter fiction, however, in which dubious figures like witches, bandits, murderers and ghosts abound. Patsy Stoneman has observed that many critics chose to dismiss these stories "as 'fancies' … or 'melodrama'" (8–9) because they did not know how to reconcile the writer's dark short fiction with their image of a caring and compassionate Elizabeth Gaskell. Benjamin Franklin Fisher, for instance, declares in a 1981 review entitled "Mrs Gaskell's Tales of Mystery and Horror" that the author's supernatural fiction is not "likely to enhance Mrs Gaskell's literary standing" (111) – a judgement which fails to acknowledge the stories' distinct engagement with questions of power and gender.[22]

Since 2000, literary scholars have been busy re-evaluating Gaskell's supernatural short fiction and have shown that her stories time and again foreground the vulnerability and marginality of women within Victorian society. Laura Kranzler, for instance, emphasises Gaskell's focus on "female characters who are victimised by the males" (xi). Similarly, Diana Wallace sees in Gaskell's short fiction "a searing proto-feminist indictment of the vulnerability of women and children within structures which support and even encourage male power and violence" (*Histories* 68). In line with these observations, Gaskell's lengthy short story "The Poor Clare", published in three instalments of *Household Words* in 1856, calls attention to the Victorian sexual double standard and to male dominance over women. In the narrative, Gaskell appropriates the motif of the *doppelgänger* to suggest female sexual repression. By presenting the *doppelgänger* as a "terrible but delicious nightmare and a wet dream of monstrous sexual agency" (Liggins, "Gendering" 49), which ultimately must be destroyed, the story not only draws attention to the denial of female sexual agency, but also hints at the impossibility of marital sexual fulfilment within the narrow confines of the Victorian moral doctrine.

The narrative is equipped with a framing device which the male homodiegetic narrator uses to introduce himself. We learn that he is now an old man who is looking back on the "extraordinary incidents" (Gaskell, "Poor

---

22   Ardel Haefele-Thomas has suggested that the "stereotype of a pure and motherly Mrs Gaskell" (Queer 48) also had its upside: "Elizabeth Gaskell was able to use her position as 'Angel of the House' to create some incredibly liberal and subversive writings; she was able to 'get away with it'" (ibid.).

Clare" 49) he was bound up with when, as a young man, he was ordered by his uncle, "an eminent attorney in London" (ibid. 61), to find out the whereabouts of Mary Fitzgerald, who inherited "some valuable estates" (ibid. 62). The story he then tells is that of Mary's daughter and his later wife Lucy who, as a young woman, was unknowingly cursed by her own grandmother Bridget. As a reason for telling Lucy's story – and his part in it – he states that he, "like most old men" (ibid. 49), is "more given to looking back upon ... [his] own career with a kind of fond interest and affectionate remembrance, than to watching the events ... immediately passing before ... [his] eyes" (ibid.). These introductory remarks are striking for several reasons. For one, we learn that the unnamed male narrator has been involved in the events he is going to relate and is thus biased. By relating the story for his wife, he further takes control over her story, thereby echoing Victorian patriarchal domination over women. It is also interesting that he seems to fondly remember the curse which has been put on Lucy. I will propose that the narrator's "affectionate remembrance" (ibid.) has mostly two motivations: Firstly, he likes to indulge in his role as saviour of "poor Lucy" (ibid.). Secondly, he has a desire to remember Lucy's sexually expressive and seductive double, which came to haunt her as a consequence of the curse.

From the narrator we learn that the story is set in the early eighteenth century and is thus distanced from the world of the Victorian audience. This process of distancing, which is reminiscent of the early Gothic novels of Anne Radcliffe, might have been a necessary means to avoid alienating the British reading audience. As Ardel Haefele-Thomas points out, "as a woman author, she may have had reason to be more cautious about setting the action of her stories 'at home'" (Queer 159). As so often with Gothic fiction, it is nevertheless possible to read Gaskell's ghost story as a direct commentary on Victorian attitudes towards gender and sexuality.

Following the narrator who relates the "events in the order in which they occurred – not that in which I became acquainted with them" (Gaskell, "Poor Clare" 49), I will first explain how Lucy came to be haunted by the double and will then return to my central argument that Gaskell's tale exposes the process of sexual repression. The story consists of three chapters. In the first chapter, we learn the background story of the curse. The narrator's own involvement in the events, however, starts later when the curse has already fulfilled itself. Hence, the narrator has not witnessed the events that occur in the first chapter but has to draw on second-hand information. This is relevant because it warns us not to take everything that he tells us for granted. Reliability is, of course, always an issue with first-person narrators, but even more so when they relate events they have not experienced themselves. The narrator presents the first chapter as the result of his research. However, more often than not, he only vaguely alludes to his sources: "people said" (ibid. 54), "many saw her" (ibid. 57), "those who knew him well" (ibid. 58). We later learn that he has met Lucy's grandmother Bridget and learns parts of the story from her and that he is in possession of letters that help him reconstruct the events. Many of his sources remain unclear though.

The chapter revolves around the "wild"[23] (Gaskell, "Poor Clare" 53) and passionate Bridget Fitzgerald and her daughter Mary who live in the household of an aristocratic family in North-East Lancashire. Even though Bridget and Mary act as servants to the family, the gentle Squire and Madam Starkey (who is Bridget's former nursling) often bend to their will so that they are "in secret the ruling spirits of the household" (ibid.). When Mary leaves her mother to become a lady's maid on the continent, Squire and Madam Starkey help the illiterate woman to stay in contact with her daughter. However, when the Squire and his wife sicken of a fever and die, Bridget is bereaved of her employers and deprived of her means of communicating with Mary. She travels abroad in search of her daughter. Without having found any trace of Mary, though, she returns to her hut months later, looking "as if she had been scorched in the flames of hell" (ibid. 57). After her return, Bridget gets into "the habit of talking to herself" and soon earns herself "the dreadful reputation of a witch" (ibid.), a figure which forms a striking contrast to the idealised "Angel in the House", as Vanessa D. Dickerson has pointed out:

> Generally understood to be a woman who sold her soul for power, the witch could be found, like the angel, at the hearth; however, she was said to brew potions there, not to boil tripe. She proffered a compelling contrast to the angel in the house, for unlike the Victorian angel, the witch consorted with demons, even engaged in sex with them. Unlike the angel, who lovingly tended the children, the witch was rumoured to have sacrificed them. Witches used their brooms to fly off to midnight meetings, not to sweep the patriarchal floor. (Dickerson 118–9)

---

23   Clare Stewart has pointed out that "wild" in Gaskell's short fiction is often a euphemism for "sexual" (*Fighting* 109).

"The Poor Clare" dwells on this idea of witchcraft when depicting Bridget as a "travel-and-sorrow-stained woman" (Gaskell, "Poor Clare" 57) who is so "brown, and scared, and fierce" (ibid.) that she must have travelled to hell and back. More particularly, Bridget can be identified as a specific type of witch which is associated with spinsterhood. She is self-reliant and straightforward, and her unwomanly withdrawal from society further works to consolidate her image as a witch. However, the idea of the demonic, child-killing witch is subverted by the love Bridget shows for her former nursling Mrs Starkey and her daughter Mary. The story also implies that Bridget does not choose to live in solitude but has been bereaved of the people for whom she cares. The only thing left to her is her daughter's little dog, who has kept her company ever since Mary left. However, even the dog is eventually taken away from her. It is shot by Squire Gisborne, a military man who stays at the estate for a few days and is frustrated after returning from an unsuccessful hunting trip. At least, that is what the narrator assumes, thereby indirectly justifying Gisborne's inhumane deed: "the gentlemen had all been out shooting, and with but little success, I believe; anyhow, Mr Gisborne had none, and was in a black humour accordingly" (ibid. 58). In her grief and anger, Bridget puts a curse on Gisborne: "You shall live to see the creature you love best, and who alone loves you ... become a terror and loathing to all" (ibid. 59). Unknowingly, Bridget curses her own granddaughter Lucy, who is Mary's and Gisborne's child. The first chapter ends with Bridget's curse and the narrator asserts that "I now come to the time in which I myself was mixed up with the people that I have been writing about" (ibid. 61).

It is later revealed that Lucy was born out of wedlock and that Mary committed suicide, presumably out of desperation. In a letter to the narrator's uncle, Gisborne states that he can "hardly find words severe enough for his own conduct" (Gaskell, "Poor Clare" 90) with regards to his behaviour towards Mary, whom he wronged and who found "a violent death" (ibid.). He expresses his belief that the curse is "working for the fulfilment of a deeper vengeance than for the death of the poor dog" (ibid.), thus acknowledging his role in Mary's suicide. Despite his own wrongdoings, however, Gisborne abandons Lucy when his daughter starts to be haunted by a sexually transgressive *doppelgänger* who is seen "dancing over the tender plants in the flower-beds" (ibid. 76) and spends time with the grooms in an "undue familiarity – all unbecoming a gentlewoman" (ibid. 77), thereby threatening Lucy's and, in consequence, Squire Gisborne's reputation. In his letter, Gisborne states that he cannot hide "the repugnance which the conduct of the demoniac creature had produced in his mind" (ibid. 90).

Gisborne's treatment of his daughter reveals the hypocrisy that underlies the attitude of the patriarchal society towards women who either refuse to assume the gendered role assigned to them or who cannot live up to the angelic ideal of womanhood. While the guilty Gisborne is free to leave his daughter and can resume his position in the military, Lucy has to suffer for his sins – just as Mary had to deal with the consequences of pre-marital sex by herself. By showing that Gisborne's actions do not have consequences for his own life, the story highlights the social injustice women have to endure in a male-dominated society.

Gisborne's guilt is also implied when Lucy's servant, Mrs Clarke, notes that "the sins of the fathers shall be visited upon the children" (Gaskell, "Poor Clare" 79), thereby referring to a passage from *The Book of Exodus* in the Old Testament. The idea that children are cursed by and have to suffer for their ancestor's deeds is one of the most popular Gothic themes. It makes its first appearance in Horace Walpole's *The Castle of Otranto* (1764) and keeps recurring in narratives like Nathaniel Hawthorne's *The House of Seven Gables* (1851) and Wilkie Collins's best-selling novels *The Woman in White* (1860), *No Name* (1862), *Armadale* (1966), and *The Moonstone* (1868).[24] In "The Poor Clare", Lucy not only has to suffer for the bad deeds of her father, who not only provoked the curse by shooting the little dog but also drove Mary Fitzgerald into suicide, thus bereaving Lucy of her mother. The seductive double which haunts Lucy can also be seen as an embodiment of Bridget's sins. This at least is suggested by the story's resolution, as we shall see.

With Gisborne having abandoned his daughter, the narrator, who sees "a pure and holy Lucy" (Gaskell, "The Poor Clare" 79) behind "another wicked, fearful self" (ibid. 77), is free to step in as the girl's rescuer. He visits Bridget and tells her that the curse she has put on Gisborne has condemned her own granddaughter to a life as a social outcast. In an attempt to undo the harm she has done, Bridget joins the ascetic order of the Poor Clares in Antwerp, Belgium. When Bridget nurses her enemy Squire Gisborne, who was wounded in combat,[25] the curse is finally lifted. In this way, the narrative highlights the pos-

---

24   It is arguably no coincidence that the theme is especially prevalent in mid-century literature when social sciences began viewing heredity as the basis of moral dysfunctions like murder, sadism, or alcoholism (Vrettos 77).

25   On the historical background of the story, see John Geoffrey Sharps in *Mrs. Gaskell's Observation and Invention*: "The later part of the narrative takes place in Antwerp between the end of the War of Spanish Succession and the beginning of the Austrian Succession. ... Mrs. Gaskell put two dates (1711 and 1718) in the body of the tale, which thus permits

sibility to "wipe out ... [the] sin of hate and vengeance" (ibid. 95) by performing "acts of love and mercy" (ibid.). By showing that only Bridget can undo the
curse, the narrative implies that, even more than Gisborne, the old woman with
her "unholy prayers" (ibid. 94) is responsible for Lucy's fate: "The spectral double
can only be exorcised by Bridget's transformation from witch into nun" (Wallace, *Histories* 82). Vanessa D. Dickerson has argued that female "power turns
into powerlessness" (129) here, for Bridget must not only "give up her proud and
powerful self, but, more importantly, she must give up her voice to become a
communal angel in the house" (Dickerson 124). The fierce and self-reliant Bridget is thus reintegrated in society. In a similar way, Lucy resumes her position
as "saintly and pure" (Gaskell, "Poor Clare" 75) soon-to-be wife of the narrator
when the curse is lifted. As so often in Victorian literature, patriarchy is restored by the eradication of inappropriate femininity, that is, in this case, the
defeat of Lucy's voluptuous double – and Bridget's metamorphosis from witch
to nun. On the surface, the message of Gaskell's tale seems obvious enough:
be good, do not transgress societal rules, and, if you do, you can find redemp-
tion by performing "acts of deepest love and purest self-devotion" (ibid. 94). It
is a message that seems to fit the above image of Elizabeth Gaskell as religious,
kind, and consoling. However, Gaskell's narrative is more complex than this.

While seemingly the result of her ancestor's sins, Lucy's seductive double
can also be interpreted as the embodiment of her repressed sexual desires. As
Enid L. Duthie stresses, Elizabeth Gaskell's "treatment of the 'doppelgänger'
motif is characteristic" (141), for the author uses the device to suggest psychic
division. While Lucy is described as a figure of purity by the male narrator, her
fearsome, sexually transgressive double symbolizes the return of a repressed
side of female identity. Thus, Lucy and her double "manifest the most fundamental split between the two sides of feminine identity so central to Victorian
ideology: the split between the 'pure', asexual ideal and the monstrous, sexual
voraciousness" (Kranzler xxv).[26] At the same time, Lucy's *doppelgänger* draws

---

some sort of chronological estimation. We may surmise that the Antwerp revolt of the
story occurred in the early seventeen-twenties" (251).

26   Laura Kranzler sees in this doubling of female identity also a link to Elizabeth Gaskell's
"own compartmentalized life" and the split she experienced "between successful writer
and committed mother, wife and community provider" (xiv). Gaskell's struggles to reconcile her career as a writer with the duties she felt were placed on her as wife and
mother are well documented. In her letters to her friends, she laments about "the distraction of children" (Gaskell, Letter to John Forster 231), the difficulties she has to write
full length novels while leading a "full household" (Gaskell, Letter to John Forster 282),

attention to the ways in which the male sexual body was confined by societal expectations. On the one hand, the narrator benefits from Lucy's demonic double because he can assume the role of the masculine rescuer who doesn't shrink "a whit" (Gaskell, "Poor Clare" 79) from Lucy but is determined to help her.[27] Thus, the ghostly appearance bolsters the narrator's masculinity. However, the *doppelgänger* also reveals his longing for the female sexual body:

> Just at that instant, standing as I was opposite to her in the full and perfect morning light, I saw behind her another figure – a ghastly resemblance, complete in likeness, so far as form and feature and minutest touch of dress could go, but with a loathsome demon soul looking out of the grey eyes, that were in turns mocking and voluptuous. My heart stood still within me; every hair rose up erect; my flesh crept with horror. I could not see the grave and tender Lucy – my eyes were fascinated by the creature beyond. I know not why, but I put out my hand to clutch it. ... I never loved her more fondly than now when – and that was the unspeakable misery – the idea of her was becoming so inextricably blended with the shuddering thought of IT. (Gaskell, "Poor Clare" 78)

Although his "flesh ... [creeps] with horror", he is "fascinated by the creature beyond" when he sees Lucy's seductive Other for the first time. He even tries to clutch Lucy's evil *doppelgänger*. This desire to touch the women "beyond" suggests that it is the "eroticism of Lucy's double which so attracts him to her" (Kranzler xxvi) and shows "his desire for possession" (Stewart, *Fighting*

---

and the visits she feels urged to pay other people, "visits that would be most charming and acceptable at any other time, but I want so much to get on with my writing" (qtd. in Martin 38). In a letter to her close friend Eliza Fox, dated April 1850, she complains about her multiple "Mes" (Gaskell, Letter to Eliza Fox 108): "I have a great number [of them], and that's the plague. ... How am I to reconcile all these warring members?" (ibid.). In light of Gaskell's letters, "The Poor Clare" can be read as a critique of the restrictions imposed on women "in a society that elevated the feminine role" as wife and mother "almost to the obliteration of any other" (Martin 38). Gaskell was aware that men do not have to split themselves in the same way: "When a man becomes an author, it is probably merely a change of employment to him. He takes a portion of that time which has hitherto been devoted to some other study or pursuit ... and another ... steps into his vacant place, and probably does as well as he. But no other can take up the quiet, regular duties of the daughter, the wife, or the mother" (Gaskell, *Life* 357), she notes in *The Life of Charlotte Brontë*.

27   It is, of course, questionable that he really does help Lucy by controlling and suppressing her sexual identity.

108). The sexual tension experienced by the narrator is further indicated by
the fact that "every hair ... [rises] up erect" (Gaskell, "Poor Clare" 78) like the
male sexual organ when he sees the *doppelgänger*. "Engulfed by the moment, he
experiences what could be described as a sexual swoon" (Stewart, *Fighting* 108).
He even forgets that Lucy is still there with him. The innocent, virginal Lucy
becomes ghost-like, something he cannot see anymore. By highlighting the
young woman's invisibility, the story foreshadows the impossibility of marital
eroticism with a sexually repressed but socially accepted Lucy. In this way, the
story draws attention to the limitations of the iconic "Angel in the House". The
narrator's desire for the sexually attractive double is further emphasised when
he admits that he "never loved her more fondly than now when – and that was
the unspeakable misery – the idea of her was becoming so inextricably blended
with the shuddering thought of IT" (Gaskell, "Poor Clare" 78). It is evident that
the narrator feels "unspeakable misery" because his desire for the seductive
Other is at odds with his moral code and can, therefore, never be fulfilled.
That this Other is in reality nothing but Lucy's repressed side of femininity
is highlighted by the fact that the narrator calls the double a "soul" (ibid. 78).
At the same time, he refers to the *doppelgänger* as "IT" (ibid.), thus presenting
Lucy's sexually transgressive side as something inhuman or even monstrous.
The narrator is both drawn to and repelled by the "loathsome demon" (ibid.).
This way, the story signals the narrator's "phobic enchantment" (Stallybrass
and White 124) and thus the extent of his own sexual repression. He senses
that it is not only Lucy's double which is deemed unacceptable by society, but
also his own desire for her unruly, spectralized sexuality.

After this encounter, the narrator does not see the *doppelgänger* again. However, he cannot forget the feeling the double has inspired in him:

> I was now apparently close on the discovery which I had striven so many
> months ago to attain. But success had lost its zest. I put my letters down, and
> seemed to forget them all in thinking of the morning I had passed the very
> day. Nothing was real but the unreal presence, which had come like an evil
> blast across my bodily eyes, and burned itself down upon my brain. (Gaskell,
> "Poor Clare" 80)

By emphasising that, after the encounter with the double, nothing but its "unreal presence" seems real to the narrator, the story highlights the artificiality
of the idealised version of femininity represented by the "pure and holy Lucy"
(Gaskell, "Poor Clare" 79). The passage also draws attention to the fact that the

narrator, just like Lucy herself, is possessed by the double. It is something that seizes his body and his mind. It has "burned itself upon [his] brain" (ibid. 80) and appears before his "bodily eyes" (ibid.).

Despite his apparent fascination with Lucy's erotic *doppelgänger*, the narrator visits Bridget and ensures that the curse is lifted. That he feels compelled to do so becomes apparent when he tells Bridget about the curse: "I love her. Yet, I shrink from her ever since that day on the moor-side. And men must shrink from one so accompanied; friends and lovers must stand afar off" (Gaskell, "Poor Clare" 88). What the narrator refers to here are not his own feelings but his awareness of societal rules which prevent him from marrying Lucy as long as her purity is overshadowed by the presence of her sexually assertive double. Here, the story turns into "a frightening depiction of the consequences of expressing female sexuality in a culture that insists that all good women are sexless angels" (Reddy 261). Even though Lucy's sexual identity is something that the narrator apparently desires (and hence does not truly shrink from), it has to be wiped out so that society does not treat Lucy as an outcast anymore. The story thus implies that it is not only Lucy's sexual drive that is suppressed but also that of the male narrator, who has to resort to "affectionate remembrance" (Gaskell, "Poor Clare" 49) in order to be reunited with Lucy's seductive *doppelgänger*.

Edith Nesbit: "The Ebony Frame" (1891)

The last story discussed in this chapter is by Edith Nesbit (1858–1924). Nesbit is a very contradictory figure. Especially the author's relationship with first-wave feminism and its icon, the New Woman, is a complicated one. Financially independent, educated, and career-oriented, the supporters of the New Woman movement not only questioned the traditional Victorian perception of women as "Angel in the House", but also threatened men's role as breadwinners (Tosh, Manliness 21). In the newspapers and the periodical press of the 1890s, the emblem of the feminist movement was ever-present. She was portrayed in novels, applauded or attacked in newspaper articles, and ridiculed in satirical verse and cartoons (Heilmann 15–6). Even though Nesbit "lived a lifestyle that many would associate with this figure – rejecting much of the Victorian ideological construct of femininity and embracing political, intellectual and sexual freedoms" (Margree, "Feminist Orientation" 425–6) – she distanced herself from the movement and satirized suffragettes in some of her children's writings.[28] Nesbit's ambivalent attitudes towards the role of women in Victorian society also seem to have puzzled her contemporaries: "She was a wonderful woman, large-hearted, amazingly unconventional, but with such strange reversions to ultra-respectable standards. She could write unconcernedly in the midst of a crowd, smoking like a chimney all the while" (qdt. in Davies, *Power* 9), the journalist Ada Elizabeth Chesterton writes in her recollection of the author, for instance. When Nesbit was asked to speak to the socialist Fabian Society about balancing motherhood and a career, she also shocked feminist members by giving a lecture on "The Natural Disabilities of Women" (Briggs, *Edith Nesbit* 356). Yet, in her private life, she acted as the breadwinner of the family after the failure of her husband's business in 1880. She wore her hair short and smoked "like a chimney" (qdt. in Davies, *Power* 9), both of which were hallmarks of the New Woman. Herself a mother of three, she also adopted the two children her husband had with his lover Alice Hoatson, who lived in their household, thus eroding Victorian ideas about marriage and family.

Edith Nesbit produced more than twenty novels (among them several children's books), a number of poems, some pieces of non-fiction, and several short stories. As in the case of Elizabeth Gaskell, it has not been until recently that Nesbit's supernatural stories have received broader scholarly attention.[29] As David Stuart Davies remarks, "[e]ven Nesbit's biographers give her ghost stories minimal treatment. Remarkably Anthea Bell and Noel Streatfield never mention them at all; while very unkindly and inaccurately Doris Langley Moore referred to them as 'singularly ineffectual and now deservedly forgotten'" (*Power* 12). Also, Julia Briggs only shortly reflects on Nesbit's supernatural fiction in her 1987 biography about the writer, which comes as a surprise considering that Briggs is also the author of *Night Visitors: The Rise and Fall of the English Ghost Story* (1977), a renowned introduction to the ghost story genre, which also informs this work.

---

28   See, for instance, *The Magic City* (1910). In the story, the protagonists Lucy and Philip travel to a world in which "girls are expected to be brave and the boys, kind" (*Magic City* 164). The children's reversal of traditional gender roles is counterbalanced by Philip's nursemaid, who follows the children and becomes a "Pretenderette". For an interpretation of the book see Amelia A. Rutledge's "E. Nesbit and the Woman Question".

29   A notable exception is Lowell T. Frye's 1998 essay "The Ghost Story and the Subjection of Women: The Example of Amelia Edwards, M. E. Braddon, and E. Nesbit."

While not devoid of the writer's "contrary impulses between sustaining and undermining the hegemony of conventional female roles" (Rutledge 236), Nesbit's supernatural writing repeatedly transgresses and questions heteronormative thinking, as recent explorations of her Gothic fiction have persuasively illustrated.[30] In her essay "The Feminist Orientation in Edith Nesbit's Gothic Short Fiction", Victoria Margree discusses several of Nesbit's Gothic stories. She concludes that "[t]he genre's licence to shock and its iconography of death and abjection seem to have provided her with a vocabulary for the expression of her most counter-hegemonic impulses in relation to gender" ("Feminist Orientation" 439). What is particularly striking about Nesbit's Gothic short fiction is the prevalence of "brutal, tragic and bleak" (Margree, "Feminist Orientation" 427) endings which often include female corpses and male violence.[31] In the following, I would like to expand on existing research by providing a feminist reading of Nesbit's "The Ebony Frame" – a story which was first published at the dawn of the New Woman movement in 1891 and which has largely been overlooked by scholars so far. I will particularly focus on the ways in which the male protagonist is emotionally and sexually frustrated with the artificial figure of the "Angel in the House".

"The Ebony Frame" tells the story of Henry Devigne, an "unappreciated journalist" (Nesbit, "Ebony Frame" 143), who is suddenly left with seven hundred pounds a year and a furnished house in Chelsea when his aunt dies. Devigne, who also serves as the narrator of the story, does not desire his girlfriend Mildred with her "chocolate-box barmaid style of prettiness" (Nesbit, "Ebony Frame" 150), but becomes obsessed with the uncanny portrait of a Pre-Raphaelite beauty in a black velvet gown, which he finds in the attic of his new home. The painting lies face to face with the portrait of a man "in a cavalier dress" (Nesbit, "Ebony Frame" 145) who bears a striking resemblance to Devigne himself who is immediately intrigued by the woman in the portrait:

This was a beautiful woman's picture, very beautiful she was. I noted all her beauties, straight nose, low brows, full lips, thin hands, large, deep, lumi-

---

30   See, for instance, Victoria Margree, "The Feminist Orientation in Edith Nesbit's Gothic Short Fiction", Nick Freeman, "E. Nesbit's New Woman Gothic", Terry W. Thompson, "'Presentiments of Evil': Sourcing Frankenstein in Edith Nesbit's 'Man-Size in Marble'", and Kathleen A. Miller, "The Mysteries of the In-Between: Re-Reading Disability in E. Nesbit's Late Victorian Gothic Fiction".

31   See, for instance, "Man-Size in Marble" (1893), "John Carrington's Wedding" (1893), and "From the Dead" (1893).

> nous eyes. ... [H]er eyes met those of the spectator bewilderingly. ... I believe it was a quarter of an hour before I could turn my eyes from her. I have never seen any other eyes like hers; they appealed, as a child's or a dog's do; they commanded, as might those of an empress. (Nesbit, "Ebony Frame" 145)

The narrator is unable to take his eyes off her but gazes at the portrait for "a quarter of an hour" (Nesbit, "Ebony Frame" 145) which is indicative of the emotional and sexual attraction he feels for the woman in the velvet gown. The fact that he uses the word "beautiful" repeatedly further emphasises his fascination with the woman. At the same time, Devigne experiences a feeling of bewilderment which implies that the woman in the portrait – and thus his desire for her – does not comply with hegemonic ideas about gender. What is also striking about the above passage is Devigne's description of the woman's eyes which are both appealing like those of a child (or a dog) and commanding like those of an empress, thereby echoing the cultural division between the child-like ideal, in need of masculine help and protection, and the head-strong, self-reliant New Woman.

The endearing beauty of the woman in the portrait is juxtaposed to the narrator's betrothed Mildred. It is clear from the onset of the story that the narrator is bored with Mildred who embodies a number of qualities ascribed to the ideal of womanhood in the Victorian period: "She was a dear, good girl, and I meant to marry her some day. It is very nice to feel that a good little woman is thinking of you – it helps you in your work – and it is pleasant to know she will say 'Yes' when you say 'Will you?'" (Nesbit, "Ebony Frame" 143). Mildred is just like women were supposed to be in the late nineteenth century: she is "dear" and "good" – and she is waiting passively for the male narrator to propose to her. The fact that he knows she will say "Yes" when he asks her to marry him suggests that there are no surprises with Mildred. It is also noteworthy that he describes her as "little", which arguably not only refers to her physical seize but might also serve as a belittlement for a woman from whom no resistance to the patriarchal order is to be expected.

Although Devigne is evidently more attracted to the woman in the portrait than he is to Mildred, he dreads meeting her gaze for a second time: "I could not forget, nor remember without singular emotion, the look in the eyes of that woman when mine first met them. I shrank from meeting that look again" (Nesbit, "Ebony Frame" 146). This reluctance to look at the portrait emphasises the narrator's awareness that the desire the woman in the portrait inspires in him is not acceptable within the Victorian moral code. However, he soon over-comes his "guilty desire" (Liggins, "Gendering" 41):

> I met her dark, deep, hazel eyes, and once more my gaze was held fixed as by a strong magic – the kind of fascination that keeps one sometimes staring for whole minutes into one's own eyes in the glass. I gazed into her eyes, and felt my own dilate, pricked with a smart like the smart of tears.
> "I wish," I said, "oh, how I wish you were a woman and not a picture! Come down! Ah, come down!" (Nesbit, "Ebony Frame" 146)

It is noteworthy that the narrator feels compelled to hold her gaze as if he were under the influence of "strong magic" (Nesbit, "Ebony Frame" 146), for, as we learn later, the woman was burned for allegedly being a witch in her lifetime. Here, the text reflects Nesbit's ambivalent attitude towards progressive female figures: on the one hand, the story showcases the danger transgressive women pose to impressionable men like the story's narrator by demonstrating the power the woman in the portrait exerts over him. Conversely, the longing for the woman in the portrait is indicative of Devigne's frustration with a society that privileges a type of femininity which cannot fulfil his emotional and sexual desires.

When the narrator voices his wish that the woman in the portrait was not a picture but a real person, the woman materialises. With the spectre, he ex-periences moments of "unspeakable happiness" (Nesbit, "Ebony Frame" 152), a state he never experienced with Mildred. It is also implied that the narrator and the spectral woman share moments of sexual bliss: "we … made such cheer each of the other as true lovers may after long parting" (Nesbit, "Ebony Frame" 148). Since the narrator is the only one who ever sees the ghostly woman, it is likely that she is nothing but a construct of his imagination, which implies that Devigne cannot satisfy his sexual desires in the real world.

After their sexual encounter, the narrator learns from the woman in the velvet gown, who calls herself "a ghost" (Nesbit, "Ebony Frame" 148), that they had been lovers in another time which suggests that he is either a reincarnation of the man in the portrait he found in the attic or a *doppelgänger*. Since he has no memories of this former life, except that he loved her and that they both suffered (ibid.), she tells him how it came that they were torn apart:

> We loved each other – ah! no, you have not forgotten that – and when you came back from the war we were to be married. Our pictures were painted

before you went away. You know I was more learned than women of that day. Dear one, when you were gone they said I was a witch. They tried me. They said I should be burned. Just because I had looked at the stars and had gained more knowledge than they, they must needs bind me to a stake and let me be eaten by the fire. (Nesbit, "Ebony Frame" 148)

The story the women relates is one of patriarchal oppression. Without the protection of her fiancé, the woman (whose name the narrator and hence the reader never learns) is vulnerable and falls victim to a society who views her with hostility. It is clear that she is regarded as a threat because of her knowledge and intelligence. Knowledge in this context is both empowering and dangerous. It sets her apart from the other "women of that day" (Nesbit, "Ebony Frame" 148), but it also leads to her violent death. The witch is portrayed as a figure of transgression here. She disobeys the rules of patriarchy by acquiring more knowledge than a woman is supposed to have. It is also implied that the woman possessed occult knowledge which she gained by "look[ing] at the stars" (ibid.). In this context, it is noteworthy that Edith Nesbit, "[l]ike her character in 'The Ebony Frame', ... sought esoteric knowledge" (Jewison 154). Like Algernon Blackwood, Nesbit was a member of the Hermetic Order of the Golden Dawn, a secret magical order that attracted many famous personages (Coulombe 348). What was considered paganism at the time the woman was tried for being a witch, was a fashionable pastime at the time in which the story is set. The narrative thus draws attention to the changing attitudes of British society towards occultism, a shift which coincides with the industrialisation and the subsequent rise of the middle class. By depicting the woman in the velvet gown as "more learned" (Nesbit, "Ebony Frame" 148) than other women of her time, the story also hints at the figure of the New Woman whose "ghost" haunted the public discourse in the 1890s. Like the woman in the velvet gown, the supporters of the feminist movement challenged the patriarchal order by demanding the same educational and career opportunities as men. The story within the story thus explores societal issues of the time in which the story was written, even though it is distanced from it in time. As has already been pointed out, this process of distancing is a typical feature of Gothic fiction and was often used as a means to comment on contemporary issues in a concealed way. The fact that the woman was burned for being a witch because her knowledge and intelligence exceeded that of the men surrounding her can thus be read as a direct commentary on contemporary attempts to undermine women's academic pursuits – including the claim that intellectual work damages a woman's uterus and makes her sterile.[32] The warning that intellectual work wrecks a woman's capacity to bear children is part of a larger discourse on degeneration which rose to the centre of national consciousness in the latter decades of the nineteenth century. However, it was also a campaign against women "who displayed any tendency to step out of their ordained sphere of innocence, purity, and submissiveness to men" (Kent 47).

Since some supporters of the feminist movement also postulated sexual liberty besides better educational and professional opportunities, the figure of the New Woman is often equated with the sexually dangerous *femme fatale* in the literary texts of the fin-de-siècle. Sally Ledger has emphasised that the depiction of the New Woman as a voluptuous man-eater has little to do with the actual women's movement, however: "Although the New Woman was constructed ... as an apostle of 'free love', firmly opposed to marriage, such a construction did not accurately reflect the position of the bourgeois women's movement in the late Victorian years" (Ledger 15). Instead, feminist campaigners like Millicent Garrett Fawcett "had their sights set on constitutional, civic, and economic rights rather than on the sexual liberation of women" (ibid.). In accordance with that, Edith Nesbit's ghostly woman is not an advocate of free love but, instead, wishes to live a long and happy life with her beloved. In the course of the story, we learn that she was even willing to sacrifice her soul so that she could be reunited with her fiancé after her execution: "The night before [the execution] ... the devil did come to me. I was innocent before – you know it, don't you? And even then my sin was for you – for you – because of the exceeding love I bore you. The devil came, and I sold my soul to eternal flame. But I got a good price. I got the right to come back, through my picture" (Nesbit, "Ebony Frame" 148). While unjustly accused of being a witch by her community, the woman in the velvet gown eventually does turn to the devil. It is clear, though, that she only does so because of the love she bears for Devine's

---

32   The warning that mental work compromises women's reproductive capacities was first uttered in 1874 by the English psychiatrist Henry Maudsley: "It will have to be considered whether women can scorn delights, and live laborious days of intellectual exercise and production, without injury to their functions as the conceivers, mothers and nurses of children. For it would be an ill thing, if it should so happen, that we got the advantages of a quantity of female intellectual work at the price of a puny, enfeebled, and sickly race" (Maudsley 204). The English author and illustrator Charles Harper warned even more dramatically that "the New Woman, if a mother at all" might people the world "with stunted and hydrocephalic children" and eventually risks "the ultimate extinction of the race" (27).

ancestor and the cruelty inflicted on her by her community. It is them who turn her into a ghost.

Nesbit's story also dwells on the myth of the fallen woman here. Nina Auerbach has pointed out that "[o]ne constant element in the myth of the fallen woman, reaching back to the Old Testament and to Milton's epic recasting of it, is the absolute transforming power of the fall. ... In Victorian revisions, it is the woman alone who is wounded, sighs, laments, and is lost" (34). This is also the case in "The Ebony Frame". While the woman was willing to take the fall for her lover, that is, to sell her soul to the devil in order to be reunited with him, Devigne hesitates when she proposes to him to also "give up ... [his] hopes of heaven" (Nesbit, "Ebony Frame" 149) so that she can transform from ghost to woman, again, and "be your wife" (ibid.). By illustrating that Devigne can enjoy moments of sexual bliss with the woman in the velvet gown but is not willing to join her in "eternal flame" (ibid. 148), the story echoes the Victorian sexual double standard which allowed men to visit prostitutes while their wives were busy cooking and cleaning at home. Devigne might enjoy the woman's voluptuousness and her sexual liberty, but she cannot become his wife.

The eponymous ebony frame works as a metaphor for the confined space of Victorian womanhood. It calls attention to the ways in which women, their (sexual) bodies, and their minds were restricted in the patriarchal society. The woman in the velvet gown transgresses these societal restrictions when she steps out of the ebony frame. It is telling that the narrator does not condemn the ghost woman but experiences a state of happiness and sexual fulfilment he can never achieve with his "Angel in the House" Mildred. This way, the story shows that men might actually desire women who "are more learned than women of that day" (Nesbit, "Ebony Frame" 148), that is, more learned than the ideal Victorian woman, whose time is consumed by occupations like stitching and other forms of needlework:

> And yet, when Mildred, too, looked at the portrait, and said, "What a fine lady! One of your flames, Mr Devigne?" I had a sickening sense of impotent irritation, which became absolute torture when Mildred – how could I ever have admired that chocolate-box barmaid style of prettiness? – threw herself into the high-backed chair, covering the needlework with her ridiculous flounces, and added, "Silence gives consent! Who is it, Mr Devigne? Tell us all about her: I am sure she has a story." (Nesbit, "Ebony Frame" 150)

In contrast to the narrator of "The Poor Clare", who praises his wife-to-be Lucy
as "pure", "holy", "saintly" and "simple" (Gaskell, "Poor Clare" 73, 75, 79) in spite
of his desire for her sexually transgressive double, the narrator of "The Ebony
Frame" disdains Mildred for her simplicity. For him, Mildred's needlework is
nothing but "ridiculous" (Nesbit, "Ebony Frame" 150) and her "chocolate-box
barmaid style of prettiness" (ibid.) far from inspiring any kind of sexual desire in him. On the contrary: the narrator is overcome by "a sickening sense
of impotent irritation" (ibid.) when he is with Mildred. The *Oxford English Dictionary* defines "impotence" as a word which has two related meanings: on the
one hand, the term signals helplessness or powerlessness. On the other hand,
it is highly charged with sexual meaning, for it describes a condition in which
a man experiences a "[c]omplete absence of sexual power" (*OED*). This feeling
of impotence stands in stark contrast to the sexual arousal and fulfilment the
narrator experiences with the ghost-woman. By emphasising the feeling of impotence, which the narrator feels when he is in the company of a woman who
embodies the predominant ideal of femininity, the story launches an attack on
Victorian binary thinking which does not allow for multiple gender and sexual identities. By highlighting the impact this exclusion of alternative forms of
gender and sexuality has on the male sexual body, the story reveals the shortcomings of heteronormative ideas about gender and sexuality.

The story takes an anti-feminist turn, however, when the burning of the
woman for being a witch is re-enacted in the present. While the narrator is out
of the house (in order to escape Mildred's company), a fire breaks out and destroys his home. He comes too late to save the portrait and with it his "own life's
joy" (Nesbit, "Ebony Frame" 152). In this way, heteronormativity is restored.

At the end of the narrative, we learn that the narrator has married Mildred
after the fire destroyed the portrait: "why have I married Mildred, and grown
stout and dull and prosperous? I tell you it is all *this* that is the dream; my dear
lady only is the reality" (Nesbit, "Ebony Frame" 152). In a way that is reminiscent
of Gaskell's "The Poor Clare", where the narrator admits that "[n]othing was real
but the unreal presence" (Gaskell, "Poor Clare" 80) of the uncanny double, the
ghost of the woman in the velvet gown appears more real to Devigne than his
actual life with Mildred. In this way, the story draws attention to the fact that
the idealised form of femininity embodied by Mildred is nothing but a social
construct, a masquerade which women wear in order to live up to social expectations, but one which suppresses their real personality. It is also implies that
the narrator has never gained happiness with Mildred but cherishes the memory of his "dear lady" (Nesbit, "Ebony Frame" 152). Much like to the narrator of

Gaskell's "The Poor Clare", Devigne has to resort to his memory in order to find sexual fulfilment.

* * *

Collectively, the stories which have been discussed in this chapter make a subversive statement about the impossibility of sexual fulfilment within the confines of the Victorian moral doctrine. By portraying characters who experience taboo sexual desires, they counteract dominant discourses about normative sexual behaviour, ultimately suggesting that sexual desire is normal and natural and should not be hushed up, pathologized, or criminalised. A recurring theme is that the protagonists vacillate between desire and disgust, thereby signalling the "unspeakability" of sexual desire. The ghostly experience in these stories eventually serves as a vehicle for the expression of a desire that cannot be satisfied otherwise.

Memory also plays a central role in all four stories. As has been pointed out previously, the figure of the ghost is necessarily concerned with memory and the collapse of the past into the present. As a revenant, the ghost is an emblem of the past, a reminder that past events, deeds, feelings, and desires can never be fully forgotten but keep hunting the present. In the stories discussed above, the ghosts also serve as a reminder of the past. In "The Real Right Thing" and "The Ebony Frame" it is the ghosts of loved ones who come back to haunt their lovers; in "The Poor Clare" the sexually transgressive *doppelgänger* is evoked by Bridget's and Squire Gisborne's past deeds; and in "Winthrop's Adventure" we encounter the ghost of a long-dead singer who stands for a past which precedes the Victorian period with its strict binary ideas of gender. Interestingly though, it is also the memory of the encounter with the ghost that is foregrounded in the stories, most notably so in "The Poor Clare" and "The Ebony Frame". While the ghosts themselves are exorcised at the end of the narratives, the memory of them – and the sexual fulfilment they stand for – remains.

Chapter 3
Weak Men: Adventure, Nationhood, and Degeneration in Imperial Ghost Stories[1]

In the ghost stories discussed so far, the British Empire is present as an underlying structure on which the concepts of Englishness and imperial masculinity are based. While seemingly marginal, this "kind of structuring absence" (Hay 10) is central for the understanding of male gender performance in many late-Victorian and Edwardian ghost stories. This is also evident in the first supernatural tale discussed in this chapter: Amelia B. Edwards's "The Phantom Coach" (1864). In the story, the unnamed male narrator sets out to prove his manly vigour but ends up representing the "direct antithesis" (Heholt, "Visible" 149) to the contemporary ideal of the imperial soldier hero. Although the story is not set in an imperial context, the narrator's actions are guided by an idea of masculinity shaped by the needs of the expanding British Empire. Yet, to fully understand the dialectical relationship between imperial ideologies and the prevalent concept of masculinity, it is also crucial to consider ghost stories that address Britain's imperial politics more directly. Therefore, the main focus of this chapter will be on two supernatural tales that make the imperial project their central concern and link the experience of masculine failure more explicitly to Britain's imperial politics: Rudyard Kipling's "The Mark of the Beast" (1890) and Arthur Conan Doyle's "The Brown Hand" (1899). There are two related issues which these stories address: one concerns the assumption of the

---

1 As pointed out previously in the introduction, parts of chapter 3 have been published before as a research article in *Humanities*, vol. 9, no. 4, Oct. 2020, titled "Haunted Oppressors: The Deconstruction of Manliness in the Imperial Gothic Stories of Rudyard Kipling and Arthur Conan Doyle". They are reprinted here with permission, alongside new, previously unpublished insights and interpretations. The original open-access version can be accessed at https://www.mdpi.com/2076-0787/9/4/122.

racial and cultural superiority of the white male imperialist over the colonised people and their supposedly savage culture and religion. The second issue relates to a feeling of crisis experienced by the white middle-class protagonists after their encounter with the colonial Other. By inverting the power structure between white colonizer and colonial Other, both stories erode the prevalent ideal of imperial masculinity with its insistence on qualities like courage, endurance and determination.

In *Rule of Darkness: British Literature and Imperialism, 1830–1914* (1988), Patrick Brantlinger describes imperial Gothic fiction as "that blend of adventure story with Gothic elements" (227). Building on this observation, this chapter shows that it is instructive to compare imperial ghost stories as a subset of imperial Gothic fiction and adventure fiction set in the colonies.[2] Not unlike ghost stories, adventure tales experienced their "golden age" in the second half of the nineteenth century and the years preceding the Great War. As Bradley Deane has pointed out, the genre replaced "the developmental narrative of the *Bildungsroman*" (Deane 101) as the dominant literary form for juvenile boys and promoted a new concept of manliness: "the decisive question of successful manliness was no longer moral growth but conduct in a limitless series of competitive trials" (ibid.). Deane even detects a "remarkable rebellion against masculine maturity" (85) in these stories. He argues that this rejection was grounded in "the period's new imperial ideologies" (ibid.) and paraded by some of the most prominent military figures of the time: "Robert Baden-Powell, who not only saw the Empire's future in the hands of his Boy Scouts but was praised for having 'always been a boy himself', Alfred Milner in South Africa, who called his circle of disciples the 'kindergarten,' and Horatio Kitchener in Egypt, who called his the 'band of boys'" (ibid.).

The rejection of masculine maturation also manifests itself in the readership of imperial adventure fiction. These stories were not only written for juveniles but "increasingly aimed at a male audience whose age was explicitly blurred" (Deane 85). This development is evident in J. M. Barrie's fin-de-siècle play *Peter Pan; or, The Boy Who Wouldn't Grow Up* (1904) whose title already suggests an unwillingness to become a man. Similarly, H. Rider Haggard's *King Solomon's Mines* (1885) is addressed to "all the big and little boys who read it" and

---

2   "Imperial romance" is also used in secondary literature as an umbrella term for stories that engage with male gender performance in the far reaches of the Empire. I chose the term "adventure fiction" because I believe that it best describes the kind of stories commonly attributed to the genre.

Sir Arthur Conan Doyle's *The Lost World* (1912) is dedicated "To the boy who's half a man / And the man who's half a boy".[3] "While women writers after George Eliot saw themselves as writing especially for other women" (Showalter, *Anarchy* 79), many male writers of the day primarily created literature about boys and men for boys and men. They "extolled the masculine and homosocial 'romance' of adventure and quest, descended from Arthurian epic" (ibid.), and imagined the Empire as a space in which men could prove themselves and excel in an exotic, untamed environment.[4] However, these tales of manly achievement and stamina often turn into narratives of failure and decay when the supernatural invades the story, as we shall see.

My central argument for the following discussion is that imperial ghost stories form an antithesis to imperial adventure fiction. Both genres situate questions of masculinity within an imperial context, but with a radically different outcome: while adventure stories affirm the belief in the imperial mission and the racial superiority of the British (especially that of the white, middle-class male) through the display of hyper-masculine heroes, imperial ghost stories establish connections between imperial decline and masculine failure. I argue that both genres are informed by theories about Britain's social, racial and national decay, which proliferated in the final decades of the nineteenth century. In order to illustrate this, the chapter is structured as follows: I first pinpoint the structure, themes and motifs of imperial adventure literature. I trace the patterns of the genre in Bracebridge Hemyng's *Jack Harckaway's Adventures Afloat and Ashore* (1872), a narrative which I believe to be representative of Victorian adventure fiction. In this context, I also look at how the ideal of masculinity was affected by the contemporary discourse on degeneration and illustrate how the heroes of adventure fiction counteract concerns about Britain's decline and reaffirm the superiority of the British race through a revitalisation of manliness. In a second step, I turn to the ghost stories presented above and examine the ways in which these tales of haunting counter adventure fiction by presenting Englishmen as hysteric, weak-willed, and powerless.

---

3   This list of literary works addressed to juvenile readers also appears in Bradley Deane's *Masculinity and the New Imperialism*, p. 85.

4   Elaine Showalter sees in the production of what she calls "the male quest romance" (Showalter, *Anarchy* 81) also an attempt to reclaim the literary market from the female writers and readers of domestic fiction. Showalter argues that "[t]he revival of 'romance' in the 1880s was a men's literary revolution intended to reclaim the kingdom of the English novel for male writers, male readers, and men's stories" (ibid. 79).

Finally, I argue that the critique of imperial masculinity inherent in Kipling's "The Mark of the Beast" and Conan Doyle's "The Brown Hand" not only reflects anxieties about the decay of the British race but also reveals concerns about the rightfulness of Britain's imperial project. Both stories anticipate themes of postcolonial Gothic literature. I propose, therefore, to situate "The Mark of the Beast" and "The Brown Hand" on the borderline between imperial Gothic and postcolonial Gothic.

The Construction of a Myth: Displays of Manliness in Imperial Adventure Fiction

In an interview conducted shortly before his death, George Alfred Henty (1832–1902), who was one of the most prolific writers of juvenile adventure fiction in the second half of the nineteenth century, acknowledges the didactic purpose of his writing: "My object has been to teach history, and still more to encourage manly and straight living and feeling among boys" (Blathwayt 8). This statement reveals that G. A. Henty had a clear vision in mind when writing his stories. He did not only intend them as entertainment but believed that his stories would equip boys and young men with knowledge and, even more importantly, with the right set of values. What Henty means by "manly and straight" can better be understood in light of his biography, which was written by his friend Manville Fenn. In *George Alfred Henty: The Story of an Active Life* (1907), Fenn comments on the feeling which Henty hoped to inspire in his readers: "He used to say that he wanted his boys to be bold, straightforward and ready to play a young man's part, not to be milksops. He had a horror of a lad who displayed any weak emotion and shrank from shedding blood, or winced at any encounter" (Fenn 334). This passage about Henty's didactic aim implies a strict societal code that sets the terms in which manliness can be described: men have to be both mentally and physically strong so that they are not rejected as weak "milksops". Accordingly, Henty saw it as his mission to teach boys how to grow into strong, self-confident and straightforward young men, who do not shy away from using violence if need be.

As the following review published in *The Daily Telegraph* in 1887 shows, "[t]his didactic aim was clearly recognised and applauded by the critics" (Richards, "Henty" 76): "Mr. Henty never loses sight of the moral purpose of his work – to enforce the doctrine of courage and truth, mercy and loving kindness, as indispensable to the making of an English gentleman" (qdt. in

Richards, "Henty" 76). It is noteworthy that the phrase "English gentleman" was a term which was less associated with gentility but more with the display of manly character traits like courage and resourcefulness in the second half of the nineteenth century.[5] Furthermore, the term draws attention to race, as Jeffrey Richards has pointed out: "Gentlemanliness is what distinguishes the Anglo-Saxon race from other races. ... Native races can be brave and their bravery acknowledged, but they are not gentlemen" (Richards, "Henty" 76). Accordingly, Henty is not only praised by *The Daily Paragraph* for promoting the necessary qualities that make for a gentleman but for teaching boys and young men what it means to be "English" at a time when Britain controlled vast parts the world.

Henty was not the only author of adventure literature for boys and young men who believed that literature could help to turn boys into strong and decisive men. In 1887, the English novelist Charlotte Mary Younge advised schools and parents to provide libraries for young male readers:

Boys especially should not have childish tales with weak morality or "washy" piety; but should have heroism and nobleness kept before their eyes; and learn to despise all that is untruthful and cowardly, and to respect womanhood. True manhood needs above all earthly qualities to be imposed on them, and books of example (not precept) with heroes, whose sentiments they admire, may also raise their tone, sometimes individually, sometimes collectively. (qdt. in Richards, Introduction 4)

Collectively, these statements indicate that "[t]he aim of juvenile literature was clearly stated for a century: it was both to entertain and instruct, to inculcate approved value systems, to spread useful knowledge, to provide acceptable role models" (Richards, Introduction 3).

---

5   The thought that a gentleman is not a gentleman by birth but someone who possesses "an aristocracy of Character" (qtd. in Smiles 382) goes back to Samuel Smiles who proposed this idea in his popular advice book *Self-Help* (1859): "Riches and rank have no necessary connexion [sic] with genuine gentlemanly qualities. The poor man may be a true gentleman, in spirit and in daily life. He may be honest, truthful, upright, polite, temperate, courageous, self respecting [sic] and self-helping, – that is, be a true gentleman. The poor man with a rich spirit is in all ways superior to the rich man with a poor spirit" (Smiles 399–400). As the century progressed, this idea gained currency in the United Kingdom. Gentlemanliness was no longer equated with gentility but with manliness.

The numerous imperial adventure tales, which were primarily published in magazines for juvenile male readers, were especially conscious in their depiction of manliness. There is a distinct formula which lies at the heart of almost every imperial adventure tale: the hero is a cool-headed, courageous, and clever adolescent boy or young man from the middle or upper class who never shrinks in the face of any challenge but faces it with determination and courage.[6] In an attempt to prove his manliness, this hero tours the world and engages in seemingly impossible quests in which his character is tried. The plot usually involves "a penetration into the imagined center of an exotic civilization, ... a place inhabited by another and darker race" (Showalter, *Anarchy* 81). The native people and the foreign country serve as "the backdrop for the white man's testing of himself" (Segal, *Slow* 173). The language in these stories is often sexualised, the countries to be conquered feminised, "to be opened up, penetrated, conquered" (ibid.). Yet (white) women almost never play a role in imperial adventure tales and if they do, they usually embody the stock character of the vulnerable woman who needs to be rescued from "the savages" by the heroic protagonist of the narrative. It is common to the heroes of adventure fiction to be confident in their belief that they know best how to solve problems: "Seldom do they ever betray a hint of uncertainty about their actions or assessments" (Boyd 59).[7] By featuring boys and/or young men who have to prove their men-

---

6   Interestingly, these stories were also popular among the increasingly literate working-class readership even though they choose young middle- and upper-class men as their heroes: "Working-class readers devoured this fiction as it took them out of themselves and allowed them to become privileged with the independence and arrogance of a Victorian hero. Hence, they placed themselves in the heroes' roles and ignored their own restricted horizons" (Boyd 49).

7   What is also evident in many adventure tales of the late-Victorian period, is a lack of Christian values like benevolence. Kelly Boyd argues that "[a]lthough authors never suggested a radical critique of society, at the same time they generally failed to conform to an evangelical vision of manners and morals" (60). This rejection of Christian values constitutes the major difference between the adventure tales of the story papers and the narratives that contributed to the Muscular Christianity movement of the mid-Victorian period. The movement, which was initiated by the English writers Charles Kingsley and Thomas Hughes, stresses the importance of bodily health and exercise, and celebrates homosocial comradeship. *Tom Brown's Schooldays* (1857), which was extremely popular among the Victorians, is set at Rugby School in the 1830s, for instance. The novel is based on Thomas Hughes's own time as a student at Rugby. Manliness for him and Kingsley "was synonymous with strength, both physical and moral" (Hall 9). The supporters of the movement believed that bodily activity enhances the

tal and physical toughness against all odds somewhere in the far-flung corners of the Empire, the genre forged a link between Britain's imperial mission and the predominant definition of masculinity.

With regards to Henty's fiction, Jeffrey Richards notes that "[t]here is comparatively little development of character. The hero normally has the necessary qualities (cool-headedness, courage under fire, resourcefulness, a sense of humour) at the outset of the book" (75). This argument can be expanded to adventure tales in general. It is also one of the major characteristics that distinguishes these stories from the more "serious" fiction for juvenile readers of the early and mid-Victorian periods. Where novels like Charles Dickens's *bildungsroman David Copperfield* (1849–1850) emphasise personal development and moral maturation, adventure tales stress the display of physical strength, resourcefulness, and bravery, combined with a boyish perkiness. While boys first had to grow up in order to become men in earlier juvenile fiction, adventure stories imply that one is not manly "by being gendered male" (Boyd 45) but by "learning to perform [the] role" (ibid.) of the cool-headed, confident, and courageous hero.

A figure who certainly knows how to perform this role is Jack Harkaway, a creation of the old Etonian and unsuccessful barrister Bracebridge Hemyng. Harkaway made his first appearance on the pages of the gender specific magazine *The Boys of England* in 1871 and would remain popular for a quarter of a century. Hemyng wrote numerous stories about Harkaway, who aged in the course of the narratives and was eventually replaced as a hero by his son and grandson.[8] The narrative which is most fruitful for the present discussion is the adventure novel *Jack Harkaway, After Schooldays; His Adventures Afloat and Ashore*, which was serialized in *The Boys of England* in 1872. In this book Jack has just finished public school and has some free time before starting his studies at Oxford. He decides to use this time to travel the world and signs on as a midshipman with a ship headed for China. With him on the ship are his best friend Harvey, his arch enemy from school, another midshipman with a questionable background, and his former teacher. Before reaching their destination, they get shipwrecked and the captain with most of the crew escapes in a lifeboat.

---

workings of the mind and thus turns a man into a better Christian – a thought that is usually absent in the adventure tales of the boys' story papers.

8   For a discussion of the sequel, see Louis James's "Tom Brown's Imperialist Sons." *Victorian Studies*, vol. 17, no. 1, Sep. 1973, pp. 89–99.

Thanks to Jack's resourcefulness, he and the other men left behind by the captain survive and are stranded on an island where they face many obstacles – among them head-hunting natives. Jack soon establishes himself as the leader of the group and overcomes all the obstacles they are confronted with.

What turns *Jack Harkaway, After Schooldays; His Adventures Afloat and Ashore* into an adventure tale par excellence is, of course, the shipwreck theme which stems from what is usually considered the first imperial adventure tale: Daniel Defoe's *Robinson Crusoe*.[9] The following passage further exemplifies the novel's preoccupation with imperial masculinity and reveals several characteristics that mark Jack as embodiment of the ideal. It depicts a dialogue between Jack and Harvey, which takes place after they have been shipwrecked in the "Chinese Sea":

> "What are we to do now?", asked Harvey.
> "I'll tell you, for I've been thinking all night. The storm is over, the ship is high if not dry, and she'll live where she is till the next storm comes."
> "When will that be?"
> "Who can say? In these beastly latitudes storms come on, of their own sweet will, at any time. The island we see before us looks as if it was deserted. All the better; there will be no niggers to eat us up."
> "Don't," said Harvey, with a shudder.
> "I didn't mean to funk you," continued Jack, "but you can't trust the inhabitants you find on those outlying islands in the China Sea. We must launch the raft, and take a lot of things on shore, and build a castle in which we can put our stores, because everything must be saved from the ship that is possible to carry away, and we have no time to lose. Another storm will finish the old 'Fairy'." (Hemyng 65–6)

First of all, this dialogue showcases Jack's composure and resourcefulness in the face of danger. While all others were not able to come up with a solution all night, Jack used the time to think of a plan which does not only offer them a way out of the water but also secures their survival ashore. He is also clever enough to realise that they must act as soon as possible, for another storm would certainly destroy the shipwrecked vessel. Accordingly, Jack is portrayed as a young man who keeps a cool head and uses his resourcefulness in order to ensure the

---

9   For an interesting article about *Robinson Crusoe* and the stories it inspired, see Green, Martin. "The Robinson Crusoe Story." *Imperialism and Juvenile Literature*, edited by Jeffrey Richards, Manchester, Manchester UP, 1989, pp. 34–52.

group's survival. Furthermore, the flippant way he talks about the inhabitants of the island who might "eat us up" shows that he knows how to perform the role of the brave and resolute hero who is not afraid of anybody – in contrast to Harvey, who shudders and asks Jack not to talk about such things. Jack's courage is pitted against the cowardice of his friend. Harvey thus serves as Jack's counter-image.

The passage, however, is not only interesting as a study of codes of manliness. It is also suffused with crude racism. Although Jack has never met the inhabitants of the island, he is convinced that they are not trustworthy. Furthermore, he implies that they might be cannibals. Hence, the indigenous people are already marked as deceitful "savages" before they make their first appearance in the book. This is not unusual for imperial adventure fiction. On the contrary: the display of an unquestioned patriotism which is entwined with a firm belief in the racial superiority of white Europeans is an integral part of the adventure tale formula. It is vital to note that such a portrayal of British manliness as superior requires the discrimination of marginalised groups. Robert Young has pointed out that "[o]ne of the main arguments of identity politics is directed not against the power structure implicit in this hierarchy, but also the fact that in this same-other relation, the identity of the other is only defined in relation to that of the same" ("Deconstruction" 200). For our purpose, it is more illuminating to turn this argument around: the white, male adventurer only gains his identity by setting himself off against the colonial Other.

G. A. Henty was particularly offensive in his tendency to exploit and reinforce racial stereotypes. In his writing, colonised people are repeatedly portrayed as "lazy, childlike, without capacity" (G. Arnold 79), as the following passage from *By Sheer Pluck: A Tale of the Ashanti War* (1884), a narrative about General Garnet Wolseley's expedition against the Ashanti in West Africa, illustrates:

> The intelligence of an average negro is about equal to that of a European child of ten years old. ... They are fluent talkers, but their ideas are borrowed. They are absolutely without originality, absolutely without inventive power. Living among white men, their imitative faculties enable them to attain a considerable amount of civilization. Left alone to their own devices they retrograde into a state little above their native savagery. (Henty 188)

This comment is made by Mr. Goodenough, an entomologist, who explains the supposed nature of the inhabitants of Western Africa to the hero of the novel as they prepare to go ashore. It is noteworthy that the native people are considered capable of acquiring "a considerable amount of civilization" when they live "among white men", according to Mr. Goodenough. By pointing out that they will remain in a state of savagery when left alone, the novel does not only render them inferior to white men, but also justifies Britain's imperial aspirations and the extension of British rule and culture all over the world. It is worth noting that Henty was aware of the propagandistic nature of adventure stories. In the interview mentioned above, he not only points out the didactic aim of his writing, but he also further boasts that his books "helped to foster the imperial spirit" (Blathwayt 8).

By reinforcing the belief in the superior position of the white Englishman, adventure tales fulfilled a crucial function at a time when theories about the national, cultural, and racial decay of the British were abundant. Towards the end of the nineteenth century, degeneration theory had developed from a discourse rooted in biology and medicine to a more general debate about racial and cultural decay. This is perhaps most evident in Max Nordau's *Degeneration*, which almost immediately caused a huge sensation after its publication in the United Kingdom in 1895.[10] In his book, "Nordau, a journalist, novelist, and a playwright rather than a scientist, refashioned a quasi-Darwinian notion that the human species could, under certain circumstances, devolve and argued that this was evident by the presence of particular literary and cultural trends" (Smith, *Demons* 15).[11] For Nordau, a degenerate person could be identified by certain "mental stigma" (Nordau 19), including emotionalism and despondency – character traits that stand in strong opposition to the ideal of imperial masculinity. By regarding effeminate emotionalism as an outward sign of degeneration, Nordau reinforces the idea that supposedly female emotions

---

10   Other examples include the aesthetic and decadent movements of the fin-de-siècle that drew "sinister analogies to Roman imperial decline and fall" (Brantlinger 230). The political activist and playwright George Bernard Shaw also attests Britain "an advanced stage of rottenness" (24) in *Fabian Essays in Socialism* (1889). Andrew Smith sees in "the ease with which the theory crossed the borders of various disciplines, with their different readerships," a sign that "the theory was always, in essence, a cultural narrative" (*Demons* 14–15).

11   Nordau explicitly launches an attack on Oscar Wilde, whose writing supposedly reveals a penchant for "immorality, sin and crime" (Nordau 320). It is a strange twist of fate that Nordau's book, which was first published in German in 1892, was translated to English and appeared in British bookstores only a few months before Oscar Wilde was sentenced to two years' hard labour for gross indecency in May 1895.

like sensitivity are unmanly and may even endanger the future well-being of a nation. He thus ties the decline of a nation to a discourse about masculinity. Yet, there is still hope, according to Nordau:

> The great majority of the middle and lower classes is naturally not *fin-de-siècle*. It is true that the spirit of the times is stirring the nations down to their lowest depths, and awaking even in the most inchoate and rudimentary human being a wondrous feeling of stir and upheaval. But this more or less slight touch of moral sea-sickness does not excite in him the cravings of travailing women, nor express itself in new aesthetic needs. (Nordau 7, emphasis in original)

While the aristocracy is singled out as clearly *"fin-de-siècle"*, the middle and working classes are capable to resist degenerate needs. In their responses to Nordau's theory, British commentators similarly emphasise the possibility of regeneration, as Egmont Hake's *Regeneration: A Reply to Max Nordau* (1895) illustrates, for example:

> No nation holds a higher responsibility than the English. Its vast possessions all over the globe, its financial and commercial supremacy, its ethical influence over all the English-speaking countries, marks it out as the standard-bearer of civilisation. … Degenerate Englishmen may still wish to meekly follow other nations, but our mission is to be practical, energetic, daring pioneers heading the march of progress. By using its great power and influence, the British nation can render invaluable service to humanity in the present crisis. (Hake 314)

By emphasising that the right attitude can put a stop to degeneration, "[t]he future of the 'State' is … linked to the vitality and courage of the individuals which compose it" (Smith, *Demons* 18) in Hake's text. This idea can be tied back to Samuel Smiles's best-selling advice book *Self-Help* (1859), in which he emphasises that "it is the energy of the individual man that gives strength to a State" (Smiles 224).[12] It is further noteworthy that Hake sees the English race as particularly capable of regeneration, thus presenting Britain not only as superior

---

12   In a similar vein, Edwin Ray Lankester presents degeneration as an imminent threat to "the white races of Europe" (Lankester 60), but one that can be prevented with mental vigour in *Degeneration: A Chapter in Darwinism* (1880).

to colonised countries but also to other Western countries – an attitude which reflects Britain's status as an imperial superpower.

This notion of masculinity also lies at the heart of many adventure tales of the time. They mimic Smiles and Hake in their assertion that a particularly English male gender performance can revitalise the nation and ensure the success of the British Empire. The following passage from *Jack Harkaway* provides a particularly revealing example in this context:

> "I wish a ship would come and take us away," said Harvey, with a sigh, as he thought of home.
> "So do I, but I don't know that I should go in her," replied Jack.
> Why not?" asked Harvey, in surprise.
> "You heard what Hunston said about a ship being wrecked on another island?"
> "Yes."
> "And an English girl being saved?" continued Jack.
> "And taken into the interior as a captive or slave or something," said Harvey.
> "That was it," replied Jack, adding, "well, I want to save that girl, and bring her away with me; and I shouldn't consider myself a man, or be happy all my life, if I had the chance of going away, and did not make something more than an effort to rescue that English girl."
> "By Jove! you're right, Jack. I always said you were a fine fellow," cried Harvey, his face speaking the admiration he felt.
> Involuntarily the boy's hands met in a cordial grasp.
> It was a silent compact between them to save the fair and unfortunate countrywoman at all hazards. (Hemyng 122–3)

By suggesting that it would reflect badly on his masculinity if he did not save a "countrywoman" from the "savages", Jack's decision to rescue the kidnapped girl is neatly tied to a discourse about manliness. It is noteworthy that Jack repeatedly calls the woman an "English girl", thus reinforcing racial boundaries. One cannot but wonder if it would have reflected badly on his masculinity if he had left a woman of colour with her kidnappers. Furthermore, the role of the woman is reduced to that of the "damsel in distress". She only serves as another means for Jack to prove his manliness.

The passage further offers an example of the sexualized language often applied in adventure fiction. By pointing out that he would not "go in her" (Hemyng 123), the ship is feminised, the boarding equated with a sexual act. The dialogue between Jack and Harvey is also interesting in terms of male homoerotic behaviour. Elaine Showalter argues that boys' fiction often "included strong if unconscious homoerotic feelings" (*Anarchy* 80). In line with this assumption, it is possible to interpret the involuntariness with which the boys' hands meet as a gesture which signals their subconscious same-sex desire, a desire which is cloaked as "a silent compact" (Hemyng 123). The word "silent" can be read as referring to the unspeakability of same-sex desire in this context. In a way that Eve Kosofsky Sedgwick has identified as typical for erotic triangles, in which homosexuality is expressed through the rivalry over a woman, the English girl serves as the conduit through which the boys' subconscious homoerotic desire is articulated.[13]

In order to save the girl, the band of boys eventually allies with another indigenous tribe. The boys thus seem to overcome their contempt for the "savage people". However, the narrative suggests that they only join forces with the inhabitants of the island in order to save the English girl. Since Jack mainly functions as the focalizer for the heterodiegetic narrator of the narrative, the reader learns what he thinks about the tribal people:

> Jack found his new friends very idle.
> They would fight, hunt, and fish, but nothing more.
> The women were made to do the principal part of the work on the island.
> All were very fond of dancing.
> The principal dance was called the minari.
> It consisted of men and women arranging themselves in two rows.
> They slowly twisted their bodies to the right and left, at the same time moving the extended arms and open hands in circles in opposite directions.
> The only motions of the naked feet were to change the weight of the body from the heel to the toe, and reverse it. (Hemyng 205)

The passage reveals Jack's presumption of a patriarchal tribal structure in which women do not work because they want to but because they are "made to do the principal part of the work" (Hemyng 205) by the male members – an assumption that reflects Jack's worldview more than it tells us about the native population. By pointing out their idleness, the passage further echoes common prejudices against tribal people, who were often seen as naturally inferior by the colonisers. Even the "principal dance" (ibid.) of the tribal people

---

13   Sedgwick bases her theory on René Girard's *Deceit, Desire, and the Novel* which illustrates that "in any erotic rivalry, the bond that links the two rivals is as intense and potent as the bond that links either of the rivals to the beloved" (*Between Men* 21).

is presented as particularly simple. The only thing they do with their "naked feet [is] to change the weight of the body from the heel to the toe" (ibid.). In this way, the culture of the native people is marked as primitive. The lack of shoes adds to their perceived savagery. In another text passage, the women of the tribe (who, of course, are very keen on marrying the white boys) are characterized as "far from being attractive" (Hemyng 204). Hence, not only the culture but also the body of the colonial Other is deemed inferior to the British. In this way, *Jack Harkaway* fuels imperialist thinking which, "as an ideology or political faith, functioned as a partial substitute for declining or fallen Christianity" (Brantlinger 228).

The final question that needs to be addressed regarding adventure fiction is: to what extent did narratives like Hemyng's *Jack Harkaway* really succeed in their mission to "foster the imperial spirit" (Blathwayt 8) and transform boys into strong men? Imperial adventure fiction is one of the most prolific genres of the latter decades of the nineteenth century and the advent of the twentieth century. Like most novels and short stories in the late Victorian era, adventure fiction was usually first serialized in magazines before being issued in hard cover. The circulation figures of journals for juvenile male readers indicate that the stories published in them reached an enormous readership: "the total circulation of the boys' story papers was well over a million a week, making them one of the most widely consumed forms of entertainment in late Victorian Britain" (Boyd 50). Accordingly, the stories published in these magazines were read by the majority of literate boys. What is even more remarkable than the sheer number of stories written for adolescents in this period, however, is the influence these tales asserted over young readers. A poll among 790 boys from selected schools conducted in the 1880s by the journalist Edward Salmon reveals that the majority of them favoured the gender specific magazine *The Boys Own Paper*. As their reason for liking the magazine, the boys – whose ages ranged from eleven to nineteen – gave "its admirable combination of instruction and amusement" (Salmon 18). They further asserted that they "place immense faith in what they read" (ibid.). This indicates that these magazines and the stories published in them had an enormous influence on the world view of their readers. Martin Green argues that adventure tales played a significant role in the shaping of the public consciousness and were even "more influential than the serious novel" (*Dreams* 49). He maintains that

the adventure tales that formed the light reading of Englishmen for two hundred years and more after *Robinson Crusoe* were, in fact, the energising myth of English imperialism. They were, collectively, the story England told itself as it went to sleep at night; and, in the form of its dreams, they charged England's will with the energy to go out into the world and explore, and conquer, and rule. (Green, *Dreams* 3)

Stephen Arata makes a similar point in *Fictions of Loss in the Victorian Fin de Siècle: Identity and Empire*: "A nation, or any imagined community, is held together in part by the stories it generates about itself" (Arata, *Fictions* 1). Arata further asserts that heroic narratives "are instrumental in the creation and maintenance of collective identities" (ibid.). The target audience of adventure tales were juvenile middle-class men – a group which was considered fundamental for the success of the imperial project. It is not surprising, therefore, that "one of the defining characteristics" of the genre "is its dual engagement with imperial discourse and issues surrounding the redefinition of middle-class masculinity" (Jamieson 75). It is safe to conclude that adventure tales provided a very useful political tool for the dissemination of qualities every man should possess or, at least, strive for in order to ensure British supremacy.

As we shall see in the next section of this chapter, stories of ghosts and other hauntings set in the British Empire also use the foreign environment in the colonies as a space for the negotiation of questions of masculinity, nationhood, and identity. However, imperial Gothic stories do not mimic the structure of adventure tales but function as a reversal of the genre. While the imperial setting is used as a testing-ground for the young hero in adventure tales, it becomes a site of personal failure in imperial ghost stories. In imperial adventure fiction, the protagonists successfully exhibit what they perceive as their "God-given right, as well as the duty, to govern and control those unable to do so for themselves" (Kantikar 194). For instance, in Robert Michael Ballantyne's *Coral Island* (1856), which relates the story of three boys who are shipwrecked in the South Pacific and subsequently marooned on an island, one of the heroes suggests to his comrades to take possession of the island by entering the service of its inhabitants: "Of course we'll rise, naturally, to the top of affairs. White men always do in savage countries" (Ballantyne 27). Similarly, in David Ker's "A Coral Prison; or, The Boy Hermits of the Indian Ocean", which was serialized in *The Boys Own Paper* from 4 October to 22 November 1890 and dwells on similar plot patterns as *Jack Harkaway*, the young heroes express the conviction that it is their right to colonise the island on which they are stranded: "we've got this island all to ourselves, and – for all we can see – we're the first white *men* that's ever put foot on it; so I reckon we've a clear right to take possession of it" ("Boy Hermits" 24, emphasis in original). The land the boys acquire is perceived as uninhabited because the native people are not seen as proper human beings, especially not as proper "*men*", as the emphasis on this term suggests. Indigenous people are repeatedly "denied the status of the human" (Byron and Punter 46) in adventure fiction: "the dangers to be encountered in the name of the spread of 'civilization' may include wild humans or human natives, but no real distinction is made between them" (ibid.). This is also the case in many imperial ghost stories, as we shall see. However, in contrast to adventure tales, the protagonists are usually shown as unable to govern the foreign countries. Instead of controlling the culture they encounter, they end up being controlled by it.

The Gothic Twist: Failing Men in Imperial Ghost Stories by Amelia B. Edwards, Rudyard Kipling, and Arthur Conan Doyle

Fears of degeneration and decay feature prominently in imperial Gothic fiction. A particularly persistent theme is the idea of "going native" (Brantlinger 230) which suggests that encounters with the supposedly savage colonial subject might lead to the degeneration of civilised Englishmen (Byron and Punter 39). Such stories are indicative of a profound xenophobia that perhaps finds its most powerful expression in Bram Stoker's *Dracula* (1897), in which the eponymous vampire threatens to invade the British motherland and people it with his kind. By presenting the foreign country, its inhabitants and their culture as something dangerous that might infect the civilised coloniser like an illness, imperial Gothic stories reinforce the binaries between civilised Western self and savage Eastern Other. Much in the same way as imperial adventure fiction, these stories thus reproduce the myth of the Orient as a place that is primarily marked by its Otherness. Accordingly, they contribute to a cultural construction of the Orient, which Edward Said has identified as fundamental to colonial power structures in his influential *Orientalism* (1978). According to Said, the tendency "to channel thought into a West and an East compartment" (*Orientalism* 46) leads to a "sense of Western power over the Orient [that] is taken for granted as having the status of scientific truth" (ibid). Imperial Gothic fiction thus reinforces a mode of thinking that is based on the binary opposition of Occident and Orient and legitimises the colonisation of Eastern countries. However, in contrast to imperial adventure fiction, the Otherness of the Orient is not used in order to reassure the British adventurers of their superior masculinity. By suggesting that the colonised people might "infect" the British colonisers with their perceived barbarism, imperial Gothic fiction implies the Englishmen's susceptibility to racial decay. Considering the tendency of Gothic writing, in general, and the figure of the ghost, in particular, to erode boundaries, it should also not surprise us to find that imperial ghost fiction does not only tend to reinforce the binary construction of Orient and Occident, but simultaneously undermines power structures between East and West.

The three ghost stories discussed in the following use elements of imperial Gothic fiction in order to dismantle the image of the courageous, cool-headed, and confident hero that imperial adventure tales so carefully construct and, in the process, make the shortcomings of the prevalent ideal of masculinity visible. While Amelia B. Edwards's story "The Phantom Coach" focuses on the inability of the protagonist to measure up to the ideal of imperial masculinity, Kipling's "The Mark of the Beast" and Conan Doyle's "The Brown Hand" present the imperial experience itself as unmanning. In all three stories, the body and mind of the white, middle-class male is shown as instable. These stories thus counter Nordau, Hake and Smile, who recognise the middle-class male as the upholder of Western civilisation.

Amelia B. Edwards's "The Phantom Coach"

The first ghost story discussed in this chapter is Amelia B. Edward's "The Phantom Coach", which was first published under the title "Another Past Lodger Relates His Own Ghost Story" in the 1864 extra Christmas number of Charles Dickens's family magazine *All the Year Round*. Edwards (1831–1892) was born Amelia Ann Blandford in London, daughter of an English banker and an Irish mother. She started writing literature in her childhood. Her poem "The Knights of Old" was published in a penny weekly when Amelia was only seven years old. Five years later, she sold her first story, "The Secret of a Clock". Edwards also showed a talent for painting and music and became one of the first female journalists in the United Kingdom in the 1850s. Besides her career as a writer, she supported the cause of woman's suffrage and became a notable traveller and archaeologist (Dalby, "Phantom"). Most of Edwards's ghost stories were published in the Christmas numbers of popular magazines.[14] Her tale "The Phantom Coach" is probably not the first story that comes to mind when talking

---

14   In his short biographical note on Amelia B. Edwards in *Shadows in the Attic: A Guide to British Supernatural Fiction, 1820–1950*, Neil Wilson notes that several of Edwards's sto-

about imperial Gothic writing. Edwards neither employs a colonial setting nor does she explicitly refer to imperial topics in her story. Also, typical elements of imperial Gothic – such as the fear that the supposedly primitive Other might infect the civilised Englishman – are missing. Nevertheless, I chose to include this story here because, of all three tales discussed in this chapter, the structure of Edwards's narrative displays the most striking similarities to imperial adventure fiction.

The struggle to conform to the hyper-masculine stereotype of the courageous, cool-headed, and confident hero celebrated in adventure stories is at the heart of "The Phantom Coach". Just like a ghost, the British Empire haunts the story as a present absence, an underlying "structure of attitude and reference" (Said, *Culture* 62) on which the ideal of masculinity is built. The story relates the tale of a newly-wed middle-class man, James Murray, who sets out on a hunting trip in the great outdoors of Northern England. Like the heroes in adventure fiction, the protagonist of Edwards's story is determined to prove his manly character in an inhospitable environment: "The wind was due east; the month, December; the place, a bleak wide moor in the far north of England" (Edwards 13). The accuracy with which the autodiegetic narrator describes the hunting conditions is reminiscent of the language explorers employ in their notebooks, thus establishing connections between their experience in the far reaches of the world and the hunting trip he undertakes "in the *far* north of England" (ibid., my emphasis). According to John MacKenzie, "[t]rapping and hunting lay at the heart of the nineteenth-century image of exploration, pioneering, and adventure" ("Hunting" 146). As such, hunting trips were often employed in juvenile literature as opportunities for the adolescent man to test himself. Naturally, the heroes of adventure fiction face unhospitable climes and wild animals with stern determination and prove their status as imperial men: "The hunter's grappling with the wild not only called for endurance and stamina, but also for qualities of 'character' admired by the Victorians, stoicism, application, command of self and followers, and the capacity to encounter high risk and triumph" (MacKenzie, "Hunting" 146). In Edwards's story, the wild moors of northern England serve as a substitute for the exotic environment in the colonies. However, in contrast to the resourceful and plucky heroes of imperial adventure fiction, James Murray lacks the necessary attributes of imperial masculinity and is unable to prove his manly character. Not only does he fail

---

ries were published anonymously. For this reason, it is "quite possible that some of her tales remain undiscovered due to their lack of attribution" (211).

to triumph and shoot a wild animal, but he also lacks the ability to maintain his orientation in an inhospitable environment and gets lost when it starts to snow. The protagonist of "The Phantom Coach" is thus already marked as unmanly at an early stage in the narrative.

In this context, it is instructive to compare the situation in which Murray finds himself with the shipwreck passage quoted earlier:

> And all this time, the snow fell and the night thickened. I stopped and shouted every now and then, but my shouts seemed only to make the silence deeper. Then a vague sense of uneasiness came upon me, and I began to remember stories of travellers who had walked on and on in the falling snow until, wearied out, they were fain to lie down and sleep their lives away. Would it be possible, I asked myself, to keep on thus through all the long dark night? Would there not come a time when my limbs must fail, and my resolution give way? When I, too, must sleep the sleep of death. Death! I shuddered. (Edwards 14)

While Jack Harkaway is not dependent on the help of others to survive on a strange island in the South China Sea, the autodiegetic narrator of "The Phantom Coach" cannot come up with a way out of his current misery but is susceptible to "a vague sense of uneasiness" (Edwards 14). He even lets his fancy get the better of him and shudders when he thinks of "stories of travellers who had walked on and on in the falling snow until, wearied out, they were fain to lie down and sleep their lives away" (ibid.). It is noteworthy that the narrator compares his situation to that of travellers, thereby indicating his identification as an explorer and adventurer. However, in contrast to Jack Harkaway, who is not even afraid of man-eating "savages" but is determined to fight them, the protagonist of Edwards's story lacks the resourcefulness, resolution, and courage characteristic of imperial masculinity. The passage thus suggests that the narrator cannot compete with the cool-headed heroes of imperial adventure fiction.

In the remainder of the story, the narrator's actions continue to stand in opposition to dominant scrips of masculinity. After stumbling about in the snow for a while, Murray encounters a "gnome-like" (Edwards 15) man with "a malicious grin" (ibid.) who brings him to his master, an eccentric astrologer, who has withdrawn from "the outer world … three-and-twenty years" (ibid. 17) ago. In a different way than Murray, the astrologer's masculine gender performance is presented as deficient according to conventional standards. While once a respected scholar, the astrologer "was branded as a visionary, held up to ridicule by [his] contemporaries, and hooted from that field of science in which [he] had laboured with honour" (Edwards 19) because of his interest in "phenomena which, under the names of ghosts, spectres, and supernatural appearances, have been denied by the sceptics" (ibid. 18). The astrologer views his exclusion from the world of science with contempt and laments the fact that "our men of science ... reject as false all that cannot be brought to the test of the laboratory table" (ibid.). His hermit-like existence in a house somewhere in the Yorkshire moors signals his status as an outcast, not only from academia but from society in general. For Lowell T. Frye, the story illustrates that "the high priests of rationalism have the power to 'exile' if not silence all who refuse to conform to orthodox modes of thinking" (179). Frye further views Murray's encounter with the man as a pivotal moment in the story, which "makes possible the supernatural experience" (Frye 177) that is to follow. While I agree with Frye that the encounter with the astrologer influences Murrays supernatural experience later in the story, I suggest that the phantoms are not real ghosts but a product of the protagonist's frenzied state of mind.

After having dinner with the astrologer, the narrator leaves his shelter to catch the night mail. The servant is ordered to accompany him to the road the night mail takes to the nearest town. Before they part, the eerie servant tells him that, nine years ago, the carriage was involved in an accident, in which six people died. For the reader, it comes as no surprise that James Murray then also finds himself surrounded by the phantoms of the former passengers when the coach finally arrives (in fact, the story's title suggests the ghostly carriage ride all along):

> I turned to the passenger on the seat beside my own, and saw – oh Heaven! How shall I describe what I saw? I saw that he was no living man – that none of them were living men, like myself! A pale phosphorescent light ... played upon their awful faces; upon their hair, dank with the dews of the grave; upon their clothes, earth-stained and dropping to pieces; upon their hands, which were the hands of corpses long buried. Only their eyes, their terrible eyes, were living; and those eyes were all turned menacingly upon me!
> A shriek of terror, a wild unintelligible cry for help and mercy, burst from my lips as I flung myself against the door, and strove in vain to open it. (Edwards 23)

What is noteworthy in this passage, besides Murray's panic (indicated by the numerous exclamation marks) and his inability to exit the coach, is the way the passengers are described. While the title of the story identifies them as phantoms, their appearance marks them as revenants who clearly show signs of death and decay. Like zombies, they literally seem to have risen from their graves with their earth-stained clothes and their rotten features. At the time when Edwards's story was published, there was no clear-cut differentiation between ghosts and zombies. In fact, the term "zombie" is a "West-African word for 'ghost'" (Botting, "Zombies" 751). It is clear though that Edwards's decaying phantoms differ from most spectres of Victorian and Edwardian literature and anticipate later depictions of zombies as "ugly, rotten and inhuman" (ibid.). What is missing, however, is a marked "desperation to feed" (ibid.), which is central to the idea of zombies today. Instead, Edwards's phantoms are described as dangerous in their perceived intention to take Murray with them to the grave. After a short ride on the phantasmal coach, the vehicle crashes and all goes dark. When Murray awakes "one morning from deep sleep" (Edwards 23), he finds out that he fell over a precipice and almost died. He has "a broken arm and a compound fracture of the skull" (ibid. 24). However, there is no trace of a coach crash.

It is left open whether the phantoms are foreign intruders or whether they are located in the mind of the ghost-seer. The story is told in retrospect by the main character himself and the reader only has access to the story through his biased narrative. There is no heterodiegetic narrator who can validate the supernatural events. Hence, on the narratological level, the story is constructed in a way that makes it impossible to tell whether the ghosts are real or not. Yet, if we look at the story more closely, there are several hints that suggest that the ghosts are a product of Murray's imagination.

As has by now been established, the astrologer's speech already "plants the idea of occult phenomena in Murray's and the reader's mind" (Frye 179) and it is more than likely that his seemingly supernatural experience is "the joint product of hypothermia and an overexcited imagination" (ibid.). It is also possible to view the ghosts as a result of the narrator's compound fracture of the skull, a medical emergency, which often causes confusion and a loss of consciousness. What should also make us suspicious is the narrator's repeated insistence on the supernatural character of the events he witnessed: "The circumstances I am about to relate to you have truth to recommend them" (Edwards 13), he emphasises in the very first sentence of the story. He goes on to tell the reader that the events happened twenty years ago, but that his "recollection of them is as vivid as if they had taken place yesterday" (ibid.). It is clear that the narrator does not want anyone to question his narrative authority: "All I entreat ... is that you will abstain from forcing your own conclusion upon me. ... I desire no arguments. My mind on the subject is quite made up, and, having the testimony of my own senses to rely upon, I prefer to abide by it" (ibid.). The narrator clearly does not want others to even consider the possibility that the ghosts are the product of his imagination, a circumstance which would reflect badly on his masculinity "at a time when theories about hallucination and its relation to the troubled psyche were in circulation" (Liggins, "Gendering" 41). As established in the introduction, hallucinations were often regarded as a sign for mental illnesses, hysteria in particular. The disease was treated as a gynaecological illness and linked to abnormalities in the female reproductive organs until well into the nineteenth century. While doctors and psychologists gradually started to diagnose men with hysteria in the second half of the nineteenth century, it still carried "the stigma of being a humiliatingly female affliction" (Showalter, *Anarchy* 106). Especially in France and Austria, a considerable number of medical publications dealing with male hysteria was published. One of the most influential works on male hysteria was written by Emile Batault, who recognised the illness in some of the patients in the Salpêtrière's special ward. In his study, Batault describes hysterical men as "timid and fearful men, whose gaze is neither lively nor piercing, but rather, soft, poetic, and languorous" (qtd. in Showalter, *Anarchy* 106). It is noteworthy that, for Batault, there is a connection between hysteria and unmanly behaviour. In order to avoid being diagnosed with this feminising malady, the narrator of "The Phantom Coach" insists that the ghosts that he saw were real.[15]

The identification of the hysteric as effeminate was widely accepted, which "made it difficult for doctors to accept the hysteria diagnosis in men who seemed conventionally virile" (Showalter, "Hysteria" 289). This is also the case in Edwards's "The Phantom Coach". At the end of the story, the narrator reveals that he told the story once before. He confided in the doctor who treated him after his adventure: "I never told my wife the fearful events which I have just related to you. I told the surgeon who attended me; but he treated the whole adventure as a mere dream born of the fever in my brain" (Edwards 24). The doctor carefully avoids calling the hysterical breakdown by its name. He rather offers an explanation that is acceptable with the contemporary

---

15   For an illuminating account on the history of hysteria, see Mark S. Micale's *Approaching Hysteria: Disease and Its Interpretations*.

ideal of masculinity: brain fever. As Valery Pedlar maintains, "[b]rain fever is a common phenomenon in nineteenth-century fiction" (64). For instance, Jonathan Harker in *Dracula* (1897) and Catherine Linton in *Wuthering Heights* (1847) also suffer from the illness. According to Pedlar, "both physicians and non-medical people believed that brain fever could be brought on by emotional shock or excessive intellectual activity" (ibid.). While recognised as an illness originating in the mind, brain fever never had the same emasculating implications as hysteria. Elaine Showalter argues that "the cultural denial of male hysteria is no accident: it's the result of avoidance, suppression, and disguise" (*Hystories* 64). Lori Jirousek even goes so far as to detect the ideal of masculinity as the source of male hysteria: "male doctors diagnosed men's neuroses to preserve acceptable masculine standards for male patients rather than examining the possibility that masculine standards themselves might cause neuroses" (Jirousek 53).

In contrast to the astrologer, Murray does not display an unwillingness to conform to normative standards of masculine behaviour in Edward's "The Phantom Coach". The story clearly implies that the protagonist is willing to assume the role of the adventurous hunter. Throughout the story, he presents himself as an ideal Victorian man who is not worried about his own life but cares about his young wife who is "breaking her heart with suspense and terror" (Edwards 19). The "thought of all suffering in store for her throughout this weary night" (ibid. 13) is so unbearable to him that he even leaves the shelter he found at the astrologer's place to catch the night mail. He thus pushes his wife into the gendered role of the vulnerable female who needs male protection. Just as in many adventure tales, women are absent from the story. Murray only refers to his wife in order to bolster his masculinity. It is apparent that he agrees with the Victorian gender roles which place him in the position of the active protector and his wife in that of the passive female. However, despite this presentation of himself as active, strong, and self-confident, he needs to be rescued in the end. Hence, Murray lacks the ability to fulfil the gendered role assigned to him. By demonstrating Murray's unsuccessful struggle to measure up to the ideal of imperial masculinity, the narrative illustrates that even if men try to conform to normative standards of masculinity, they might be unable to do so.

While imperial adventure tales propagate that the right attitude automatically turns boys into resourceful and courageous young men, Edward's tale suggests that this attitude might turn into a destructive force and wreck the male adventurer. Even the life-threatening accident does not lead Murray to question an ideal that made him go out into a lonely moor with his gun in deepest winter and risk his life in the first place. He cannot free himself from the gender expectations of his time but is haunted by his ambition to conform to the ideal. In this way, Edwards's tale makes apparent the pitfalls of a hegemonic concept of gender.

Rudyard Kipling: "The Mark of the Beast"

The second supernatural story discussed in this chapter takes us to one of the most important colonial possessions of the Empire: British India. "The Mark of the Beast" is not only set in India, but it was also written by an author who could draw on first-hand experience when writing about the country: Rudyard Kipling. It is difficult to imagine a writer more entangled with the British Empire than Rudyard Kipling. Among his Anglo-Indian contemporaries, the Indian-born author and journalist had "a reputation for knowing more about the colonial underworld than the police did" (Arata, *Fictions* 163). For British readers, his writings gave an insight into the distant culture and frame of mind of Indian people, as the following quote from an unsigned review about Kipling's short story collection *Plain Tales from the Hills* (1888), published in the *Daily News* on 2 November 1889, illustrates: "It may safely be said that *Plain Tales from the Hills* will teach more of India, of our task there, of the various peoples whom we try to rule, than many Blue Books" (Lang 48). By explaining the foreign Other to British readers, Kipling's writings fulfilled a significant cultural function that served the colonial mission. Naturally, this perception of Kipling as spokesman for the British imperial task has strongly influenced the reception of his writings. However, there is more to Kipling than "[t]his familiar image ... as popular apologist for the dominant ideology" (Arata, *Fictions* 151). Especially his early Gothic fiction betrays a markedly ambivalent attitude towards the imperial project. This ambivalence is evident in Kipling's "The Mark of the Beast", which was initially rejected for publication in England in 1886 with the strong recommendation to "instantly ... burn this detestable piece of work" (qdt. in Hamilton 133). This strong reaction to the story is indicative of the story's potential to alienate and offend English reading audiences. Eventually, the story was published in two instalments in the *Pioneer*, the Allahabad newspaper, in 1890 (Davies, *Strange* ix). In a way, the story thus had to go "colonial" in order to be voiced.

Rather than a story about ghosts and phantoms, "The Mark of the Beast" is a narrative about possession.[16] It relates the tale of three Englishmen in British India who become entangled in supernatural happenings when one of them pollutes the statue of a Hindu deity. The story is told by an unnamed homodiegetic narrator who is spending New Year's Eve in a British club with his friends Strickland, a policeman, and Fleete, who recently "owned a little money and some land in the Himalayas" (Kipling, "Mark" 3) and whom the narrator describes as "a big, heavy, genial, and inoffensive man" (ibid.) with a limited knowledge of the indigenous population of North India.

At the beginning of the story, British India is presented by the narrator as a place where Englishmen can celebrate their Englishness in an exclusively male environment:

On New Year's Eve there was a big dinner at the club, and the night was ex-cusably wet. When men foregather from the uttermost ends of the Empire, they have a right to be riotous. ... It was a very wet night, and I remember that we sang 'Auld Lang Syne' with our feet in the Polo Championship Cup, and our heads among the stars, and swore that we were all dear friends. Then some of us went away and annexed Burma, and some tried to open up Sudan and were opened up by Fuzzies in that cruel scrub outside Suakim, and some found stars and medals, and some were married, which was bad ... . (Kipling, "Mark" 3–4)

The narrator's remarks serve several functions: First of all, they imply that he, Strickland, and Fleete belong to a privileged group of white, middle-class men. More specifically, they are presented as "'clubbable' men, the type of empire builder who would no doubt establish a club at any convenient meeting point in the colonial world" (W. Hughes 12). Women are absent from this environment, just as in many adventure tales of the period. It is a telling absence that "implicitly warns of the debilitating effects of woman" (Stott 70). The narra-tor only indirectly refers to women when he states that some of the men got married at some point after the New Year's Eve party at the club in India. By calling marriage a "bad" (Kipling, "Mark" 4) thing, the narrator identifies het-

---

16   As established in the introduction, the ghost story is not a clearly defined genre. This work considers supernatural tales which have a moment of haunting at the core of the narrative – be that in the form of actual ghosts, imagined ones, Doppelgängers, or pos-sessions.

erosexual bonds as a threat to male comradeship.[17] Furthermore, the reference
to the stars and medals men can earn themselves in the far-flung corners of
the British Empire highlights the opportunities for individual advancement in
the colonies. It is also noteworthy that the men sing Robert Burn's "Auld Lang
Syne' with … [their] feet in the Polo Championship Cup" (ibid.), for the song as
well as the game point to the ways in which the British Empire absorbs the culture of its possessions and dependencies: while "Auld Lang Syne" is originally a
Scots-language poem, the game of polo was imported to the United Kingdom
from India. Finally, the narrator attempts to excuse Fleete's behaviour later
that evening by pointing out that the night is "excusably wet" (ibid. 3) and that
they "have a right to be riotous" (ibid.). He further emphasises the "inoffensive"
(ibid.) nature of his friend.

This characterisation of Fleete is contested by his actions as the story progresses. On their way back from the party at the club, the drunken Englishman
runs up the stairs of a Hindu temple and offends Hindu priests by "gravely

---

17   A story that even more explicitly warns of the perceived threat women pose to male
friendship is Kipling's "The Man Who Would Be King", which was published two years
previous to "The Mark of the Beast". "The Man Who Would Be King" is often attributed
to the adventure genre. It relates the story of two men, Daniel Dravot and Peachey
Carnehan, who embark on a journey to Kafiristan, a region of Afghanistan that "no Englishman has ever been through" (Kipling, "King" 201) and plan to become the rulers
of the region: "we will subvert that King and seize his Throne and establish a Dynasty"
(ibid.). The two men make a pact to stay away from liquor and women, "black, white,
or brown" (ibid. 203), so that they do not "get mixed up with one or the other harmful" (ibid.). The potentially dangerous influence of women (English and foreign) is thus
heightened from an early point in the narrative. The two men succeed in their quest
and Dan becomes the ruler of the Kafirstani, who believe him to be a god. However,
Dan eventually breaks his pact with Peachey and requires a wife. Dan's infidelity to
Peachey is soon punished, for Dan's chosen bride is so afraid of her future husband
that she bites him, thus revealing that Dan, who starts bleeding, is a human being.
Dan is decapitated by the Kafirstani. Peachey brings back his head, but also dies soon
after that. "The Man Who Would Be King" is a story about a failed adventure. It is still
possible, though, to read the tale as an affirmation of imperial masculinity, for the
story strongly implies that the male adventurers only fail because Dan cannot resist the
appeal of women and betrays his symbolic marriage with another man: "Dan's real
crime is not his exploitation of the Kafirstani, but his emotional betrayal of Peachey
and his violation of their contract of male marriage" (Showalter, Anarchy 94). The message of the story is clear: male adventurers must stay away from women. The story
elevates homosocial bonds between men and thus indirectly justifies the exclusion of
women from homosocial institutions in Victorian Britain.

grinding the ashes of his cigar-butt into the forehead of the red stone image of Hanuman[,] … the Monkey God" (Kipling, "Mark" 4). He justifies his vandalism by alluding to a passage in Revelation, Chapter 13, in which the "Beast out of the Earth", which is commonly identified as the Anti-Christ, requires those who worship him to wear a mark on the right hand or the forehead: "Shee that? Mark of the B-beasht! *I* made it. Ishn't it fine?" (ibid., emphasis in original), Fleete slurs after his deed. By putting a mark on the statue's forehead, he identifies Hanuman as a disciple of Anti-Christ and, in extension, implies that the local population worships a false prophet. In this way, Fleete degrades the indigenous religion and indirectly justifies the missionary idea of British imperialism. Fleete's branding of the statue of Hanuman further evokes connotations of branding as a mark of belonging. By branding the Hindu deity, Fleete draws attention to the status of India as British domination and thereby reinforces his position as white coloniser. In this context, the mark can also be interpreted as a metaphor for the success of the British Empire which leaves its mark on every culture the British conquer. Fleete's branding of the statue is thus a demonstration of British superiority in more than one way: it highlights British supremacy and presents Christianity as the only true religion.[18]

Until this point in the story, the narrative shows striking parallels to imperial adventure fiction. British India is presented as "the site of 'masculinist imaginings' in which men [can] enjoy homosocial comradeship in physically challenging, arduous circumstances far from … the damaging influences of 'the feminine'" (Beynon 31). The particularly English character of the white male adventurers is pitted against the supposedly uncivilised character of the indigenous people who worship a false prophet. What primarily marks the three men in Kipling's story as superior is their status as white men: "being a White Man, for Kipling and for those whose perceptions and rhetoric he influenced, was a self-confirming business. One became a White Man because one *was* a White Man; … [b]eing a White Man was therefore an idea and a reality" (Said, *Orientalism* 227, emphasis in original). By stressing the inferiority of the foreign people

---

18   Ardel Haefele-Thomas has made a similar point. In their article "That Dreadful Thing That Looked Like a Beautiful Girl: Trans Anxiety/Trans Possibility in Three Late Victorian Warewolf Tales" Haefele-Thomas argues that Fleete uses Hanuman as an ashtray, thus expressing his disregard for the foreign culture: "Metaphorically speaking, Kipling could very well be making a much grander political point about the ways the English continually disrespected and defiled India" (Haefele-Thomas, "Dreadful" 102). Haefele-Thomas does not point out the problematic implications of branding, however.

and their culture, the Englishmen invariably gain in strength. As Edward Said has remarked in *Orientalism*, the dualism between superior West and inferior East points to the workings of power structures in general: "Such strength and such weakness are as intrinsic to Orientalism as they are to any view that divides the world into large general divisions, entities that coexist in a state of tension produced by what is believed to be a radical difference" (Said, *Orientalism* 45). As will be shown in the following, the intrusion of the supernatural into the story unsettles these dualisms.

Western superiority starts to be threatened when Fleete is cursed by a naked, faceless leper, who emerges from behind the statue of Hanuman and, in revenge for his disrespect of the god, leaves a mark on Fleete's breast. In the following, the Englishman's character regresses to that of a beast within a day: first, he shows a craving for raw meat; he then develops an aversion to bright lights; eventually, there seems nothing left of a human being:

> [W]e saw Fleete getting out of the window. He made beast-noises in the back of his throat. He could not answer us when we shouted at him. He spat. I don't quite remember what followed, but I think that Strickland must have stunned him with the boot-jack or else I should never have been able to sit on his chest. Fleete could not speak, he could only snarl, and his snarls were those of a wolf, not of a man. The human spirit must have been giving way all day and have died out with the twilight. We were dealing with a beast that had once been Fleete.
> … We bound this beast with leather thongs of the punkah-rope, and tied its thumbs and big toes together, and gagged it with a shoehorn, which makes a very efficient gag if you know how to arrange it. (Kipling, "Mark" 9)

Fleete's transgression to a beast is reminiscent of a werewolf transformation. "Fleete is no longer just a human or just an animal, but a hybridized combination of both" (Haefele-Thomas, "Dreadful" 103). As with adventure fiction, it is instructive to read Kipling's story in light of late-Victorian anxieties about degeneration and their entanglement with Darwinian theories of evolution. Darwin's findings in *The Decent of Man, and Selection in Relation to Sex* (1871) formed the basis for concerns about the possibility of social, racial, and cultural decay, "for if humans could evolve, it was thought they could also *devolve* or degenerate, both as nations and individuals" (Spencer 311). However, as Kathleen Spencer has observed, "Darwinian evolutionary theory blurred the boundaries between human and animal in not one but two ways: by the famous argument that humans and apes had a common ancestor, but also by the implied hierarchy at the end of *The Decent of Man* which leads from the ape-like ancestor through primitive peoples to civilized Europeans" (Spencer 310). Within this hierarchy, indigenous people occupy a liminal position between human and animal – a position which justified their often-inhumane treatment under British rule. As a werewolf, Fleete similarly becomes a hybrid figure and thus loses his status as a human being. This development is underscored by a shift of the personal pronoun from "he" to "it" in the above passage.

The colonised Other is presented as responsible for Fleete's transgression. "The Mark of the Beast" thus expresses the concern that the racially superior white man might become infected by the Otherness of the foreign country and regress to the barbaric – a theme which Melissa Edmundson has identified as characteristic for stories by male writers of colonial Gothic fiction (*Colonial* 8). This fear of "going native" (Brantlinger 230) reflects a quintessentially Western point of view in which the colonised subjects are characterised by their Otherness. "The Mark of the Beast" is thus closely linked to a Eurocentric world view and the Western construction of the Orient as exotic and potentially monstrous. As Edward Said has pointed out, "European culture gained in strength and identity by setting itself off against the Orient as a sort of surrogate and even underground self" (*Orientalism* 3). The depiction of the foreign culture as something alien and dangerous justifies the imperial mission in that it presents the colonised peoples as savages who must be tamed and controlled. The imperial project is thus cloaked as a civilising mission intended to bring peace and culture to the colonies.

However, it would be short-sighted to view "The Mark of the Beast" solely as a warning about the corrupting and potentially dehumanising influences of the foreign Other. Said's concept of orientalism not only as a Western strategy to enforce power structures but also as a projection of repressed desires and anxieties (*Orientalism* 8) provides a useful approach to understanding how ideas about the imperial Other ultimately say more about the colonisers than about the colonized subjects. While the colonial Other is presented as the source of Fleete's regress, the story similarly stresses the susceptibility of the English middle-class man to racial decay. In this way, "The Mark of the Beast" mirrors *fin-de-siècle* anxieties about the degeneration of the English race. In this context, it is perhaps worth noting that the narrative counters the prevailing assumption that the degenerate is marked by outward signs, for Fleete's regress is shown as a mental rather than a physical progress.[19] "The Mark of the Beast" thus suggests that "appearances might provide no real indication of the personality within" (Buzzwell).

The story also problematises Fleete's reckless attitude towards the foreign culture and religion. This is another point where this "adventure story with Gothic elements" (Brantlinger 227) departs from most non-supernatural fiction set in the colonies. In most adventure fiction, the contempt for and ignorance towards supposedly savage peoples is part of the masculine identity of the white, male adventurer. David Ker's "A Coral Prison; Or, The Boy Hermits of the Indian Ocean" serves as a good example in this context. In the story, the boys repeatedly violate the religious traditions of the indigenous people and penetrate sacred spaces. For instance, they ignore the request not to approach the tomb of a "Mohammedan saint" (Ker 85), who is buried on the summit of a mountain in the centre of the island. However, instead of being punished for their behaviour, the boys are rewarded for their disrespect towards the native culture. When a tsunami hits the island, they are spared from certain death only because of having climbed the sacred mountain, whereas the death of the native population is presented as a Godly punishment. The indigenous people are referred to as "doomed" (Ker 118) by the heterodiegetic narrator and the storm that precedes the tsunami is described as "the thunder of heaven" (ibid.). The religiously tinted language applied here suggests that the native population is rightly wiped from the face of the earth. The "The Mark of the Beast" counters such stories that present the violation of the foreign religion as acceptable and even desirable by showing that Fleete's violation of religious sanctity has fatal consequences.

"The Mark of the Beast" also dwells on anxieties about Britain's national decline which intensified towards the *fin de siècle*. Although the British Empire

---

19   The notion that degeneracy is "potentially lurking within certain types of physiology" (Smith, "Degeneration" 175) was developed by the French psychiatrist B. A. Morel, who coined the term *dégénérescence* in the 1850s (Ledger and Luckhurst 1). Morel looked for answers to mental diseases in heredity and, in the process, established a theory of social decay. In line with Morel, the Italian physician Cesare Lombroso developed the notion of criminal atavism according to which the criminal could be distinguished by a set of facial anomalies. For Lombroso, features reminiscent of apes like a sloping forehead or unusually big ears mark the born criminal as degenerate and savage. Andrew Smith has observed that these theories "ultimately culminate[d] in a movement for eugenic regulation" (Smith, "Degeneration" 175).

continued to expand its frontiers and its influence over the world, particularly in Africa, its supremacy was contested by the rise of other political and economic powers such as Germany and the United States and by a series of military setbacks in the colonies and possessions (Arata, "Occidental" 622). What also came as a shock to Victorian society was the death of the military hero General Charles George Gordon, who was defeated in Khartoum in 1885 by a Muslim leader, the Mahdi. Many Victorians interpreted the death of the national idol as a sign that the empire was being undermined by the "lower" races (Showalter, *Anarchy* 5). By showcasing the supernatural power of the colonised Other, on the one hand, and the defencelessness of the Englishman against this power, on the other hand, "The Mark of the Beast" reverses colonial power structures. In this context, it is noteworthy that the healthy middle-aged Englishman is cursed by a naked leper whose "disease was heavy upon him" (Kipling, "Mark" 5). While the man's nakedness marks him as uncivilised, his disease implies weakness and decay. Being defeated by a sick leper has the effect of unmanning the supposedly superior Englishman. It further adds to the story's horror that the Hindu deity Hanuman is commonly depicted as a man with the face and tail of a monkey. By emphasising the supernatural power of the god's disciple and the impotence of the Western man, the story does not only imply the possibility of devolution but reverses the hierarchical order between human and ape altogether.

As the story continues, Western superiority is further eroded. In an attempt to cure Fleete, Strickland and the narrator consult a doctor who diagnoses the Englishman with rabies – a disease which, as Ardel Haefele-Thomas has pointed out, "destroys the boundaries between human and animal since all mammals can be fatally affected equally" ("Dreadful" 103). Fleete's liminal position is thus further emphasised. The doctor declares that there is no cure for Fleete's condition. His inability to help Fleete showcases "the story's insistence upon the impotence of Western rationality as paradigm of civilisation and progress, and the power of the native supernatural culture" (Generani 27). Eventually, Strickland and the narrator are forced to believe in the superiority of the foreign culture:

> So Dumoise [the doctor] left, deeply agitated; and as soon as the noise of the cart-wheels had died away, Strickland told me, in a whisper, his suspicions. They were so wildly improbable that he dared not say them aloud; and I, who entertained all Strickland's beliefs, was so ashamed of owning to them that I pretended to disbelieve. (Kipling, "Mark" 10)

The passage reveals that both Strickland and the narrator suspect that the leper has bewitched Fleete. However, the Englishmen are ashamed of their suspicions. While Strickland can only utter them in a whisper, the narrator even pretends to disbelieve him, which suggests that they are both aware that their acceptance of the foreign religious power reflects badly on their status as Western men. By believing in the leper's supernatural abilities, the two Englishmen admit the superior power of the cultural Other. In this way, the narrative reverses the colonial hierarchical order and reveals British supremacy as illusory.

Eventually, the two men see no other option but to capture the leper and torture him into lifting the curse:

> Strickland wrapped a towel round his hand and took the gun-barrels out of the fire. I put the half of the broken walking stick through the loop of fishing-line and buckled the leper comfortably to Strickland's bedstead. I understood then how men and women and little children can endure to see a witch burnt alive; for the beast was moaning on the floor, and though the Silver Man had no face, you could see horrible feelings passing through the slab that took its place, exactly as waves of heat play across red-hot iron – gun-barrels for instance.
> Strickland shaded his eyes with his hands for a moment and we got to work. This part is not printed here. (Kipling, "Mark" 12)[20]

This is an immensely dense passage that allows for a number of readings. First of all, the narrator's refusal to reveal the extent of their torture suggests that he is not willing to disclose the brutality of British rule in India. He indirectly invites the readers to fill the gap left by him with their own thoughts. As Gustavo Generani has observed, "[t]here is no imperial civilising mission in those behaviours, but plain barbarism" (25). It is noteworthy, however, that the narrator is careful not to present their actions as barbaric, but justifies their brutality by comparing the torture to the burning of a witch, an event that was usually witnessed by "men and women and little children" (Kipling, "Mark" 12), as the narrator points out. The torture is thus presented as something that they only "endure" (ibid.) because they are convinced of the rightfulness of their actions. In addition, the comparison highlights the leper's similarities with a witch. Like

---

20   Earlier in the story, the narrator explains that he is referring to the leper as "the Silver Man" because the illness has affected the man's skin to a degree that makes it appear "like frosted silver" (Kipling, "Mark" 5).

a witch, he put a curse on a human being and is thus justly punished. By high-lighting the supposed monstrosity of the indigenous culture and the danger it poses for civilisation, the story emphasises the necessity of Britain's imperial intervention and even presents torture as a legitimate means to control the de-monic power of the Other: "Although Fleete is the first aggressor, the narration shows him as a victim whose suffering vindicates the torture of the Other. It is a position founded on an implicit argument: that British barbarism is justified by the influence of a barbarian context" (Generani 30). Nevertheless, the pas-sage betrays the men's brutality, for the narrator sees "the Silver Man" (Kipling, "Mark" 12) express "horrible feelings" (ibid.). In this context, the narrator's as-surance that he "buckled the leper *comfortably* to Strickland's bedstead" (ibid. 12, my emphasis) can only be understood as crude sarcasm. It is also worth noting that Strickland and the narrator duplicate Fleete's crime by branding the leper with gun-barrels. The act of branding here can be understood as an attempt to re-establish British superiority over the colonised Other. At the same time, the two Englishmen acknowledge the superior power of the Hindu man by tor-turing him into lifting the curse. Hence, the passage simultaneously reinforces and erodes the binary oppositions between civilised Englishman and barbaric Other, coloniser and colonised, victim and aggressor.

While the two Englishmen succeed in their mission to help Fleete, it is not glory that they get as a reward:

> [Strickland] caught hold of the back of a chair, and, without warning, went into an amazing fit of hysterics. It is terrible to see a strong man overtaken with hysteria. Then it struck me that we had fought for Fleete's soul with the Silver Man in that room, and had disgraced ourselves as Englishmen for ever, and I laughed and gasped and gurgled as shamefully as Strickland, while Fleete thought that we had both gone mad. … [I]t is well known to every right-minded man that the gods of the heathen are stone and brass, and any attempt to deal with them otherwise is justly condemned. (Kipling, "Mark" 13–14)

In contrast to the heroes of imperial adventure tales, who are able to sustain their gentlemanly vigour in the face of any challenge, Strickland and the nar-rator do not come through their adventure unscathed. On the contrary, they "disgrace [themselves] as Englishmen" (Kipling, "Mark" 14) in more than one way. The above quotation reveals that the two agents of empire regress to an un-manly state when they are overtaken by hysteria, an illness which was strongly associated with femininity, as was pointed out earlier. Furthermore, they accept the authority of the "gods of the heathen" (ibid.) in order to rescue Fleete, something which is "justly condemned" (ibid.) as the narrator concludes. By acknowledging the superior power of the foreign religion, the two Englishmen have embarked on a "shameful regress into superstition" (Sage 15) and damaged their status as "right-minded man" (Kipling, "Mark" 14). British India is thus presented as a site of personal failure.

Arthur Conan Doyle: "The Brown Hand"

The last story discussed in this chapter is by Arthur Conan Doyle (1859–1930), an author who is today mainly known for the creation of the most popular detective of all time. Conan Doyle wrote four novels and over fifty short stories about the eccentric detective Sherlock Holmes. The rest of his vast oeuvre is often overshadowed by this popular figure. Yet Conan Doyle wrote "numerous novels and tales, plays, poems, histories, pamphlets on various issues, propaganda for spiritualism, and even a co-authored libretto" (Watts xii). Besides his literary career, he worked as a physician. This profession repeatedly took him to the British colonies. Soon after his graduation from Edinburgh University in 1881, he served as a medical officer on the steamer *Mayumba*, for instance, which commuted between Liverpool and the west coast of Africa. He also volunteered as a doctor in South Africa during the Second Boer-War, "tending the sick and wounded, at least once coming under heavy artillery fire" (ibid. x). Although he later defended the imperial mission in South Africa, Conan Doyle believed – "unlike the many imperialists of the day" (ibid. xii) – that indigenous people should be left "unmolested and at peace" (qdt. in Stashower 47). In the "The Brown Hand" Conan Doyle seems to dwell on his personal experiences as both a doctor and an Englishman who has travelled the world.

In the ghost story, a British physician, Sir Dominick Holden, who has earned a reputation as "the most distinguished Indian surgeon of his day" (Conan Doyle, "Brown" 71) in British India, is punished for his ignorance towards the religion and culture of the indigenous people. While still in colonial service, Holden becomes haunted by the ghost of an Afghan whose hand he amputated and kept as a fee for his services, despite the man's belief that "the body should be reunited after death and so make a perfect dwelling for the spirit" (ibid. 79). Holden returns to England, but the phantom keeps troubling the English surgeon: "when I tell you that for four years I have never passed one single night, either in Bombay, aboard ship or here in England, without my sleep being broken by this fellow, you will understand why it is that I am a wreck of my former self" (ibid. 78), he confides to his nephew, Dr Hardacre, who functions as the homodiegetic narrator of the story. In very much the same way in which Kipling's "The Mark of the Beast" explores the idea that English gentlemen might be contaminated by Eastern ideas in the colonies, "The Brown Hand" illustrates what can happen to men in the far-flung corners of the British empire: they might be reduced to a wreck of their former selves. Furthermore, "The Brown Hand" deals with the anxiety that the outward movement of British imperialism might be reversed and "that England itself will be invaded and contaminated by the alien world" (Byron and Punter 39–40). Hence, both stories dwell on imperial Gothic motifs that reinforce the Othering of the foreign culture by presenting it as an evil force. However, at the same time, they also make a statement about British imperialism and illustrate that the white man's ignorance towards the traditions and religion of the colonised people is responsible for their misfortune.

When Holden relates the story to his nephew, he justifies his actions thus:

> After much persuasion he consented to the operation, and he asked me, when it was over, what fee I demanded. The poor man was almost a beggar, so that the idea of a fee sounded absurd, but I answered in jest that my fee should be his hand and that I proposed to add it to my pathological collection.
> To my surprise he demurred very much to the suggestion, and he explained that according to his religion it was an all-important matter that the body should be reunited after death and so make a perfect dwelling for the spirit. The belief is, of course, an old one, and the mummies of the Egyptians arose from an analogous superstition. I answered him that his hand was already off, and asked him how he intended to preserve it. He replied that he would pickle it in salt and carry it about with him. I suggested that it might be safer in my keeping than his, and that I had better means than salt for preserving it. On realising that I really intended to keep it carefully, his opposition vanished instantly. "But remember, sahib," said he, "I shall want it back when I am dead." I laughed at the remark and so the matter ended. (Conan Doyle, "Brown" 79)

Even though Holden emphasises that he asked for the hand "in jest" (Conan Doyle, "Brown" 79), the fact that he eventually persuades the Afghan to accept his deal indicates that he considers the hand of a brown man as a valuable contribution to his pathological collection. In this way, the brown hand is both objectified and exoticized. The story thus testifies to the Othering of colonised people (and their body parts) in the British Empire. "Also, the literal taking of the hand relates as well to the metaphorical taking of the hand in a marriage ceremony, a common British description of the relationship between England and India under British Imperialism" (Hay 136). It is further noteworthy that Holden attempts to cloak his desire to possess the brown hand under a guise of generosity, for he emphasises that "the idea of a fee sounded absurd" (Conan Doyle, "Brown" 79). The story thus provides an interesting allegory to British expansionism, which was often presented by its supporters as a civilising mission rather than a means to extend Britain's political and economic power.[21] Even the Afghan's explanation that his religion demands the reunification of the body after death does not prompt Dominick Holden to change his mind. Instead, he abandons the man's concerns as mere "superstition" (ibid.). The religious beliefs of the foreign culture are thus presented as something which must not be taken seriously. The fact that Holden light-heartedly rejects the Afghan's warning that he shall want the hand back when he is dead is further indicative of his disregard for the foreign culture. In his attitude to recklessly ignore the traditions of the native population, Dominick Holden resembles the heroes of adventure literature like Jack Harkaway or the boys in Ker's "A Coral Prison". However, in contrast to these adventurers, Holden eventually pays the price for his ignorance towards the foreign culture.

When the Afghan's ghost starts to haunt the surgeon, he realises that the spirit can only be put to rest if the Afghan is reunited with his missing hand – a seemingly impossible task, for the hand was destroyed in a fire in Holden's house in Bombay. Holden could only save a part of his pathological collection, which our narrator describes thus: "I glanced over them and saw that they were of a very great value and rarity from a pathological point of view: bloated organs, gaping cysts, distorted bones, odious parasites – a singular exhibition of the products of India" (Conan Doyle, "Brown" 76). India is presented here as a place rife with the marks of disease and decay. The story thus establishes

---

21 For instance, in a speech delivered at the annual dinner of the Royal Colonial Institute in March 1897, the British statesman and then Secretary of State for the Colonies, Joseph Chamberlain, maintains that British rule has "brought security and peace and comparative prosperity to countries that never knew these blessings before" (Chamberlain 139). He even justifies British warfare by pointing out that "[y]ou cannot have omelettes without breaking eggs; you cannot destroy the practices of barbarism, of slavery, of superstition, which for centuries have desolated the inferior [sic] of Africa, without the use of force" (ibid. 140).

connections between India and degeneration theory. The fact that the narrator uses the phrase "products of India" in order to describe the collection suggests an attitude towards the colonised people similar to that which Karl Marx calls "the fetishism of commodities" (Marx 81) in *Capital: A Critique of Political Economy* (1867). According to the German philosopher and socialist, objects are "'haunted' by the labour it took to produce them, as the capitalist processes by which the object came into existence are thrust out of sight in a consumerist market" (Bissell, *Haunted Matters* 28–9). The exploitation of the workers who produced the commodity is obscured and substituted by a fetishism for them (Marx 83, 86–87). This is also the case in "The Brown Hand". Rather than seeing the "products" for what they are – organs and body parts that belong to actual human beings –, they are regarded as curiosities that contribute to a valuable and rare collection. The fact that they tell stories about loss and suffering is thrust out of sight. The appearance of the ghost in Conan Doyle's narratives reverses this process. In a way that conforms to Jacque Derrida's concept of hauntology, according to which history refuses to be forgotten, the Afghan's ghost makes apparent that Holden's "products of India" (Conan Doyle, "Brown" 76) are haunted by the people they once belonged to and by their stories.

Dominic Holden has been haunted by the Afghan's ghost for four years when he finally confides in his nephew, who is himself a physician and a member of the illustrious Society for Psychical Research.[22] By this time, the nightly appearance of the ghost has left its mark on Dominick Holden:

> His figure was the framework of a giant, but he had fallen away until his coat dangled straight down in a shocking fashion from a pair of broad shoulders. ... [T]he appearance and bearing of the man were masterful, and one expected a certain corresponding arrogance in his eyes, but instead of that I read a look which tells of a spirit cowed and crushed, the furtive, expectant look of a dog whose master has taken the whip from the rack. (Conan Doyle, "Brown" 73)

---

22   Founded in London in 1882, the Society for Psychical Research (SPR) was the most prominent association which devoted itself to the investigation of paranormal phenomena in the late-Victorian and Edwardian periods. It brought together renowned public figures like Robert Louis Stevenson, Arthur Conan Doyle, Sigmund Freud, and Gustav Jung with fellows of the Universities of Cambridge and Oxford. Shane McCorristine suspects that it was through "their intellectual quality, ... as well as their consistent will-to-investigate, [that] these figures established psychical research as a profoundly influential cultural constant in the late Victorian and Edwardian culture" (104).

In contrast to imperial adventure tales, where the young hero engages in a dangerous quest or journey in the colonies and returns to the United Kingdom a better and stronger man, Dominick Holden's return is marked by physical decay: the way the coat dangles down from Holden's shoulders is described by the narrator as "shocking" (Conan Doyle, "Brown" 73), thus indicating his bodily collapse. Holden's physical weakness is accompanied by "a look which tells of a spirit cowed and crushed" (ibid.). The surgeon's regress is thus presented as both a physical and a mental process. Considering prevailing anxieties about the future of the colonial project, it is possible to read Holden's regression as an allegory for the crumbling British Empire that is being eroded by foreign powers and starts to wither like the old man in Conan Doyle's narrative.[23]

As has been pointed out in the introduction, the figure of the ghost was often employed by women writers to critique women's liminal, ghost-like position within Victorian society. In "The Brown Hand", Conan Doyle provides us with a similar metaphor. Akin to the Afghan's ghost, Dominick Holden is reduced to the ghost of his former self: "My nerve was a byword in India. Even the Mutiny never shook it for an instant. And yet you see what I am reduced to – the most timorous man, perhaps, in all this country of Wiltshire" (Conan Doyle, "Brown" 75). This short passage reveals that the ghostly appearance of the Afghan has robbed the once so brave doctor, who could not even be unsettled by "the Mutiny" (ibid.), of his manly vigour and "reduced" (ibid.) him to a "timorous man" (ibid.). It is noteworthy that the surgeon uses the word "reduced" in this context which evokes associations to theories of degeneration. This association is further forged by the description of Dominick Holden's look as that of a "dog whose master has taken the whip from the rack" (ibid. 73).

The ghostly further serves to demonstrate the return of the imperial repressed in "The Brown Hand". By detecting Dominick Holden's ignorance towards the colonised people as the source of his decline, the story questions the rightfulness of the imperial mission. The surgeon's disregard for the Afghan's culture is reminiscent of Fleete's contempt towards the Indian people and their religion. By showing what the consequences of contempt and ignorance towards the culture of the imperial Other might look like, "The Brown Hand" criticises the arrogance and ignorance of the British colonisers. In addition, the

---

23   Simon Hay similarly argues that the description of Dominick Holden "is indicative of a whole set of imperial anxieties, in which Holden's body stands in allegorically for the British Empire, that the story sets out to address" (136).

story "articulates profound anxieties about Western scientific practices" (Macfarlane 82) and hints at the coloniser's macabre and racist interest in what is called "the products of India" (Conan Doyle, "Brown" 76) earlier in the story. The encounter with the Afghan is related by Holden himself. Hence the reader cannot be certain whether the amputation was necessary in the first place. Like the Afghan man himself, we can only take Dominick Holden's word for it. There is nobody who could confirm the doctor's diagnosis. The story thus opens up a space for speculations about the rightfulness of the amputation. By implying that the operation might not have been necessary, the story again points to the dehumanisation and objectification of the foreign Other, whose bodily integrity is subordinated to Holden's scientific interests. It adds to the story's horror that Holden cannot fulfil his promise to keep the hand safe.

The Afghan's "position as undifferentiated object of imperial intervention continues" (Macfarlane 83) as the story progresses. In an attempt to satisfy the restless spirit, Holden's nephew organises a brown man's hand and puts it in one of the glass jars that Holden uses for his pathological collection. However, Dr Hardacre's first attempt to help his uncle fails because he did not even think of getting the correct hand. While the ghost is missing its right hand, Hardacre took the left hand of an Indian man, who was lying dead in a British hospital. It is noteworthy that Hardacre duplicates his uncle's deed. He recklessly takes the hand of a man of colour. Aside from the nationality, the reader does not get any information about the dead man. His personal history is thrust out of sight. Eventually, Hardacre succeeds in his mission. Once the ghost finds the right hand of another brown man in the jar, he is satisfied and disappears. By suggesting that any brown hand will do, the body of the colonised Other is objectified yet again. In addition, the story implies the superior intelligence of the white doctor, who can trick the Afghan, who, in turn, is depicted as stupid and easily satisfied. To a certain extent, the story thus rehabilitates the image of the superior, middle-class Englishman.

The recovery of white, middle-class masculinity is also implied by Holden's recovery at the end of the story. Like Fleete in "The Mark of the Beast", Dominick Holden regains his manliness when the haunting is lifted: "He had suddenly turned younger by twenty years at the least. His eyes were shining, his features radiant, and he waved one hand in triumph over his head" (Conan Doyle, "Brown" 82). Both stories thus suggest that revitalisation is possible. Nevertheless, the men's temporary regression blurs the binary divisions between civilized Western self and savage Eastern Other.

According to Ruth Heholt and Joanne Ella Parsons, "post-colonialism looks at the process that 'othered' and 'abnormalised' colonised people in relation to a dominant white ideal of the normal" (13). In "The Mark of the Beast" and "The Brown Hand" it is also the body of the white, middle-class male that is othered and abnormalized. While Fleete regresses to a liminal state between human and wolf, Holden is reduced to a ghost-like existence. In this way, the stories not only suggest the Englishmen's susceptibility to degeneration, but also stress that the agents of Empire do not go unpunished. The imperial repressed return to haunt their oppressors. The supernatural punishment is self-inflicted in both stories. The white colonisers Fleete and Dominick Holden are shown as responsible for their misery. Their feeling of racial and moral superiority and their ignorance towards the traditions of the foreign culture are identified as highly problematic. My intention is not to suggest that these stories fully grasp the extent of the violation experienced by the colonised people through Britain's interference with their culture. Being written from a quintessentially British perspective, they could never do so. Nevertheless, they question Britain's imperial politics and the ideal of manliness which was forged by it. Furthermore, Kipling's and Conan Dole's imperial Gothic tales display the cruelty of Britain's imperial practices. This cruelty is revealed in the torture scene in Kipling's "Mark of the Beast". It also underlies the doctor's insistence on keeping the hand of a poor Afghan man in Conan Doyle's "The Brown Hand". Both stories thus illustrate the consequences of British imperialism – for both the colonised people and the British intruders.

By problematising the consequences of British imperial rule, "The Mark of the Beast" and "The Brown Hand" address a topic which repeatedly recurs in postcolonial Gothic fiction, a sub-genre of the Gothic which "often centres on the unresolved conflict between imperial power and former colony" (Newman 86). As Gina Whisker has noted, the "[p]ostcolonial is variously understood as referring to the period after colonialism, and undercutting and operating against the values of colonialism" (511). According to this definition, the postcolonial exclusively deals with the aftermath of colonialization. Postcolonial Gothic would then chronologically supersede imperial Gothic fiction. Stories like "The Mark of the Beast" and "The Brown Hand" problematise this notion of the postcolonial as referring to the time after colonialism only. Although these stories were written in the colonial period, they offer profound critiques of Britain's imperial project.

Ella Shohat has drawn attention to the ambivalence inherent in the prefix "post". In "Notes on the 'Post-Colonial'" she argues that the prefix in postcolonial is both epistemological and chronological, indicating "the notion of a movement beyond" and signalling "a passage into a new period and a closure of a certain historical event or age" (Shohat 101). To attribute "The Mark of the Beast" and "The Brown Hand" thoroughly to imperial Gothic fiction would be to ignore their potential to go *beyond* the idea of imperialism. Both stories use the potential of the Gothic to transgress boundaries in order to reveal the consequences of British imperialism.

In this context, it is useful to employ Derrida's hauntolgical concept, again, and what he calls the "spectrality effect" (48) in *Spectres of Marx*.[24] As a revenant, "the specter is the future, it is always to come" (ibid.). Accordingly, the ghost is a being "whose very nature is to violate chronological time" (Margree, *British* 2). It therefore erodes our understanding of a linear development of history and draws our attention to the fact that the present and the future are inevitably entangled with the past. The spectre's nature to undo "this opposition, or even this dialectic, between actual, effective presence and its others" (Derrida 48) is what

---

24   It is important to be aware that Derrida's *Specters of Marx* has been subject to much critical debate, especially in the field of postcolonial studies. Gayatri Chakravorty Spivak, for instance, criticises Derrida for his Western worldview and the neglect of subaltern women in her response to Derrida's work, "Ghostwriting" (1995). According to Spivak, Derrida offers us "the best of the West" (Spivak 68). Derrida also fails to see systematic connections between capitalism and colonialism, as Spivak remarks: "he cannot know the connection between industrial capitalism, colonialism, so-called postindustrial capitalism, neocolonialism, electrified capitalism, and the current financialization of the globe, with the attendant phenomena of migrancy and ecological disaster" (ibid.). In "Reconciling Derrida: 'Specters of Marx' and Deconstructive Politics", Aijaz Ahmad also points out that Derrida's deconstructivist ideas have been used by anti-Marxist scholars (see esp. pp. 92–102). While Ahmad acknowledges that Derrida himself is certainly not right-wing, he maintains that "Derrida's own deconstructionist project ... unwittingly *contributed* to openings for resurgence of a fully-fledged right-wing intelligentsia" (98, emphasis in original). By contrast, Robert Young defends Derridean deconstruction and argues that Derrida "developed deconstruction as a procedure for intellectual and cultural decolonization" (193). He further maintains that the idea of reinterpretation, which is at the core of deconstruction, has been used by postcolonial theorists: "postcolonial history uses this technique against the historical narrative of colonialism that has hitherto been presented" (Young, "Deconstruction" 196). While I find the above criticism justified, I believe that Derrida's hauntological discourse provides a useful framework for the understanding of ghosts, in general, and the ghost story, in particular. I also believe that Derrida's framework can be extended to marginalized groups, even if Derrida fails to do so himself.

Derrida calls the "spectrality effect". Derrida's insistence on a "looping circularity of history" (Punter, "Spectral Criticism" 262) underscores the notion that the postcolonial is already present in the colonial moment. According to Gina Wisker, "postcolonial experience is inevitably haunted by a colonial past; ... and traces of the legacy of silence, pain, humiliation, and dispossession ... reappear in spectral figures" (511). The figure of the ghost in Conan Doyle's story is particularly significant in this context, for it signals that colonialization is not over with colonisers like Dominick Holden leaving the country but that the present is always affected by the past. The ghost of the mutilated Afghan returns to reclaim what has been taken from him by the coloniser Dominick Holden, thus reminding the doctor of his colonial deeds.

Several Gothic scholars have also argued against a definition of the postcolonial Gothic as a literary movement that begins only "after the departure of the invasive power source" (Hughes and Smith 1). James Procter and Angela Smith problematise the distinction between imperial Gothic and postcolonial Gothic in their essay "Gothic and Empire", for example. They argue that texts written within the colonial period can "offer a critique of the empire from within" (Procter and Smith 97). In "Defining the Relationship between Gothic and the Postcolonial", William Hughes and Andrew Smith propose to locate "the onset of the postcolonial at the point in which indigenous culture, with its power structures, has its integrity violated by external (cultural or physical) interference" (Hughes and Smith 1). They claim that

> the Gothic is, and has always been, *post*-colonial, and this is where, in the Gothic text, disruption accelerates into change, where the colonial encounter – or the encounter which may be read or interpreted through the colonial filter – proves a catalyst to corrupt, to confuse or to redefine the boundaries of power, knowledge and ownership. (Hughes and Smith 1)

In line with this argument, "The Mark of the Beast" and "The Brown Hand" expose, criticise, and reverse power structures. It would be highly problematic, however, to completely attribute "The Mark of the Beast" and "The Brown Hand" to the postcolonial Gothic. As pointed out above, both stories simultaneously erode and reinforce the binaries West/East, civilised/savage, ruler/subject. They are thus marked by an ambivalent treatment of the colonial encounter. I suggest, therefore, to situate them on the borderline between imperial Gothic and postcolonial Gothic – along with other colonial Gothic literature critical of the imperial project like Joseph Conrad's *Heart of Darkness*.[25] It is important to see "The Mark of the Beast" and "The Brown Hand" not only as Western texts that replicate the stereotypical depiction of the East as savage and monstrous, but as profound "responses to cultural guilt" (Arata, "Occidental" 623). By detecting the men's ignorance towards the colonised people as the source of their decline, these narratives question the ideal of manliness which these men display. In this way, they problematise the recklessness which constitutes a significant part of imperial masculine identity in colonial adventure fiction.

* * *

All three tales discussed above invert the success-formula of the imperial adventure tale and, in the process, reveal the shortcomings of white middle-class masculinity. They do so in markedly different ways. Amelia B. Edwards's "The Phantom Coach" focuses on the protagonist's inability to prove his manly vigour in an inhospitable environment. While imperial adventure fiction suggests that it is possible to master every situation with a plucky and brave attitude, Edward's tale illustrates that men's eagerness to conform to the idea of imperial masculinity might actually bring them into dangerous and life-threatening situations. Although not explicitly mentioned, the British Empire is present in the story as a sort of underlying "structure of attitude and reference" (Said, *Culture* 62). Rudyard Kipling's "The Mark of the Beast" and Arthur Conan Doyle's "The Brown Hand" more directly explore the effects of Britain's imperial politics. Both stories use a colonial setting in order to blur the binary divisions between West and East, civilised and savage, ruler and subject – dualisms which are clear-cut in colonial adventure stories, where the white adventurer is able to prove his manly stamina and resourcefulness against the backdrop of the foreign country and its supposedly untamed, uncivilised inhabitants. In contrast to the stock figure of the young adventurer, Kipling's

---

25   Melissa Edmundson has made a similar point: "this book ... seeks to expand our current understandings of imperial literature by focusing on women's responses to empire as an important bridge between imperial Gothic texts of the nineteenth and twentieth centuries and postcolonial Gothic literature of the later twentieth and twentieth-first centuries" (Edmundson, *Colonial* 2). Edmundson justifies her reading by pointing out that "many nineteenth- and twentieth-century Colonial Gothic texts – and, I would argue, particularly ones written by women – were progressive critiques of power structures" (ibid. 6)

and Conan Doyle's imperialists become inflicted by the "Otherness" of the foreign country and regress to a lesser state of being. Both stories are tales of decline that call our attention to the contemporary discourse about individual, cultural, and national degeneration. They are thus expressions of the same cultural anxiety that informed some of the most well-known Gothic texts of the late-nineteenth century, including Robert Louis Stevenson's *Dr. Jekyll and Mr. Hyde*, Bram Stoker's *Dracula*, and Joseph Conrad's *Heart of Darkness*. By unsettling the hierarchical relationship between Western coloniser and Eastern subject, these stories also anticipate characteristics of post-colonial fiction and voice concerns about the inhumane treatment of the indigenous population in the colonies.

Chapter 4
Male Scepticism and Paternal Ghost-Seeing: Science and Spiritualism in the Ghost Story

The ghost stories we have discussed so far focus on men who fail to adhere to contemporary standards of masculinity and experience their transgression as shameful. For these men, ghost-seeing is not a positive thing, but, instead, evokes associations with femininity and/or madness, thereby threatening the status of the bourgeois male at a time when men were expected to display mental and physical toughness. While some of the stories have confronted us with "real" ghosts, the boundaries between illusion and reality were markedly blurred in other stories, thus suggesting that the male protagonists might be haunted by a distorted picture of manliness rather than actual ghosts. Visual experience is shown as potentially unreliable in these stories, reflecting on the psychological state of the ghost-seer rather than representing reality.

The texts discussed in this chapter give the relationship between men and ghost-seeing an additional twist, firstly by challenging the notion of reality itself as it was defined by Victorian "materialist, masculine, patriarchal culture" (R. Jackson xvii), and secondly by suggesting that ghost-seeing might actually be empowering for men and initiate a redefinition of male gender identity. In order to illustrate this, the chapter is divided into two sections. In the first section, we will look at Bram Stoker's "The Judge's House" (1891) and Lettice Galbraith's "In the Séance Room" (1893). Both stories were published in the early 1890s, a time in which unprecedented developments in engineering and science had irrevocably transformed everyday life and sparked a widespread belief in scientific advancement and progress. For many people, scientific epistemology replaced religious paradigms of knowledge and – in analogy to imperialism – functioned as a substitute for the faith in God in an increasingly secular world.[1] "The Judge's House" and "In the Séance Room" engage critically with the Victorian enthusiasm for scientific knowledge and materialism by indicating the inefficiency of natural laws and reason in the face of supernatural forces. In both stories, we encounter sceptical male materialists from professional middle-class backgrounds who flatly dismiss the possibility of ghosts and haunting – with fatal consequences. By suggesting that there are phenomena that evade rational explanation, Galbraith's and Stoker's narratives challenge the male protagonists' notions of reality which are restricted "to what is familiar and under rational control" (R. Jackson xvii). Ultimately, the punishment for the men's disbelief in the supernatural is death.

In contrast to these doomed figures, the male protagonists we will encounter in the second section of this chapter overcome their initial scepticism towards the supernatural and acquire a spiritual awareness which opens up a path for a new concept of masculinity that includes the acceptance of supposedly female character traits like tenderness and sensitivity as part of masculine gender identity. My analysis in this section focuses on Margaret Oliphant's "The Open Door" (1882) and Rudyard Kipling's "They" (1904). I have chosen these two stories because they address a key aspect of what I will call the New Man (in analogy to the New Woman movement of the 1890s): fatherhood. While Oliphant's story showcases a military man who is forced to redefine his gender identity in order to rescue his son, Kipling's tale features a protagonist who embarks on a spiritualist journey in order to find a way to deal with the loss of his child. My central argument in this section is based on Sarah Bissell's observation that the experience of witnessing a spectre does not necessarily have "a shattering or feminising effect on male protagonists" ("Reconstructing" 63) in nineteenth-century literature. However, while Bissell argues that the "ghostly encounters enable the male protagonists to develop a form of spiritual sensitivity which strengthens rather than undermines their embodiment of traditionally masculine traits" (ibid.), my reading of Oliphant's "The Open Door" and Kipling's "They" suggests a departure from dominant perceptions of masculinity in favour of a new concept of manliness

---

1   Richard Noakes has made a similar point and observed that the late-Victorian "period has been called 'the age of science', a period of increasing belief that the cosmos was governed by immutable natural laws rather than capricious supernatural agencies or divine whim" (Noakes 23).

that accommodates qualities traditionally associated with the realm of the mother such as love, nurture, and compassion.[2]

A topic which resurfaces in both sections of this chapter is the relationship between science and spiritualism. Rather than being marked by mutual rejection and hostility, as might be presumed, the relationship between the two was rather ambiguous. Spiritualism rose to popularity in Britain during the 1850s and remained "a conspicuous ... part of Victorian cultural life, with its mediums, ... societies and private and public séances" (Noakes 26) for the rest of the century. While some scientists wholeheartedly rejected the idea that the spirits of the dead can connect with the living through mediums, others were inclined to believe in the possibility of spirit communication. Together with psychic investigators, supporters of spiritualism even sought to place supernatural encounters on a scientific footing. They thought it possible that "the erratic phenomena of the séance could be reduced to natural laws" (Noakes 24) and that "scientific epistemology would verify the materiality of the unseen" (Owen xvii). As Alex Owen points out in her influential *The Darkened Room: Women, Power, and Spiritualism in Late Victorian England* (1989), this endeavour "was actually less odd than it might seem, for throughout the [nineteenth] century scientists were continuing to push back the boundaries of what was known about matter. ... Many believers argued that spiritualism provided scientific evidence for the spirit's survival after death, and did not perceive science as inimical to spiritualist beliefs" (xvi). The belief in the possibility of spirit communication was also fostered by the fact that advancements in science and technology were themselves experienced as supernatural by many people: "Disembodied voices over the telephone, the supernatural speed of the railway, near-instantaneous communication through telegraph wires: the collapsing of time and distance achieved by modern technologies ... was often felt to be uncanny" (Brown et al. 1). From the supposedly "mysterious powers of electricity" it was only a small step to "the baffling feats of mesmerists and apparently real communications from the dead elicited by Spiritualist mediums" (ibid.).

---

2   Bissell also investigates Kipling's "They" in her essay "Reconstructing Masculinity in Charlotte Riddell's 'The Open Door' and Kipling's 'They'" (2017). Coincidentally, the second story under consideration in her essay, Riddell's "The Open Door" (1882), was published in the same year and bears the same title as the story discussed by Margaret Oliphant in this chapter.

Although men did not "constitute an unimportant minority of believers" (Owen xii), spiritualism was commonly associated with femininity.[3] Women were regarded as "particularly gifted" (Owen 1) in spirit communication and thus became mediums more often than their male contemporaries. It was partly a woman's coding as a self-less, sensitive, and caring "Angel in the House" that paved the way for women's engagement in spiritualism: "female mediumship was predicated in part on a nineteenth-century view of women as morally and spiritually refined creatures who were particularly suited to the negation of self which mediumship demanded" (Owen 12). In contrast to women's perceived link to self-negation, sensitivity, and spirituality, "the association of masculinity with reason, authority, and resolve was consolidated" (Tosh, *Man's Place* 47). The stories discussed in the following undermine this association of men with science and rationality, on the one hand, and of women with spiritualism and emotionality, on the other hand. While Bram Stoker's "The Judge's House" and Lettice Galbraith's "In the Séance Room" critique a concept of masculinity which is based solely on reason/rationality and social status, Margaret Oliphant's "The Open Door" and Rudyard Kipling's "They" feature male protagonists who reconcile science and/or reason with occult forms of knowledge, thus suggesting a concept of masculinity that is not perceived as antithetical to feminine emotionalism.

Ghostly Punishments: Supernatural Forces and the Limits of Scientific Epistemology in Bram Stoker's "The Judge's House" and Lettice Galbraith's "In the Séance Room"

In this section, I will discuss the ways in which Bram Stoker's "The Judge's House" and Lettice Galbraith's "In the Séance Room" problematise the elevation of rational materialism as a basis for male gender performance. The male characters whom we will encounter here belong to a scientific community that values reason above all and embraces rationality and social status as hallmarks of ideal male gender performance. They represent a rational masculinity that differs from the ideal of imperial masculinity insofar as it marginalises

---

3   As Alex Owen has maintained, men were actually just as involved as women in the spiritualist movement: "The numerous accounts of personal séance experiences, together with the published records of local spiritualist societies, suggest that as many men as women were attracted to spiritualism." (Owen xii).

qualities such as courage and self-sacrifice, which are central to the ideal of the brave soldier hero, in favour of an intellectual mindset and scientific knowledge.

While not as omnipresent in popular fiction as the ideal of imperial masculinity, there are nevertheless numerous characters in Victorian and Edwardian literature who exemplify the concept of rational masculinity. For instance, the popular figure of the private detective with his methods of deduction and logical reasoning is closely tied to this idea of masculinity. It is noteworthy, however, that private detectives like Sherlock Holmes use their abilities to help others, thus encouraging readers to embrace rationality as a basis for their actions. By contrast, the male protagonists in Stoker's and Galbraith's stories focus on their own well-being, especially in Galbraith's "In the Séance Room", in which we encounter a man who is even willing to murder a vulnerable young woman to secure his own social advancement. Furthermore, the men's ability to employ a rational mindset is presented as arrogant and ultimately self-destructive in Stoker's and Galbraith's narratives. "The Judge's House" and "In the Séance Room" thus function to illustrate the shortcomings of rational masculinity.

Both stories dwell on a narrative formula that is followed by many ghost stories of the period. At the core of these stories is a "stanch rationalist" (Bissell, "Science" 42) who sets out to find a reasonable explanation for a seemingly supernatural occurrence, but whose "worldview is profoundly shaken by the narrative's close" (ibid. 40). In the course of this work, we have come across this classic ghost story plot several times, for instance in H. G. Well's "The Red Room", Algernon Blackwood's "The Empty House", and Lettice Galbraith's "A Ghost's Revenge". In those stories, "the materialist doubters are silenced, and some moralising is made to the effect that there are more things in heaven and earth ... than are dreamt of in the narrow secular philosophies" (Baldick xv). In an uncanny twist of this archetype, the male rationalists presented in the following must not only acknowledge the unexplained but also pay for their ignorance towards the supernatural with their lives.

Bram Stoker's "The Judge's House"

The first story discussed in this chapter is by the Irish author Bram Stoker (1847–1912). Not unlike Arthur Conan Doyle, whose "The Brown Hand" (1899) has been discussed in the previous chapter, Stoker's vast corpus – thirteen novels, two biographies, one play, and numerous short stories as well as articles – is today largely overshadowed by the creation of a single literary figure: Dracula. In contrast to Conan Doyle and his Sherlock Holmes stories, however, *Dracula* (1897) was only "relished … as a good potboiler but never made Bram Stoker or his monster famous" (Auerbach and Skal ix) during the author's lifetime. It was but "one of many fantastic adventure stories pitting manly Englishmen against foreign monsters" (ibid.) and thus "seemed commonplace" (ibid) in the late nineteenth century.

However, just as the figure of the vampire itself, Stoker's *Dracula* had a vigorous afterlife. Besides Frankenstein's monster, there is arguably no other figure in literature that has inspired more adaptations and crossed more genres and media than the eponymous vampire from Stoker's novel. According to Kate Hebblethwaite, it is a "paradox" (xi) that even though Stoker "wrote so much, … so much should in turn be written about such a small section of his work" (ibid.). Nina Auerbach and David J. Skal have argued that Dracula's popularity can partly be ascribed to his being "an adaptable monster" (ix). What Auerbach and Skal mean by that is not only Dracula's adaptability to other media, but the vampire's potential to "be at home everywhere" (ibid.). Dracula differs from other monsters in that he does not wear obvious marks of deformity. Furthermore, he has the ability to blend into English society as if it were his own: he speaks English fluently and is familiar with the customs of the foreign country. And, most importantly, as an ancient creature, the vampire knows how to adapt to different times.

Given *Dracula's* undying popularity throughout the twentieth and twenty-first centuries, it is perhaps not surprising that the vampire narrative has also been at the focus of academic research, while the rest of Stoker's writing has received little critical attention. However, I concur with Hebblethwaite that it is important also to consider other sections of Stoker's work: "Far from the rather slapdash image that Stoker's fiction beyond *Dracula* has generated, such works can be seen to be the product of deep thought, research and a profound understanding of the society in which he lived" (Hebblethwaite xiii). In the following, I will provide a reading of Stoker's eerie ghost story "The Judge's House". The narrative was first published in 1891 in *The Illustrated Sporting and Dramatic News* and was then republished in *Dracula's Guest, and Other Weird Stories*, a collection of short Gothic stories by Stoker compiled in 1914, two years after the author's death.

"The Judge's House" belongs to what has been described as "a particularly lurid and creepy kind of fiction" (qdt. in Luckhurst, Introduction 3) in an obituary published after Stoker's death in 1912 in *The Times*. The story incorporates some of the most common plot devices and figures of Victorian Gothic writing: a haunted house, an uncanny portrait, and a bunch of rats. What turns "The Judge's House" into a horrific tale, however, is not Stoker's use of well-known stock features of the Gothic, but the story's insistence on "the inefficacy of pure reason" (Reiter 230). The narrative focuses on Malcom Malcomson, a Cambridge student who is seeking some peace and quiet in order to study for the Mathematical Tripos. For this purpose, he takes the train to "some unpretentious little town where there would be nothing to distract him" (Stoker, "Judge's House" 109) and rents an old house that "has been so long empty that some kind of absurd prejudice has grown up about it" (ibid. 110). The house is said to be haunted by the phantom of a cruel old judge, who "was held in great terror on account of his harsh sentences and his hostility to prisoners" (ibid.) during his lifetime. Malcomson's decision to move into the old house is not affected by the rumours though and also the fact that the house is crowded with rats, which have been regarded as harbingers of death from the middle ages onwards, cannot put him off. He hires a woman to clean up the place and then starts his extensive studying.

Malcomson's motivation to rent the house despite its reputation and the uncanny presence of the rats is rooted in an urge to find a place that "satisfie[s] his wildest dreams regarding quiet" (Stoker, "Judge's House" 109) where nothing and nobody can distract him from his mathematical studies. It is an urge that comes close to an obsession and impacts his bodily and mental health, as we shall see later. The location of the house is so remote that the narrator adds to its description that "quiet was not the proper word to apply to it – desolation was the only term conveying any suitable idea of its isolation" (ibid.), thereby emphasising the fact that there is nobody close-by who could help Malcomson should he be in trouble. It is thus established from early on in the narrative that the solitude Malcomson seeks might be dangerous.[4]

Malcomson is not worried by the house's location, however. When the local inn owner, Mrs Witham, begs him not to stay the night in the Judge's House, the Cambridge student replies that a man like him cannot be scared by what he perceives as ridiculous rumours:

---

4   Commenting on the meaning of the name Malcom, which "refers to a follower of Saint Columba" (Reiter 237), Geoffrey Reiter has remarked that it can be interpreted as "bad calm" (whereas the prefix "mal-" is Latin for "bad" and "com" is phonetically close to "calm"). The name thus implies that his seclusion from society is harmful for Malcomson.

The good creature was so manifestly in earnest, and was so kindly in her intentions, that Malcomson, although amused, was touched. He told her kindly how much he appreciated her interest in him, and added: "But, my dear Mrs Witham, indeed you need not be concerned about me! A man who is reading for the Mathematical Tripos has too much to think of to be disturbed by any of these mysterious 'somethings', and his work is of too exact and prosaic a kind to allow of his having any corner in his mind for mysteries of any kind. Harmonical Progression, Permutations and Combinations, and Elliptic Functions have sufficient mysteries for me!" (Stoker, "Judge's House" 111)

The passage suggests that there is no room for "mysterious 'somethings'" (Stoker, "Judge's House" 111) in the world view of a mathematician who has a rational outlook on life and only believes in things that can be reduced to "exact" (ibid.) natural laws. He does not even consider the possibility of ghosts and haunting; instead, he dismisses Mrs Witham's concern as superstitious nonsense.

The passage also highlights the entanglement of Victorian science with dominant middle-class masculinity. There is a marked arrogance inherent in Malcomson's attitude towards Mrs Witham. He is touched by her concern for his well-being, but finds her belief in the supernatural amusing. By pointing out that his mind is too preoccupied with mathematics to worry about "mysteries of any kind" (Judge's House 111), Malcomson sets himself apart from the inn owner as a representative of the working class who is not practiced in logical thinking. By listing mathematical terminology, Malcomson presents the discipline as "the evident referent of logical reasoning" (González 19) and further reinforces his superior position as a well-educated Cambridge student. The passage thus displays Malcomson's feeling of superiority as a white, educated, middle-class male who sees himself as more sophisticated than the local population. By exposing the arrogance that comes with privilege, the tale "critiques a system that reserves educational resources to the wealthy and middle-class" (Lynch 79–80).

In this context, it is also relevant that Malcomson's counterpart is not only a member of the working class, but also a woman. Despite the advances in women's rights in the second half of the nineteenth century, scientific research was still a field dominated by a privileged group of white, middle-class men. The near absence of women from this field of research was in part the result of an educational system that supported upper- and middle-class men – first at the boarding schools and later at the universities. These inequalities in educational and work opportunities for men and women – women were not allowed to practice medicine until 1877, for instance (Ohri 256) – were accompanied by a social discourse that furthered the association of men with rationality and of women with emotionality and functioned as an excuse for the exclusion of women from the world of science.[5] This gendered dualism is represented by Malcomson and Mrs Witham in the story. However, instead of reaffirming the supposedly superior position of the bourgeois materialist, Malcomson's reliance on rationalism is exposed as pure hubris in the course of the story.

Before moving on, however, it is worth having another look at the passage quoted above and Malcomson's reference to his mathematical exercises as "mysteries" (Stoker, "Judge's House" 111). Geoffrey Reiter suggests that Malcomson presents his mathematical studies as the basis for his epistemology by calling them "mysteries", which means *sacramentum* in Latin: "his equations and texts represent the sacraments of his rationalistic belief system" (Reiter 238). Reiter's argument here is that the Cambridge student is aware of the Latin word and consciously makes use of this knowledge – a knowledge which Mrs Witham does not possess. There is certainly some truth to the idea that Malcomson is seeking to present his mathematical studies as the basis for his rational worldview in an encoded way, thereby further distancing himself as an educated member of the middle class from Mrs Witham and her limited knowledge. However, it is also possible to read Malcomson's statement as a hint at the potential of mathematics to mystify and haunt a person's mind. This reading is reinforced as the story progresses, for Malcomson repeatedly loses track of time and space when he is engrossed in his studies.

Malcomson spends three nights in the old judge's house. However, far from being able to work without any distraction, his studies, which continue until late in the night, are interrupted by the noise the rats make: "How busy they were! And hark to the strange noises! Up and down behind the old wainscot, over the ceiling and under the floor they raced, and gnarled, and scratched!" (Stoker, "Judge's House" 113), Malcomson complains on the first night in the building. The exclamation marks used in the description of the rats' activity are indicative of the quality of the noise, on the one hand, and the irritation Malcomson experiences, on the other hand. Looking about the dining room,

---

5   It is perhaps worth noting that this discourse continues to shape our cultural reality to this day and results in more men than women becoming scientists and mechanics.

which serves as a study for the student, he notices two things: "some old pictures on the walls ... coated so thick with dust and dirt that he could not distinguish any detail of them" (ibid.) and "the rope of the great alarm bell on the
roof, which hung down in a corner of the room on the right-hand side of the
fireplace" (ibid.). Later in the story, Malcomson discovers that one of the pictures shows the former owner of the house, an old judge, and that the rope is
the very same "which the hangman used for all the victims of the Judge's judicial rancour" (ibid. 118). Malcomson's fate as another victim of the judge's atroc-
ity is thus foreshadowed. Yet, on his first night in the old house, Malcomson is
neither bothered by the portrait nor the rope. What upsets him most is the appearance of a gigantic rat which looks at him with "cruel eyes" (ibid. 114) and
does not stir when he tries to chase it away.

Despite the disturbance caused by the rats, Malcomson eventually manages to focus on his mathematical studies and is soon "so immersed in his
work that everything in the world, except the problem he was trying to solve,
passed away" (ibid. 113). This is one of the passages in which Malcomson's extensive studying is addressed. It is a state of mind in which he is completely
immersed in his mathematical problems. The world "passe[s] away" (Stoker,
"Judge's House" 113), leaving him in a sort of parallel universe. In another passage, Malcomson is described as having "lost himself in his propositions and
problems" (ibid. 116), thus suggesting that he even forgets about his own existence when absorbed in his studies. Rather than forming an adequate foundation for epistemology, Malcomson's studies are thus presented as a form of
escapism.

"The Judge's House" further suggests that his excessive studying has turned
Malcomson into an addict. Time and again, his physical and mental dependence on "strong tea" (ibid. 118) is pointed out in the story. For instance, the
Cambridge student waits until the "tea began to have its effects of intellectual
and nervous stimulus" (ibid. 113) before he starts studying on the first night
in the judge's house, and, later in the story, Mrs Witham shows herself concerned about Malcomson's habit and asks the local doctor to advise him "to give
up the tea and the very late hours" (ibid. 118). Given the availability of drugs
such as opium and cocaine in nineteenth-century Britain, it is even possible
that "strong tea" (ibid. 118) is used as a code word here and that Malcomson's

consumption of the beverage stands in for the abuse of another, stronger substance.[6]

The mentally taxing work also seems to have an impact on Malcomson's health, for when he meets Mrs Witham after his first night in the judge's house, she is concerned about his well-being: "'You must not overdo it, sir. You are paler this morning than you should be. Too late hours and too hard work on the brain isn't good for any man!'" (Stoker, "Judge's House" 114). However, Malcomson shrugs off Mrs Witham's concerns and studies just as extensively on the second night in the judge's house. As before, Malcomson is disturbed by the big rat. In what might have been a turning point in his understanding of the world, Malcomson throws books at the vermin, seeking to hit the creature fatally:

> He raised a book in his right hand, and, taking careful aim, flung it at the rat. The latter, with a quick movement, sprang aside and dodged the missile. He then took another book, and a third, and flung them one after another at the rat, but each time unsuccessfully. At last, as he stood with a book poised in his hand to throw, the rat squeaked and seemed afraid. This made Malcomson more than ever eager to strike, and the book flew and struck the rat a resounding blow. It gave a terrible squeak, and turning on its pursuer a look of terrible malevolence, ran up the chairback and made a great jump to the rope of the alarm bell and ran up it like lightning. … [Malcomson] picked up the books one by one, commenting on them as he lifted them. "*Conic Sections* he does not mind, nor *Cycloidal Oscillations*, nor the *Principia*, nor *Quaternions*, nor *Thermodynamics*. Now for the book that fetched him!" Malcomson took it up and looked at it. As he did so, he started, and a sudden pallor overspread his face. He looked round uneasily and shivered slightly, as he murmured to himself:
> "The Bible my mother gave me! What an odd coincidence." (Stoker, "Judge's House" 116–7)

While Malcomson's study books prove useless, his ancestral Bible is presented as an adequate weapon against the evil rat – "a symbolic triumph of faith over logic" (Hebblethwaite xxi), as Kate Habblethwaite has noted. The rat squeaks

---

6   Several well-known authors, such as Charles Dickens, Wilkie Collins, and Elizabeth Barrett-Browning, are known for having taken opium and references to drugs are not uncommon in nineteenth-century literature (Ruston). For instance, Sherlock Holmes lists "cucaine [sic] injections" (Conan Doyle, "Sherlock" 133) as one of his "little weaknesses" (ibid).

and exhibits fear, thus illustrating that the Christian faith provides a powerful "resource[...] to ward off [the] distinctly supernatural evil" (Reiter 230) represented by the rat. Reason is thus pitted against the supernatural threat represented by the rat, on the one hand, and against religion as a basis for epistemology, on the other hand. Malcomson is unable to shed his rational scepticism, however. Though at first affected by the discovery that the only book which hit the rat turns out to be the Bible he received from his mother, Malcomson decides to view it as "an odd coincidence" (Stoker, "Judge's House" 117). The fact that Malcomson received the Bible from his mother also suggests a conflict between the generations. The act of giving a Bible to one's child can be seen as an attempt to impart a certain set of values onto the next generation. However, the Bible represents a religious worldview that conflicts with Malcomson's rationalism. He does not even consider using the book as a protection when the judge eventually materialises on Malcomson's third night in the haunted house.

Returning from a stroll through the town, Malcomson finds that his house cleaner, who has left the building again in the meantime, has dusted the pictures in the dining room and that one of them is a portrait of the old judge:

> It was of a judge dressed in his robes of scarlet and ermine. His face was strong and merciless, evil, crafty, and vindictive, with a sensual mouth, hooked nose of ruddy colour, and shaped like the beak of a bird of prey. The rest of the face was of a cadaverous colour. The eyes were of peculiar brilliance and with a terribly malignant expression. As he looked at them, Malcomson grew cold, for he saw there the very counterpart of the eyes of the great rat. (Stoker, "Judge's House" 120)

The portrait provides several hints at the judge's ghostly existence. As a phantom, the judge is both dead and alive. While the "cadaverous colour" (ibid.) of his face is indicative of the judge's demise, the peculiarly bright eyes and the strong expression suggest his supernatural power as an undead creature. The comparison of his nose with the beak of a bird of prey further suggests the judge's status as predator, on the one hand, and Malcomson's position as his prey, on the other hand. However, the most obvious sign of the judge's supernatural presence is the resemblance between the judge's eyes and those of the great rat. As in the scene in which Malcomson is throwing books at the rat, the student's bodily reaction signals that he subconsciously understands that there is an evil presence in the house which cannot be explained away with logical reasoning. He grows cold, apparently shocked by the discovery. However, instead of fully acknowledging the supernatural power of the judge, Malcomson tries to find a rational explanation for the uncanny resemblance between the rat and the judge and suspects that his "nerves must have been getting into a queer state" (ibid. 121) because of the tea he had been drinking. In an effort to calm his nerves, Malcomson "mixe[s] himself a good stiff glass of brandy and water and resolutely [sits] down to his work" (ibid.).

Too late, Malcomson notices that the gigantic rat has reappeared and gnarled off the end of the alarm bell rope. Looking up from his work, he further discovers that the portrait of the judge is empty: "Malcomson, almost in a chill of horror, turned slowly round, and then he began to shake and tremble like a man in a palsy. … There, on the great high-backed carved oak chair sat the Judge in his robes of scarlet and ermine, with his eyes glaring vindictively" (Stoker, "Judge's House" 122). Picking up the loose piece of rope, the judge ties a noose, throws it around Malcomson's neck and hangs the student on the alarm bell rope. Paralysed by fear, Malcomson is incapable of defending himself and dies.

Given Malcomson's excessive studying, his addiction to "strong tea" (Stoker, "Judge's House" 118), and the isolated position of the judge's house, it is tempting to surmise that Malcomson has not been murdered by a revenant but suffered a mental breakdown and committed suicide. The ghostly figure of the judge would then be a construct of Malcomson's frenzied state of mind. The story's conclusion, however, contradicts such a reading and testifies to the supernatural power of the judge:

> When the alarm bell of the Judge's House began to sound a crowd soon assembled. Lights and torches of various kinds appeared, and soon a silent crowd was hurrying to the spot. They knocked loudly at the door, but there was no reply. They burst in the door, and poured into the great dining-room, the Doctor at the head.
> There at the end of the rope of the great alarm bell hung the body of the student, and on the face of the Judge in the picture was a malignant smile. (Stoker, "Judge's House" 123–24)

The judge in the picture now wears "a malignant smile" (ibid.). This change in the judge's expression hints at the fact that he has actually stepped out of the portrait and resumed his "judicial rancour" (Stoker, "Judge's House" 118).

The narrative does not provide us with poetic justice. On the contrary, the "supernatural forces are not agents of a cosmic justice but of a human evil so persistent that it refuses to die" (Senf, "Three" 296–7). Kate Hebblethwaite suggests that the judge's cruel triumph at the end of the narrative "connects the story with the Gothic genre's long-established subversion of 'conventional' powers of right and wrong, for instance in William Godwin's *Caleb Williams* (1794) and Mary Shelley's *Frankenstein* (1818; 1831)" (xxi).[7]

The comparison between Stoker's "The Judge's House" and Godwin's *Caleb Williams* is particularly fruitful because both narratives address arbitrary patriarchal power and expose flaws in the judicial system. In *Caleb Williams*, members of the working class are repeatedly punished for things they have not done. First, two servants are unjustly convicted and executed for the murder of Barnabas Tyrell, a wealthy but tyrannical landowner, who has really been killed by his neighbour Ferdinando Falkland. When Falkland's servant Caleb discovers his master's secret, Falkland accuses him of theft, whereupon Caleb is sent to prison. Just like the two servants before, Caleb falls victim to a judicial system that fails to punish the real culprit and is used by the powerful as a means of despotism and oppression. The novel therefore has often been read as a commentary on the legal system that does not protect innocent people from arbitrary power. "The Judge's House" similarly subverts the execution of "legitimate social power" (Senf, "Tracing" 13) by featuring "a cruel judge who uses the law to control others rather than achieve justice" (ibid.). Just as in *Caleb Williams*, the system fails to protect the innocent from the arbitrary power executed by the judge. Unlike Falkland, however, who is haunted by guilt and eventually dies, the judge not only abuses his power but takes pleasure in his evil deeds. Also, the judge's actions are not motivated by a secret that needs to remain hidden. There is no personal connection between the judge and his victims. The judge therefore represents a dangerous masculinity that is rooted in hatred and malice.

There is also a parallel between the protagonists of the two narratives, for, like Caleb Williams, Malcom Malcomson is partly responsible for his fate. While Caleb Williams does not accept certain boundaries in his thirst for

---

7   Antonio Ballesteros González also comments on the similarities of "The Judge's House" with Godwin's and Shelley's famous works, which have often been discussed together in academia, partly because Mary Shelley was William Godwin's daughter. For more information, see González's "Portraits, Rats and Other Dangerous Things: Bram Stoker's 'The Judge's House'", esp. p. 27.

knowledge and intrudes the privacy of his master, Malcomson's rejection of anything that cannot be reduced to natural laws proves fatal in "The Judge's House". As Geoffrey Reiter has adequately pointed out, "the judge is an evil that can be exorcised" (Reiter 241). Yet, Malcomson is too limited in his worldview to understand that the Bible his mother gave him provides a powerful weapon against the supernatural evil. In ignoring his ancestral Bible as a representative of "the only forces capable of overcoming evil influences" (González 23), Malcomson "appears to lack faith in both God and family" (Senf, "Three" 297) and is therefore defenceless against the supernatural power of the judge.

Furthermore, Stoker's story is reminiscent Joseph Sheridan Le Fanu's "An Account of Some Strange Disturbances in Aungier Street" (1853). Like "The Judge's House", Le Fanu's story involves the ghost of a cruel judge, a gigantic rat, and a hanging rope. Commenting on the similarities between the two stories, Walter Kendrick points out that "only amnesia or plagiarism can account for the resemblance" (193) of the two stories. He maintains that Stoker must have read Le Fanu's tale somewhere: "two stories that center on a hanging judge reincarnated as a giant rat in a spooky old house can hardly have arisen from separate bursts of genius" (ibid.). However, while the protagonists of Le Fanu's story escape the noose of the murderous revenant in the end, Stoker's tale confronts the reader with a more shocking ending. Le Fanu's tale is also not as concerned with the shortcomings of scientific epistemology. Hence, "it would be misleading to imply that, in displaying similarities with Le Fanu's work, Stoker was merely plagiarizing his ideas" (Hebblethwaite xviii). Nevertheless, Stoker seems to have been inspired by the work of his Irish fellow-countryman. His famous *Dracula* (1897) and his short story "Dracula's Guest" (1914), which was published posthumously by Stoker's wife and presumably constitutes a chapter from *Dracula* which was excluded from the novel before publication, also display similarities with Le Fanu's vampire narrative *Carmilla* (1872). As Carol Senf has pointed out, there are also some striking similarities between Stoker's and Le Fanu's lives: "Even though they are members of different generations (Le Fanu was born in 1814 and died in 1873 while Stoker was born in 1847 and died in 1912), the two were Dublin residents, graduates of Trinity College, members of the Anglo-Irish Ascendancy, lawyers who never practiced law, friends of the William Wilde family, and creators of ghost stories" (Senf, "Three" 293). [8]

---

8   For a detailed analysis and comparison of Stoker's "The Judge's House" and Le Fanu's "An Account of Some Strange Disturbances in Aungier Street", see Carol Senf's "Three

"The Judge's House" is also not unlike *Dracula* in that it juxtaposes modern science, here represented by pure mathematics, against the supernatural, ultimately suggesting that the world cannot be reduced to scientific laws. In *Dracula*, "the human characters ... surround themselves with modern gadgets and skills – shorthand, typewriters, dictating machines, cameras – but they must learn to combat an ancient enemy with ancient beliefs: wild Eastern superstitions ... and, with Van Helsing as medium, the Catholicism that was anathema to the enlightened secularism of sophisticated Victorians" (Auerbach and Skal x). Van Helsing explicitly criticises Dr Seward for his rationalist worldview: "it is the fault of our science that it wants to explain all; and if it explain not, then it says there is nothing to explain" (*Dracula* 171). While the human characters in *Dracula* eventually succeed in their mission to destroy the monster, Malcomson does not understand that his rationalism is inadequate to explain the presence of "the rat with the Judge's baleful eyes" (Stoker, "Judge's House" 121).

By illustrating the shortcomings of a purely rational epistemology, Stoker's tale promotes an idea of reality that encompasses the seemingly inexplicable. Furthermore, the story critiques a concept of masculinity that links manliness, social status, and reason. Time and again, Malcomson ignorantly rejects the warnings of the local inn keeper and looks down upon her because of her supposed inability to exercise rationality. By presenting the male protagonist's disbelief in the supernatural as misguided, the story reveals Malcomson's superior attitude, which is based on his social status and rational perspective, as pure hubris.

Lettice Galbraith's "In the Séance Room" (1893)

"In the Séance Room" is the second story by Lettice Galbraith discussed in this book. As previously pointed out, Galbraith and her ghost stories have almost disappeared from collective memory, even though her tales were widely read in the 1890s. The reason for this neglect may be that Galbraith did not publish any more stories after the 1890s and that, in contrast to her short fiction, her longer pieces of writing were not best-sellers. In any case, Galbraith's career as a writer was successful but short-lived. Her ghost story "In the Séance Room" was first published in Galbraith's popular ghost story collection *New Ghost Stories* in 1893. Just as "A Ghost's Revenge", which has been analysed in the first

---

Ghost Stories: 'The Judge's House', 'Some Strange Disturbances in Aungier Street', and 'Mr. Justice Harbottle'".

chapter of this work, "In the Séance Room" is preoccupied with questions of gender and power and exposes the social vulnerability of women in Victorian society. In the story, Valentine Burke, a London gynaecologist and magnetiser, has to do away with his lover Katharine Greaves to secure his marriage with the wealthy Elma Lang. He hypnotises Katharine and compels her to jump into Regent's Canal in London. When a park-keeper rushes to help the drowning girl, Valentine Burke jumps into the water instead, thus secretly ensuring her death and presenting himself as a brave, if unsuccessful, hero. Burke's cruel and selfish deed is exposed four years later when he attends a séance in London as a psychical researcher intent on proving that the medium, Madame Delphine, is a fraud. However, far from proving to be a charlatan, the medium summons the ghost of Katharine who exposes Burke as her murderer. Deprived of his reputation and with his marriage about to end, Burke commits suicide.

In contrast to "The Judge's House", Galbraith's "In the Séance Room" provides the reader with a satisfying ending, in which justice is ensured by a higher power. This power is hinted at from early on in the narrative. When Burke abuses his occult abilities in order to hypnotise Katharine Greaves and tells her to drown herself, the heterodiegetic narrator states that "[n]o living soul, save the 'sensitive' on whom he was experimenting, heard those words, but they were registered by a higher power than that of the criminal court, damning evidence to be produced one day against the man who had prostituted his spiritual gift to mean and selfish ends" (Galbraith, "Séance" 194). From the moment Burke commits his reckless deed, it is clear he will eventually pay the price for his cruelty. The "damning evidence" (ibid.) hinted at by the narrator is a diamond ring which Burke received as an engagement gift from Elma Lang and which Katharine pulled off his finger before she drowned. When Katharine materialises during the séance, she holds out the ring to Burke. The ring is both a proof that the drowned girl from Regent's Canal has really come back from the dead and a symbol for Burke's tendency to value money more than the life of a human being.

What is also noteworthy about the above quote is the comparison between the "criminal court" and the "higher power" (Galbraith, "Séance" 194). It takes the supernatural to punish Burke for his deed, for nobody suspects the gynaecologist after Katharine's death and he thus evades the criminal court. Just as in *Caleb Williams* and "The Judge's House", the justice system is thus presented as defective. The narrator further refers to Burke's own "spiritual gift" (ibid.) and makes clear that he will not only be punished for the murder of a vulnerable young woman but for the abuse of his mesmeric abilities. The heterodiegetic narrator thus uses their authority to foreshadow events and instruct the reader on how to read the story that is to come. Most of the time, however, Burke functions as internal focalizer and we perceive the events through his perspective.

Though apparently gifted with the power of mesmerism, Burke does not perceive his ability as a "spiritual gift" (Galbraith, "Séance" 194), but views it as a scientific technique that he applies in order to control people and to make his way up in Victorian society:[9]

> The ordinary routine of his profession bored him. That he might eventually succeed as a ladies' doctor was tolerably certain. For a young man with little influence and less money, he was doing remarkably well; but Burke was ambitious, and he had a line of his own. He dabbled in psychics, and had written an article on the future of hypnotism which had attracted considerable attention. He was a strong magnetiser, and offered no objection to semi-private exhibitions of his powers. ... In that section of society which interests itself in occultism Burke saw his way to making a big success.
> Meanwhile, as man cannot live on adulation alone, the doctor had a living to get, and he had no intention whatever of getting it by the labour of his hands. He was an astute young man, who knew how to invest his capital to the best advantage. His good looks were his capital, and he was about to invest them in a wealthy marriage. (Galbraith, "Séance" 198)

The passage suggests that Burke does not come from a wealthy family and is thus dependent on his profession as a gynaecologist to make a living. Burke strives for more, however. Instead of being a "man with little influence and less money" (Galbraith, "Séance" 198), he wants to have money without having to get it "by the labour of his hands" (ibid.). By explicitly referring to the hands as tools used to practice work, the narrative draws attention to the "physicality of labor" (Zandy 2) and evokes associations with the working class whose members are often reduced to their "working parts" (ibid. 1), hands in particular. Considering that Burke is a gynaecologist and thus belongs to the middle class, this emphasis might seem misplaced. However, it draws attention to the fact that Burke is not wealthy at this point in the narrative and that he, as a physician, must also rely on the labour of his hands – a necessity that he wishes to

---

9   Hypnosis was (and is) not only practised by spiritualists but also by psychologists who used it as a form of therapy. For more information on the topic, see Carlos S. Alvarado's "Nineteenth-Century Hysteria and Hypnosis: A Historical Note on Blanche Wittmann" (2009).

overcome. Burke is "ambitious" (Galbraith, "Séance" 198) and he is eager to rise up in society. Besides his career as "a ladies' doctor" (ibid.), he practises magnetism because he believes that it is in the "section of society which interests itself in occultism" (ibid.) where he can make a success and climb up the social ladder.

However, more than on his profession and his powers as a magnetiser, Valentine Burke relies on his good looks and intends "to invest them in a wealthy marriage" (Galbraith, "Séance" 198). Hence, the narrative inverts the classic marriage plot in which a pretty girl secures herself a wealthy husband. Despite this apparent gender role reversal, however, Burke is not being pushed into a feminised position. Instead of being dependent on a rich wife and her family, he wants to marry the orphaned but wealthy Elma Lang and take control of her fortune, thus securing himself power and autonomy. There are no feelings involved in his decision to entice Elma into marriage. All that matters to him is that she is "sufficiently pretty" (ibid. 190) and wealthy. Burke is thus presented as someone who judges women according to their value for his social reputation. His motivation for marrying Elma is entirely motivated by his desire to become "the possessor of a charming wife and a large fortune" (ibid. 192). By contrast, Katharine Greaves represents a "wreck of womanhood" (Galbraith, "Séance" 192) to Burke because she cannot further his advancement in London society but would bring him "poverty and disgrace" (ibid.). He cannot even feel pity for the woman who has fallen in love with him. Instead, he is "nauseated" (ibid.) by her devotion. When his love affair with Katharine endangers his marriage to Elma, Burke justifies his plan to kill her by pointing out that, as a fallen woman, she has lost her reputation, and hence all that made life worth living: "Why should she not die? Her life was over, a spoiled, ruined thing. There was nothing before her but shame and misery. She would be better dead" (ibid. 193). By using Katharine's damaged social status as an excuse for his deed, the story problematises the vulnerability of women in Victorian society. While Burke "never cared much about her" (Galbraith, "Séance" 192), Katharine has fallen for him and believes that he will marry her. Hence, Burke has clearly taken advantage of Katharine. Nevertheless, it is the girl who must take the blame. As Indu Ohri has maintained, "Galbraith condemns the sexual double standard" (271) of late-Victorian society which treats women as outcasts when they have transgressed societal rules and codes of sexual conduct, whereas men can have premarital sex without having to worry about the consequences.

While Burke gains power through their marriage, Elma, who "had full control of her fortune of thirty thousand pounds" (Galbraith, "Séance" 190) until that point, loses her autonomy. We learn from the narrator that she makes "an admirable wife, interesting herself in [Burke's] studies, and assisting him materially in his literary work" (ibid. 196). Hence, Elma not only helps Burke achieve wealth and social status, but also becomes his research assistant.

Nevertheless, Elma feels a "vague distrust" (Galbraith, "Séance" 196) towards Burke, "bred of an instinctive feeling that her husband was not what he seemed to be" (ibid.). She then also turns her back on him when she learns that her husband murdered a woman and that her "wretched fortune supplied the motive for the crime" (ibid. 202). By pointing out that Elma senses that there is something amiss with Burke, the story highlights the importance of intuition, described as "instinctive feeling" (ibid. 196) in the story. This ability to sense the real nature of people stands in opposition to the cold rationality with which Burke plans Katharine's murder and ensnares Elma into marriage.

While initially furthering his prosperity and social ascent, Burke's cold rationality eventually brings about his downfall when he attends a séance as part of a test committee that was formed to examine a "medium of extraordinary power [who] had flashed like a meteor into the firmament of London society" (Galbraith, "Séance" 196). Burke's participation in a test committee for spiritual phenomena is modelled on the psychical researchers of the Society for Psychical Research (SPR). The members of the SPR had different opinions on the psychic and paranormal phenomena they investigated. While some where "sympathetic to or intrigued by spiritualism" (Owen xvii) and thought it possible that spirits "embodied an unknown kind of matter" (ibid.), others were resolved to prove that "spiritualism was mere hocus pocus" (ibid. xv). Burke belongs to the latter group. Four years have passed since Katharine's death. He has made his way up in society and has become "an authority on psychic phenomena" (Galbraith, "Séance" 196). However, he only pretends to believe in supernatural occurrences and abuses his authority as "the idol of the 'smart' women who played with the fashionable theories and talked glibly on subjects the very A B C of which was far beyond their feeble comprehension" (ibid.). While the text clearly targets the gullibility of Burke's bunch of admirers, who are ironically labelled "smart", the heterodiegetic narrator "is more scornful of Burke's deceiving them with false occult teachings" (Ohri 272). Burke uses society's interest in occultism in order to gain attention and he is convinced that the London medium, Madame Delphine, is doing the very same thing:

"What do you really think of it?"

"Humbug, of course; but the difficulty is to prove it."

"Mrs Thirlwall declares that the fifth appearance last night was undoubtedly her husband. I saw her today; she was quite overcome."

"Mrs Thirlwall is a hysterical fool."

"But your theory admitted the possibility of materialising the intense mental –"

Burke leaned back in the carriage, laughing softly.

"My dear child, I had to say something."

"Valentine," she cried, sorrowfully, "is there no truth in anything you say or write? Do you believe in nothing?"

"Certainly. I believe in matter and myself, also that the many fools exist for the benefit of a minority with brains. When I see any reason to alter my belief, I shall not hesitate to do so. If, for instance, I am convinced that I see with my material eyes a person whom I know to be dead, I will become a convert to spiritualism. But I shall never see it." (Galbraith, "Séance" 197)

The passage shows Burke's tendency to look down on women. The physician assumes a paternalistic role when he refers to Elma as "My dear child" (Galbraith, "Séance" 197), a belittling phrase which implies that Elma is immature and less competent than he is. It is also telling that he calls Mrs Thirlwall "hysteric" (ibid.), thus reinforcing Victorian associations of women with mental illnesses. Furthermore, the passage highlights Burke's willingness to take advantage of others. He expresses the conviction that his intellect entitles him to deceive "the many fools [that] exist for the benefit of a minority with brains" (ibid.). For the doctor, supernatural appearances are nothing but figments of the imagination and only "hysterical fool[s]" (ibid.) fall for "humbugs" (ibid.) like Madame Delphine. He only believes in "matter" (ibid.) and in what he can see with his "material eyes" (ibid.). This emphasis on materiality in Burke's explanation to Elma is indicative of his rational mindset. A man like him has a too factual approach to the world to even consider the possibility of ghosts and other supernatural phenomena.

Burke's worldview is profoundly shaken, however, when the ghost of Katharine Greaves materialises during the séance:

Suddenly the stillness was broken by a shriek of horror. It issued from the lips of the medium, who … saw more than she expected, and crouched terror-stricken in the chair to which she was secured by cords adjusted by the test committee. The presence which had appeared before the black curtain was ... a woman in dark, clinging garments – a woman with wide-opened, glassy eyes, fixed in an unalterable stony stare. It was a ghastly sight. All the concentrated agony of a violent death was stamped on that awful face.

Of the twenty people who looked upon it, not one had power to move or speak.

Slowly the terrible thing glided forward, hardly touching the ground, one hand outstretched, and on the open palm a small, glittering object – a diamond ring!

It moved very slowly, and the second or so during which it traversed the space between the curtain and the seats of the audience seemed hours to the man who knew for whom it came.

Valentine Burke sat rigid. He was oblivious to the presence of spectators, hardly conscious of his own existence. Everything was swallowed up in a suspense too agonising for words, the fearful expectancy of what was about to happen. Nearer and nearer 'it' came. Now it was close to him. He could feel the deathly dampness of its breath; those awful eyes were looking into his. The distorted lips parted – formed a single word. Was it the voice of a guilty conscience, or did that word really ring through and through the room – 'Murderer!'

For a full minute the agony lasted, then something fell with a sharp click on the carpet-less floor. The sound recalled the petrified audience to a consciousness of mundane things. They became aware that 'it' was gone. (Galbraith, "Séance" 199–200)

As in other ghost stories involving female spectres – Elizabeth Gaskell's "The Poor Clare" and Galbraith's "A Ghost's Revenge", for instance – Katharine's ghost is referred to as "it". While highlighting the phantom's liminal status as something not quite human, it is striking that particularly female ghosts are labelled as "it", thus suggesting that their transgressive behaviour, which counteracts the role of the caring mother and supportive wife, defeminises them. Furthermore, Katharine's ghost is not unlike other spectres in Victorian and Edwardian fiction in that it appears in order to expose a crime that the police were unable to solve, thus taking revenge on her murderer. It is worth noting, however, that Katharine is dependent on the occult power of another woman to materialise. In this way, the story highlights the importance of "female solidarity" (Ohri 275). Katherine's ghost then, in turn, also liberates Burke's wife Elma "from a stifling marriage, so she is not enslaved to Burke the way his unfortunate lover was" (ibid. 275–6). Finally, Elma ensures that Katharine's death is avenged. After the séance, she hypnotises Burke to find out the whole truth about the woman's murder, thus using the same technique Burke applied to control Katharine. In a letter to Burke at the end of the narrative, Elma suggests Burke's death as "the only thing that is left to us" (Galbraith, "Séance" 202). After reading the letter, the doctor shoots himself. His death restores Elma's independence. While she subordinated herself to her husband during their marriage, she can now reclaim her fortune. Elma even obtains authority over Burke, who follows her orders without hesitation. It is part of the story's engagement with questions of justice that the doctor dies in the same way his victim did: by being ordered to commit suicide.

The title of the story suggests that the space of the séance room plays a significant role in the narrative. As we learn earlier in the narrative, the séance takes place in Madame Delphine's drawing room – a space commonly coded as feminine through its furniture and decoration, but nevertheless a space used by both sexes. It is in this space that "the female characters recover their power" (Ohri 273). Through the séance, the women turn the room into an exclusively female space in which the male intruder is brought to justice. This female revenge, the story implies, is made possible through Burke's ignorance towards the supernatural that makes him attend the séance in the first place. Burke's limited scientific gaze is juxtaposed to Madame Delphine's ability to see the truth and conjure up Katharine's ghost. "In the Séance Room" thus portrays the conflict between scientific materialism and occultism as a battle between the sexes. The occult power of the medium humbles Burke who, until that point in the narrative, prided himself on his supposedly superior understanding of the world.

The stories discussed in the next section also erode binary ideas about gender. However, they differ from the other narratives discussed in this dissertation insofar as they do not contend themselves with disclosing the shortcomings of hegemonic masculinity but point the way towards an alternative concept of manliness which embraces empathy and sensitivity as an important part of masculine gender identity.

Spectral Revelations and Manly Sentiment: Margaret Oliphant's "The Open Door" and Rudyard Kipling's "They"

Susan Schaper has noted that in Victorian haunted house narratives, male and female psychic researchers "could employ their respective powers to neutralize the disconcerting effects of an unaccommodating past" (Schaper 12).

For female characters, this means they are often able to "subdue household ghosts with their feminine compassion" (ibid.), while men rely on "masculine strength, intellect, and self-discipline" (ibid.) in order to exorcise ghosts. Clearly, the qualities highlighted by Schaper correspond to the Victorian separate spheres ideology and such stories work to further establish the idea that humankind can be divided "into two quite different elements" (Tosh, *Man's Place* 47). The ghost stories analysed in the following counteract the idea that men can count on their "masculine athleticism, rational faculties, and educated expertise" (Schaper 12) in their encounters with the supernatural. Instead, the protagonists of Oliphant's "The Open Door" and Kipling's "They" must turn to qualities traditionally associated with women, mothers in particular: intuition, compassion, and empathy. Both stories focus on the male protagonist's relationship with (ghost)children, thereby stressing the importance of paternal involvement. Ultimately, these stories propose a departure from traditional ideas about masculinity in favour of a new concept that reconciles qualities generally associated with femininity with masculine gender performance.

Margaret Oliphant's "The Open Door" (1882)

Margaret Oliphant (1829–97) is arguably the most prolific writer discussed here. The Scottish author wrote ninety-eight novels, more than fifty short stories, twenty-six books of non-fiction, over 300 articles and reviews, and a posthumously published autobiography (McCarthy, "Love" 97.). Oliphant was partially driven to write out of financial necessity, especially after the death of her husband in 1859, which left her as the sole breadwinner of the family (Makala 118). She also supported her brothers Willie and Frank as well as the latter's family with the money she earned from her writing. Oliphant's remarkable literary productivity has often been frowned upon by critics who maintained that the quantity of her output has affected the quality of her work. Virginia Woolf, for instance, comments very harshly on Oliphant in her feminist essay *Three Guineas* (1938): "Mrs. Oliphant sold her brain, her very admirable brain, prostituted her culture and enslaved her intellectual liberty in order that she might earn a living and educate her children" (139).[10] Oliphant was well aware that her productivity did not further her status as a writer: "It

---

10   Commenting on "Woolf's anger at Oliphant's career" (Blair 127), Emily Blair has maintained that Woolf's pointed comments about Oliphant also reflect on Woolf herself

has been my fate in a long life of production to be credited chiefly with the equivocal virtue of industry, a quality so excellent in morals, so little satisfactory in art" (qtd. in McCarthy, "Haunting" 106), she complains in the preface to her novel *The Heir Presumptive and the Heir Apparent* (1891). In her autobiography, Oliphant counters her critics by highlighting that writing for her was first and foremost a passion that also happened to bring her the money she urgently needed to make a living: "I have written because it gave me pleasure, because it came natural to me, because it was like talking and breathing, besides the big fact that it was necessary for me to work for my children" (Oliphant, *Autobiography* 4). By comparing writing to breathing, Oliphant not only expresses the ease with which writing came to her but equates it with something that is essential to keep her alive, thus highlighting the importance writing had for her – emotionally and as a means to earn a living.[11] In line with Oliphant's comments, Elizabeth McCarthy has warned not to regard the author's "immense literary output and financial hardships as unhappy bedfellows", but to acknowledge her "creative integrity" (McCarthy, "Haunting" 106). With regards to Oliphant's supernatural fiction, McCarthy writes that her stories are "distinct and diverse" (McCarthy, "Love" 99). While "suspenseful and unnerving" (ibid.), on the one hand, "they emphasise the themes of familial love, loss, mourning, guilt and the less than entirely successful role of religious faith in comforting the bereaved" (ibid.).

Compared to the rest of her oeuvre, Oliphant produced comparatively few ghost stories. She only started writing them at the age of fifty and wrote "little more than a dozen" (McCarthy, "Love" 99) of them. Oliphant also did not feel the same ease and creativity regarding this particular genre but could only write tales of the supernatural on rare occasions. As she confesses in a letter to her publisher William Blackwood, "[t]hey are not like any others. I can produce them only when they come to me" (Oliphant, *Autobiography* 321). This reluctance to write ghost stories may have been conditioned by Oliphant's own experiences with maternal loss (she outlived not only her husband but also

---

and express an "anxiety about the nineteenth-century woman writer who makes a deliberate compromise by producing both texts and children" (ibid.).

11   Margaret Oliphant was not the only woman who wrote to earn a living. As Lowell T. Frye has noted, "authorship was one of the few professions available to middle-class women" (167) at the time and numerous women "wrote to support themselves" (ibid.) – among them authors discussed in this work, including Amelia Edwards, Charlotte Riddell, E. Nesbit, and Margaret Oliphant.

her six children, three of whom died as infants). This is at least suggested by the prevalence of dead and/or severely ill children in Oliphant's ghost writing. Her ghost story "The Open Door", which was first published in January 1882 in *Blackwood's Edinburgh Magazine*, is no exception. The story features both a dead youth, Willie, whose restless spirit is seeking to be reunited with his mother, and a young boy, Roland, who is troubled by the grieving ghost and, as a consequence, develops a life-threatening brain fever.

While certainly "an example of a wider pre-occupation in Oliphant's ghost stories with themes of loss and mourning" (Margree, *British* 40), "The Open Door" also engages with questions of masculinity. As we shall see, the story presents both the rational man of science as well as the imperial soldier hero as impotent when it comes to family matters and the protection of children. The story focuses on Roland's father, Colonel Henry Mortimer, and his mission to soothe Willie's ghost to rescue his own son. In the following, I will illustrate how the encounter with the ghostly sets in motion an emotional development that transforms Mortimer from a self-confident man of action and combat into a caring and compassionate father who abandons science and reason as a foundation for epistemology in favour of traditionally female forms of knowledge, such as intuition and empathy.

The story starts with the return of Colonel Mortimer and his family from India to Britain, where they move into Brentwood Estate, a country mansion close to Edinburgh. The fact that Mortimer has a high military rank and has served in the colonies indicates that he has defended the British Empire in oversea wars and is equipped with the necessary male attributes of courage, determination, and self-discipline. Mortimer, who serves as homodiegetic narrator of the story, is pleased to settle down with his family in Scotland, where they can enjoy "the greenness, the dewiness, the freshness of the northern landscape ... pouring in vigour and refreshment" (Oliphant, "Open" 152) after their time in "[t]he warmth of the Indian suns" (ibid.). He also finds pride in the ruins of a former building, which can be found in the park that surrounds the country mansion. Mortimer describes them as the remains of "a much smaller and less important house than the solid Georgian edifice which we inhabited. The ruins were picturesque, however, and gave importance to the place" (ibid.). What strikes him most is an open doorway: "A door that led to nothing – closed once perhaps with anxious care, bolted and guarded, now void of any meaning" (ibid.), he points out. We quickly discover, however, that Mortimer's description is not quite accurate because the vacant doorway is far from "void of any meaning" but will develop into the locos of his troubles.

Yet, at this point in the narrative, Mortimer is confident that his children will thrive in this environment which seems to combine the advantages of the countryside with the comforts of the close-by city of Edinburgh.

While Mortimer is willing to provide for his daughters as many "masters and lessons ... as they required" (Oliphant, "Open" 150) and is eager "to see them improve upon their mother" (ibid.), it is his son, Roland, whom he ascribes "the most precious life on earth" (ibid. 162). The reader learns that Roland's brothers have died prematurely from fever: "The lad was doubly precious to us, being the only one left us of many." (ibid. 150), Mortimer is worried, however, that life in India has had a softening effect on Roland. Mortimer describes him as "fragile in body ... and deeply sensitive in mind" (ibid.) and complains that his son "has never known anything more invigoration than Simla" (ibid.). It is telling that Mortimer attributes Roland's delicate nature to the living conditions in India, thereby indirectly fostering the assumption that the native population of India is naturally inferior to and less manly than the British colonisers who are used to "the brisk breezes of the North" (ibid.).[12] Hoping that the "pale-faced boy" (ibid.) would gain "something of the brown and ruddy complexion of his schoolfellows" (ibid.), Mortimer and his wife decide to let Roland ride to school in Edinburgh on his pony.

Given Mortimer's military background and his own representation of heteronormative masculinity, his wish to see Roland acquire manly grit can be interpreted as the ambition of a father who wants his son to measure up to the ideal of imperial masculinity. Yet, it might also express the anxiety of a parent who has already lost several sons and wants the only one left him to be strong enough to resist the fever that killed his brothers. Still, Mortimer wants his son to toughen up. The ride to school and back has the opposite effect, however. Instead of gaining strength, Roland falls ill. Mortimer is away in London when he is informed about his son's illness. Having spent some days with old friends from his time in military service, Mortimer returns to his club where several letters and telegrams await him:

> I was absent in London when these events began. In London an old Indian plunges back into the interests with which all his previous life has been as-

---

12   For a nuanced discussion of the role of colonial masculinity in the 1880s and 1890s in British India and the establishment and exploitation of stereotypes about Indian men as a strategy of colonial rule, see Mrinalini Sinha's *Colonial Masculinity: The "Manly Englishman" and the "Effeminate Bengali" in the Late Nineteenth Century*.

sociated, and meets of friends at every step. I had been ... enjoying the re-
turn to my former life ... and had missed some of my home letters. ... I was
about to open one of these, when the club porter brought me two telegrams.
... I opened, as was to be expected, the last first, and this was what I read:
'Why don't you come or answer? For God's sake, come. He is much worse'"
(Oliphant, "Open 153).

The passage not only reveals Roland's illness but also marks Mortimer as an
absent father who, even after having retired, spends his days away from his
family and does not tend to his parental duties. Mortimer's absent fatherhood
mirrors the behaviour of many men between 1860 and the First World War.
Homosocial institutions flourished in this period. Many upper- and middle-
class men went from the male environment at the public schools to the equally
male-dominated universities or the military. Even married men often spent
their time away from their families in the numerous gentlemen's clubs, which
were, for all intents and purposes, "extensions of the male communities of the
public schools and universities" (Harrison 97). For those men, homosocial institutions came to replace family life. As Brian Harrison notes, "this was an age
of bachelors, or of married men who spent a large part of their lives as if they
were bachelors" (97). John Tosh talks of a "flight from domesticity" (Man's Place
170) – a term which not only implies a departure from an ideal of masculinity
that required, as its counterpart, the idealised idea of the "Angel in the House",
but which also suggests an outright rejection of the female-dominated sphere
of the family home.[13] "The Open Door" critiques men's domestic escapism by
showing that Mortimer is not there for his family when he is most needed.
Since he has been "circulating among some half-dozen of" (Oliphant, "Open"
153) his old friends, Mortimer even missed his letters and telegrams, thereby
making it impossible for his wife to communicate with him. His wife's frustration about Mortimer's absence is apparent in her telegram.

Mortimer rushes back to Brentwood house and discovers his son has developed a life-threatening brain fever. Roland, who has been anxiously waiting
for his father to return home, confides in Mortimer that, on his ride back from
school, he heard the moaning voice of a spirit crying "Oh, mother, let me in!

---

13   Tosh rightly warns not to exaggerate this rejection of the domestic family home: "The
turn away from marriage was class-specific. It did not affect the working class, nor the
lower middle class, for whom the close of the century was the acme of domesticity"
(Manliness 206). However, the "flight from domesticity" (Tosh, Manliness 206) was a reality for many upper- and middle-class men.

oh, mother, let me in" (Oliphant, "Open" 157) in the ruins which lie close to the manor house. Mortimer is instantly convinced that his son is suffering from hallucinations: "My blood got a sort of chill in my veins at the idea that Roland should be a ghost-seer; for that generally means a hysterical temperament and weak health and all that men most hate and fear for their children" (ibid. 158). As in other stories discussed in the course of this work, ghost-seeing – or hearing, in this case – is regarded as a trick of the mind and attributed to poor physical health and mental instability. The prevalent association of hysteria with madness and femininity stigmatises Roland as both mentally ill and effeminate. The fact that Mortimer feels not only fear after Roland's confession but also disdain signals that he is not only worried about his son but also disapproves of the boy's unmanly conduct. What troubles him even more, however, is the fact that Roland asks him to help the spectre.

> "... It was something – in trouble. Oh, father, in terrible trouble!"
> "But, my boy," I said – I was at my wits' end – "if it was a child that was lost, or any poor human creature – But, Roland, what do you want me to do?"
> "I should know if I was you," said the child, eagerly. "That is what I always said to myself – 'Father will know.' ..." ...
> I do not know that I ever was in a greater perplexity in my life; ... [i]t is bad enough to find your child's mind possessed with the conviction that he has seen – or heard – a ghost. But that he should require you to go and help that ghost, was the most bewildering experience that had ever come my way. ... [T]hat I should take up his ghost and right its wrongs, and save it from its trouble, was such a mission as was enough to confuse any man. (Oliphant, "Open" 158)

Mortimer experiences the encounter with his son as "most bewildering" (Oliphant, "Open" 158). For one, Roland expects him to see something that Mortimer believes to be the product of his son's imagination. Furthermore, the boy's request challenges his understanding of fatherhood at a time when people thought that "too great an emotional closeness with sons would undermine their self-reliance and moral autonomy, that manly independence which was expected to be evident by the age of twelve" (Tosh, *Manliness* 141).[14] This is at least suggested by Mortimer's assertion that his son's expectations would

---

14   By contrast, there was "less reason for the father to impose constraint or distance on a daughter" (Tosh, *Manliness* 141) because of women's lifelong association with domesticity.

"confuse any man" (Oliphant, "Open" 158). It is a request that would usually fall into the realm of the mother who was seen as responsible for the emotional upbringing of the child. Elizabeth McCarthy has noted that Roland is begging his father to open his mind "[m]uch in the same way as the spectral voice the boy hears pleads with its mother" ("Love" 100). But it is not only open-mindedness that Roland asks from Mortimer. He also appeals to his father's ability to master difficult situations. "I should know if I was you" (Oliphant, "Open" 158), Roland says to his father, thus appealing to Mortimer's resourcefulness. Military man that he is, Mortimer then also refers to his son's request as a "mission" (ibid.)

Roland is already so sick at this point in the narrative that his appearance resembles that of a ghost with eyes that "were like blazing lights projecting out of his white face" (Oliphant, "Open" 155). Since his son might die (and become a ghost himself) if he does not do anything, Colonel Mortimer decides to investigate the supernatural appearance. Before setting out on his "mission" (ibid. 158), Mortimer is careful to emphasise that, as a "sober man" (ibid.), he does "[o]f course ... not believe in ghosts" (ibid.), thus highlighting that a belief in a supernatural realm has no place in his worldview.

As so often in Victorian ghost fiction, the middle-class man first "looks to the servants for information regarding the local lore and superstitions" (Makala 120) and finds out that, according to them, "the certainty that the place was haunted was beyond doubt" (Oliphant, "Open" 161) and that some people "had seen the darkness moving" (ibid.) in the months of November and December. However, fearing that they should be "the laughing-stock of a' [sic] the country-side" (ibid. 163), they never asked "the minister and the gentry" (ibid.) to investigate the supernatural occurrences. "'[T]hey just laugh in your face. Inquire into the thing that is not! Na, na, we just let it be'" (ibid.), a servant woman explains to Mortimer. The servant woman in Oliphant's tale is referring to what Lowell T. Frye had termed "the social power of rationality" (181). As we have already seen in Bram Stoker's "The Judge's House", this power works to set the educated upper and middle classes apart from the "unlearned person" (Oliphant, "Open" 163), as the servant woman calls herself, thus expressing her class consciousness and knowledge of her low social status.[15] Colonel Mortimer is not willing to accept the limitations set by scientific rationalism,

---

15   For an exploration of class issues in Oliphant's narrative, see also Melissa Edmundson Makala's *Women's Ghost Literature in Nineteenth-Century Britain*, pp. 118–131.

however, because he apprehends that he might lose Roland if he cannot provide a satisfying answer for his son: "I feared that even a scientific explanation of refracted sound, or reverberation, or any other of the easy certainties with which we elder men are silenced, would have very little effect upon the boy" (Oliphant, "Open" 162). While he would have been satisfied with a rational explanation himself, he is aware that Roland cannot be "silenced" (ibid.) in the way "elder men" (ibid.) can. By using the word "silenced" (ibid.) in this context, the story again hints at the oppressive power of scientific discourse, which can also be directed against the middle class itself.

To get to the bottom of the mystery, Colonel Mortimer decides to visit the ruins after nightfall. To his surprise, he soon starts to hear the wailing voice of the ghost: "I sprang back, and my heart stopped beating. Mistaken! No, mistake was impossible. I heard it as clearly as I hear myself speak; a long, soft, weary sigh, as if drawn to the utmost, and emptying out a load of sadness that filled the breast" (Oliphant, "Open" 165). While Mortimer first ascribed Roland's encounter with the ghost to the boy's weak and effeminate nature, he is immediately convinced that the spirit is real and not just a trick of the mind when he hears the voice himself.

While he apparently trusts his own senses, Colonel Mortimer soon learns that hearing ghosts also threatens the status of a distinguished military man like him. When he confides in the local doctor, John Simson, the medical man jibes at him and announces that ghosts are like an "epidemic. When one person falls victim to this sort of thing, it's safe as can be – there's always two or three" (Oliphant, "Open" 170), thus suggesting that Mortimer, much like his effeminate son, has been affected by "the freaks our brains are subject to" (ibid.). As has already been pointed out, "vision's status as the primary means of knowing the world" (Bissell, "Science" 42) was increasingly questioned in the nineteenth century. In the story, vision is substituted by another sense: hearing – a sense which is commonly regarded as even more susceptible to deception than sight. This is also suggested by John Simson: "'It's all bosh about apparitions. I never have investigated the laws of sound to any great extent, and there is a great deal in ventriloquism that we don't know much about'" (ibid. 177), the doctor says to Mortimer, convinced that there must be some kind of trick behind the moaning voice in the ruins.

With regards to Margaret Oliphant's supernatural fiction, Esther Schor has remarked that the confrontation with "the unexplained figure often leads to an uncanny exchange of roles: as the ghostly figure assumes authority, the interpreters take on the aura of the irrational" (91). In "The Open Door", the association of ghost-seeing with mental instability and the irrational threatens to demasculinise Mortimer – despite his military achievements and his high social status. Mortimer is particularly bothered by John Simson, who makes him "look like a credulous fool" (Oliphant, "Open" 172). Mortimer's comment reveals that he fears his reputation might be damaged by the ghost-hunt. The story thus suggests that the military man is still haunted by a normative idea of masculinity that he is eager to fulfil at this point in the narrative. At the same time, Mortimer knows he must shed his manly pride and his "masculine ratio-nality must be supplemented by a certain level of spiritual awareness" (Bissell, "Reconstructing", 76) in order for him to be able to help the spirit and thus save his son: "In my mind there was no longer any indifference to the thing, what-ever it was, that haunted these ruins. My scepticism disappeared like mist. I was as firmly determined that there was something as Roland was" (Oliphant, "Open" 165). It is noteworthy that Mortimer not only starts believing in the exis-tence of the ghost, but, just like his son, he feels empathy for the spirit. Unlike Roland, however, Mortimer does not fall ill. Nevertheless, he experiences the wailing as almost unbearable, "a sound that made one's blood curdle, full of human misery" (ibid.). Mortimer is determined to put the poor spirit to rest: "I did not know if it was man or woman; but I no more doubted that it was a soul in pain than I doubted my own being; and it was my business to soothe this pain – to deliver it, if that was possible" (Oliphant, "Open" 174). Colonel Mortimer refrains from fighting against the spirit that threatens his son's life, which would have been the most natural reaction for a man with his military background. Unlike the soldier who "is created to fight" (qtd. in MacKenzie, *Popular Imperialism* 2), as Thomas Carlyle has put it, it becomes his "business to soothe ... pain" (Oliphant, "Open" 173–74). The ghostly thus functions to set in motion an emotional development that leads to the acceptance of qualities usually associated with the realm of the mother, empathy and compassion in particular. Mortimer's willingness to assume the traditional role of the mother is implied by the usage of the word "deliver" in the quote above, a term which evokes associations with childbirth.

After his first encounter with the spirit, Mortimer revisits the ruins in the following nights, and each time he is accompanied by a different man: first, he goes with his butler Bagley, a military man who served under Mortimer in In-dia; then, he is joined by John Simson; finally, he approaches the ruins with the local minister, Dr Moncrieff. Each time, they hear the restless spirit, "unhappy, moaning, crying, before the vacant doorway, which no one could either shut or open more" (Oliphant, "Open" 168). The vacant doorway here is of course a metaphor for the liminal state of the spirit, which is "earthbound", as Oliphant has so aptly put it in one of her other ghost stories.[16] Just like Roland, the butler, whom Mortimer describes as a brave soldier who is "not supposed to fear anything – man or devil" (ibid. 164), faints and is bed-stricken after the encounter with the ghost – in spite of his embodiment of normative masculinity. Dr Simson, as might have been assumed, is also of little help. When Mortimer asks him to accompany him to the ruins, he is hesitant to do so, arguing that "'it would ruin me for ever if it were known that John Simson was ghost hunting'" (ibid. 170), thus highlighting the threat ghost-seeing poses to his representation of rational masculinity. Mortimer replies: "'There it is, … you dart down on us who are unlearned with your phonetic disturbances, but you daren't examine what the thing really is for fear of being laughed at. That's science!'" (ibid.), thereby launching an attack on science at large. Thus challenged, Simson agrees to join Mortimer, but not without pointing out that a man of science like him will never believe in the existence of ghosts and other supernatural phenomena: "The thing has delusion on the front of it. It is encouraging an unwholesome tendency even to examine. What good could come of it? Even if I am convinced, I shouldn't believe" (ibid.).

The last sentence of Simson's statement is particularly striking as it contrasts conviction with belief. While both terms have a similar meaning, the word "belief" is commonly associated with a person's (religious) faith. By contrasting the two terms, Simson highlights his rejection of forms of knowledge that are not based on rational materialism. It comes as no surprise that the doctor then also does not believe in the supernatural character of the ghostly voice, even after having heard it for himself: "He recovered with a spring, and in a moment, from the awe-stricken spectator he had been, became himself sceptical and cynical" (Oliphant, "Open" 181). Simson insists that there must be some rational explanation for the seemingly supernatural occurrence: "'One thing is certain, you know, there must be some human agency'" (ibid.), he contends – much to Mortimer's annoyance: "These scientific fellows, I wonder people put up with them as they do, when you have no mind for their cold-blooded confidence" (ibid. 177), he criticises the tendency of scientists to scorn everything that cannot be reduced to natural laws. For the doctor, the experience of ghost-seeing not only stands in opposition to dominant scripts of masculinity, but effectively destroys men: "You've disabled this poor fellow of yours and

---

16   Oliphant's story "Earthbound: A Story of the Seen and Unseen" was published in Fraser's Magazine two year prior to "The Open Door".

made him ... a lunatic for life", he says to Mortimer after Bagley's breakdown. Sarah Bissell has remarked that ghost stories repeatedly "present doctors as well meaning but potentially arrogant in their logical worldview" ("Science" 42). This is also the case in "The Open Door". Dr Simson fulfils the role of the "materialist doubter" (Baldick xvi) in the story, whose confidence in the laws of science is ultimately shown as ineffective and misguided. As Roland complains, "that fellow's a doctor, and never thinks of anything but clapping you into bed" (Oliphant, "Open" 157), thus indicating the doctor's limited ability to help him get better.[17]

Mortimer ultimately joins forces with the local minister, Dr Moncrieff, who identifies the spirit as that of a former inhabitant of the house, a troublesome lad who returned home to find that his mother had died and whose restless spirit is now caught in an endless re-enactment of his homecoming. The minister, "absorbed in anxiety and tenderness" (Oliphant, "Open" 179), tells the spirit that his mother is not here: "You'll find her with the Lord. Go there and seek her, not here" (ibid.). The minister fulfils the role of the exorcist in the narrative. While showing empathy for Willi's lost spirit, he also commands him the leave the place of haunting: "'I forbid ye! Cry out no more to man. Go home, ye wandering spirit! ... Go home to the Father – the Father! Are you hearing me?' Here the old man sank down upon his knees, his face raised upwards, his hands held up with a tremble in them" (ibid.). Moncrieff's gesture suggests that the clerical man calls upon God in his attempt to free the ruins from Willi's ghost. Involuntarily, Mortimer also drops on his knees, thus supporting Moncrieff in exorcising the place from the ghost. Eventually the men succeed. It is important to note that the men do not defeat but console "the poor lost spirit" (Oliphant, "Open" 175) by showing pity and tenderness – character traits usually ascribed to the feminine sphere. For them, it is "a poor fellow-creature in misery, to be succoured and helped out of his trouble" (ibid. 183). In exorcising the ruins from Willi's ghost, the men also free the boy's earthbound soul. At the same time, the liberation of the spirit serves as a metaphor for Mortimer's liberation from a distorted ideal of masculinity. By the end of the story, he has not only developed a spiritual awareness but accepted sensitivity and tenderness as part of his masculine identity. Thus, the story proposes an idea of masculinity

---

17   In Rudyard Kipling's "The Mark of the Beast", which has been discussed in the previous chapter, the doctor is also incapable of helping Fleete, who is gradually degenerating into a wild animal.

and fatherhood which defies the concept of imperial masculinity with its stern rejection of supposedly feminine virtues.

Despite the story's emphasis on character traits traditionally coded as feminine, "The Open Door" clearly presents ghostbusting as a male preserve, as Susan Schaper has noticed: first, "Roland dismisses his mother as a prospective exorcist, asking his father to give succor to the ghost. Mortimer in turn is assisted by men. ... Indeed, only men hear and respond to Willie's ghost calling out for 'Mother'" (Schaper 9). It is worth noting in this context, that the minister asks Willi's ghost to stop looking for his mother on earth but to "[g]o home to the Father – the Father!" (Oliphant, "Open" 179). While clearly a synonym for God, the emphasis on "Father" can also be understood as a request to accept the significance of the father figure for a child's emotional development and well-being. John Tosh has argued that, together with the separate spheres ideology, the strict dichotomy between male and female, "energy and repose, intellect and feeling ... cut the moral pretensions of men in the home down to size, and their significance as parents was correspondingly diminished. ... The feminine home was the place for nurture and love, the masculine world for restless energy and rationality" (*Man's Place* 47). Hugh Cunningham even talks of a "subordinate position" (69) of fathers and Jackie C. Horne sees their role as being "eclipsed by that of the mother" (73) in the Victorian period. By demonstrating that only men are able to help Willi's ghost and free him from being earthbound, the story works against the "elevation of the Angel Mother" (Tosh, *Man's Place* 47) and stresses the importance of paternal involvement.

Rudyard Kipling's "They" (1904)

Rudyard Kipling's "They" is the last ghost narrative investigated in this book. The story differs vastly from Kipling's earlier tale "The Mark of the Beast" (1890), which has been discussed in the previous chapter. While "The Mark of the Beast" is set in India in an imperial, markedly masculine environment that is characterised by the absence of both women and children, "They" takes place in England and, besides the male narrator, the main characters are a blind spinster and a bunch of (ghost)children. While not without imperial undertones, the focus of "They" lies on paternal bereavement and grief.

The tale is narrated by an autodiegetic narrator who encounters a bunch of children while driving through the countryside with his car. He stops at a remote house with a flourishing garden, where he meets a blind woman who is apparently taking care of the children. It is not until the end of the story that the narrator realises that the children are ghosts. This revelation reminds him of his own paternal loss. However, in contrast to other male ghost-seers – Dominic Holden in Conan Doyle's "The Brown Hand" and the narrator of Edward's "The Phantom Coach", for instance – the experience of ghost-seeing does not lead to the protagonist's mental and physical collapse. On the contrary, the encounter with the spectral children helps him to allow grief and to come to terms with the loss of his child. The story thus explores the idea that men can overcome traumatic experiences by admitting emotion and spiritual sensitivity.

Most critics and biographers of Kipling's work have suggested that the story deals with the author's own grief over the loss of his daughter Josephine, who died of pneumonia in 1899 at the age of six. Angus Wilson, for instance, claims that the story "is almost a direct fantasy of Kipling's longing to see and touch his daughter again" (264). William Dillingham has also pointed to the autobiographical elements in "They", arguing that the story constitutes "a surprisingly personal work from the pen of a writer who as a rule recoiled at the very thought of publicly exposing his innermost being" (408). As Dillingham contends, Kipling never fully recovered from Josephine's death and kept having vivid visions of his daughter – much like the narrator of "They" who is able to see the ghostly bodies of deceased children.[18] It is, of course, tempting to read the story in light if Kipling's own traumatising experience of paternal loss. However, the focus of my reading will be on how the text promotes what Sarah Bissell has called a "rehabilitated version of masculinity" ("Reconstructing" 64), which diverges from the then dominant idea of manliness as rational, resilient, and self-reliant.[19]

Interestingly, the story begins with an affirmation of established gender norms by portraying the protagonist as a potent motorist who is exploring the British countryside with his car. As Sean O'Connell has maintained, the car at the turn of the century was an "essentially male tool" (46) in more than one

---

18   Kipling's visions of his deceased daughter Josephine are well documented. In a letter, Kipling's father writes about how his son told his mother about the visions. For more information see William B. Dillingham's "Kipling: Spiritualism, Bereavement, Self-Revelation, and 'They'" (2002) and Charles Carrington's *Rudyard Kipling: His Life and Work* (1950), in particular the memoir by Kipling's daughter Elsie, which is published as an epilogue to the book.

19   While I find it problematic to build an analysis solely on an author's personal life, I believe that the contextualisation of literary texts can be instructive and further support an interpretation that is based primarily on close reading.

way: "In the first instance, the car's association with the engineering industry implanted the car in a world of masculine language of engineers and en-
trepreneurs. Second, the pioneering spirit of its early protagonists also lend
itself to a sense of masculine endeavour" (O'Connell 45). The car was thus something that was literally man-made; it also served to reaffirm the manliness of
those who owned and controlled the modern technology. Kipling was a car en-
thusiast himself and saw driving as a daring adventure, especially when the
technology was not yet refined. As he maintains in a letter to the newspaper
journalist Alexander Bell Filson Young, "any fool can wait to buy the invention
when it is thoroughly perfected; but the men to reverence, to admire, to write
odes and erect statues to are those Prometheuses and Ixions ... who chase the
inchoate idea to fixity up and down the King's Highway" (Kipling, Letter to Filson Young 150). This "sense of masculine endeavour" (O'Connell 45) that Kipling
associated with cars is also inherent in his ghost story. For one thing, the narrator presents his outings with the car as an excursion into unknown territory
where he finds "hidden villages" (Kipling, "They" 66) and "miraculous brooks"
(ibid.), as if he was discovering a new country somewhere in the far reaches of
the British Empire. Furthermore, the narrator is presented as someone who
can master the new technology. When the car breaks down halfway through
the story, he gets out his repair kit and starts working on the engine. As Bissell
has remarked, his "willingness to perform physical labour" ("Reconstructing"
73) lends him a certain "sense of class-neutrality" (ibid.). At the same time, his
"interest in the device's mechanical workings posits it as a symbol of his manliness" (ibid.) and stresses the narrator's embodiment of important masculine
virtues, such as resourcefulness and self-reliance. This image of the motorist
as manly and potent is further reinforced by the fact that the narrator uses the
female pronouns "she" (Kipling, "They" 71), "her" (ibid.), and "herself" (ibid. 70)
in order to refer to the car, thereby gendering the vehicle female. Besides the
sexual connotations evoked by the car's feminisation and the narrator's position as the driver of the car, the story reinforces ideas of men as active and in
control, while women, here symbolised by the car, passively obey.

However, there are also early hints in the story that suggest that the narrator does not embody the hegemonic ideal of masculinity propagated by Victorian imperialist ideology but that he represents a modern man at the turn of
the century who explicitly distances himself from the misguided ideas of the
past. When Miss Florence confides in him that people laugh at her "about *them*"
(Kipling, "They" 73, emphasis in original), the narrator gets angry. Although he
has not yet realised that the children are ghosts and therefore does not under-

stand that people ridicule Miss Florence for her belief in spirit communication, he calls them "savages" (ibid.) and muses about "the more than inherited (since it is also carefully taught) brutality of the Christian peoples, beside which the mere heathendom of the West Coast nigger is clean and restraint" (ibid.). While the choice of words the narrator uses is highly problematic from our perspective, it is nevertheless remarkable that he calls Christian people "savages" (ibid.) and condemns their "brutality" (ibid.) as more problematic than "the mere heathendom" (ibid.) of indigenous people, thereby reversing the cultural narrative propagated by imperialist ideology which sees indigenous people as naturally inferior to the white British colonisers. According to Bissell, the narrator's "privileging of non-white ideology posits him as a relatively progressive figure" ("Reconstructing" 73).

Also, the relationship between the narrator and his car takes a turn as the story advances. While he is at first presented as in control of the modern technology, he later contends that it is not his own will that takes him back to the house one month after his first visit but that his "car took the road of her own volition" (Kipling, "They" 71). While there are no other hints in the narrative that the car might actually be somehow supernatural and in possession of willpower, it is nevertheless telling that the narrator suggests that it was the car with her supposedly female (and feminine) character that made him revisit the house, for it highlights his consciousness of traditional gender norms. At this point in the story, the narrator is not aware of the ghostly nature of the children, and he cannot explain the attraction the house has for him. It is an irrational longing that he associates with femininity and that he cannot (yet) reconcile with his notion of proper masculine behaviour.

Besides the car's larger association with a "rugged, down-to-earth and utilitarian masculinity" (O'Connell 63), it is also presented as a means to make contact with the spectral children in the story. When the narrator first arrives at the remote house where the ghost-children reside, the blind owner, Miss Florence, asks him "to take your car through the gardens, once or twice – quite slowly" (Kipling, "They" 68) to give the children a chance to see the modern vehicle. It is worth noting that the garden with its remoteness and stunning beauty is reminiscent of the Garden of Eden and thus serves as an early hint at the children's unearthly nature. Appropriately enough, the narrator then also refers to the proposed tour through the garden as a "sacrilege" (Kipling, "They" 68), but starts the engine nonetheless, eager to impress the children. Later in the story, the narrator also consciously utilises the car to attract the children's attention. When the car breaks down close to the manor house upon his second visit, he takes out more tools than necessary for his repairs: "I confess now that I put it out to attract them. I don't need half those things really" (ibid. 72), he admits to Miss Florence. The car "is thus recoded as a desirable object with which one might forge pseudo-parental relationships" (Bissell, "Reconstructing 73). The narrator's eagerness to get in contact with the children is relevant insofar as it highlights his longing to resume the role of the father.

It is then also the direct encounter with one of the spectral children that eventually sets in motion the narrator's recognition of a spiritual sensitivity as part of his male gender identity. The narrator is back at Miss Florence's house for the third time. This time, he leaves his car behind and enters the building. Inside, he and Miss Florence chase the children who seem to be playing hide and seek with the two adults. They are interrupted by the appearance of one of Miss Florence's tenants who seeks to talk about his business with the blind woman "man to man" (Kipling, "They" 82). The narrator is present during their conversation and witnesses how Miss Florence, who initially seemed dependent on the help of others because of her disability, assumes the authority of a landowner who declines her tenant's request to build a new stable at her expense: "'You are overstocked already. Dunnett's Farm never carried more than fifty bullocks … . You've sixty-seven … . You've broken the lease in that respect. You're dragging the heart out of the farm'" (ibid.), Miss Florence points out, thereby revealing that she does not only know how to talk about business "man to man" (ibid.), but that she also has a profound knowledge about farming and farm management. Not unlike Miss Gostock in Charlotte Riddell's "Nut Bush Farm", which has been discussed in the first chapter of this work, Miss Florence is presented as a propertied woman whose ability to handle business transgresses familiar gender scripts of the time. However, while Miss Gostock is demonised by the male narrator of "Nut Bush Farm" for her supposedly inappropriate behaviour, Miss Florence's participation in the masculine world of business and landownership is not frowned upon. One reason for this may be her motherly attitude towards the ghost-children. Just like Miss Gostock, Miss Florence has never married and "neither born nor lost" (ibid. 83) a child, as she points out to the narrator. Nevertheless, she makes her house a home for spectral children and even equips it with children's toys like a doll's house, a rocking-horse and "a gilt wooden cannon" (ibid. 80). "[T]hey were all I should ever have. And I love them so!" (ibid. 83), she explains her devotion to the children at the end of the narrative, thereby stressing the important role these children have in her life. Through this focus on childcare and love, Miss Florence is presented as someone who also incorporates attributes stereotypically attributed to women. By showing that she can reconcile her role as a landowner and businesswoman with (spectral) motherhood, the story undermines binary constructions of gender and proposes a modern idea of womanhood that is not restricted to the domestic sphere. Furthermore, Miss Florence's embodiment of motherhood without ever having born a child points to alternatives to heterosexual marriage.

Interestingly, it is at this point of the narrative when Miss Florence is shown as resolute and straightforward that the narrator can also surmount the gender role restrictions imposed on men in the period. While his host is still talking to her tenant, the narrator feels how one of the children takes his hand and gives him a kiss:

> The little brushing kiss fell in the centre of my palm – as a gift on which the fingers were, once, expected to close: as the all-faithful half reproachful signal of a waiting child not used to neglect even when grown-ups were busiest – a fragment of the mute code devised very long ago.
> Then I knew. And it was as though I had known from the first day when I looked across the lawn at the high window.
> I heard the door shut. The woman turned to me in silence, and I felt that she knew.
> What time passed after this I cannot say. I was roused by the fall of a log, and mechanically rose to put it back. Then I returned to my place in the chair very close to the screen.
> "Now you understand," she whispered, across the packed shadows.
> "Yes, I understand—now. Thank you."
> "I—I only hear them." She bowed her head in her hands. "I have no right, you know—no other right. I have neither borne nor lost—neither borne nor lost!"
> "Be very glad then," said I, for my soul was torn open within me.
> "Forgive me!"
> She was still, and I went back to my sorrow and my joy. (Kipling, "They" 83)

The narrator understands that the children are ghosts and that he can see them because of his own loss. This revelation sets in motion an emotional process. The narrator can finally shed the stiff upper lip and admit grief over the death of his child. His soul is "torn open" (Kipling, "They" 83), but the memory of his deceased child is not altogether experienced as devastating but brings him both "sorrow and ... joy" (ibid.). Bissell speaks of a "frustrated paternity which can only find solace in the spiritual" ("Reconstructing" 73). The story thus proposes that ghost-seeing can be a good thing for men and initiate what Bret E. Carroll has called "an emotionally expressive and domestically engaged style of man-hood" (3) in his study on spiritualism and masculinity. Because of the accep-tance of emotions as part of masculine identity, Carroll contends, "Spiritualist ideology and ritual provided ideal theoretical and physical settings for [the] re-thinking of masculinity" (5). Carroll draws particular attention to the subject of male grief in this context: "male Spiritualists used grief as a didactic rhetori-cal and emotional device to stimulate Victorian men, and through them wider middle-class culture, to a reorientation of manhood" (Carroll 7). In Kipling's story, the spectral encounter sets in motion such a development. By the end of the narrative, the narrator represents a male gender identity that accommo-dates both emotion and a spiritual sensitivity.

It is well established that Kipling was sceptical towards spiritualism and publicly distanced himself from the spiritualist community to which some of his friends and his sister Alice "Trix" MacDonald Fleming belonged (Dilling-ham 403–4). However, as William Dillingham has pointed out, "he did not con-sider all mediums to be charlatans and all claims about psychic phenomena to be spurious" (404). There is also no "hint in the story of fakery or of men-tal unbalance, no suggestion whatever that the children might be hallucina-tions" (Dillingham 408). In this respect, "They" differs from most other ghost stories of the period which maintain a certain ambiguity or explicitly suggest the mental instability of the ghost-seer. The experience of ghost-seeing is also not experienced as horrifying in Kipling's narrative but "instigates a healing process" (Bissell, "Reconstructing" 74). This is at least suggested at the end of the narrative when the narrator decides not to revisit Miss Florence and her ghost children. While his repressed grief held him back and made him revisit Miss Florence's house, the acceptance of emotion and the pain of loss makes it possible for him to finally move on.

* * *

The aim of this chapter has been to illustrate the ways in which Victorian and Edwardian ghost stories question a worldview that is solely built on scientific materialism. Instead, they propose an idea of reality that goes "beyond the blinkered limits of male science, language, and rationalism" (R. Jackson xviii). By challenging dominant ideas "of what is possible or 'true'" (ibid. xvi), these stories also manage to raise consciousness about gender norms and expose a toxic masculinity that is harmful for both men and women.

The stories which have been discussed in the first section of this chapter "offer a twist on the idea that the male characters' rationality or their bourgeois status makes them superior to women who practice [or believe in] the supernatural" (Ohri 259). While Malcom Malcomson is punished for his disregard for everything that cannot be reduced to scientific laws and his dismissive attitude towards the local inn keeper, Mrs Witham, Valentine Burke's recklessness against women and his scepticism towards the occult are presented as the source of his decline. What both stories share is that the men's unwillingness to believe in the supernatural is presented as narrow-minded, arrogant, and potentially dangerous – especially for themselves. Both men end up being destroyed by the supernatural forces they have so ignorantly rejected. By presenting women and their spiritualist sensitivity as "productive alternatives to rationalism" (Bissell, *Haunted Matters* 71), both stories not only question scientific epistemology but undercut male superiority.

The stories discussed in the second section combat "the growing marginalization of British fatherhood" (Horne 74) in the second half of the nineteenth century in that they stress the importance of emotional involvement not only on the part of the mother but also on the part of the father. While Roland in "The Open Door" reaches out to his father and requests him to help the restless spirit, the unnamed narrator in "They" can only come to terms with the loss of his child when he establishes an emotional, quasi-parental link with a bunch of ghost children. Both texts thus challenge the notion of unemotional fatherhood and paternal non-involvement and encourage a form of masculinity that diverges from the dominant ideal of imperial masculinity which was primarily marked by a "dissociation from the feminine" (Tosh, *Man's Place* 47). The encounter with spectral children plays an important role in both stories. While Mortimer is able to enter the realm of the mother by showing affection and tenderness to the earthbound spirit of a boy longing to be reunited with his mother in Oliphant's narrative, the ghostly kiss in Kipling's story makes it possible for the unnamed narrator to finally admit his long-supressed grief. Most importantly, the feminised form of masculinity promoted in both stories is ultimately not experienced as shameful by the protagonists and thus provides men with an alternative to more aggressive forms of manhood. Given the raise of the New Woman movement towards the end of the nineteenth century with its stress on traditionally male attributes as part of women's gender identities, this alternative concept of masculinity can appropriately be referred to as the "New Man".

Conclusion

In the past, research on the ghost story has largely focused on either ghost stories written by men but with no particular attention to questions of gender and sexuality or on ghost stories by female authors with an emphasis on how women used the form as a means to question their role(s) within society. *Spectres of Masculinity: Manhood in Victorian and Edwardian Ghost Stories, 1860 – 1914* complements current scholarly accounts on the ghost story by interrogating what has mostly been overlooked: men and displays of masculinity in the genre. As this book has shown, this blind spot in research on the literary ghost story has not occurred because there is nothing to say about men and masculinity in the genre. On the contrary, the fact that most narrators are male in the ghost stories of the Victorian and Edwardian periods should have tipped off scholars that masculinity is an issue in these tales. I believe that the primary reason for the long neglect of the male narrative perspective lies in the social and cultural invisibility of normative masculinity. We are not used to looking at what is presented to us as the norm but are conditioned to register everyone who diverges from this norm – people of colour, people with disabilities, and women in general, to name just a few.[1] In an attempt to counter this development, I have looked at those who have usually assumed the role of the spectator, but who are not used to being gazed at: white, middle-class men.

In my work, I have sought to identify some of the most important issues that haunted men in the period between 1860 and 1914 in Great Britain. These include compulsive heterosexuality, imperial shame and guilt, fears of degeneration and reverse colonisation, fears about "the unexpected power and agency of women" (Margree, *British* 194), and anxieties about the role of the

---

1   On the cultural and social invisibility of the white, male body see, for instance, Anthony Easthope in *What a Man's Gotta Do: The Masculine Myth in Popular Culture* (1986), Jonathan Rutherford in *Male Order: Unwrapping Masculinity* (1988), and Ruth Heholt and Joanne Ella Parsons in *The Victorian Male Body* (2018).

father at a time when men were mostly absent from the domestic realm. An idea that figures centrally in most of the ghost stories I have looked at is the role model of the mentally and physically strong soldier hero, an "ultimate male fantasy"[2] (Lackaff and Sales 67) which was fuelled by the needs of the British Empire and defined in opposition to ideas about femininity. Time and again, we have met male protagonists who struggle to live up to this paragon of manliness, but ultimately fail to do so. What remains is a feeling of shame and distress. By leaving a loophole for a rational explanation of the seemingly supernatural occurrences, many ghost stories suggest that, rather than being haunted by "real" ghosts, the male protagonists are haunted by a distorted picture of masculinity.

I have also looked at femininity, especially at characters who transgress the image of the good and proper housewife. My focus was on why and how these female figures appear monstrous to the male narrators and what this tells us about the identity crisis experienced by those men. Two female figures stood out repeatedly in the ghost stories I have interrogated: the sexually liberated femme fatale and the propertied woman, two female figures that are marked by their self-reliance and assertiveness – traits which stand in opposition to the idea of women as passive and dependent on their male relatives and which gave cause for male gender insecurity at a time which saw a growing agitation for women's rights.

In all chapters, my analysis of Victorian and Edwardian ghost fiction was informed by an interdisciplinary approach that connects ghost story criticism with masculinity studies, philosophy, sociology, historical science, architecture, and psychology. The first chapter looked at male discomfort and gendered domestic spaces in late-Victorian and Edwardian haunted house narratives. While clearly drawing attention to fears about female dominance and power, these stories also show how men "lose their confidence, become oppressed, doubtful, unsure of their status, vulnerable to swings of emotion" (Uglow xvi) within the domestic space and are thus pushed into a feminised position. My

---

2   I have borrowed the term from Derek Lackaff's and Michael Sales's article about comic books because it also perfectly describes the ideal of imperial masculinity. For one, it is a fantasy, a myth that cannot be reached by normal men who are "just" human and not superhuman. Furthermore, both the archetypical superhero (Superman, for instance) and the imperial soldier hero reinforce heteronormative ideas. They are male, heterosexual, white, hyper-physical, and cisgender and they embody white supremacist thinking (Gavaler 77, 179).

second chapter focused on what I have termed "spectral sexualities", that is to say on love and desire that was deemed unnatural or even unlawful at the time when these stories were written, namely homosexuality and the longing for the sexually attractive and aggressive woman. The ghosts who appear in these stories stand in allegorically for the male protagonists' sexual fantasies and desires. Chapter three then turned to colonial ghost stories and illustrated how these tales function to simultaneously blur and reinforce the binary divisions between West and East, civilised and savage, ruler and subject. The chapter also showed how the ghost story genre works as a reversal of the success-formula of imperial adventure fiction, thereby expressing fears about masculine failure and imperial decline. Finally, in my last chapter, I looked at the relationship between science and spiritualism and illustrated how writers used the spectral to criticise the idea of rational masculinity, on the one hand, and sought to negotiate a new concept of manhood that emphasises the importance of fatherhood and qualities such as compassion and tenderness, on the other hand.

It is not my intention to suggest that my work covers everything there is to say about men and depictions of masculinity in the literary ghost story. Considering the complexity of the genre and the diversity of authors who have contributed to it, it is more than likely that there are aspects this work has not dealt with. An aspect that I have not looked at in depth is the male ghost body, for instance. I focused on men who see ghosts and not on men who are or become ghosts. Is the male phantom an emasculated figure, a shadow of his former self, or is he determined, aggressive, and able to possess and control others? This question, and the socio-cultural implications it entails, still needs answering.[3] For this reason, I hope that my work can encourage further research in the field.

At his point, I would like to draw attention again to what has been labelled imperial masculinity and the event that presumably started its decline as the prevalent concept of masculinity: The Great War. Several critics have suggested that the romanticising of the frontier as a place where men could prove their manliness and enjoy homosocial comradeship only lasted as long as the horrors of war were only known to a minority of the population, namely to those who actually fought in the wars in which the British Empire was entangled. As John

---

3   In her article "Visible yet Immaterial: The Phantom and the Male Body in Ghost Stories by Three Victorian Women Writers" Ruth Heholt addresses this question. While necessarily limited to only a few authors (namely Catherine Crowe, Rhoda Broughton, and Edith Nesbit), Heholt's article opens the door for further research on the topic.

Tosh has pointed out, "[t]he problem was that military masculinity was associated with an image of war which was completely at variance with the reality to be found" (*Masculinity* 4). John Beynon likewise notes that "[a]fter the carnage of Passchendaele and Somme, ... the idea that war was a glorious game played by gentlemen could never again be taken seriously" (50). The war thus "killed off the bachelor gentleman" (Skovmand 54), as Michael Skovmand has put it.[4] Of course, elements of imperial masculinity have lived on to this day. Especially in modern day sports displays of manly vigour and homosocial solidarity are a daily fare that is, surprisingly, hardly ever commented on by the press. It is, in fact, also an image that can be revitalised in times of war, as the war in Ukraine has shown, where president Volodymyr Zelenskiy has impressed the world with his bravery and will to fight and turned from a former comedian and actor into a manly role model and hero of the nation. Nevertheless, critics are right in contending that in Great Britain the figure of the military soldier hero has never again been as omnipresent as it was in the late-Victorian and Edwardian eras. While the trauma of the Great War has certainly had an impact on male gender identities in Great Britain, the decline of imperial masculinity is, of course, also linked to the British Empire, which started to crumble after the First World War. As Beynon maintains, "the disintegration of the British Empire ... deprived [the imperial man] of his role" (50).

Several scholars have suggested that the ghost story as a popular literary form suffered a similar fate, that there was a period in which the genre flourished before it started its decline. This period, many critics agree, coincides with the heyday of the British Empire – much like the image of the imperial soldier hero. Michael Cox and R. A. Gilbert, for instance, write in their introduction to *The Oxford Book of English Ghost Stories* (1986) that "[t]he golden age of Empire was also the golden age of the English ghost story" (xiii) and Philip

---

4   Skovmand's term refers to the kind of man for whom marriage was a burden and who rather spent his time in the company of other men – be that in a gentlemen's club or the military. There were, in fact, numerous role models for this type of man in the military. Many empire builders of the day remained bachelors like Horatio Herbert Kitchener and Charles George Gordon, "or else married well after their empire-building days were over" (Tosh, *Manliness* 206) like Robert Baden-Powell. Kitchener even refused to accept married officers under his command in the Sudan campaign of 1897–8 (ibid.). The bachelor gentleman as an ideal was further established by such figures as Sherlock Holmes and Dr Watson, who lived in what Skovmand calls "the blessed garden of Leisured Bachelorhood" (46).

van Doren Stern asserts that there has never been "such of flood of [ghost sto-ries] within so short a period" (qdt. in Sullivan 3) as there was at the turn of the century. In their introduction to *The Victorian Gothic: An Edinburgh Companion* (2012), Andrew Smith and William Hughes have reinforced this claim, arguing that "the Victorian period seems ... to have represented something of a heyday for the ghost story" ("Locating" 3).

Julia Briggs has maintained that the First World War brought an end to the golden age of the ghost story: "the horrors of the ghost story now sud-denly appeared childish, trivial and of no account" (Briggs, *Night Visitors* 165) next to the brutally real horrors of the war, "the charnel-house trenches full of rats, skeletons and mouldering corpses" (ibid.). A ghost story like Walter Scott's "The Tapestried Chamber" (1828), which arguably ignited the ghost story genre in the 1820s, almost seemed to mock reality with its claim that for the general who features as the story's protagonist the experience of ghost-seeing is "far more testing ... than going into battle" (Briggs, *Night Visitors* 165). Such stories, Briggs contends, lost their appeal at a time when "modern technology had transformed the battlefield into something very like a vision of hell itself" (ibid.).

A look at ghost fiction from the time after 1914 shows, however, that the form adjusted to the horrors of the war rather than being in decline. The Great War produced ghosts of its own, as Siegfried Sassoons's description of a di-vision coming back from the Somme offensive in France, in which countless British soldiers lost their lives, illustrates: "with an almost spectral appearance, the lurching brown figures flitted past with slung rifles and heads bent for-ward under basin-helmets. ... [I]t was as though I watched an army of ghosts" (84). Rather than envisioning palpable ghosts that haunt the soldiers, Sassoon uses the metaphor of the ghost to suggest that, though still alive, the war has turned these men into spectres, mere phantoms of their former selves. At the same time, the war is the ultimate ghost that haunts the soldiers. Much like Sassoon, who wrote about his own wartime experiences in his autobiographi-cal novel *Memoirs of an Infantry Officer* (1930), many men who fought in the war were certainly haunted for life by what they had experienced.

Considering the genre's long preoccupation with the workings of the hu-man psyche and the status of the ghost as something that is coming back, an "anachronistic intrusion of the past into the present" (Luckhurst, *Trauma* 93), it is not surprising that authors used the ghost story to relay "the deep psychic trauma caused by war" (Foley 320). Oliver Onions's "The Rope in the Rafters" (1935), for instance, deals with traumatic memory by centring on a war veteran,

Hopley, who is both mentally disturbed and disfigured to the extent that his lover cannot look at him anymore. Physically and mentally impaired, the veteran represents the antithesis to healthy masculinity. Much like the soldiers in the quote above, Hopley is haunted by his memories and, at the same time, is ghostlike himself. While in a hotel in the French countryside, where he is supposed to gain some strength, Hopley is then also haunted by what appears to be an actual ghost to him. It is unclear though whether the spectre is real or a product of the man's damaged psyche. What the story clearly shows is the spectrality of trauma. Trauma, Hopley's fate shows, works like "a form of possession or haunting" (Edmundson, "Haunting" 55) and the ghost embodies "the idea of the persistence of traumatic memory" (Luckhurst, *Trauma* 93). Onions's story thus suggests the ghostliness of war in more than one way.[5]

While Onion's story depicts the dark aspects of the war, there are also supernatural tales from the trenches that utilise the "motif of supernatural aid" (Kokot 228), thereby "constructing patriotic myths" (Foley 320) that supported the war effort. A prominent example is Arthur Machen's "The Bowmen" (1914), a tale about the spectral appearance of bowmen from the Battle of Agincourt[6] who, led by St. George, help the Allies during a battle "that was for a time in awful danger, not merely of defeat, but of utter annihilation" (Machen 23–4). Several critics have argued that Machen's story has inspired the "Angel of Mons", a divine figure that was supposedly seen during the battle at Mons by British and French soldiers who believed that God was supporting their armies against the German troops (cf. Foley, cf. Kokot).

Rudyard Kipling, whose only son, John, went "missing" (a term which became something of a codeword for "dead and buried in a mass grave") during the war, also utilized the ghost story for patriotic purposes. In "'Swept and Garnished'" (1915), for instance, an elderly German woman in Berlin is haunted by the ghosts of murdered Belgian children. Kipling's story was inspired by reports about German atrocities in Belgium and exposes what is arguably seen as the worst of all war crimes, the murder of innocent children, thereby

---

5   Oliver Onions's "The Rope in the Rafters" is not the only wartime ghost story to deal with shell shock and wartime injuries. Other examples are D. H. Lawrence's "The Thimble" (1915) and H. D. Everett's "The Perplexing Case" (1920).

6   The Battle of Agincourt took place in 1415 during the Hundred Years War between England and France. The English won the battle unexpectedly. For more information see, for instance, Clifford J. Rogers's "The Battle of Agincourt" in *The Hundred Years War*, part 2.

dehumanising the German enemy. Another story that dwells on the so-called "Rape of Belgium" is H. D. Everett's "Over the Wires" (1920). The tale is narrated through the perspective of a British army captain who receives ghostly calls from his beloved, a Belgian girl who is raped by German soldiers and then dies. It is left open whether she has committed suicide or has been killed by the men – the former is strongly suggested though by the girl's assertion that she would rather have been killed like her aunt, who was stabbed by the soldiers, than having to endure mass rape: "they dragged the Tante and me away. But the Tante could not go fast enough to please them. They stabbed her in the back with their bayonets, and left her bleeding and moaning, lying in the road to die. Oh, if only they had killed me too. Don't ask me – never ask me – what they did to me!" (Everett, "Wires" 127). As Melissa Edmundson has noticed, the rape is unspeakable in Everett's tale ("Haunting" 58). It is a weapon that deeply shames the victim who feels that only death can ensure that she is "washed clean" (Everett, "Wires" 126). While clearly a tale about women's suffering in times of war, "Over the Wires" also relates the tale of a military man who proves himself on the front, but is ultimately unable to protect those he loves most (Edmundson, "Haunting" 58).

Finally, there are also Great War ghost stories that depict the return of dead soldiers to their loved ones like Violet Hunt's "Love's Last Leave" (1925), a story about Gussy and her sister Aggie, the latter of whom becomes pregnant when their husbands, the brothers George and Willy Leclerc, return from the front for Christmas. Being called back to duty, Willy must leave his wife Aggie after only one night. We then learn that Willy has died in the war around the time of his visit. Since nobody has seen the soldier during his visit except for Aggie, it is unclear whether the man's ghost has returned to Aggie and fathered the child or whether she has actually spent the night with her sister's husband George. This ambiguity is not resolved throughout the story (although the title suggests Willy's ghostly return) and Aggie and her adolescent son Peter eventually drown themselves. Stories like "Love's Last Leave" were not written by and for the men on the front lines, but by and for those who were left behind, those who had to live in uncertainty as to whether their sons, brothers, fathers, and husbands had died. As Melissa Edmundson has rightly remarked, such stories shift the spotlight from the front lines and stress "shared experience and shared trauma" ("Haunting" 56).

In summary, it can be said that the Great War clearly did not exorcise the literary ghost. Far from it, the horror of the war led to a new wave of ghost fiction. As my brief discussion of wartime ghost narratives has indicated, these stories have much to say about men and ideas of masculinity. Hence, there certainly is potential for further research on questions of masculinity and the ghost story genre.

As recent research on women's ghost writing has illustrated, female authors also picked up the ghost story in the interwar years to address concerns about female self-determination and "contemporary notions of modernity" (Margree, *British* 148). Paul March-Russell, for instance, claims that the genre was "in transition" (21) after the First World War, "becoming a seedbed for that other rich and strange phenomenon known as Modernism" (ibid.). Among the women writers who employed the ghost story in the transitionary period between the wars are Virginia Woolf, May Sinclair, Eleanor Scott, Violet Hunt, and Elizabeth Bowen, to name but a few. Also, as Cox and Gilbert have acknowledged, writers took up "the challenge of the ghost-story form ... after the Second World War" (*English* xiv). The Jewish writer Isaac Bashevis Singer, for instance, wrote powerful ghost narratives about the aftermath of the holocaust. Also, writers like Cynthia Asquith, Robert Aickman, and L. T. C. Rolt contributed to the genre after the Second World War. It is true, though, that the classical ghost story became less ubiquitous in the latter decades of the twentieth century and is today almost insignificant as a genre in the literary marketplace. This decline goes hand in hand with – and might actually be explained by – "the shrinking of the magazine market" (Liggins et al., *British* 211).

However, while the ghost story as it was established in the nineteenth century may almost have disappeared today, ideas of haunting and spectrality have not. As Sarah Bissell has pointed out, "Neo-Victorian fiction continually employs motifs of haunting, and much modern theory utilizes spectrality as a potent symbol through which to understand history, literature, and intertextuality" ("Science" 47). Also, the figure of the literary ghost has come back in many shapes and forms and entered other genres and media as the short story ceased to provide a suitable home for it, among them television series, films, video games, and pop songs. It is true that ghosts have been somewhat eclipsed by other Gothic figures such as the vampire and the zombie in popular film and fiction in the last decades. In particular, the figure of the "good" vampire, which was introduced by Anne Rice in *Interview with the Vampire* (1976), has been immensely popular ever since the publication of Stephenie Meyer's romantic *Twilight* series (2005–2020). Nevertheless, there have been some notable ghost narratives. Toni Morrison, for instance, has used the figure of the ghost as "a collective reminder of past trauma and in

order to challenge notions of social belonging and racial marginalization"
(Beville 451) in her acclaimed novel *Beloved* (1987). More recently, Vera Brosgol
has taken up the tradition of women's ghost writing in her graphic novel
Anya's Ghost (2011). In the book, the eponymous heroine falls into a dry well
where she meets the ghost of Emily, a girl who died there 90 years earlier.
When Anya is rescued, Emily starts following her and soon becomes obsessed
with Anya's life. Brosgol's graphic novel is a modern ghost story in more than
one way: most importantly, it uses the supernatural for social commentary
by illustrating how ideas about beauty impact Anya's body image. This is
particularly foregrounded by the artwork of the graphic novel which shows
that Anya's perception of her body diverges from the way other people view
her. The story demonstrates that beauty standards work as a mechanism of
control that defines and confines women's bodies and lives – much like the
ideal of domestic femininity in the nineteenth century. Furthermore, *Anya's
Ghost* calls the reader's attention to the identity issues of immigrants. Anya,
who has immigrated to the US from Russia with her mother and brother,
avoids bringing Russian food to school and even tells her love interest that
her surname is Brown instead of Borzakovskaya. The ghostly Emily serves
as Anya's mirror in the graphic novel. By asking seemingly naïve questions
about Anya's attitude towards her Russian heritage, she draws attention to
the ways in which heteronormative thinking impacts identity formation. In
addition to the socio-cultural commentary, Brosgol's work actively engages
with typical plot patterns of the ghost story. While *Anya's Ghost* constitutes
an archetypical story about haunting, in which the ghost attempts to control
the protagonist, the text breaks with stock features of the genre elsewhere:
in a twist of the classic ghost story plot, in which the ghost returns in order
to expose its murderer, Emily's ghost exists because of a crime that she has
committed during her lifetime. Brosgol thus plays with the expectation of the
reader.

There have also been some notable ghost films, such as M. Night Shyamalan's *The Sixth Sense* (1999), in which the protagonist does not know that he
has died and come back as a ghost. The idea that a ghost is unaware of its death
is not new. We have come across such a ghost in Margaret Oliphant's "The Open
Door", for instance, where the ghost of a prodigal son returns to his mother after the woman's death and begs to be left into a house that is not inhabited any
more. However, what gives *The Sixth Sense* an additional turn of the screw is the
fact that the audience is as oblivious to the truth as the protagonist. We only
learn at the end of the film that Dr Malcom Crowe (played by Bruce Willis) has

been dead the whole time and what we perceived as real were his memories and ghostly interactions with the living.[7] More recent examples of films that centre on ghosts are Rob Savage's horror film *Host* (2020), in which a malignant spirit is called during a video call on Zoom at the beginning of the COVID-19 pandemic, and the Netflix series *The Haunting of Bly Manor* (2020), a modern adaptation of Henry James's well-known *The Turn of the Screw* (1898).

Collectively, these examples show that the ghost is a potent figure that can never fully be exorcised. As ghost story writer Elisabeth Bowen remarked in 1952, ghosts "adapt themselves well, perhaps better than we do, to changing world conditions – they enlarge their domain, shift their hold on our nerves and, dispossessed of one habitat, set up house in another" (Bowen 7). As long as humankind exists, ghosts will thus continue to haunt us.

---

7   Alejandro Amenábar's Gothic film *The Others* (2001), which stars Nicole Kidman as the leading actress, follows a similar plot pattern. It is not until the end that we know that the protagonists are, in fact, ghosts.

Bibliography

Primary Sources

Acton, William. *The Functions and Disorders of the Reproductive Organs*. London, J. & A. Churchill, 1875, pp. 212–13.

Almond, H. H. "The Public School Product." *The New Review*, vol. 16, London, 1897, pp. 84–98. *ProQuest*, https://search.proquest.com/docview/6534005 ?fromopenview=true&pq-origsite=gscholar&imgSeq=1. Accessed 26 Feb. 2025.

Almond, H. H. "Athletics and Education." *Macmillan's Magazine*, vol. 43, London, R. Clay, Sons, and Taylor, 1881, pp. 283–94. *Internet Archive*, https://archive.o rg/details/macmillansmagazi43macmuoft/page/294/mode/2up. Accessed 26 Feb. 2025.

Baker Brown, Isaac. *On the Curability of Certain Forms of Insanity, Epilepsy, Catalepsy, and Hysteria in Females*. London, Robert Hardwicke, 1866.

Baldwin, Louisa and Lettice Galbraith. *The Shadow on the Blind and Other Stories*. Edited by David Stuart Davies, London, Wordsworth Editions, 2007.

Ballantyne, R. M. *The Coral Island: A Tale of the Pacific Ocean*. 1856. London, Ward, Lock & Co, 1901.

Barrie, J. M. *Peter Pan; or, The Boy Who Wouldn't Grow Up*. Project Gutenberg Australia. Feb. 2003. http://gutenberg.net.au/ebooks03/0300081h.html. Accessed 26 Feb. 2025.

Beard, George. *American Nervousness: Its Causes and Consequences*. New York, G. P. Putnam's Sons, 1881. *Internet Archive*, https://archive.org/details/americ annervousnoobearuoft/page/n7/mode/2up. Accessed 26 Feb. 2025.

Blackwood, Algernon. "The Empty House." *The Oxford Book of English Ghost Stories*, Oxford, Oxford UP, 1987, pp. 222–35.

Bodkin, A. H. and Frederick Mead. *The Criminal Law Amendment Act, 1885*. Shaw and Sons, 1885. *Internet Archive*, https://archive.org/details/criminallawam enoobodkgoog/page/n6/mode/2up. Accessed 26 Feb. 2025.

Bowen, Elizabeth. "Introduction to *The Second Ghost Book*." *The Green Book: Writings on Irish Gothic, Supernatural and Fantastic Literature*, no. 9, 2017, pp. 7–10. Jstor, https://www.jstor.org/stable/48536135?seq=1. Accessed 26 Feb. 2025.

Braddon, Mary Elizabeth. *Lady Audley's Secret*. Edited by Lyn Pykett, Oxford, Oxford UP, 2012.

Breuer, Josef and Sigmund Freud. *Studies in Hysteria*. Translated by Nicola Luckhurst, London, Penguin, 2004.

Brontë, Anne. *The Tenant of Wildfell Hall*. Edited by Herbert Rosengarten, Oxford, Oxford UP, 1998.

Brontë, Charlotte. *Jane Eyre*. Edited by Margaret Smith, Oxford, Oxford UP, 2000.

Brontë, Emily. *Wuthering Heights*. London, Penguin, 1994.

Brosgol, Vera. *Anya's Ghost*. New York, First Second Books, 2011.

Burke, Edmund. *A Philosophical Enquiry into the Origin of Our Ideas of the Sublime and Beautiful*. London, R. and J. Dodsley, 1757. *Internet Archive*, https://arch ive.org/details/enqphilosophicalooburkrich/page/n1/mode/2up. Accessed 26 Feb. 2025.

Chamberlain, Joseph. "The True Conception of Empire." *The Fin de Siècle. A Reader in Cultural History c. 1880–1900*, edited by Sally Ledger and Rodger Luckhurst, New York, Oxford UP, 2000, pp. 137–141.

Collins, Wilkie. "The Unknown Public." *My Miscellanies*, vol. 1, London, Sampson Low, Son, & Co, 1863, pp. 169–191. *Internet Archive*, https://archive.org/ details/mymiscellaniesoicoll/page/190/mode/2up?view=theater&ui=emb ed&wrapper=false. Accessed 26 Feb. 2025.

Conan Doyle, Arthur. *The Adventures of Sherlock Holmes*. London, George Newnes, 1892. *Internet Archive*, https://archive.org/details/adventuresofsh eroo1892doyl/page/n5/mode/2up?q=weaknesses. Accessed 26 Feb. 2025.

Conan Doyle, Arthur. "The Brown Hand." *Tales of Unease*, St. Ives, Wordsworth, 2000, pp. 71–85.

Conan Doyle, Arthur. *'The Lost World' and Other Stories*, St Ives, Wordsworth, 2010.

Conrad, Joseph. *Heart of Darkness*. Edited by Paul B. Armstrong, New York, W. W. Norton, 2016.

Crenshaw, Kimberlé. "Demarginalizing the Intersection of Race and Sex: A Black Feminist Critique of Antidiscrimination Doctrine, Feminist Theory and Antiracist Politics." *University of Chicago Legal Forum*, vol. 1989, no. 1, 1989, pp. 139–167.

Crowe, Catherine. *The Night-Side of Nature: or, Ghosts and Ghost-Seers*. New York, B. B. Mussey & Co, 1850. *Internet Archive*, https://archive.org/details/nightsi denatureoocrowgoog/page/n8/mode/2up?q=productive. Accessed 26 Feb. 2025.

Darwin, Charles. *On the Origin of Species*. Cambridge, Massachusetts, Harvard UP, 1964.

Darwin, Charles. *The Decent of Man*. John Murray, 1896.

Dickens, Charles. "A Curious Dance Round a Curious Tree." *Charles Dickens' Uncollected Writings from* Household Words *1850–1859*, edited by Harry Stone, vol. 2, Bloomington, Indiana UP, 1968, pp. 381–91.

Dickens, Charles. *A Christmas Carol and Other Christmas Writings*. London, Penguin, 2003.

Dickens, Charles. "A Christmas Tree." *A Christmas Carol and Other Christmas Writings*. London, Penguin, 2003, pp. 231–47.

Dickens, Charles. *David Copperfield*. London, Penguin, 1994.

Dickens, Charles. Letter to Mrs Gaskell. 25. Nov. 1851. *The Letters of Charles Dickens: The Pilgrim Edition*, edited by Madeline House et al., vol. 6, Oxford, Clarendon Press, 1988, pp. 545–6.

Dickens, Charles. Letter to Mrs Gaskell. 6 Nov. 1852. *The Letters of Charles Dickens: The Pilgrim Edition*, edited by Madeline House et al., vol. 6, Oxford, Clarendon Press, 1988, pp. 798–800.

Dickens, Charles. Letter to Mrs Gaskell. 4 Dec. 1852. *The Letters of Charles Dickens: The Pilgrim Edition*, edited by Madeline House et al., vol. 6, Oxford, Clarendon Press, 1988, pp. 815–6.

Dickens, Charles. *The Haunted House*. Mineola, Dover Publications, 2008.

Dickens, Charles. *The Letters of Charles Dickens: The Pilgrim Edition*. Vol. 6, edited by Madeline House et al., Oxford, Clarendon Press, 1988.

Dickens, Charles. "The Trial for Murder." *The Complete Ghost Stories of Charles Dickens*. New York, Franklin Watts, 1983, pp. 289–98. *Internet Archive*, https://archive.org/details/completeghoststoodick/page/298/mode/2up. Accessed 26 Feb. 2025.

Derrida, Jacques. "Archive Fever: A Freudian Impression." *Diacritics*, vol. 25, no. 2, summer 1995, pp. 9–63.

Derrida, Jacques. *Specters of Marx*. 1993. Translated by Peggy Kamuf, New York, Routledge, 2006.

Edwards, Amelia B. "The Phantom Coach". *The Oxford Book of English Ghost Stories*, edited by Michael Cox and R. A. Gilbert, Oxford, Oxford UP, 1987, pp. 13–24.

Ellis, Havelock. *Man and Woman: A Study of the Human Secondary Sexual Characters*. London, Walter Scott, 1894. *Internet Archive*, https://ia800201.us.archive.org/20/items/manandwoman00elligoog/manandwoman00elligoog.pdf. Accessed 26 Feb. 2025.

Ellis, Havelock. *Studies in the Psychology of Sex: Sexual Inversion*. Philadelphia, F. A. Davis Company, 1901. *Internet Archive*, https://archive.org/details/sexualinversion00elligoog/page/n8/mode/2up. Accessed 26 Feb. 2025.

Everett, H. D. "Over the Wires." *The Crimson Blind and Other Stories*, Ware, Wordsworth, pp. 125–34.

Everett, H. D. "The Perplexing Case." *The Crimson Blind and Other Stories*, Ware, Wordsworth, pp. 167–76.

Foucault, Michel. *Discipline and Punish: The Birth of the Prison*. Translated by Alan Sheridan, New York, Vintage Books, 1979.

Foucault, Michel. *The History of Sexuality: Vol. 1: An Introduction*. New York, Vintage Books, 1990.

Freud, Sigmund. "The Uncanny." *The Standard Edition of the Complete Psychological Works of Sigmund Freud*, translated and edited by James Strachey et al., vol. 17, London, Random House, 2001, pp. 219–56.

Galbraith, Lettice. "A Ghost's Revenge." *The Shadow on the Blind and Other Stories*. London, Wordsworth Editions, 2007, pp. 219–37.

Galbraith, Lettice. "In the Séance Room." *The Shadow on the Blind and Other Stories*. London, Wordsworth Editions, 2007, pp. 189–203.

Galbraith, Lettice. *The Blue Room and Other Ghost Stories*. Edited by Richard Dalby, Mountain Ash, Sarob Press, 1999. *Richard Dalby Library*, https://richarddalbyslibrary.com/products/lettice-galbraith-the-bruce-room-and-other-ghost-stories-sarob-press-1999?variant=3632466165787. Accessed 26 Feb. 2025.

Galbraith, Lettice. "The Missing Model." *The Shadow on the Blind and Other Stories*. London, Wordsworth Editions, 2007, pp. 205–18.

Gaskell, Elizabeth. Letter to Eliza Fox. 17 Nov. 1851. *The Letters of Mrs Gaskell*, edited by J. A. V. Chapple and Arthur Pollard, Manchester, Mandolin, 1997, pp. 171–3.

Gaskell, Elizabeth. Letter to Eliza Fox. April 1850. *The Letters of Mrs Gaskell*, edited by J. A. V. Chapple and Arthur Pollard, Manchester, Mandolin, 1997, pp. 107–10.

Gaskell, Elizabeth. Letter to John Forster. April 1853. *The Letters of Mrs Gaskell*, edited by J. A. V. Chapple and Arthur Pollard, Manchester, Mandolin, 1997, pp. 230–1.

Gaskell, Elizabeth. Letter to John Forster. 14 May 1854. *The Letters of Mrs Gaskell*, edited by J. A. V. Chapple and Arthur Pollard, Manchester, Mandolin, 1997, pp. 282–3.

Gaskell, Elizabeth. *The Life of Charlotte Brontë*. New York, Harper, 1900. *Internet Archive*, https://archive.org/details/lifeofcharlotteb00gask/page/n13/mode /2up. Accessed 26 Feb. 2025.

Gaskell, Elizabeth. "The Grey Woman." *Gothic Tales*, edited by Laura Kranzler, London, Penguin Books, 2000, pp. 287–340.

Gaskell, Elizabeth. "The Old Nurse's Story." *Curious, If True. Strange Tales*, edited by Jenny Uglow, London, Virago Press, 1995, pp. 1–25.

Gaskell, Elizabeth. "The Poor Clare." *Gothic Tales*, edited by Laura Kranzler, London, Penguin Books, 2000, pp. 49–102.

Godwin, William. *Caleb Williams*. New York, Oxford UP, 1998.

Gramsci, Antonio. *Selections from the Prison Notebooks*. London, Lawrence & Wishart, 1971.

Greg, W. R. *Why Are Women Redundant?* London, Trübner, 1869. *Internet Archive*, https://archive.org/details/whyarewomenredu00greggoog/page/ n2/mode/2up. Accessed 26 Feb. 2025.

Haggard, H. Rider. *King Solomon's Mines*. New York, Longmans, Green & Company, 1901. *Internet Archive*, https://archive.org/details/kingsolomonsmin0 0hagggoog/page/n6/mode/2up. Accessed 26 Feb. 2025.

Hake, Egmont. *Regeneration: A Reply to Max Nordau*. London, Archibald Constable, 1895. *Internet Archive*, https://archive.org/details/cu31924029763012/pa ge/n4. Accessed 26 Feb. 2025.

Halberstam, Jack. *Female Masculinity*. Durham, Duke UP, 2018.

Hardy, E.J. *How to Be Happy Though Married: Being a Handbook to Marriage by a Graduate in the University of Matrimony*. London, T Fisher Unwin, 1887. *Internet Archive*, https://archive.org/details/howtobehappythou00hard/page/n5 /mode/2up. Accessed 26 Feb. 2025.

Harper, Charles. *Revolted Woman: Past, Present, and to Come*. London, Elkin Mathews, 1894.

Hemyng, Bracebridge. *Jack Harkaway: After Schooldays*. 1872. Chicago, M. A. Donohue and Company.

Henty, G. A. *By Sheer Pluck: A Tale of the Ashanti War*. London, Blackie and Son, 1884.

Host. Directed by Rob Savage, performance by Haley Bishop, Vertigo Films, 2020.

Hughes, Thomas. *Tom Brown's Schooldays and Tom Brown at Oxford.* Ware, Wordsworth, 1993.

Hunt, Violet. "Love's Last Leave." *The Complete Uneasy Tales,* London, William Heinemann, pp. 81–164.

James, Henry. Letter to Francis Boott. 11 Oct. 1895. *Henry James: Selected Letters,* edited by Leon Edel, Cambridge, Massachusetts, Harvard UP, 1987, p. 293.

James, Henry. "The Real Right Thing." *Ghost Stories of Henry James,* edited by David Stuart Davies, Ware, Wordsworth Editions, 2008.

James, Henry. *The Turn of the Screw.* Edited by Deborah Esch and Jonathan Warren, Norton, 1999.

Ker, David: "A Coral Prison; Or, The Boy Hermits of the Indian Ocean. A Tale of the Maledive Isles." *The Boy's Own Annual,* vol. 13, 1891, pp. 6–8, pp. 23–27, pp. 40–42, pp. 56–58, pp. 70–72, pp. 85–86, pp. 100–101, pp. 117–18.

Kerr, David. *The Gentleman's House: Or, How to Plan English Residences, from the Parsonage to the Palace.* London, John Murray, 1865. *Internet Archive,* https://archive.org/details/gentlemanshouse01kerrgoog/page/n4/mode/2up. Accessed 26 Feb. 2025.

King, Stephen. *The Shining.* New York, Anchor Books, 2012.

Kipling, Rudyard. Letter to Alexander Bell Filson Young. April 1904. *The Letters of Rudyard Kipling,* edited by Thomas Pinney, vol. 3, Basingstoke, Palgrave Macmillan, 1996, pp. 149–152.

Kipling, Rudyard. "'Swept and Garnished.'" *Strange Tales,* London, Wordsworth, 2006, pp. 170–77.

Kipling, Rudyard. "The Man Who Would Be King." *Under the Deodars, The Phantom Rickshaw, Wee Willie Winkie,* Doubleday, Page & Company, 1914, pp. 189–236. *Internet Archive,* https://archive.org/details/underdeodarspha02kiplgoog/mode/2up. Accessed 26 Feb. 2025.

Kipling, Rudyard. "The Mark of the Beast." *Strange Tales,* Ware, Wordsworth, 2006, pp. 3–13.

Kipling, Rudyard. "They." *Strange Tales.* Ware, Wordsworth, 2006, pp. 66–84.

Lankester, E. Ray. *Degeneration: A Chapter in Darwinism.* London, Macmillan, 1880. *Internet Archive,* https://archive.org/details/degenerationchap00lank/page/n6. Accessed 27 Feb. 2025.

Lavater, Ludwig. *Of ghostes and spirites walking by nyght.* London, Thomas Creede, 1596. *Internet Archive,* https://archive.org/details/ofghostesspirite0olava/page/n3/mode/2up. Accessed 27 Feb. 2025.

Lawrence, D. H. "The Thimble." *Phoenix II: Uncollected, Unpublished, and Other Prose Works*, edited by Warren Roberts and Harry T. Moore, New York, Viking, pp. 53–63. Internet Archive, https://archive.org/details/uncollecte dunpuboooounse/page/n5/mode/2up. Accessed 27 Feb. 2025.

Lee, Vernon. *Hauntings and Other Fantastic Tales*, edited by Catherine Maxwell and Patricia Pulham, Peterborough, Broadview, 2006.

Lee, Vernon. "Winthrop's Adventure." *The Virago Book of Victorian Ghost Stories*, edited by Richard Dalby, London, Virago Press Limited, 1988, pp. 105–34.

Le Fanu, Joseph Sheridan. "Ghost Stories of Chapelizod." *Ghost Stories and Mysteries*, edited by E. F. Bleiler, New York, Dover, 1975, pp. 116–35.

Le Fanu, Joseph Sheridan. "An Account of Some Strange Disturbances in Aungier Street." *The Oxford Book of Victorian Ghost Stories*, Oxford, Oxford UP, 2003, pp. 19–36.

Machen, Arthur. "The Bowmen." *Angels of Mons: The Bowmen and Other Legends of the War*, New York, G. P. Putnam's Sons, 1915, pp. 23–32. *Internet Archive*. https://archive.org/details/angelsmonsbowmeoomachgoog/page/n 8/mode/2up. Accessed 27 Feb. 2025.

Maudsley, Henry. "Sex in Mind and Education." *Popular Science Monthly*, New York, D. Appleton and Company, 1874, pp. 198–215. *Internet Archive*, https://a rchive.org/details/popularsciencem0051874newy/page/n5/mode/2up. Accessed 27 Feb. 2025.

Marx, Karl. *Capital: A Critique of Political Economy*. New York, The Modern Library, 1906. *Internet Archive*, https://archive.org/details/capitalcritique001 marx/page/n3 /mode/2up. Accessed 27 Feb. 2025.

Meyer, Stephenie. *The Twilight Saga*. Little, Brown, 2022, 7 vols.

Morrison, Toni. *Beloved*. New York, Knopf, 1993.

Nordau, Max. *Degeneration*. 1892. London, William Heinemann, 1898. *Internet Archive*, https://archive.org/details/degeneration0onordiala/page/n3. Accessed 27 Feb. 2025.

Nesbit, Edith. "The Ebony Frame." *The Power of Darkness: Tales of Terror*, edited by David Stuart Davies, Ware, Wordsworth, 2006, pp. 143–52.

Nesbit, Edith. *The Magic City*. London, Macmillan, 1910. *Internet Archive*, https:// archive.org/details/TheMagicCity/page/n11/mode/2up. Accessed 27 Feb. 2025.

Oliphant, Margaret. "The Open Door." *The Virago Book of Victorian Ghost Stories*, edited by Richard Dalby, London, Virago Press, 1988, pp. 150–84.

Oliphant, Margaret. *The Autobiography and Letters of Mrs M. O. W. Oliphant*. Edited by Marry Coghill, Edinburgh and London, William Blackwood and

Sons, 1899. *Internet Archive*, https://archive.org/details/Autobiography_an d_Letters_of_Mrs_MOW_Oliphant/page/n3/mode/2up. Accessed 27 Feb. 2025.

Onions, Oliver. "The Rope in the Rafters." *The Dead of Night: The Ghost Stories of Oliver Onions*, London, Wordsworth, 2010, pp. 377–508.

Patmore, Coventry. *The Angel in the House Books I & II: The First Editions Collated with His Original Holograph Manuscript*, edited by Patricia Aske and Ian Anstruther, London, Haggerston, 1998.

Rice, Anne. *Interview with the Vampire*. New York, Ballantine Books, 1988.

Riddell, Charlotte. "Nut Bush Farm." *The Collected Ghost Stories of Mrs J. H. Riddell*. New York, Dover Publications, 1977, pp. 1–37.

Riddell, Charlotte. "The Old House in Vauxhall Walk." *The Collected Ghost Stories of Mrs J. H. Riddell*. New York, Dover Publications, 1977, pp. 85–101.

Riddell, Charlotte. "The Open Door." *The Collected Ghost Stories of Mrs J. H. Riddell*. New York, Dover Publications, 1977, pp. 38–84.

Said, Edward W. *Culture and Imperialism*. New York, Vintage Books, 1994.

Said, Edward W. *Orientalism*. London, Penguin Books, 2003.

Sassoon, Siegfried. *Memoirs of an Infantry Officer*. London, Faber & Faber, 1983. *Internet Archive*, https://archive.org/details/memoirsofinfantr00sieg/page /n3/mode/2up. Accessed 27 Feb. 2025.

Scott, Walter. "Novels of Ernest Theodore Hoffman." *Miscellaneous Prose Works of Sir Walter Scott*, vol. 6, Paris, Baudry's European Library, 1838, pp. 340–72.

Scott, Walter. "The Tapestried Chamber." *The Oxford Book of English Ghost Stories*, Oxford, Oxford UP, 1986, pp. 1–12.

Shakespeare, William. *Hamlet*. New York, Henry Holt and Company, 1914. *Internet Archive*, https://archive.org/details/shakespeareshaml01shak/page/n 5/mode/2up. Accessed 27 Feb. 2025.

Shaw, George Bernard. "Economic." *Fabian Essays in Socialism*, London, The Fabian Society, 1889, pp. 3–29.

Smiles, Samuel. *Self-Help*. London, John Murray, 1876. *Internet Archive*, https://archive.org/details/in.ernet.dli.2015.220299/page/n1. Accessed 27 Feb. 2025.

Stevenson, Robert Louis. *Dr, Jekyll and Mr. Hyde*. Edited by Katherine Linehan, New York, W. W. Norton, 2003.

Stevenson, Robert Louis. *"Virginibus Puerisque", and Other Papers*. London, C. K. Paul & Co. *Internet Archive*, https://archive.org/details/buspuerisstevvirgin irich/page/4/mode/2up. Accessed 27 Feb. 2025.

Stoker, Bram. *Dracula*. Edited by Nina Auerbach and David J. Skal, New York, W. W. Norton, 1997.

Stoker, Bram. "The Judge's House." *The Oxford Book of English Ghost Stories*, Oxford, Oxford UP, 1987, pp. 109–124.

The Haunting of Bly Manor. Created by Mike Flanagan, Intrepid Pictures, Amblin Television and Paramount Television Studios, 2020.

The Others. Directed by Alejandro Amenábar, performance by Nicole Kidman, Warner Sogefilms and Studio Canal, 2001.

The Sixth Sense. Directed by M. Night Shyamalan, performance by Bruce Willis, Buena Vista Pictures, 1999.

Wells, H. G. "The Red Room." *The Oxford Book of English Ghost Stories*, Oxford, Oxford UP, 1987, pp. 172–79.

Wharton, Edith. "Afterward." *The Ghost Stories of Edith Wharton*, New York, Scribner Paperback Fiction, 1997, pp. 58–91.

Wilde, Oscar. *The Picture of Dorian Gray*. Edited by Michael Patrick Gillespie, New York, W. W. Norton, 2007.

Woolf, Virginia. "The Supernatural in Fiction." *Collected Essays*, vol. 1, London, Hogarth Press, 1966, pp. 293–6.

Woolf, Virginia. *Three Guineas*. New York, Harcourt, Brace and Company, 1938. *Internet Archive*, https://archive.org/details/threeguineas00wool/page/n7/mode/2up. Accessed 27 Feb. 2025.

Secondary Sources

Abraham, Nicolas. "Notes on the Phantom: A Complement to Freud's Metapsychology." Translated by Nicholas Rand, *Critical Inquiry*, vol. 13, no. 2, Winter 1987, pp. 287–292.

Ackroyd, Peter. *The English Ghost: Spectres Through Time*. London, Chatto & Windus, 2010.

Adams, James Eli. "Victorian Sexualities." *A Companion to Victorian Literature and Culture*, edited by H. F. Tucker, Oxford, Blackwell, 1999, 125–38.

Ahmad, Aijaz. "Reconciling Derrida: 'Specters of Marx' and Deconstructive Politics." *Ghostly Demarcations: A Symposium on Jacques Derrida's Specters of Marx*, London, Verso, 1999, pp. 88–109.

Allen, Dennis W. "Young England: Muscular Christianity and the Politics of the Body in *Tom Brown's Schooldays*." *Muscular Christianity: Embodying the Victo-*

rian Age, edited by Donald E. Hall, Cambridge, Cambridge UP, 1994, pp. 114–32.

Allott, Miriam. *Elizabeth Gaskell*. Harlow, Longman Group, 1960.

Alvarado, Carlos S. "Nineteenth-Century Hysteria and Hypnosis: A Historical Note on Blanche Wittmann." *Australian Journal of Clinical & Experimental Hypnosis*, vol. 37, no. 1, 2009, pp. 21–36.

Arata, Stephen. *Fictions of Loss in the Victorian Fin de Siècle*. Cambridge, Cambridge UP, 1996.

Arata, Stephen. "The Occidental Tourist: *Dracula* and the Anxiety of Reverse Colonisation." *Victorian Studies*, vol. 33, no. 4, 1990, pp. 621–45.

Arnold, Catharine. *The Sexual History of London: From Roman Londinium to the Swinging City – Lust, Vice, and Desire Across the Ages*. New York, St. Martin's Press, 2010.

Arnold, Guy. *Held Fast for England: G. A. Henty – Imperialist Boys' Writer*. London, Hamish Hamilton, 1980.

Ashley, Mike. "Ghost Stories." *The Encyclopedia of Fantasy*, edited by John Clute and John Grant. London, Orbis, 1997, pp. 403–7.

Auerbach, Nina and David J. Skal. Preface. *Dracula*, edited by Nina Auerbach and David J. Skal, New York, W. W. Norton, 1997, pp. ix-xiv.

Auerbach, Nina. "The Rise of the Fallen Woman." *Nineteenth-Century Fiction*, vol. 35, no. 1, 1980, pp. 29–52.

Baldick, Chris. Introduction. *The Oxford Book of Gothic Tales*. Oxford, Oxford UP, 2009, pp. xi–xxiii.

Basham, Diana. *The Trial of Woman: Feminism and the Occult Sciences in Victorian Literature and Society*. Basingstoke, Palgrave, 1992.

Bauer, Gero. *Houses, Secrets, and the Closet: Locating Masculinities from the Gothic Novel to Henry James*. Bielefeld, transcript, 2016.

Beccalossi, Chiara. *Female Sexual Inversion: Same-Sex Desires in Italian and British Sexology, c. 1870–1920*. Palgrave Macmillan, 2012.

Bennett, Andrew and Nicholas Royle. *An Introduction to Literature, Criticism, and Theory*. New York, Routledge, 2014.

Berger, Anna. "Haunted Oppressors: The Deconstruction of Manliness in the Imperial Gothic Stories of Rudyard Kipling and Arthur Conan Doyle." *Humanities*, vol. 9, no. 4, Oct. 2020. MDPI, https://www.mdpi.com/2076-078 7/9/4/122. Accessed 27 Feb. 2025.

Beville, Maria. "Postmodern Ghost Stories." *The Routledge Handbook to the Ghost Story*, edited by in Scott Brewster and Luke Thurston, London, Routledge, 2018, pp. 445–453.

Beynon, John. *Masculinities and Culture*. Philadelphia, Open UP, 2002.

Bissell, Sarah. *Haunted Matters: Objects, Bodies, and Epistemology in Victorian Women's Ghost Stories*. 2014. U of Glasgow, PhD dissertation. *University of Glasgow*, http://theses.gla.ac.uk/6402/. Accessed 27 Feb. 2025.

Bissell, Sarah. "Reconstructing Masculinity in Charlotte Riddell's 'The Open Door' and Rudyard Kipling's 'They'." *Victoriographies*, vol. 4, no. 1, 2014, pp. 62–78.

Bissell, Sarah. "The Ghost Story and Science." *The Routledge Handbook to the Ghost Story*, edited by Scott Brewster and Luke Thurston, London, Routledge, 2018, pp. 40–48.

Blair, Emily. *Virginia Woolf and the Nineteenth-Century Domestic Novel*. New York, State U of New York P, 2007.

Blathwayt, Raymond. "How Boys' Books are Written: A Talk with Mr. G. A. Henty." *Great Thoughts from Master Minds*, vol. 2, Oct. 1902, pp. 8–10.

Bleiler, E. F. "Mrs. Riddell, Mid-Victorian Ghosts, and Christmas Annuals." Introduction. *The Collected Ghost Stories of Mrs. J. H. Riddell*, by Charlotte Riddell, New York, Dover Publications, pp. v-xxvi.

Botting, Fred and Dale Townshend. Introduction. *Gothic: Critical Concepts in Literary and Cultural Studies*, vol. 3, London, Routledge, 2004.

Botting, Fred. *Gothic*. New York, Routledge, 1996.

Botting, Fred. "Zombies." *The Encyclopedia of the Gothic*, edited by William Hughes et al., John Wiley & Sons, 2016, pp. 751–7.

Boyd, Kelly. *Manliness and the Boys' Story Paper in Britain: A Cultural History 1855–1940*. Basingstoke, Palgrave Macmillan, 2003.

Brake Laurel and Julie F. Codell. "Encountering the Press." Introduction. *Encounters in the Victorian Press: Editors, Authors, Readers*. Basingstoke, Palgrave Macmillan, 2005, pp. 1–7.

Brantlinger, Patrick. *Rule of Darkness: British Literature and Imperialism, 1830–1914*. Ithaca, Cornell UP, 1988.

Bray, Alan. *Homosexuality in Renaissance England*. London, Gay Men's Press, 1982.

Briggs, Julia. *Edith Nesbit. A Woman of Passion*. Chalford, Tempus, 2007.

Briggs, Julia. *Night Visitors: The Rise and Fall of the English Ghost Story*. London, Faber, 1977.

Briggs, Julia. "The Ghost Story." *A New Companion to the Gothic*. Wiley-Blackwell, 2012, pp. 176–85.

Bronfen, Elizabeth. "Abjection." *The Encyclopaedia of the Gothic*, edited by William Hughes, David Punter, and Andrew Smith, Chichester, Wiley Blackwell, pp. 1–4.

Brown, Nicola, Carolyn Burdett, and Pamela Thurschwell. Introduction. *The Victorian Supernatural*, edited by Nicola Brown et al., Cambridge, Cambridge UP, pp. 1–19.

Buchbinder, David. *Masculinities and Identities*. Melbourne UP, 1994.

Budd, Michael Anton. *The Sculpture Machine. Physical Culture and Body Politics in the Age of Empire*. London, Macmillan, 1997.

"Burke's *A Philosophical Enquiry into the Origin of our Ideas of the Sublime and Beautiful*." *The British Library*, https://www.bl.uk/collection-items/burkes-a -philosophical-enquiry-into-the-origin-of-our-ideas-of-the-sublime-an d-beautiful. Accessed 21 April 2023.

Bussing, Ilse M. "Sequestered Spaces and Defective Doors in Tales by Collins and Riddell." *Ilha do Desterro/Florianopolis*, no. 62, 2012, pp. 99–125.

Butler, Judith. *Gender Trouble: Feminism and the Subversion of Identity*. London, Routledge, 1990. *Internet Archive*, https://archive.org/details/butler-gende r-trouble/page/n1/mode/2up. Accessed 16 May 2025.

Buzzwell, Greg. "Gothic Fiction in the Victorian Fin de Siècle: Mutating Bodies and Disturbed Minds." *British Library*, 15 May 2014, https://www.bl.uk/ro mantics-and-victorians/articles/gothic-fiction-in-the-victorian-fin-de-si ecle. Accessed 21 April 2023.

Byron, Glennis and David Punter. *The Gothic*. Oxford, Blackwell, 2004.

Carrington, Charles. *Rudyard Kipling: His Life and Work*. London, Macmillan, 1950. *Internet Archive*, https://archive.org/details/rudyardkiplinghi0000ca rr/page/n7/mode/2up. Accessed 25 Feb. 2025.

Carroll, Bret E. "'A Higher Power to Feel.' Spiritualism, Grief, and Victorian Manhood." *Men and Masculinities*, vol. 3, no. 1, July 2000, pp. 3–29.

Castle, Terry Castle. *The Apparitional Lesbian: Female Homosexuality and Modern Culture*. New York, Columbia UP, 1993.

Castle, Terry Castle. *The Female Thermometer: Eighteenth-Century Culture and the Invention of the Uncanny*. Oxford, Oxford UP, 1995.

Cavaliero, Glen. *The Supernatural and English Fiction*. Oxford, Oxford UP, 1995.

Cocks, H. G. *Nameless Offences*. London, I. B. Tauris, 2003.

Cocks, H. G. "Secrets, Crimes and Diseases, 1800–1914." *A Gay History of Britain. Love and Sex Between Men Since the Middle Ages*, edited by Matt Cook, Oxford, Greenwood World Publishing, 2007, pp. 107–144.

Cohen, Ed. "Writing Gone Wilde: Homoerotic Desire in the Closet of Representation." *PMLA*, vol. 102, no. 5, Oct 1987, pp. 801–813.

Cohen, William. *Sex Scandal: The Private Parts of Victorian Fiction*. London, Duke UP, 1996.

Colby, Vineta. *Vernon Lee: A Literary Biography*. London, U of Virginia P, 2003.

Connell, R. W. *Masculinities*. Berkeley, U of California P, 1995.

Connell, R. W. and James W. Messerschmidt. „Hegemonic Masculinity: Rethinking the Concept." *Gender and Society*, vol. 19, no. 6, Dec. 2005, pp. 829–59.

Coulombe, Charles A. "Hermetic Imagination: The Effect of The Golden Dawn on Fantasy Literature." *Mythlore: A Journal of J.R.R. Tolkien, C.S. Lewis, Charles Williams, and Mythopoeic Literature*, vol. 21, no. 2, 1996, pp. 346–355.

Cox, Michael and R. A. Gilbert. Introduction. *The Oxford Book of English Ghost Stories*, Oxford, Oxford UP, 1986, pp. ix-xvii.

Cox, Michael and R. A. Gilbert. Introduction. *The Oxford Book of Victorian Ghost Stories*, Oxford, Oxford UP, 2003, pp. ix-xx.

Crane, Diana. *Fashion and Its Social Agendas: Class, Gender, and Identity in Clothing*. Chicago, U of Chicago P, 2000.

Crompton, Louis. *Homosexuality & Civilization*. Harvard UP, 2003.

Cunningham, Hugh. *Children and Childhood in Western Society Since 1500*. New York, Routledge, 2021.

Dalby, Richard. Introduction. *The Phantom Coach: Collected Ghost Stories*, by Amelia B. Edwards, Kindle ed., Ash-Tree Press, 2012.

Davies, David Stuart. Introduction. *Strange Tales*, by Rudyard Kipling, St Ives, Wordsworth, 2006, vii-xiii.

Davies, David Stuart. Introduction. *The Power of Darkness: Tales of Terror*, by Edith Nesbit, Ware, Wordsworth, 2006, pp. 7–13.

Davis, Adrienne D. and Stephanie M. Wildman. "Language and Silence: Making Systems of Privilege Visible." *Santa Clara Law Review*, vo. 35, no. 3, 1995, pp. 881–906.

Deane, Bradley. *Masculinity and the New Imperialism: Rewriting Manhood in British Popular Literature, 1870–1914*. Cambridge, Cambridge UP, 2014.

Denisoff, Dennis. "'Vernon Lee': Violet Paget." *Nineteenth-Century British Women Writers*, edited by Abigail Burnham Bloom, London, Aldwych Press, 2000, pp. 249–251.

Dickerson, Vanessa D. *Victorian Ghosts in the Noontide: Women Writers and the Supernatural*. Columbia, U of Missouri P, 1996.

Dillingham, William B. "Kipling: Spiritualism, Bereavement, Self-Revelation, and 'They'." *English Literature in Transition 1880–1920*, vol. 45, no. 4, 2002, pp. 402–25.

Downing, Lisa. *The Cambridge Introduction to Michel Foucault*. Cambridge, Cambridge UP, 2008.

Duthie, Enid L. *The Themes of Elizabeth Gaskell*. London, Macmillan, 1980.

Easthope, Anthony. *What a Man's Gotta Do: The Masculine Myth in Popular Culture*. London, Paladin, 1986.

Edmundson, Melissa (see also Makala, Melissa Edmundson). Foreword. *The Blue Room and Other Tales: The Ghost Stories of Lettice Galbraith*, edited by Alastair Gunn, Wimbourne Books, 2023, pp. 1–2.

Edmundson, Melissa. "'The Cataclysm We All Remember': Haunting and Spectral Trauma in the First World War Supernatural Stories of H. D. Everett." *Women's Writing*, vol. 24, no. 1, 2017, pp. 53–6.

Edmundson, Melissa. *Women's Colonial Gothic Writing, 1850–1930*. Palgrave Macmillan, 2018.

Eldridge, C. C. *Victorian Imperialism*. London, Hodder & Stoughton, 1978.

Ellis, Kate Ferguson. *The Contested Castle: Gothic Novels and the Subversion of Domestic Ideology*. Urbana, U of Illinois P, 1989.

Ellmann, Richard. *Oscar Wilde*. London, Vintage, 1988.

Faderman, Lillian. *Surpassing the Love of Men: Romantic Friendship and Love Between Women from the Renaissance to the Present*, New York, William Morrow and Company, 1981.

Feltwell, Tom. "Counter-Discourse Activism on Social Media: The Case of Challenging 'Poverty Porn' Television." *Computer Supported Cooperative Work*, vol. 26, 2017, pp. 345–385.

Fenn, Manville G. *George Alfred Henty: The Story of an Active Life*. London, Blackie and Son, 1907.

Fennell, Phil. *Treatment Without Consent: Law, Psychiatry and the Treatment of Mentally Disordered People Since 1845*. London, Routledge, 1996.

Ferguson, Christine. "Recent Studies in Nineteenth-Century Spiritualism." *Literature Compass*, vol. 9, no. 6, 2012, pp. 431–40.

Fisher, Benjamin Franklin. "Mrs Gaskell's Tales of Mystery and Horror." *Studies in Short Fiction*, vol. 18, 1981, pp. 110–11.

Fletcher, John. "The Haunted Closet: Henry James's Queer Spectrality." *Textual Practice*, vol. 14, no. 1, 2000, pp. 53–80.

Floyd, Kevin. "Masculinity Inside Out: The Biopolitical Lessons of Transgender and Intersex Studies." *Constructions of Masculinity in British Literature from the Middle Ages to the Present*, edited by Stefan Horlacher, New York, Palgrave Macmillan, 2011, pp. 33–48.

Foley, Matt. "The Ghosts of War." *The Routledge Handbook to the Ghost Story*, edited by in Scott Brewster and Luke Thurston, London, Routledge, 2018, pp. 319–27.

Freeman, Nick. "E. Nesbit's New Woman Gothic." *Women's Writing*, vol. 15, no. 3, 2008, pp. 454–69.

Freeman, Nick. "Haunted Houses." *The Routledge Handbook to the Ghost Story*, edited by Scott Brewster and Luke Thurston, New York, Routledge, 2018, pp. 328–37.

Frye, Lowell T. "The Ghost Story and the Subjection of Women: The Example of Amelia Edwards, M. E. Braddon, and E. Nesbit." *Victorians Institute Journal*, vol. 26, 1998, pp. 167–209.

Furneaux, Holly. "Victorian Sexualities." *The British Library*. 15 May 2014. https://www.bl.uk/romantics-and-victorians/articles/victorian-sexualities. Accessed 5 September 2022.

Gatens, Moira. *Imaginary Bodies: Ethics, Power and Corporeality*. London, Routledge, 1996.

Gavaler, Chris. *Superhero Comics*. London, Bloomsbury, 2018.

Generani, Gustavo. "Kipling's Early Gothic Tales: The Dialogical Consciousness of an Imperialist in India." *Irish Journal of Gothic and Horror Studies*, vol. 15, 2016, pp. 20–43.

George W. Stocking, Jr. *Race, Culture, and Evolution: Essays in the History of Anthropology*. London, Collier-Macmillan, 1968.

Gettmann, Royal A. "Vernon Lee: Exponent of Aestheticism." *Prairie Schooner*, vol. 42, no. 1, spring 1968, pp. 47–55.

González, Antonio Ballestros. "Portraits, Rats and Other Dangerous Things: Bram Stoker's 'The Judge's House'." *That Other World: The Supernatural and the Fantastic in Irish Literature and its Contexts*, edited by Bruce Stewart, Gerrards Cross, Colin Smythe, 1998, pp. 18–29.

Gray, Margaret K. Introduction. *Margaret Oliphant: Selected Short Stories of the Supernatural*, Edinburgh, Scotting Academic Press, 1985.

Green, Martin. *Dreams of Adventure, Deeds of Empire*. New York, Basic Books, 1979.

Green, Martin. "The Robinson Crusoe Story." *Imperialism and Juvenile Literature*, edited by Jeffrey Richards, Manchester, Manchester UP, 1989, pp. 34–52.

Groot, Joanna de. "'Sex' and 'Race': The Construction of Language and Image in the Nineteenth Century." *Sexuality and Subordination*, edited by Susan Mendus and Jane Rendall, London, Routledge, 1989, pp. 89–128.

Gunn, Alastair. "A Biography of Lettice Galbraith." *The Blue Room and Other Tales: The Ghost Stories of Lettice Galbraith*, edited by Alastair Gunn, Wimbourne Books, 2023, pp. 175–92.

Haefele-Thomas, Ardel. "That Dreadful Thing That Looked Like a Beautiful Girl: Trans Anxiety/Trans Possibility in Three Late Victorian Warewolf Tales." *TransGothic in Literature and Culture*, edited by Jolene Zigarovich, New York, Routledge, 2018, pp. 97–116.

Haefele-Thomas, Ardel. *Queer Others in Victorian Britain: Transgressing Monstrosity.* Cardiff, U of Wales P, 2012.

Haley, Bruce. *The Healthy Body and Victorian Culture.* Cambridge, Massachusetts, Harvard UP, 1978.

Hall, Donald E. "Muscular Christianity: Reading and Writing the Male Social Body." Introduction. *Muscular Christianity: Embodying the Victorian Age*, Cambridge, Cambridge UP, 1994, pp. 3–13.

Hall, Donald E, editor. *Muscular Christianity: Embodying the Victorian Age.* Cambridge: Cambridge UP, 1994.

Hamilton, Ian. "Kipling's First Story." *Kipling: Interviews and Recollections*, edited by Harold Orel, London, Macmillan, 1983, pp. 130–4.

Hanman, Natalie. "Eve Kosofsky Sedgwick and Judith Butler Showed Me the Transformative Power of the Word Queer." *The Guardian*, 22 August 2013, https://www.theguardian.com/commentisfree/2013/aug/22/judith-butler-eve-sedgwick-queer. Accessed 27 Feb. 2025.

Harrison, Brian. *Separate Spheres: The Opposition to Women's Suffrage in Britain.* London, Croom Helm, 1978.

Hay, Simon. *A History of the Modern British Ghost Story.* Palgrave Macmillan, 2011.

Hebblethwaite, Kate. Introduction. *Dracula's Guest and Other Weird Stories*, London, Penguin, 2006.

Heholt, Ruth and Joanne Ella Parsons. "Visible and Invisible Bodies." Introduction. *The Victorian Male Body*, Edinburgh, Edinburgh UP, 2018, 1–22.

Heholt, Ruth. *"Raising Crime from the Dead: Revenge and Retribution in 'Real' Ghost Stories."* Captivating Criminality 6: Metamorphoses of Crime: Facts and Fictions, June 2019, Universita Chieta-Pescara, Italy. Conference paper.

Heholt, Ruth. "Science, Ghosts and Vision: Catherine Crowe's Bodies of Evidence and the Critique of Masculinity." *Victoriographies*, vol. 4, no. 1., 2014, pp. 46–61.

Heholt, Ruth. "Visible yet Immaterial: The Phantom and the Male Body in Ghost Stories by Three Victorian Women Writers." *The Victorian Male Body*, edited by Ruth Heholt and Joanne Ella Parsons, Edinburgh, Edinburgh UP, 2018, pp. 148–168.

Heilmann, Ann. *New Woman Fiction: Women Writing First-Wave Feminism.* London, Macmillan Press, 2000.

Henson, Louise. "Investigations and Fictions: Charles Dickens and Ghosts." *The Victorian Supernatural*, edited by Nicola Brown et al., Cambridge, Cambridge UP, 2005, pp. 44–63.

Hobson, J. A. Excerpt from *Imperialism: A Study. The Fin de Siècle: A Reader in Cultural History c. 1880–1900*. Oxford, Oxford UP, 2000, pp. 162–66.

Hoeveler, Diane Long. "Homospectrality in Henry James's Ghost Stories." *Henry James and the Supernatural*, edited by Anna Despotopoulou and Kimberly C. Reed, Palgrave Macmillan, 2011, pp. 113–36.

Hopkins, Annette B. "Dickens and Mrs. Gaskell." *Huntington Library Quarterly*, vol. 9, no. 4, August 1946, pp. 357–385.

Horlacher, Stefan. "Masculinity Studies: Contemporary Approaches and Alternative Perspectives." *Beyond Gender: An Advanced Introduction to Futures of Feminist and Sexuality Studies*, edited by Greta Olson et al., London, Routledge, 2018, pp. 52–78.

Horne, Jackie C. *History and the Construction of the Child in Early British Children's Literature*. London, Routledge, 2016.

Hotz-Davies, Ingrid. "Not Drowning but Waving: On the Problem of Understanding Utterances in Henry James's *The Pupil*." *Dimensionen der Zweisprachenforschung: Festschrift für Kurt Kohn*, edited by Michaela Albl-Mikasa et al., Tübingen, Narr, 2009, pp. 277–88.

Hughes, William and Andrew Smith. "Defining the Relationship between Gothic and the Postcolonial." Introduction. *Gothic Studies*, vol. 5, no. 2, Nov. 2003, pp. 1–6.

Hughes, William and Andrew Smith. "Locating the Victorian Gothic." Introduction. *The Victorian Gothic: An Edinburgh Companion*, edited by William Hughes and Andrew Smith, Edinburgh, Edinburgh UP, 2012, pp. 1–14.

Hughes, William. "Men, Masons and Melancholy: The Singularly Masculine Ghost Stories of Rudyard Kipling." *Victoriographies*, vol. 4, no.1, 2014, pp. 5–23.

Hyde, H. Montgomery. *The Cleveland Street Scandal*. New York, Coward, McCann & Geoghegan, 1976. *Internet Archive*, https:// archive.org/details/clevelandstreets0000hyde/mode/2up. Accessed 27. Feb. 2025.

"Impotence." *Oxford English Dictionary*. https://www.oed.com/view/Entry/92644?redirectedFrom=impotence#eid. Accessed 27. Feb. 2025.

Jackson, Earl. "Explicit Instruction: Teaching Male Gay Sexuality in Literature Classes." *Professions of Desire: Lesbian and Gay Studies in Literature*, edited by George E. Haggerty and Bonnie Zimmerman, New York, Modern Language Association of America, 1995.

Jackson, Rosemary. Introduction. *What Did Miss Darrington See? An Anthology of Feminist Supernatural Fiction*, edited by Jessica Amanda Salmonson, New York, The Feminist Press, 1989, pp. xv-xxxv.

Jagose, Annamarie. "Masculinity Without Men: Annamarie Jagose Interviews Judith Halberstam About Her Latest Book, Female Masculinity." *Genders*, April 1999. *Genders*, Masculinity Without Men: Annamarie Jagose interviews Judith Halberstam About Her Latest Book, Female Masculinity | Genders 1998–2013 | University of Colorado Boulder.

James, Henry. "Miss Braddon." *Notes and Reviews by Henry James*. Cambridge, Massachusetts, Dunster House, 1921, pp. 108–16.

James, Louis. "Tom Brown's Imperialist Sons." *Victorian Studies*, vol. 17, no. 1, Sep. 1973, pp. 89–99.

Jamieson, Theresa. "Working for the Empire: Professions of Masculinity in H. G. Well's *The Time Machine* and R. L. Stevenson's *The Strange Case of Dr Jekyll and Mr Hyde*." *Victorian Network*, vol. 1, no. 1, 2009, pp. 72–91.

Janes, Dominic. *Picturing the Closet: Male Secrecy and Homosexual Visibility in Britain*. Oxford, Oxford UP, 2015.

Jewison, Cathy. "Picturing the Future: The Feminist Orientation of Portraiture in 'The Ebony Frame' and an Example of Victorian Spirit Art." *Vides*, vol. 4, Spring 2016, pp. 152–61. *Open Educational Resources*, 11 July 2016, https://open.conted.ox.ac.uk/resources/documents/picturing-future-feminist-orientation-portraiture-ebony-frame-and-example. Accessed 16 Nov. 2022.

Jirousek, Lori. "Haunting Hysteria: Wharton, Freeman, and the Ghosts of Masculinity." *American Literary Realism*, vol. 32, no.1, Fall 1999, pp. 51–68.

Joshi, S. T. "Algernon Blackwood" *The Routledge Handbook to the Ghost Story*, edited by Scott Brewster and Luke Thurston, New York, Routledge, 2018, pp. 116–23.

Junker, Christine. "The Domestic Tyranny of Haunted Houses in Mary Wilkins Freeman and Shirley Jackson." *Humanities*, vol. 8, no. 2, 2019, pp. 1+. *Humanities*, https://www.mdpi.com/2076-0787/8/2/107. Accessed 27 Feb. 2025.

Kahane, Claire. "Hysteria, Feminism, and the Case of The Bostonians." *Feminism and Psychoanalysis*, edited by Richard Feldstein and Judith Roof, Ithaca, Cornell UP, 1989, pp. 280–297. *Internet Archive*, https://archive.or g/details/feminismpsychoano000unse/page/280/mode/2up. Accessed 27. Feb. 2025.

Kane, Mary Patricia. *Spurious Ghosts: The Fantastic Tales of Vernon Lee.* Rome, Carocci, 2004.

Kanitkar, Helen. "'Real, True Boys': Moulding the Cadets of Imperialism." *Dislocating Masculinity: Comparative Ethnographies*, edited by Andrea Cornwall and Nancy Lindisfarne, London, Routledge, 1994, pp. 183–95.

Kaplan, Morris B. *Sodom on the Thames: Sex, Love, and Scandal in Wilde Times.* Ithaca, Cornell UP, 2005.

Kendrick, Walter. *The Thrill of Fear: 250 Years of Scary Entertainment.* New York, Grove Weidenfeld, 1991.

Kent, Susan. *Sex and Suffrage in Britain, 1860–1914.* Princeton, Princeton UP, 1987.

Killeen, Jarlath. "Gendering the Ghost Story? Victorian Women and the Challenge of the Ghost Story." *The Ghost Story from the Middle Ages to the Twentieth Century*, edited by Helen Conrad O'Briain and Julie Anne Stevens, Chippenham, Four Court's Press, 2010, pp. 81–96.

Kimmel, Michael S. "Invisible Masculinity." *Society*, vol. 30, no. 6, Sep. 1993, pp. 28–35.

King, Stephen. *Danse Macabre.* New York, Berkley Books, 1981.

Kokot, Joanna. "From the Angels of Mons to the Revolt of Animals: Arthur Machen's *The Terror.*" *The Lives of Texts: Exploring the Metaphor*, edited by Andrzej Kowalczyk and Katarzyna Pisarsk, Newcastle, Cambridge Scholars Publishing, 2012, pp. 227–245.

Kranzler, Laura. Introduction. *Gothic Tales*, edited by Laura Kranzler, London, Penguin Books, 2000, pp. xi–xxxiv.

Kristeva, Julia. *Powers of Horror: An Essay on Abjection.* New York, Columbia UP, 1992.

Kruger, Kate. *British Women Writers and the Short Story, 1850–1930.* New York, Palgrave Macmillan, 2014.

Kruger, Steven F. "Queer Theory." *A Companion to Literary Theory*, edited by David H. Richter, John Wiley & Sons, 2018, pp. 336–47.

Kucich, John. *Repression in Victorian Fiction: Charlotte Brontë, George Eliot, and Charles Dickens.* Berkeley, U of California P, 1987.

L'Esperance, Jean. "Doctors and Women in Nineteenth-Century Society: Sexuality and Role." *Health Care and Popular Medicine in Nineteenth-Century England*, edited by John Woodward and David Richards, New York, Holmes & Meier, 1977, pp. 105–27.

Lackaff, Derek and Michael Sales. "Black Comics and Social Media Economics." *Black Comics: Politics of Race and Representation*, edited by Sheena C. Howard and Ronald L. Jackson II, London, Bloomsbury, 2013, pp. 65–78.

Lang, Andrew. "An Indian Story-Teller." *Rudyard Kipling: The Critical Heritage*, edited by Roger L. Green, London, Routledge, 1971, pp. 47–8.

Ledger, Sally and Roger Luckhurst, editors. *The Fin de Siécle: A Reader in Cultural History c. 1880–1900*. Oxford, Oxford UP, 2000.

Ledger, Sally. *The New Woman: Fiction and Feminism at the Fin de Siècle*. Manchester, Manchester UP, 1997.

Leighton, Angela. *On Form: Poetry, Aestheticism, and the Legacy of a Word*. Oxford, Oxford UP, 2007.

Liggins, Emma et al. *The British Short Story*. Basingstoke, Palgrave Macmillan, 2011.

Liggins, Emma. "Gendering the Spectral Encounter at the Fin de Siècle: Unspeakability in Vernon Lee's Supernatural Stories." *Gothic Studies*, vol. 15, no. 2, Nov. 2013, pp. 37–52.

Liggins, Emma. *The Haunted House in Women's Ghost Stories: Gender, Space and Modernity, 1850–1945*, Cham, Palgrave Macmillan, 2020.

Luckhurst, Roger. Introduction. *The Cambridge Companion to* Dracula. Cambridge, Cambridge UP, 2018, pp. 1–8.

Luckhurst, Roger. *The Trauma Question*. London, Routledge, 2008.

Lustig, T. J. "Jamesian Ghosts: Romance and History." *The Routledge Handbook to the Ghost Story*, edited by in Scott Brewster and Luke Thurston, London, Routledge, 2018, pp. 142–49.

Lyall, Edna. "Mrs Gaskell." *Women Novelists of Queen Victoria's Reign: A Book of Appreciations*. London, Hurst and Blackett, 1897, pp. 117–45.

Lynch, Eve M. "Spectral Politics: The Victorian Ghost Story and the Domestic Servant." *The Victorian Supernatural*, edited by Nicola Brown et al., Cambridge, Cambridge UP, pp. 67–86.

Macfarlane, Karen E. "Here Be Monsters: Imperialism, Knowledge and the Limits of Empire." *Text Matters*, vol. 6, no. 6, 2016, pp. 74–95.

MacKenzie, John M. "Hunting and the Natural World in Juvenile Literature." *Imperialism and Juvenile Literature*, edited by Jeffrey Richards, Manchester, Manchester UP, 1989, pp. 144–173.

MacKenzie, John M. *Popular Imperialism and the Military*. Manchester, Manchester UP, 1992.

Maines, Rachel P. *Technology of Orgasm: Hysteria, the Vibrator, and Women's Sexual Satisfaction*. Baltimore, John Hopkins UP, 1999.

Makala, Melissa Edmundson (see also Edmundson, Melissa). *Women's Ghost Literature in Nineteenth-Century Britain*. Cardiff, U of Wales P, 2013.

Mandal, Anthony. "The Ghost Story and the Victorian Literary Marketplace." *The Routledge Handbook to the Ghost Story*, edited by in Scott Brewster and Luke Thurston, London, Routledge, 2018, pp. 29–39.

Mangan, J. A. *"Manufactured" Masculinity. Making Imperial Manliness, Morality and Militarism*. London, Routledge, 2012.

Mangan, J. A. *The Games Ethic and Imperialism: Aspects of the Diffusion of an Ideal*. London, Frank Cass, 1998.

Mangan, J. A. and James Walvin, editors. *Manliness and Morality: Middle-Class Masculinity in Britain and America*. Manchester, Manchester UP, 1987.

March-Russell, Paul. Introduction. *Uncanny Stories*, London, Wordsworth Editions, 2006, pp. 7–21.

Margree, Victoria. *British Women's Short Supernatural Fiction, 1860–1930*. Cham, Palgrave Macmillan, 2019.

Margree, Victoria. "The Feminist Orientation in Edith Nesbit's Gothic Short Fiction." *Women's Writing*, vol. 21, no. 4, 2012, pp. 425–443.

Margree, Victoria. "(Other)Worldly Goods: Gender, Money and Property in the Ghost Stories of Charlotte Riddell." *Gothic Studies*, vol. 16, no. 2, Nov 2014, pp. 66–85.

"Marriage: Property and Children." *UK Parliament*, www.parliament.uk/about /living-heritage/transformingsociety/private-lives/relationships/overvie w/propertychildren/. Accessed 27 Feb. 2025.

Martin, Carol A. "Gaskell's Ghost's: Truth's in Disguise." *Studies in the Novel*, vol. 21, no. 1, Spring 1989, pp. 27–39.

Matterson, Stephen. "'The Consecration of His Enterprise': Henry James' 'The Real Right Thing'." *The Ghost Story from the Middle Ages to the Twentieth Century*, edited by Helen Conrad O'Briain and Julie Anne Stevens, Chippenham, Four Court's Press, 2010, pp. 203–15.

McCarthy, Elizabeth. "Haunting Memories: Death, Mourning, and Memory in the Ghost Stories of Margaret Oliphant." *The Routledge Handbook to the Ghost Story*, edited by in Scott Brewster and Luke Thurston, London, Routledge, 2018, pp. 106–155.

McCarthy, Elizabeth. "'This Voice out of the Unseen': Love, Death and Mourning in the Writing of Margaret Oliphant." *The Ghost Story from the Middle Ages to the Twentieth Century*, edited by Helen Conrad O'Briain and Julie Anne Stevens, Chippenham, Four Court's Press, 2010, pp. 97–111.

McCorristine, Shane. *Spectres of the Self: Thinking About Ghosts and Ghost-Seeing in England, 1750–1920*. Cambridge, Cambridge UP, 2010.

Micale, Mark S. *Approaching Hysteria: Disease and Its Interpretations*. Princeton, Princeton UP, 1995.

Miller, Kathleen A. "The Mysteries of the In-Between: Re-Reading Disability in E. Nesbit's Late Victorian Gothic Fiction." *Journal of Literary and Cultural Disability Studies*, vol. 6, no. 2, 2012, pp. 143–57.

Mitchell, B. R. *British Historical Statistics*. Cambridge, Cambridge UP, 1988.

Mitchell, Juliet. *Psychoanalysis and Feminism: A Radical Reassessment of Freudian Psychoanalysis*. London, Penguin, 2000.

Moody, Nickianne. "Visible Margins: Women Writers and the English Ghost Story." *Image and Power: Women in Fiction in the Twentieth Century*, edited by Sarah Sceats and Gail Cunningham, London, Longman, 1996, pp. 77–90.

Murphy, Geraldine. "Publishing Scoundrels: Henry James, Vernon Lee, and 'Lady Tal'." *Henry James Review*, vol. 31, no. 3, Fall 2010, pp. 280–287.

Nemesvari, Richard. "Manful Sensations: Affect, Domesticity and Class Status Anxiety in East Lynne and Aurora Floyd." *The Victorian Novel and Masculinity*, edited by Phillip Mallett, Basingstoke, Palgrave Macmillan, 2015, pp. 88–115.

Newman, Judie. "Postcolonial Gothic: Ruth Prawer Jhabvala and the Sobhraj Case." *MFS Modern Fiction Studies*, vol. 40, no. 1, Spring 1994, pp. 85–100.

Newsome, David. *Godliness and Good Learning*. London, John Murray, 1961.

Noakes, Richard. "Spiritualism, Science and the Supernatural in mid-Victorian Britain." *The Victorian Supernatural*, edited by Nicola Brown, Carolyn Burdett and Pamela Thurschwell, Cambridge, Cambridge UP, 2004, pp. 23–43.

Norton, Rictor. *Mother Clap's Molly House: The Gay Subculture in England 1700–1830*. London, Gay Men's Press, 1992.

Norton, Rictor. "The Term Homosexual." *A Critique of Social Constructionism and Postmodern Queer Theory*, 1 June 2002, http://rictornorton.co.uk/social14.htm. Accessed 27 Feb. 2025.

O'Connell, Sean. *The Car and British Society: Class, Gender and Motoring, 1896–1939*. Manchester, Manchester UP, 1998.

Ohri, Indu. "'A Medium Made of Such Uncommon Stuff': The Female Occult Investigator in Victorian Women's Fin-de-Siècle Fiction." *Preternature: Critical and Historical Studies on the Preternatural*, vol. 8, no. 2, 2019, pp. 254–82.

Owen, Alex. *The Darkened Room: Women, Power, and Spiritualism in Late Nineteenth Century England*. London, Virago Press, 1989.

Palmer, Paulina. *The Queer Uncanny: New Perspectives on the Gothic*. Cardiff, U of Wales P, 2012.

Pedlar, Valerie. *The Most Dreadful Visitation: Male Madness in Victorian Fiction*. Liverpool, Liverpool UP, 2006.

Perkin, Joan. *Women and Marriage in Nineteenth-Century England*. London, Routledge, 1989.

Procter, James and Angela Smith. "Gothic and Empire." *The Routledge Companion to Gothic*, edited by Catherine Spooner and Emma McEvoy, London, Routledge, 2007.

Prosser, Jay. *Second Skins: The Body Narratives of Transsexuality*. New York, Columbia UP, 1998.

Punter, David. "Spectral Criticism." *Introducing Criticism at the 21st Century*, edited by Julian Wolfreys, Edinburgh, Edinburgh UP, 2002, pp. 259–78.

Punter, David. "The English Ghost Story." *The Routledge Handbook to the Ghost Story*, edited by in Scott Brewster and Luke Thurston, London, Routledge, 2018, pp. 179–87.

Pykett, Lyn. "Sensation and the Fantastic in the Victorian Novel." *The Cambridge Companion to the Victorian Novel*, Cambridge, Cambridge UP, 2005, pp. 192–211.

Pykett, Lyn. *Wilkie Collins*. Oxford, Oxford UP, 2006.

Radcliffe, Anne. "On the Supernatural in Poetry." *New Monthly Magazine*, vol. 16, no. 1, 1826, pp. 145–152. *Internet Archive*, https://archive.org/details/dli.ben gal.10689.14225/page/n159/mode/2up. Accessed 27 Feb. 2025.

Reddy, Maureen T. "Female Sexuality in 'The Poor Clare': The Demon in the House." *Studies in Short Fiction*, vol. 21, no. 3, 1984, pp. 259–65.

Reeser, Todd W. "Concepts of Masculinity and Masculinity Studies." *Configuring Masculinity in Theory and Literary Practice*, edited by Stefan Horlacher, Leiden, Brill, 2015, pp. 11–38.

Reeser, Todd W. *Masculinities in Theory*. Chichester, Wiley-Blackwell, 2010.

Reiter, Geoffrey. "Malcom Malcomson's Bible: Rival Epistemologies in Bram Stoker's 'The Judge's House'." *Christianity & Literature*, vol. 66, no. 2, 2017, pp. 230–243. *Project Muse*, https://muse.jhu.edu/article/73856. Accessed 27 Feb. 2025.

Richards, Jeffrey. Introduction. *Imperialism and Juvenile Literature*, edited by Jeffrey Richards, Manchester, Manchester UP, 1989, pp. 1–11.

Richards, Jeffrey. "With Henty to Africa." *Imperialism and Juvenile Literature*, edited by Jeffrey Richards, Manchester, Manchester UP, 1989, pp. 72–106.

Robbins, Ruth. "Apparitions Can Be Deceptive: Vernon Lee's Antrogynous Spectres." *Victorian Gothic: Literary and Cultural Manifestations in the Nineteenth Century*, edited by Ruth Robbind and Julian Wolfreys, Basingstoke, Palgrave, 2000, pp. 182–200.

Rogers, Clifford J. "The Battle of Agincourt." *The Hundred Years War*, part 2, edited by L. J. Andrew Villalon and Donald J. Kagay, Leiden, Brill, 2008, pp. 37–132.

Ruston, Sharon. "Representations of Drugs in 19th-Century Literature." *British Library*, 15 May 2014, https://www.bl.uk/romantics-and-victorians/articles/representations-of-drugs-in-19th-century-literature#footnote9. Accessed 2 April 2023.

Rutherford, Jonathan. Introduction. *Male Order: Unwrapping Masculinity*. London, Lawrence and Wishart, 1988, 3–20.

Rutledge, Amelia A. "E. Nesbit and the Woman Question." *Victorian Women Writers and the Woman Question*, edited by Nicola Diane Thompson, Cambridge, Cambridge UP, 1999, pp. 223–40.

Sage, Victor. "Empire Gothic: Explanation and Epiphany in Conan Doyle, Kipling and Chesterton." *Creepers: British Horror and Fantasy in the Twentieth Century*, edited by Clive Bloom, London, Pluto Press, 1993, pp. 3–23.

Salmon, Edward. *Juvenile Literature As It Is*. London, Henry J. Drane, 1888.

Sanders, Valerie. *The Brother-Sister Culture in Nineteenth-Century Literature: From Austen to Woolf.* Basingstoke, Palgrave, 2002.

Sausman, Justin. "James, Henry." *The Encyclopedia of the Gothic*, edited by William Hughes et al., John Wiley & Sons, 2016, pp. 366–8.

Schaper, Susan E. "Victorian Ghostbusting: Gendered Authority in the Middle-Class Home." *The Victorian Newsletter*, Fall 2001, pp. 6–13.

Schmidt, Leonie. Editor's Introduction. "Masculinity Studies: Contemporary Approaches and Alternative Perspectives." *Beyond Gender: An Advanced Introduction to Futures of Feminist and Sexuality Studies*, edited by Greta Olson et al., London, Routledge, 2018, p. 52.

Schor, Esther H. "The Haunted Interpreter in Oliphant's Supernatural Fiction." *Margaret Oliphant: Critical Essays on a Gentle Subversive*, edited by D. J. Trela, Selinsgrove, Susquehanna UP, 1995, 90–112.

Sedgwick, Eve Kosofsky. *Between Men: English Literature and Male Homosocial Desire*. New York, Columbia UP, 2006.

Sedgwick, Eve Kosofsky. *Epistemology of the Closet*. 1990. Berkeley, U of California P, 2008.

Sedgwick, Eve Kosofsky. "'Gosh Boy George, you must be awfully secure in your masculinity'." *Constructing Masculinity*, edited by Maurice Berger et al., New York, Routledge, 1995, pp. 11–20.

Segal, Lynne. "Back to the Boys? Temptations of the good Gender Theorist." *Textual Practice*, vol. 15, no. 2, 2001, pp. 231–50.

Segal, Lynne. *Slow Motion: Changing Masculinities, Chancing Men*. London, Virago Press, 1992.

Senf, Carol. "Three Ghost Stories: 'The Judge's House', 'Some Strange Disturbances in Aungier Street', and 'Mr. Justice Harbottle'". *Reflections in a Glass Darkly: Essays on J. Sheridan Le Fanu*, edited by Gary William Crawford, New York, Hippocampus Press, 2011, pp. 293–308.

Senf, Carol. "Tracing the Gothic through Stoker's Short Stories." Introduction. *Bram Stoker*. Cardiff, U of Wales P, 2010, pp. 1–30.

Seville, Catherine. "Copyright." *The Cambridge History of the Book in Britain: Vol. 6 1830–1914*, edited by David McKitterick, Cambridge, Cambridge UP, 2010.

Shanley, Mary Lyndon. *Feminism, Marriage and the Law in Victorian England: 1850 –1895*. London, I. B. Tauris, 1989.

Sharps, John Geoffrey. *Mrs. Gaskell's Observation and Invention: A Study of Her Non-Biographic Works*. Linden Press, 1970.

Shohat, Ella. "Notes on the 'Post-Colonial'." *Social Text*, no. 31/32, 1992, pp. 99–113.

Showalter, Elaine. "Hysteria, Feminism, and Gender." *Hysteria Beyond Freud*, edited by Sander L. Gilman et al., Los Angeles, U of California P, 1993, pp. 286–344.

Showalter, Elaine. *Hystories: Hysterical Epidemics and Modern Culture*. Chatham, Picador, 1997.

Showalter, Elaine. *Sexual Anarchy: Gender and Culture at the Fin the Siècle*. London, Bloomsbury, 1991.

Showalter, Elaine. "Victorian Women and Insanity." *Madhouses, Mad-Doctors, and Madmen: The Social History of Psychiatry in the Victorian Era*, edited by Andrew Scull, Philadelphia, U of Pennsylvania P, 1981, pp. 313–226.

Sinfield, Alan. *Literature, Politics, and Culture in Postwar Britain*. London, Continuum, 2004.

Sinha, Mrinalini. *Colonial Masculinity: The "Manly Englishman" and the "Effeminate Bengali" in the Late Nineteenth Century*. Manchester, Manchester UP, 1995.

Skovmand, Michael. "The Mystique of the Bachelor Gentleman in late Victorian Masculine Romance." *Broadening the Context*, edited by Michael Green, London, John Murray, 1987, pp. 45–59.

Smajic, Srdjan. *Ghost-Seers, Detectives, and Spiritualists: Theories of Vision in Victorian Literature and Science*. Cambridge, Cambridge UP, 2010.

Smith, Andrew. "Degeneration." *The Encyclopedia of the Gothic*, edited by William Hughes, David Punter, and Andrew Smith, 2013, pp. 174–76.

Smith, Andrew. "Hauntings." *The Routledge Companion to Gothic*, edited by Catherine Spooner and Emma McEvoy, New York, Routledge, 2007.

Smith, Andrew. *The Ghost Story, 1840–1920: A Cultural History*. Manchester, Manchester UP, 2010.

Smith, Andrew. *Victorian Demons: Medicine, Masculinity and the Gothic at the Fin de Siècle*. Manchester, Manchester UP, 2004.

Spencer, Kathleen. "Purity and Danger. *Dracula*, the Urban Gothic, and the Late Victorian Degeneracy Crisis." *Gothic. Critical Concepts in Literary and Cultural Studies*, edited by Fred Botting and Dale Townshend, London, Routledge, 2004, pp. 304–330.

Spivak, Gayatri Chakravorty. "Ghostwriting." *Diacritics*, vol. 25, no. 2, 1995, pp. 64–84.

Stallybrass, Peter and Allon White. *The Politics and Poetics of Transgression*. Ithaca, Cornell UP, 1986.

Stashower, Daniel. *Teller of Tales: The Life of Sir Arthur Conan Doyle*. New York, Henry Holt and Company, 1999.

Stewart, Clare. *Fighting Spirit: Victorian Women's Ghost Stories*. 2000. U of Glasgow, PhD dissertation. *University of Glasgow*, http://theses.gla.ac.uk/1610/. Accessed 27 Feb. 2025.

Stewart, Clare. "'Weird Fascination': The Response to Victorian Women's Ghost Stories." *Feminist Readings of Victorian Popular Texts*, edited by Emma Liggins and Daniel Duffy, Aldershot, Ashgate, 2001, pp. 108–125.

Stocking, George W., Jr. *Race, Culture, and Evolution: Essays in the History of Anthropology*. London, Collier-Macmillan, 1968.

Stone, Sandy. "The Empire Strikes Back: A Posttranssexual Manifesto." *The Transgender Studies Reader*, edited by Susan Stryker and Stephen Whittle, New York, Routledge, pp. 221–35.

Stott, Rebecca. "The Dark Continent: Africa as Female Body in Haggard's Adventure Fiction." *Feminist Review*, no. 32, 1989, pp. 69–89.

Sullivan, Jack. *Elegant Nightmare*. Athens, Ohio UP, 1978.

Syrotinski, Michael. *Deconstruction and the Postcolonial: At the Limits of Theory*. Liverpool, Liverpool UP, 2007.

"The Scandal of Cleveland Street." *Pall Mall Gazette*, 20 November 1889, p. 6. *The British Newspaper Archive*, https://www.britishnewspaperarchive.co.uk/vie wer/BL/0000098/18891120/016/0006?browse=true. Accessed 27 Feb. 2025.

Thompson, Terry W. "'Presentiments of Evil': Sourcing Frankenstein in Edith Nesbit's 'Man-Size in Marble.'" *CEA Critic*, vol. 73, no. 2, 2011, pp. 91–100.

Todorov, Tzvetan. *The Fantastic: A Structural Approach to a Literary Genre*. Translated by Richard Howard, Ithaca, Cornell UP, 1973.

Tosh, John. *A Man's Place: Masculinity and the Middle-Class Home in Victorian England*. New Haven, Yale UP, 1999.

Tosh, John. "Hegemonic Masculinity and Gender History." *Masculinities in Politics and War: Gendering Modern History*, Manchester, Manchester UP, 2004, pp. 41–58.

Tosh, John. Introduction. *Masculinity: Men Defining Men and Gentlemen, 1560–1918: Sources from the Bodleian Library*, part 2, Marlborough, Adam Matthews Publications, 2002, pp. 1–4.

Tosh, John. *Manliness and Masculinities in Nineteenth-Century Britain×: Essays on Gender, Family and Empire*. Routledge, 2016.

Uglow, Jennifer. Introduction. *The Virago Book of Victorian Ghost Stories*. Edited by Richard Dalby, London, Virago Press Limited, 1988, pp. ix–xvii.

Urbach, Henry. "Closets, Clothes, disClosure." *Assemblage*, vol. 30, 1996, pp. 62–73.

Vance, Norman. *The Sinews of the Spirit: The Ideal of Christian Manliness in Victorian Literature and Religious Thought*, Cambridge, Cambridge UP, 1985.

Vicinus, Martha. *Intimate Friends: Women Who Loved Women, 1778–1928*. London: U of Chicago P, 2006.

Vidler, Anthony. *The Architectural Uncanny: Essays in the Modern Unhomely*. London, MIT Press, 1992.

Vrettos, Athena. "Victorian Psychology." *A Companion to the Victorian Novel*, edited by Patrick Brantlinger and William B. Thesing, Massachusetts, Blackwell, 2002, pp. 67–83.

Walker, Lynne. "Home Making: An Architectural Perspective." *Signs*, vol. 27, no. 3, Spring 2002, pp. 823–835.

Walker, Nathalie. *Configurations of the Female Closet: 1800–1930*. Tübingen, Tübingen Library Publishing, 2019.

Wallace, Diana. "Uncanny Stories: The Ghost Story as Female Gothic." *Gothic Studies*, vol. 6, no. 1, 2004, pp. 57–68.

Wallace, Diana. *Female Gothic Histories: Gender, History and the Gothic*. Cardiff, U of Wales P, 2013.

Warwick, Alexandra. "Victorian Gothic." *The Routledge Companion to Gothic*, edited by Emma McEvoy and Catherine Spooner, New York, Routledge, 2007, pp. 29–37.

Watts, Cedric. Introduction. *"The Lost World" and Other Stories*, by Sir Arthur Conan Doyle, Ware, Wordsworth, 2010, pp. vii-xxiv.

Weber, Carl J. "Henry James and His Tiger-Cat." *PMLA*, vol. 68, no. 4, Sep 1953, pp. 672–687.

Whisker, Gina. "Postcolonial Gothic" *The Encyclopedia of the Gothic*, edited by William Hughes, David Punter, and Andrew Smith, 2013, pp. 511–14.

White, Chris. *Nineteenth-century Writings on Homosexuality: A Sourcebook*. London, Routledge, 1999.

Willard, Thomas. "Blackwood, Algernon (1869–1951)." *The Handbook of the Gothic*, edited by Marie Mulvey-Roberts, Chippenham, Palgrave Macmillan, 2009.

Williams, Anne. *Art of Darkness: A Poetics of Gothic*. Chicago, U of Chicago P, 1995.

Wilson, Angus. *The Strange Ride of Rudyard Kipling: His Life and Works*. New York, Viking, 1978.

Wilson, Neil. *Shadows in the Attic: A Guide to British Supernatural Fiction, 1820–1950*. London, The British Library, 2000.

Wolfreys, Julian. *Victorian Hauntings: Spectrality, Gothic, the Uncanny and Literature*. Basingstoke, Palgrave, 2002.

Wynne, Debora. *The Sensation Novel and the Victorian Family Magazine*. Basingstoke, Palgrave, 2001.

Young, Robert J. C. "Deconstruction and the Postcolonial." *Deconstructions: A User's Guide*, edited by Nicholas Royle, Basingstoke, Palgrave, 2000, pp. 187–210.

Young, Robert J. C. *Postcolonialism: An Historical Introduction*. Chichester, Wiley Blackwell, 2016.

Zandy, Janet. *Hands: Physical Labor, Class, and Cultural Work*. New Brunswick, Rutgers UP, 2004.

Zorn, Christa. *Vernon Lee: Aesthetics, History, and the Victorian Female Intellectual*. Athens, Ohio, Ohio UP, 2003.